The Complete

FRESHWATER FISHERMAN

STRATEGIES, TECHNIQUES, AND TIPS FOR CATCHING MORE FISH

© Copyright 2006
Creative Publishing international, Inc.
18705 Lake Drive East
Chanhassen, Minnesota 55317
1-800-328-3895
www.creativepub.com

Printed in China
10 9 8 7 6 5 4 3 2 1

President/CEO: Ken Fund
Publisher: Winnie Prentiss

Contributing Photographers: Bill Buckley/The Green Agency: pp.
278-279; Dwight Kuhn p. 12TL; Chris Munchow: P. 46; Dale C.
Spartas: p. 11BC; Joseph R. Tomelleri (www.americanfishes.com):
fish identification illustrations.

CONTENTS

The book staff traveled to Castaic Lake in California to catch and photograph giant largemouth bass.

In developing this book, the writers, editors and researchers traveled from Alaska to Mexico to fish with veteran guides and nationally known tournament anglers. The tips and techniques they uncovered are fully explained in these pages through hundreds of full-color how-to photographs and an interesting, easy-to-understand text. The following paragraphs highlight a few of the most memorable book staff fishing adventures.

Introduction

Arkansas Catfish – A rustic houseboat owned by Ralph Griffin, "The Cat Man," was home to the book staff for an amazing week of trotlining, jug fishing and limblining. The staff traveled by jon boats throughout the Three Rivers Country – the region where the White, Arkansas and Mississippi rivers converge – and learned how Ralph successfully catches big blue and flathead catfish.

Mexico Largemouths – The photo crew spent 10 incredible days bass fishing with local guides on Lake Guerrero, Mexico. Creek channels, weedbeds, timber, brush and man-made features all held bass on this sprawling reservoir. According to the staff, the best part of the adventure was putting the cameras down and getting in on the explosive action. After a couple of days the crew was missing thumbprints from lip-landing and unhooking big largemouths.

Canada Muskies and Walleyes – A 1¹/₂-hour boat ride to the outpost camp on beautiful Lac Suel in Ontario, Canada, was home for the staff's northwoods muskie/walleye trip. This huge body of water is known for producing trophy muskies. During the week, the crew learned and used various techniques to catch and photograph several muskies, including a 35-pound giant on the last night of their stay.

The walleye fishing was Canadian walleye fishing at its finest as the staff located fish on nearly every reef and point. And thanks to the fine Lac Suel guides, the staff learned a number of different presentations tailored for reservoir walleyes.

Western Lake Trout – Flaming Gorge Reservoir, located on the Wyoming-Utah border, brought the staff in search of trophy lake trout. Local guide Cliff Redmon provided the fishing information needed to land several of the giant lakers Flaming Gorge is known for, and also introduced the crew to great kokanee salmon and smallmouth bass fisheries available at "The Gorge."

Kentucky Mixed Bag – Kentucky provided the staff with a number of fishing opportunities on scenic Lake Cumberland. Working closely with local guide and fishing expert Randall Gibson, the staff gathered information over a 2-week period on how to catch eight different fish species. During their stay, the staff was stationed on a houseboat in the heart of the best fishing. The trophy striped bass fishing was the highlight of the trip, as the staff worked closely with a crew from *In-Fisherman* magazine to discover little-known striper secrets.

These trips are only a small sampling of the dozens and dozens of fishing adventures the staff enjoyed while putting together this book. As you turn these pages, you can be assured that the fishing tips and techniques you're learning come from North America's finest fresh-water anglers.

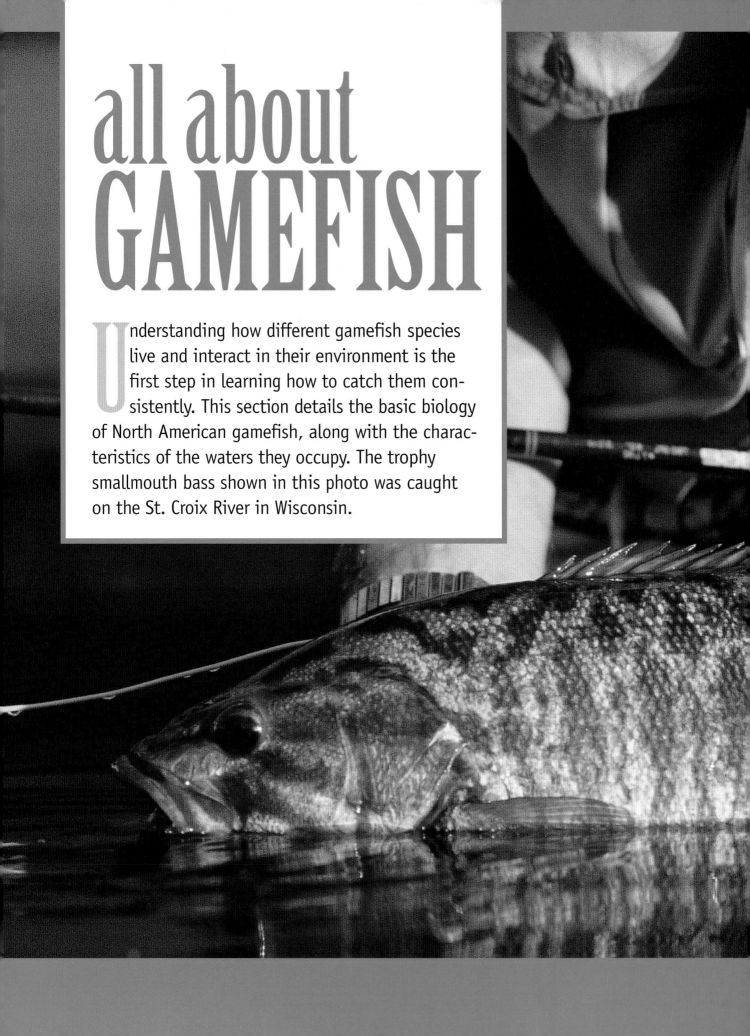

all about
GAMEFISH

Understanding how different gamefish species live and interact in their environment is the first step in learning how to catch them consistently. This section details the basic biology of North American gamefish, along with the characteristics of the waters they occupy. The trophy smallmouth bass shown in this photo was caught on the St. Croix River in Wisconsin.

Fish Basics

You don't have to be a fisheries biologist to be a successful angler. However, without a solid understanding of how fish use their senses to feed and avoid predators, you'll have a difficult time finding and catching fish consistently. Likewise, you need to know how the spawning season affects gamefish location and behavior in all bodies of water.

Nares

Fish Senses

Fish are fine-tuned to their watery world. In addition to the usual senses of most animals – vision, hearing, taste and smell – they have a unique sense, the lateral line. It enables them to find food and detect danger even when they are unable to see.

LATERAL LINE. Nerve endings along a fish's sides (see crappie above) sense vibrations in the water, helping fish determine the speed, direction of movement, and even size of predators and prey. In murky water, the lateral line is more important to a fish's survival than its eyes. Not only does it enable fish to find food and escape predators, it also helps them detect fixed objects and swim smoothly in compact schools.

VISION. Like humans, fish see brightness and color by means of tiny receptors, called rods and cones, in the retina. Rods sense light intensity; cones identify color.

Most fish, particularly shallow-water species like largemouth bass, have good color vision. In bright light near the surface, they can detect much the same range of color as humans. But some fish cannot see the full color spectrum. Walleyes, for instance, see all colors as some shade of red or green.

Water filters out color, so fish in the depths cannot see the spectrum of colors visible at the surface.

Red is first to disappear; yellow, next; and blue, last. Anglers working deep water soon learn that the most effective colors are usually blues and greens. Even if fish cannot see a certain color, however, they can still identify the object. They see it as a shade of gray, or they may respond to a flash of light reflected from it. This ability, combined with the lateral-line sense, explains why brightness and action of a lure are often more important than its color.

The distance fish can see in water depends on its clarity. In extremely clear water, fish can spot objects more than 100 feet away, but in very murky water, they can see only a few inches.

Lateral line

The usual range of vision for lake-dwelling fish is 10 to 20 feet.

Fish can see above-water objects through a window in the water's surface. Because of the way light rays bend when entering the water, fish can actually see above-water objects to the side of their direct line of vision. Therefore, anglers should keep a low profile when approaching fish, to keep from being detected.

Eye placement gives fish a wide field of vision. They can see in all directions, except straight down and straight back. To judge distance, a fish must

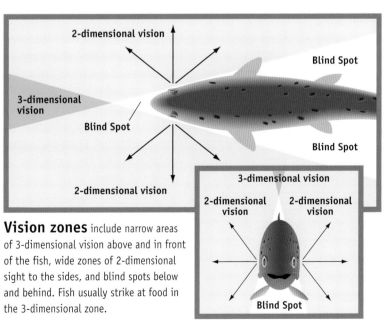

Vision zones include narrow areas of 3-dimensional vision above and in front of the fish, wide zones of 2-dimensional sight to the sides, and blind spots below and behind. Fish usually strike at food in the 3-dimensional zone.

How Gamefish View the Outside World

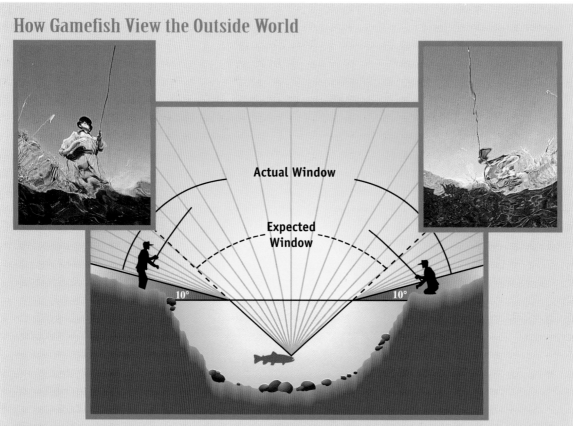

Light rays entering the water vertically are not bent at all, so trout clearly see objects directly above them. Rays entering the water at an angle are bent; the lower the angle, the more the distortion. Because of this bending, the actual window of view is much wider than the expected window. Although both anglers in the diagram above are out of the expected window, the trout can still see them. The angler on the left (top left photo), however, is more clearly visible than the one on the right (top right photo), because the light rays reflecting off him into the water are not bent as much. To get completely out of the trout's window, you would have to stay in the purple zone, at an angle of about 10° above the water's surface. If you're 40 feet from the edge of the window, you can stand up without being seen; at 20 feet, you would have to kneel.

turn to view an object with both eyes. Some fish, like northern pike, have sighting grooves on their snout that broaden their field of three-dimensional vision.

Overhead objects are easy for most fish to see, even at night. A shallow-running lure shows up well against the surface; a deep runner is much harder to see at night because it does not stand out against the bottom.

HEARING. Fish hear sound with a system different from that used to detect vibrations. Although they lack external ears, they have an inner ear that functions much like that of a human. Tiny bones in the inner ear pick up sound, and semicircular canals help maintain balance.

SMELL. Fish have a highly developed sense of smell. Odors are detected by the nasal sac inside the snout. Water is drawn into a front opening, or nare (crappie, p. 8), passed through the nasal sac and expelled through the back nare.

Salmon, hundreds of miles at sea, track the odor of water from their home stream, enabling them to return to spawn at the precise spot where their lives began. Odors also alert fish to the presence of predators or prey. When attacked by a predator, baitfish emit a chemical that warns other baitfish to flee. In a laboratory experiment, a small volume of water from a tank containing northern pike was poured into a tank containing perch. The perch immediately showed signs of distress and scattered. Spawning salmon will retreat downstream when they detect the water-borne odor of a human or bear.

Despite their ability to detect odors, most predator fish rely more heavily on other senses to find food. Odors dissipate slowly in water, and if the current is from the wrong direction, the odor won't be detected at all. Vision and the lateral-line sense, on the other hand, enable fish to detect prey almost instantaneously.

TASTE. The sense of taste is of minimal importance to most gamefish. Notable exceptions are bullheads and catfish. Their skin, and especially their whiskers, or barbels, have taste-sensitive cells that enable them to test food before eating it.

Scent products are controversial among fishermen. Some believe they're effective on all fish species; others say only scent-oriented fish, like catfish, respond to them.

Bullheads and catfish use their whiskers, or barbels, to test food before eating it.

How Senses Affect Fishing Strategy

Understanding the senses of gamefish and adjusting your fishing tactics accordingly will definitely improve your success. For instance, experienced anglers avoid banging their tackle box on the boat floor because they know fish can easily detect the sound and vibration. Bass anglers use lures with rattles to attract largemouths in muddy water, and pike anglers rely on flashy baits in clear water. Trout fishermen, understanding the concept of the fish's window, stay low when approaching the streambank. Channel catfish anglers, knowing their quarry has a strong sense of smell and taste, use stinkbaits – the smellier the better.

Foods & Feeding

Fish learn by trial and error what is edible and what is not. Young fish approach unfamiliar food with caution and often eject the morsel several times

How Food Affects Fish Behavior

Baitfish hatched in spring become large enough to interest predator fish by midsummer. This explains why fishing slows down in the latter part of the summer and remains slow well into the fall. Then, fishing begins to pick up again as predators reduce numbers of young-of-the-year baitfish.

Insect hatches may cause fish to temporarily change diets. Walleyes, for example, may stop eating perch and switch to mayfly nymphs.

Windblown algae can be a clue to fish location. Baitfish grazing on algae attract larger fish that do not hesitate to feed in the shallow, discolored water.

Understanding the Food Chain

Algae, or phytoplankton, are tiny plants that constitute the basic link in the aquatic food chain. They come in many shapes, as shown in this high-power-microscope photograph. Zooplankton (arrow) are tiny animals that graze on algae.

Minnows and other small fish eat zooplankton. Some fish, however, bypass this link in the food chain by feeding directly on algae.

Small predators, such as crappies, consume minnows and other small fish. However, they may feed directly on large zooplankton.

Large predators, such as northern pike, eat whatever food is available. Most prefer slim-bodied prey, because it's easy to swallow. But when such food is scarce, they do not hesitate to take deep-bodied prey.

before swallowing it. But once they learn what is acceptable, they become much less cautious about eating similar items.

Over their lifetime, fish build up a long list of acceptable foods and, among these, a set of preferred items. However, many of their favorite foods, such as insects, are usually available for only brief periods. At other times, fish cannot afford to be so choosy and must eat whatever nature will give them.

Not all fish feed in the same way. Northern pike, for example, grab their prey crosswise, puncturing it with long, sharp teeth until it stops struggling. A pike then turns the prey and begins to swallow it headfirst. If the prey is too large to be swallowed completely, a pike swallows as much as it can, letting the tail protrude from its mouth while the front end is being digested. Sometimes the tail still protrudes from the pike's mouth 24 hours after the prey was struck.

Other gamefish, like largemouth bass, inhale small foods. The bass opens its mouth quickly to suck in water and the food. It then forces the water out the gills while it either swallows or rejects the object. Bass can expel food as quickly as they inhale it, so anglers must set the hook immediately when using small lures or baits.

Bass usually grab large prey, then turn the food to swallow it headfirst. This explains why anglers who use large golden shiners, frogs or salamanders wait a minute or more before setting the hook.

Spawning Behavior

The spawning period, which takes place in early spring for most gamefish, is the single greatest annual influence on fish location and behavior. In general, gamefish leave the depths and move into warmer shallow water to spawn. After spawning is complete, gamefish move back to deeper water to recuperate. Of course, it's far more complicated than that. For an example of what actually takes place during this period, read the smallmouth bass case study below. You can find detailed spawning information for other species in the various chapters of the section, "How to Catch Freshwater Fish."

Note: In some states and on certain bodies of water, the fishing season is closed to protect spawning fish, so check the regulations for your area. Many anglers believe that catching spawners is detrimental to the long-term welfare of the fish population. For this reason, these anglers voluntarily release any spawning fish to help keep fish populations strong.

Largemouth bass spawn on a nest. The male bumps and nips the female, stimulating her to deposit her eggs. Then the male covers the eggs with his sperm, or milt.

Case Study — Smallmouth Bass Spawning Behavior

Smallmouth bass can spawn successfully in lakes or streams, and the areas they choose for spawning in streams differ very little from the areas they choose in lakes.

A spawning site is near an object like a rock or log which shelters it from strong current or wave action. Such an object also makes it easier for a male to guard the nest because predators cannot sneak in from behind. Nests are usually in water 2 to 4 feet deep, although they have been found in water as deep as 20 feet. Smallmouth almost always nest on sand, gravel or rubble and avoid mud bottoms.

Males begin building nests in spring, when the water temperature stabilizes above 55°F. The male uses his tail to fan out a circular nest with a diameter about twice as great as his own length. On a rubble bottom, he simply sweeps debris off the rocks. But on a sand or gravel bottom, he fans out a depression from 2 to 4 inches deep. A male nests in the same general area each year and will sometimes use the same nest.

Females move into the vicinity of the nest a few days later. When a male spots a female, he rushes toward her and attempts to drive her to the nest. At first, she swims away, but she returns again later. Eventually, the male coaxes her to the nest. Spawning usually occurs at a water temperature of 60° to 65°F, about 3 degrees cooler than the typical spawning temperature of largemouth bass.

As the spawning act begins, the fish lie side by side, both facing the same direction. Then the female tips on her side to deposit her eggs and the male simultaneously releases his milt. Females deposit an average of 7,000 eggs per pound of body weight.

The female leaves after spawning, but the male remains and vigorously guards the nest against any intruders. He will attack fish much larger than himself and may even bump a wading fisherman who gets too close. The amount of time required for hatching depends on water temperature. At 54°F, the eggs hatch in 10 days; at 77°, 2 days. On the average, 35 percent of the eggs hatch.

The male guards the fry on the nest for 5 to 7 days and usually continues to guard them for another week or two after the school leaves the nest. Of the fry that leave the nest, only about 10 percent survive to fingerling size (3 to 5 inches long).

Fishermen can destroy smallmouth nests by stepping on them or by catching the guarding male. If panfish are numerous, they quickly consume the eggs or fry once the male is gone. In one study, a single bluegill ate 39 smallmouth fry when the male was momentarily driven away.

A Fish's World

From the day fish hatch as fry, they are constantly tested on their ability to survive. They need cover to avoid larger fish, fish-eating birds, aquatic mammals and other predators. Even with good cover, nature takes a heavy toll. Some fish lay as many as 100,000 eggs. Less than one-third may hatch and, of these, only three or four fish may reach adulthood. Adult fish use cover to help protect their nests, so that they do not have to guard all sides of it.

Adult fish also require cover to escape predators. Perch, for example, hide in weeds to avoid walleyes and northern pike. Weeds also help camouflage perch, so they can dart out to grab minnows or other prey.

Many kinds of fish move from shallow to deep water on a daily basis. This explains why cover adjacent to deep water generally holds more fish than cover far up on a shallow flat.

Another basic rule: broad-leaved weeds make better cover than narrow-leaved varieties. They provide more shade and better concealment from predators. Narrow-leaved weeds usually hold only small fish. Similarly, newly flooded trees, with all the small branches intact, make better cover than

older trees, with most of the small branches rotted away.

Cover is just as important in moving water as it is in still water. Boulders, logs, bridge pilings or any objects that break the current and create eddies are gamefish magnets.

Where it is legal, fishermen often sink coniferous trees or brush piles to attract fish. Another option is to build an artificial fish attractor, such as a stakebed (left), which is built with 1x2 uprights attached to a 4x8-foot frame made from 2x4s.

Freshwater Basics

Fresh waters differ in many ways. Color and clarity are two conditions which can be easily seen. Less obvious, though more important to fish, are temperature, oxygen level and fertility. Together, these factors determine the type and amount of fish in a lake and what part of the lake they inhabit.

Temperature

Each fish species requires a certain range of water temperatures in which to live, grow and reproduce. Fish fall into three categories, according to temperature preferences (chart, right). Coldwater fish are limited to lakes that provide a refuge of cold, oxygenated water in the heat of summer. Coolwater species fare best in waters with intermediate summer temperatures, but without long periods of high temperatures. Warmwater species thrive in lakes where temperatures are high all summer.

Oxygen

The water in which fish live must have ample dissolved oxygen. Water absorbs oxygen when it comes in contact with the air. This is why flowing waters rarely have low oxygen levels.

Oxygen is also added by aquatic plants. Fish extract oxygen as water passes through their gills. Crappies, northern pike, perch and especially bullheads tolerate lower oxygen levels than most gamefish.

Fertility

The fertility of any body of water is determined mainly by the amount of dissolved nitrogen and phosphorus. Just as the amount of fertilizer in the soil determines crop yields, the fertility level of a body of water determines how many pounds of fish it can produce. Fertile lakes have high levels of these nutrients; sterile lakes, low levels. The higher the fertility level, the heavier the algal bloom. Because algae is the basic link in the aquatic food chain, fertile lakes produce the largest fish crops.

Fertility also determines the kind of fish a body of water can support. Coldwater fish like trout cannot survive for long in fertile lakes. Dead plants and algae are rapidly decomposed by bacteria, which consume large amounts of oxygen, forcing the fish into shallow water. There, the high temperature would soon kill coldwater fish.

In shallow, highly fertile lakes, oxygen is used up rapidly in winter, and in years of heavy snow cover, aquatic plants do not receive enough sunlight to replenish the supply. Eventually, the lake undergoes winterkill, commonly called "freeze-out," and nearly all the fish die from oxygen starvation.

High-fertility lakes are common in nutrient-rich farmlands, where fertilizers are routinely applied. Runoff carries the nutrients into nearby lakes, where they fuel heavy algal blooms. Low-fertility waters are usually surrounded by bedrock or nutrient-poor lands. Rains carry in few nutrients to fuel algal growth, so the water stays clear and fish production is low.

Gamefish Temperature Preferences (° F)

GAMEFISH SPECIES	TEMPERATURE PREFERENCE
● Lake Trout	50
● Brook Trout	54
● Chinook Salmon	55
● Coho Salmon	55
● Cutthroat Trout	55
● Rainbow Trout	55
● Brown Trout	60
● Muskellunge	67
● Yellow Perch	68
● Walleye	69
● Northern Pike	70
● Smallmouth Bass	70
● Crappie	71
● Striped Bass	72
● Largemouth Bass	73
● Bluegill	75
● White Bass	76
● Bullhead	78
● Channel Catfish	78
● Flathead Catfish	80

● Coldwater ● Coolwater ● Warmwater

Temperature preferences of common gamefish species are shown above. But fish are not always found in water of the preferred temperature. If food is more plentiful in warmer or cooler water, that's where the fish will be.

Fertility levels of lake types are reflected by the amount of algae, which, in turn, determines the kinds of fish life. Although most fish species are found in more than one lake type, those shown above are most typical.

Seasonal Movements

As the seasons pass, fish adjust to natural changes in lakes, reservoirs and ponds. Fish movement is keyed to two factors: dissolved oxygen and water temperature. Throughout the year, fish seek the zone in a lake that comes closest to satisfying both of these needs.

To understand how lakes change, it's important to know what happens to water at different temperatures. Water becomes lighter when warmed and heavier when cooled. But water has a unique property. When it cools below 39°F, it becomes lighter. This ensures that a lake's bottom water stays warmer than the surface during winter.

Because of this property of water, most lakes form three separate layers in summer. The upper layer, called the

Spring

○ Dissolved Oxygen   ☐ Warm Water
☐ Cool Water   ☐ Cold Water

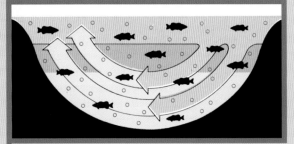

Early spring. The ice has melted. Runoff and the sun's rays rapidly warm a thin layer of water at the surface. As it warms, it absorbs oxygen from the air. Fish are drawn to the warm, oxygen-rich shallows.

Spring turnover. When the surface water warms to 39°F, it sinks. Soon all water in the lake is 39°F, so density is the same from top to bottom. Wind easily mixes the water, spreading oxygen. Fish may be anywhere.

Late spring. Warmer, lighter surface water starts to separate from cooler, heavier water below. Bottom water has oxygen, but is too cold for most fish. A strong wind can still mix the lake and scatter fish to any depth.

Summer

Early summer. Three distinct layers form: the epilimnion, or warm surface layer; the hypolimnion, or cold bottom layer; and between them, the thermocline, where the temperature drops fast. Fish select a comfortable depth.

Midsummer. Temperature layers become more distinct. The deepest part of the hypolimnion begins to lose oxygen. Coldwater fish are forced into the upper part of the hypolimnion, even though the water is too warm.

Late summer. Surface water has enough oxygen, but is too warm for many fish. The hypolimnion has lost much of its oxygen. Coldwater fish edge into the thermocline where warmer temperatures may kill them.

epilimnion, is warmer, lighter water that is easily circulated by the wind. As it mixes, it renews its oxygen supply. Meanwhile, the cold, heavy bottom layer, or *hypolimnion*, becomes stagnant and may lose its oxygen. Separating the two layers is the *thermocline*, a zone where the temperature drops very fast. In very shallow lakes, however, these layers may not form because the entire body of water is mixed by the wind.

These diagrams show the annual cycle of a moderately fertile lake in a northern climate. Seasonal fish movement is different in other types of lakes.

For example, infertile lakes do not lose oxygen in the depths, so fish are not forced into the shallows in summer or winter.

In extremely fertile lakes, low oxygen levels restrict fish to the shallows most of the year, with the exception of spring and fall turnover periods, when they may be found anywhere.

Fall

Early fall. Cool nights lower the surface temperature. The margin between epilimnion and thermocline is less distinct. The hypolimnion remains unmixed and without oxygen. Many fish move to the cool shallows.

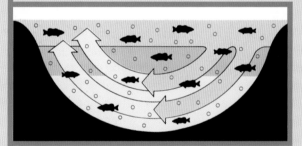

Fall turnover. The surface water cools even more and begins to sink. The thermocline disappears. Soon, water at the surface is the same temperature as bottom water. Wind mixes the layers, scattering fish.

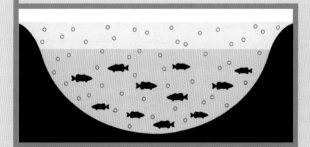

Late fall. The entire lake continues to cool, though faster at the surface. As the surface water drops below 39°F, it becomes lighter, so it floats on the warmer, deeper water. Fish move to the warmer water.

Winter

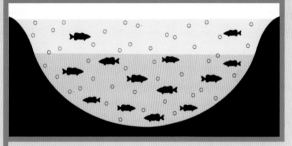

Early winter. Ice forms on a cold, still night, though the lake may reopen if milder days return. Fish may be found at any depth, but most stay in deep water where the temperature is warmer.

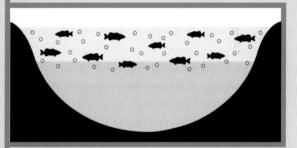

Midwinter. Thick ice and snow reduce the amount of sunlight reaching aquatic plants, so they cease to produce oxygen. Decaying plants and animals on the bottom consume oxygen, forcing fish to the oxygen-rich shallows.

Late winter. Ice and snow cover grows thicker. The low oxygen band widens. Soon, only the extreme upper layer has enough oxygen. A late winter thaw may bring oxygen into the lake. If not, it winter-kills.

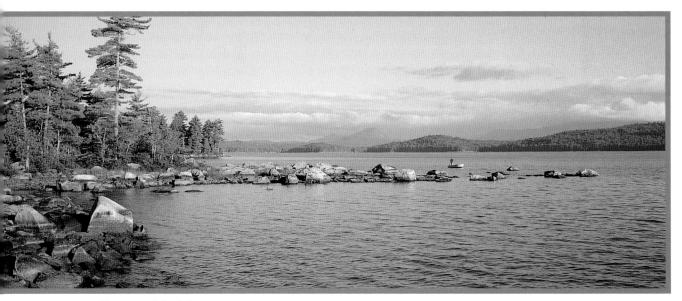

Oligotrophic lakes are the favorite destination for many anglers looking to experience the wilds of the Far North. It's not uncommon to spot moose feeding in the shallow bays of these large lakes, or hear nearby timberwolves howling during the night.

Water Types

Natural Lakes

Every natural lake is unique, the end product of a host of factors that combine to shape its character, including its fish population. Important elements are geographic location, size and shape of the basin and water fertility, which is the basis for the lake-classification system that follows.

OLIGOTROPHIC LAKES. Because the lands surrounding oligotrophic, or infertile, lakes release few nutrients, the water is quite sterile. Most oligotrophic lakes are located on the Canadian Shield, a vast rock-bound area that covers eastern Canada and dips into the northern states from Minnesota to Maine. Oligotrophic lakes, which are also called trout lakes by many anglers, are deep and cold, and usually have rocky basins with sparse weed growth. Some oligotrophic lakes are found at high elevations, where the climate is cold. Coldwater species, such as trout, predominate. Some of these lakes are stocked with stream trout; others, including many in the Far North, have natural lake trout. Because their fish are slow to grow and mature, these lakes can withstand only light fishing pressure.

MESOTROPHIC LAKES. These lakes are located primarily in the northern United States and southern Canada. However, they can be found most anywhere on the continent. Mesotrophic lakes are slightly more fertile than trout lakes, with basins of rock, gravel and sand, and sparse to moderate weed growth. These lakes have trout in the depths and coolwater or warmwater fish, such as walleyes, bass or panfish, in shallower water.

EUTROPHIC LAKES. These fertile lakes are surrounded by nutrient-rich soils that add large amounts of nitrogen, phosphorus and other fertilizing elements. They are typically found in agricultural areas in the southern two-thirds of the United States, although there are many in the North. Eutrophic lakes usually have a high percentage of mud bottom and heavy weed growth. Algal blooms on some eutrophic lakes reduce water clarity to the point where plants grow only in the shallows. These bodies of water are best suited for warmwater species, such as bass, northern pike, sunfish and roughfish. If walleyes are present, they're usually stocked.

Every lake is oligotrophic when first formed. But as time passes, aquatic plants and animals die and their remains form a layer of organic ooze on the bottom. As this layer thickens, the lake becomes shallower and is more easily warmed by the sun. Plant growth increases, and the water becomes more fertile, edging into the mesotrophic category. As ooze continues to accumulate, the lake becomes eutrophic.

Eutrophic lakes can offer excellent fishing close to home. In fact, many of the largest largemouths and panfish ever taken came from eutrophic lakes near large towns and cities in the southern and southeastern United States.

Eventually, the water becomes too shallow for fish. This process, called aging, may take thousands of years.

Ponds & Pits

About one-fourth of all freshwater fishing is done in these small lakes, most of which are man-made. There are nearly 3 million farm ponds in the United States alone, constructed mainly for cattle watering, irrigation or erosion control. Most ponds are made by bull-dozing or blasting a basin, or by damming a small stream. Ponds are also created by beavers damming small watercourses, and by floods digging scour holes adjacent to streams.

Pits are generally deeper than ponds. They fill with water after various types of sand-gravel or mining operations have been discontinued. Strip-mining for coal, for instance, often leaves pits more than 50 feet deep. Iron-ore pits may be more than 500 feet deep.

Farm ponds are commonly stocked with largemouth bass and bluegills. Channel catfish are popular in southern farm ponds. As a rule, any pond that freezes over in the winter should be at least 12 feet deep over one-fourth of its area to prevent winterkill. Shallower ponds can be aerated to prevent wintertime fish kills.

Beaver ponds along coldwater streams often hold trout; those along warmwater streams, a mixture of species, such as bass, pike, sunfish and crappies.

Iron-ore pits often have an ample supply of deep, cold, well-oxygenated water ideal for growing trout and even salmon. Shallower pits usually hold bass and panfish.

Gravel pits and quarries usually have clear, relatively infertile water. Deep pits are sometimes stocked with trout; shallower ones, bass and bluegills, or catfish. Shallow pits can be managed for trout only if they are spring-fed. Even then, they may have to be aerated in winter.

Strip pits may be stocked with bass and panfish, trout or even catfish. But many newer pits are fairly unproductive, due to their steep banks and acidic water.

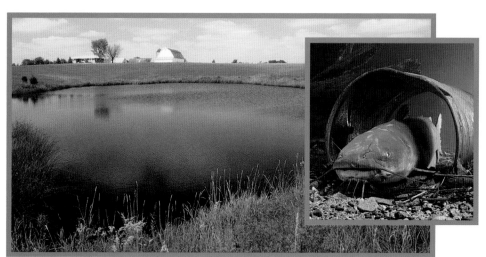

A farm pond is a great place to take a kid on his or her first fishing trip. These small bodies of water often hold a surprising number of channel catfish (inset), panfish and largemouth bass.

Swampland reservoirs are some of the most scenic bodies of water in all of North America. For example, when you fish on Lake Bistineau in Louisiana (shown below), you'll be treated to a jungle of flooded cypress trees overgrown with Spanish moss.

Man-made Lakes

Also called reservoirs or impoundments, man-made lakes are formed by damming rivers. In some respects, man-made lakes are much like natural lakes, but in other ways, they're very different. Like natural lakes, they often stratify into temperature layers. And they can be classified by fertility (p. 15) in the same way as natural lakes. But unlike natural lakes, reservoirs seldom lack oxygen in the depths, because of the moving water.

Man-made lakes tend to be longer and narrower than natural lakes, and there is usually a noticeable current at the upper end. The current carries in large quantities of sediment, meaning that their basins fill in much more quickly than those of natural lakes. Fluctuations in river flow cause dramatic changes in water level, meaning that aquatic plants are less abundant and baitfish crops less stable than in natural lakes.

Fishermen generally categorize man-made lakes in one of the seven types discussed below.

EASTERN MOUNTAIN RESERVOIRS are found in hilly or mountainous terrain. These deep, steep-sided lakes may be called hill-land, highland or cove reservoirs. The main lake is more than 100 feet deep and the creek arms may be several miles long. These waters are best suited to warmwater fish like largemouth and smallmouth bass, crappies and stripers, but some deeper ones also hold trout.

FLATLAND RESERVOIRS are surrounded by flat or gently rolling land and typically have depths of only 30 to 60 feet over most of their area. The main basin is relatively wide, and the creek arms short. These fertile lakes usually have good populations of largemouth bass, crappies, sunfish, catfish and white bass.

SWAMPLAND RESERVOIRS have maximum depths seldom exceeding 25 feet. These warm, weedy, highly fertile lakes are

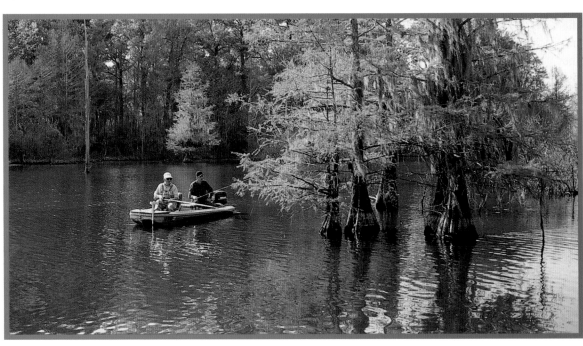

A FISH'S WORLD

often low in clarity. They support the same fish species as flatland reservoirs, but the fish run shallower because of the low clarity and lack of oxygen in the depths. These lakes seldom have distinct creek arms.

CANYON RESERVOIRS have a long, narrow main body more than 200 feet deep, and long, narrow creek arms. These lakes, which are cold, clear and low in fertility, have sharp-sloping shorelines and are better suited to rainbow, brown or lake trout than to warmwater fish like largemouth bass. Between spring and fall, canyon reservoirs may be drawn down more than 100 feet to generate power.

DESERT RESERVOIRS, found in the Southwest, are at least 100 feet deep. They have a large storage capacity for supplying water to cities and agricultural areas. Rich desert soils make the water quite fertile. Most desert reservoirs have good numbers of largemouth bass, with some white bass, crappies, catfish, smallmouth bass or striped bass.

PRAIRIE RESERVOIRS have warm, shallow, fertile water on the upper end and deep, cold, infertile water on the lower, so they support a wide variety of fish life, ranging from catfish to salmon. Creek arms tend to be small and short. Water levels fluctuate greatly, depending on long-term rainfall cycles.

CANADIAN SHIELD RESERVOIRS usually have bedrock basins and are very low in nutrients. Most are deep and cold, with a highly irregular bottom and numerous islands and reefs. Many such reservoirs have "two-story" fisheries, with warmwater fish like walleyes and northern pike in the upper layer, and coldwater fish like lake trout in the lower.

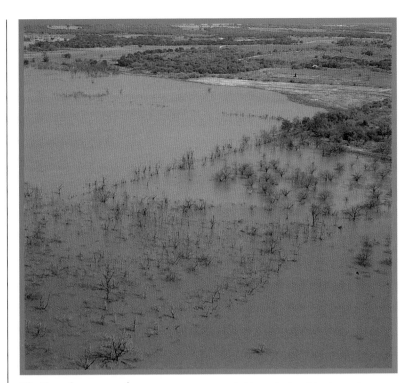

Flatland reservoirs are typically surrounded by agricultural lands, so these lakes receive large quantities of nutrients, which means there are abundant crops of baitfish (primarily shad) and fast-growing gamefish. Timber and brush provide the main cover for fish. These shallow reservoirs rank among the top trophy largemouth waters in all of the United States.

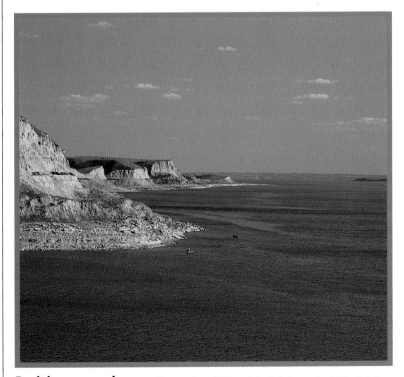

Prairie reservoirs can offer excellent fishing. Lake Sakakawea in North Dakota (above), for example, is famous for its trophy-caliber walleyes and northern pike. The light fishing pressure, combined with an abundance of smelt for food, explains why the fish grow so large.

Rivers & Streams

Beyond every bend in a river or stream lies a new fishing challenge. One moment, the water may flow slowly over nearly level ground; the next, it may turn into a churning rapids as it plummets over steep terrain.

Most streams and small rivers have the riffle-run-pool sequence explained below. This sequence may not be as noticeable in very large streams or streams with a very slow current. Nevertheless, fish recognize the different habitat types and so can the angler with a well-trained eye.

Species such as largemouth bass, crappies, catfish and walleyes spend most of their time in deep pools. Smallmouth bass and trout also inhabit pools but may be found in runs if the current is not too swift. Riffles are usually too shallow to provide enough cover for large fish, although they are important morning and evening feeding areas for many river species. Small gamefish and minnows stay in riffles through the day.

The slope or gradient of the streambed is one of the many factors that determine what kind of fish live in a particular river or stream. Others include water quality, bottom type and depth. The overriding factor, however, is water temperature.

Warmwater streams are home to such species as largemouth and smallmouth bass, white bass, walleyes, catfish and carp. Coldwater streams are best suited to species like trout, steelhead, salmon, grayling and whitefish.

The Riffle-Run-Pool Sequence

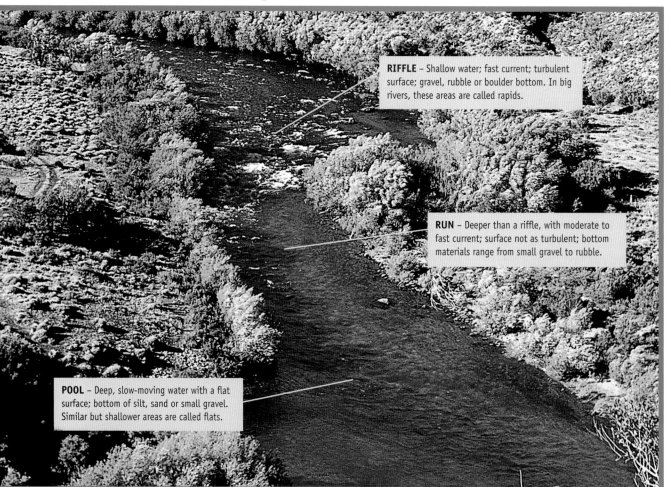

RIFFLE – Shallow water; fast current; turbulent surface; gravel, rubble or boulder bottom. In big rivers, these areas are called rapids.

RUN – Deeper than a riffle, with moderate to fast current; surface not as turbulent; bottom materials range from small gravel to rubble.

POOL – Deep, slow-moving water with a flat surface; bottom of silt, sand or small gravel. Similar but shallower areas are called flats.

Fast water in a riffle excavates a deeper channel, or run, immediately downstream. As current digs the run deeper, the velocity slows, forming a pool. Because of the slower current, sediment is deposited at the pool's downstream end, raising the streambed and channeling the water into a smaller area. With the flow more constricted, the current speeds up, forming another riffle. The sequence then repeats. In most streams, this riffle-run-pool pattern is repeated about once for every seven stream widths. In other words, a new riffle, run and pool sequence would be repeated about every 140 feet in a stream 20 feet wide.

The Mechanics of Moving Water

Why does a fish lie upstream of a boulder when there is a noticeable eddy on the downstream side? Why does it choose a feeding spot on the bottom when most of its food is drifting on the surface? And why does a floating lure cast near the bank drift more slowly than one in midstream?

Questions like these have a direct bearing on your ability to find and catch fish in moving water. Answering them correctly requires a basic understanding of stream hydraulics.

A fish often holds on the upstream side of the boulder because an eddy forms upstream of an object as well as downstream. A fish chooses a feeding spot on the bottom because friction with bottom materials slows the current to as little as one-fourth the speed in the center of the stream (top right). Similarly, a lure next to the bank drifts more slowly than one in midstream, because friction with the bank slows the current.

Current speed varies within the stream cross section. The light blue area (1) has slow current; the medium blue (2), moderate current; the dark blue (3), fast current. Water in the fast zone moves up to four times as fast as that in the slow zone. For purposes of illustration, the fast zone is depicted in the middle of the stream, but it could occur in any part of the stream's cross section, depending on the shape of the channel.

Eddies form both upstream and downstream of a boulder. Many anglers do not realize that there is an eddy on the upstream side; they work only the downstream eddy, overlooking many fish. Eddies also form downstream of points, sharp bends, islands and obstacles such as bridge pilings.

Undercuts occur in meandering streams because current flowing to the outside of a bend becomes swifter, eroding the streambank. At the same time, current on the opposite side of the stream slackens, depositing sediment and forming a bar or point. In almost all cases, the outside bends and eddies below the bars and points hold the most fish.

Plunge pools form at the base of a falls as a result of the cascading water. Plunge-pool depth may exceed the distance from the crest of the falls to the water level. A dugout often forms at the base of the falls, creating one of the best fish feeding and resting spots in the stream, especially for large fish.

fishing EQUIPMENT

Matching your fishing equipment to the species you're after and the technique you're using will greatly increase the day's catch. From boats, rods, reels and lures to fishing lines and bobbers, this section will detail which products are the best choice for whatever type of fishing you plan to do. The anglers in this photo are heading out for a day of catfishing on the White River in Arkansas.

Rods & Reels

Fishing rods and reels can be divided into the five basic categories discussed below, and within each of those groups are many subcategories, based on specific kinds of use. Bass fishermen, for example, often

Success comes from picking the right rod and reel for the job.

carry a selection of different baitcasting outfits for such uses as pitchin', flippin', crankbaiting and grub fishing. Similarly, many walleye fishermen carry different spinning outfits rigged for slip-sinker fishing, slip-bobber fishing and jigging.

Your rod and reel selection depends not only on the size of fish you'll be catching, but on the size of your lure or bait. A tiny, lightweight spinner, for instance, would be easy to cast with a light spinning outfit and 4-pound monofilament line, but casting would be nearly impossible with a heavy baitcaster and 17-pound monofilament.

As anglers gain experience and their fishing interests diversify, their inventory of rod-and-reel combinations usually grows. It's not unusual for avid anglers to own more than a dozen fishing outfits.

The basic information that follows is intended to help you select the type of fishing outfit that best suits your needs:

SPINCASTING. Many inexperienced anglers prefer spincasting gear, because it's backlash-free and the enclosed spool prevents much of the snarling associated with spinning gear. But the closed face also increases line friction, reducing casting distance. Spincast reels also have low gear ratios and, as a result, they don't retrieve a lot of line with each turn of the handle, which makes it very difficult to properly fish lures such as spinnerbaits and buzzbaits. While spincasting outfits are excellent tools to teach beginning anglers the mechanics of casting, fishermen should begin learning how to master spinning and baitcasting equipment as soon as possible.

SPINNING. Ideal for distance casting and tossing light lures, a spinning outfit includes an open-face reel, which has a bail that flips open to allow line to flow easily off a fixed spool. The rod has large guides to minimize line friction. Spinning tackle is highly versatile, and with no rotating spool, it cannot backlash. It is not the best choice, however, when using heavy monofilament line, which tends to spring off the spool and cause tangles.

BAITCASTING. Baitcasting gear excels for casting accuracy, because you can "thumb" the spool to stop the lure precisely where you want it. And a baitcasting outfit handles heavy monofilament and braided lines better than a spinning outfit. Baitcasting reels have a push button or thumb bar that frees the spool so you can cast without the reel handle turning. Although backlashing can be a problem because of the rotating spool, innovations such as magnetic anti-backlash devices have greatly reduced the problem. Baitcasting rods are generally stiffer and have smaller guides than spinning rods.

TROLLING. These outfits provide the line capacity needed for downrigger or longline trolling with heavy line. The large, rugged level-wind reels usually have smooth star drags. Trolling rods vary from long and limber, for downrigger trolling, to short and stiff, for trolling with big plugs.

FLYCASTING. A fly rod is designed to cast a thick fly line, which in turn pulls along a 7- to 10-foot monofilament leader and a fly. The long rod, usually measuring 7$\frac{1}{2}$ to 9 feet, flexes over its entire length to help pick up and propel the fly line. The fly reel has no function in casting; it serves mainly to store the line.

Selecting the best rod for a particular type of fishing can be a highly confusing task. Besides the basic considerations – length, power and action – anglers should also pay attention to rod sensitivity. The explanations that follow will simplify the rod-selection process.

What to Look for in a Fishing Rod

LENGTH. A long rod is generally better for distance casting and controlling the lure, but a short rod may be needed in tight quarters. In the past,

short rods were needed to achieve the desired degree of stiffness, but with the space-age materials now available, it's possible to achieve the same stiffness in a longer fishing rod. As a result, the trend is toward increasing rod length.

ACTION. The action of a rod refers to where it bends. Action, which is primarily determined by degree of taper of the rod shaft, is usually rated as slow, medium, fast, extra-fast, etc.

Fast-action rods are the best choice when you need a responsive tip for twitching a surface lure or detecting subtle strikes when jigging. A fast tip also gives you a quicker, stronger hook-set. Medium-action rods are ideal for live-bait fishing, because the fish is less likely to feel resistance from the soft tip and drop the bait. Slow-action rods work like a shock absorber, cushioning the fight of a big fish so it won't break the line.

POWER. A rod's power is the amount of force required to bend it. Some manufacturers

Rod-and-reel types include: (1) spincasting, (2) spinning, (3) baitcasting, (4) trolling and (5) flycasting.

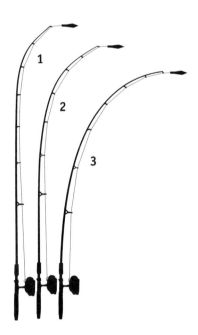

Rod action is shown in the above illustration by pulling equally on different rods of the same power. A fast-action rod (1) bends mainly near the tip; a medium-action (2), over the front half; and a slow-action (3), over the entire rod length.

rate power only as light, medium, heavy, medium-heavy, etc., while others use a numerical 1 to 10 system, with 1 being the lightest. The heavier the lure and the larger the fish, the more powerful the rod you'll need.

Light rods bend backward, or load, under the weight of a light lure. The force generated by the rod whipping forward makes casting easier. Heavy rods are needed for heavy lures. A light rod would not have the power to whip the lure forward or to sink the hooks into a big fish's jaws. Obstacles such as thick weedbeds or timber make it necessary to use a heavy rod, so you can stop a fish's run and keep it away from snags.

Perhaps the biggest factor confusing the rod-selection process is misuse of the terms power and action among sales clerks, writers and even some manufacturers. They commonly refer to a light-action rod, for instance, when they really mean light-power. Before buying a rod, make sure the salesperson understands these terms.

SENSITIVITY. A rod's sensitivity is the ability it has to telegraph vibrations from the line down the rod and on to the hand. Sensitivity is determined by the material the rod is made of, the rod's action and the physical weight of the rod.

A graphite rod, for example, transmits vibrations better than a fiberglass rod. When comparing two rods made from the same material, the rod with the fastest action is usually the most sensitive. And finally, when comparing two rods of the same material with identical actions, the rod that weighs the least will be the most sensitive.

What to Look for in a Fishing Reel

Selecting the right reel for your style of fishing can be confusing. For the best performance from any kind of fishing outfit, the reel must be balanced with the rod. If you use a reel that weighs too much for the rod, the outfit will feel butt-heavy. Not only will you have problems casting, the heavy butt will take away from the sensitivity of the tip. Conversely, a reel that is too light for the rod will make the outfit feel tip-heavy, and your wrist will soon tire from trying to hold the rod up.

SPINNING. The spool of a spinning reel does not turn when you cast; the line simply flows off the end of the spool once the bail is opened. Reels come with either manual bails or bail triggers, which allow you to open the bail using one hand. A front drag is smoother and more reliable than a rear drag. A front drag employs washers that press on a large, flat surface, much like disk brakes on a car. A rear drag applies pressure on a small-diameter drive shaft, explaining why the drag may seem jerky. Some fishermen, however, prefer rear-drag reels because the drag is easier to adjust while fighting a fish.

SPINCASTING. A favorite among beginning anglers, these inexpensive reels are much like spinning reels, except the spool is covered to minimize tangling problems. The push-button style is used with a baitcasting rod; the underspin style, with a spinning rod. When selecting a spincasting reel, look for one with a smooth drag. The most inexpensive models often have sticky drags, resulting in many broken lines.

BAITCASTING. Used primarily for fishing with heavier lines and lures, baitcasting reels have smooth, dependable drag systems designed to handle big fish. Round reels hold the most line and have either a thumb-bar spool release or a push-button spool release. Low-profile reels feature a thumb-bar spool release and are more comfortable to palm (above) during the retrieve. Modern baitcasting reels feature spool-braking systems that almost totally eliminate backlashes.

TROLLING. These large-capacity, level-wind reels are used mainly for longline trolling. They may hold several hundred yards of 20- to 30-pound monofilament. Because they do not have an anti-backlash mechanism, they should not be used for casting. Some trolling reels have a digital line counter that enables you to return your lure to the precise depth should you catch a fish.

FLY FISHING. The primary function of the fly reel is to hold the fly line while casting. However, some of the more sophisticated fly reels feature adjustable disc-drag systems, which help fight powerful fish such as steelhead and striped bass. Most fly reels have an exposed spool rim that allows you to apply additional drag tension by pressing the palm of your open hand against the rim.

Lines & Knots

Line Types

MONOFILAMENT LINES. Used in both spinning and baitcasting, mono is inexpensive, easy to cast and nearly invisible in water. Its major drawback is the high stretch factor.

You can select from many types and colors of mono. Plastic-worm or jig fishermen, who detect strikes by watching for a line twitch, may favor fluorescent mono when fishing discolored water but would probably use clear or green mono in clearer water. Anglers who fish rocky bottoms prefer abrasion-resistant mono. Live-bait fishermen use thin, flexible mono for a natural presentation. Don't buy cheap, off-brand mono. It weakens quickly, tends to be very kinky and may have thin spots.

BRAIDED LINES. Braided lines have little stretch, so they work well for telegraphing bites and getting strong hook-sets. In the past, nylon and Dacron® were the only choices in braided-line materials. But today, fishermen can opt for space-age fibers, such as Spectra® and Kevlar®, which have even less stretch and a much thinner diameter for their strength. Modern braided lines are three to four times as strong as mono of equal diameter.

Nylon and Dacron lines, because of their thick diameter, are used mainly on baitcasting reels and for backing on fly reels. Modern braided lines, however, work well with spinning gear.

FLY LINES. Level lines have the same diameter over their entire length. Although they are inexpensive, level lines are hard to cast. Double-taper lines, with a level middle section and gradual tapers at each end, allow a delicate presentation. When one end wears out, the line can be reversed for economy. Weight-forward lines have a short, thick belly behind the tapered front end; the rear portion is tapered to a long, thin section, called running line. The up-front weight makes it easier to punch into a strong wind and make longer casts. Shooting-head lines are similar to weight-forward lines, but the running line is monofilament. They cast farther than other lines.

Most fly lines float, but full-sinking or sink-tip types are available. All shooting-head lines sink. Line weight designations range from 1 (lightest) to 12 (heaviest). For best casting performance, the line must be matched to the weight designation on the rod.

WIRE LINES. Single-strand and braided-wire lines, used mainly for deep-trolling or jigging, have no stretch, but kink easily. Some braided-wire lines are coated with plastic to reduce kinkiness. Wire lines are also used to make leaders for toothy gamefish, such as northern pike and muskies.

Lead-core lines, commonly used for deep-trolling, are more flexible than other wire lines, but their thick diameter requires a large reel. Most lead-core is color-coded so you can easily monitor your fishing depth.

Knots

Your fishing line is only as strong as the knots used in tying it. All knots weaken line to some degree, and some knots cut the line strength in half.

The knots on the following pages are good choices for the purposes described, though many other knots can be substituted. Avoid using knots that put sharp

Line wear is evident by comparing electron microscope photos of new monofilament line (left) with used line (right). Abrasion, sunlight and airborne chemicals deteriorate line, so it pays to replace it regularly.

bends in your line, because those bends may fracture under stress (right).

The ability to tie good knots will save you from losing countless lures and fish. Below are some important knot-tying tips:

• Choose knots that are easy to tie; even the strongest knots will fail if not tied properly.

• All knots will weaken with use. Get in the habit of tying new knots before every trip, and retie knots frequently.

• Moisten the knot before snugging it up. This reduces the friction that can cause slight abrasions when you pull the knot tight.

• Snug up the knot with a smooth, strong pull. Do not be timid about testing it. Better it should break while being tied than after hooking a big fish.

• Leave a little extra line when clipping the tag end. Some knots slip slightly just before they break, and extra line is good insurance.

Tie knots with care. A slight scratch from a nail clipper is barely visible to the naked eye. But shown 40 times actual size, the nick appears as a large rupture in the line's skin.

Retie should an overhand knot accidentally form in your line or leader. An overhand knot has a very sharp bend (arrow), and will usually cause the line to fail at about 50 percent of its rated strength.

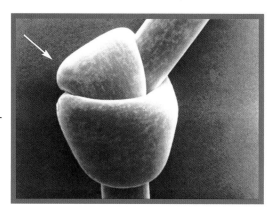

Arbor Knot — Line to spool: strength 60%

The Arbor Knot should be used for attaching your line to the spool of your fishing reel. (1) Loop the line around the spool, then (2) tie an overhand knot around the standing line to form a loose slip knot. (3) Tie an overhand knot in the free end and snug it up. (4) Pull firmly on the standing line until the knot in the free end snugs up against the slip knot. The Arbor Knot will not slip when you wind line onto the spool.

Trilene Knot — Attaching hook to line: strength 90%

The Trilene Knot is one of the easiest knots for novice anglers to learn how to tie. Experts also like the knot because it can be easily tied at night in complete darkness. (1) Slide your line through the hook eye, and repeat, entering the line from the same direction and being sure to form a double loop at the hook eye, as shown. (2) Wrap the tag end around the standing line four or five times, moving away from the hook. (3) Pass the tag end back through the double loop at the hook eye, moisten, pull the knot tight against the hook eye, and trim the tag end (4).

Duncan Loop — Lure to loop: strength 90%

The Duncan Loop allows a hook or crankbait to swing freely on a loop for maximum wobble. (1) Slide your line through the hook eye, and form a loop in the tag end as shown. (2) Pass the tag end through the loop, winding around the standing line and top section of the loop four or five times while moving away from the hook. (3) Moisten the line and pull the tag end to tighten the knot. (4) Slide the knot to the desired position by pulling on the standing line, and trim the tag end.

Blood Knot — Splicing lines of similar diameter: strength 65%

The Blood Knot works great for splicing two lines of similar diameter. (1) Cross the two sections of line to be joined, and then wrap one tag end around the standing part of the other line five to seven times, depending on line diameter. (2) Pass the tag end back between the two lines. (3) Wrap the other tag end in the same manner, and bring it back through the same opening. (4) Pull the standing lines to tighten knot; trim.

Palomar Knot — Attaching hook to line: strength 90%

The Palomar Knot is easy and fast to tie and handy for attaching hooks, swivels and other terminal tackle to your fishing line. It is especially popular with anglers using braided fishing lines. (1) Double about 6 inches of line and pass through the eye of the hook. (2) Tie a simple overhand knot in the doubled line, letting the hook hang loose. Avoid twisting the lines. (3) Pull the end of the loop down, passing it completely over the hook. (4) Pull both ends of the line to draw up the knot. Trim excess.

Dropper Loop Knot — Attaching a dropper line: strength 90%

The Dropper Loop provides a handy attachment point for a dropper line when fishing with several hooks. (1) Form a loop in the line, and wrap the end overhand seven times through the loop. (2) Keep open the midpoint where the turns, or twists, are being made. A pencil inserted in the middle turn helps keep the strands separated so this can be done easily. (3) Hold the other side of the loop and pull it through the opening. Stick your finger through the loop so it does not pull back through. (4) Hold the loop with your teeth, and pull gently on both ends of the line, making the turns gather and pack down on either side of the loop. (5) Tighten with a hard pull on both ends of the line.

Improved Clinch Knot — Attaching hook to line: strength 90%

The Improved Clinch Knot is for attaching leaders and lines to hooks and swivels. The knot is easy to tie and retains nearly all of the line's original strength. (1) Pass end of the line through eye of hook or swivel. (2) Pull about 6 inches of line through and double it back against itself. Twist five to seven times. (3) Pass end of the line through the small loop formed just above the eye, then through the big loop just created. Be careful coils don't overlap. (4) Pull tag end and main line so that coiled line tightens against the eye. Trim excess.

Terminal Tackle

You can spend a small fortune on a boat equipped with all the modern electronics and outfit yourself with the best rods and reels, but if you don't have the right terminal tackle, you won't catch as many fish as you should.

Novice anglers often make the mistake of overrigging – using terminal tackle that is too heavy for the type of fishing they're doing – because they don't want to risk losing a fish to a bent hook or snap. But heavy terminal tackle makes your bait look unnatural and interferes with its action, so you get fewer bites. The best policy is to select the lightest terminal tackle suitable for the conditions.

A finicky walleye, for instance, may turn up its nose at a nightcrawler rigged on a size 2 hook attached to a snap-swivel. But it will eagerly suck in the same worm rigged on a size 6 short-shank hook tied directly to monofilament line.

In some situations, however, delicacy is not an issue. An aggressive pike or muskie will take a foot-long baitfish rigged on the biggest hook attached to the heaviest snap, and will swim leisurely away with the bait, towing a float the size of a tennis ball.

As a rule, use the smallest hook feasible. Small hooks penetrate quicker than big hooks. Small hooks also allow better live-bait presentations.

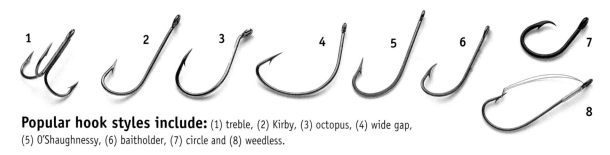

Popular hook styles include: (1) treble, (2) Kirby, (3) octopus, (4) wide gap, (5) O'Shaughnessy, (6) baitholder, (7) circle and (8) weedless.

Sharp Anglers Use Sharp Hooks

Sharp hook points penetrate better and catch more fish than dull ones. When a point breaks or gets dull, you can simply tie on a new hook. But don't be misled into thinking a new hook is always a sharp hook. Cheap hooks are often made of soft, poor-quality steel and are poorly sharpened (left photo). Even new, high-quality hooks dull quickly when dragged through rocks or debris.

Examine your hook frequently to see if it needs sharpening. One simple method is to draw the hook's point across a fingernail. A sharp hook leaves a light scratch and digs into the nail. A dull hook "skates" across the nail without digging in. When necessary, touch up the point using a hook file.

Another option is to use "chemically sharpened" hooks (right photo). Many manufacturers offer a line of hooks made of a finer grade steel and then dipped in a chemical bath, which gives the hook a supersharp point. These hooks can be twice as expensive as conventional hooks, but if you want sharp hooks out of the package, they are the best option. The bottom line – make it a point to keep all your hooks needle sharp.

Carry your terminal tackle in a rig box with plenty of small compartments. That way, you can quickly find the appropriate float, sinker, hook or attachment device for most situations.

Popular sinker styles include: (1) bank, (2) pyramid, (3) rubbercore, (4) bead-chain, (5) split-shot, (6) Bait-Walker, (7) bottom bouncer, (8) egg, (9) bell, (10) walking, (11) bullet.

Popular slip-bobber styles include: (1) glow, (2) lighted, (3) weighted, (4) antenna and (5) balsa. Popular fixed bobbers include: (6) round plastic, (7) heavy current and (8) spring-lock.

Fishing Boats

A good fishing boat must be designed for the type of waters you fish, and it should be laid out and rigged for your style of fishing. A jon boat, for instance, may be ideal for fishing a small river, but its low profile makes it unsafe for use on a large lake. A bass boat is perfect for casting, but the transom is too low for backtrolling on a windy day. Console steering offers comfort, easy steering and good visibility while speeding from spot to spot, but tiller steering gives you better boat control for trolling.

Boats with flat, open floors and comfortable swivel seats allow anglers to move about easily while casting or fighting a fish.

Modern boats are commonly rigged with many sophisticated accessories. Besides depth finders and other electronics, they're often equipped with front and rear trolling motors, live wells, bilge pumps, anchor winches, spotlights, on-board chargers and even such luxury items as AM-FM marine-band cassette players.

On these pages are photographs and descriptions of the most popular types of fishing boats used by freshwater anglers.

Bass boat. The ultimate in speed and fishing comfort, these luxurious boats are often rigged with 150- to 250-hp outboards and can reach speeds exceeding 70 mph.

Deep-V. Often called walleye boats, these boats are ideal for fishing large, windswept lakes. Console- or tiller-operated, many of these boats are rigged with small-horsepower "kicker" motors for trolling.

Semi-V. These 12- to 16-foot boats are inexpensive, yet versatile. Larger, deeper models are used on big lakes, while smaller ones are often used as "car-toppers" to fish waters with poor access.

Jon boat. Rugged and stable, yet inexpensive, the jon boat has a very shallow draft, making it an excellent choice for shallow, stumpy backwaters, marshy lakes and rock-strewn rivers.

Canoe. Light and easy to paddle, a canoe allows you to fish small lakes, ponds and rivers where access is difficult. Small outboards can be used on square-stern canoes or standard canoes with a motor bracket.

Float tube (left) **and kick boat** (right). These small one-person watercraft are lightweight, easily transported and ideal for exploring small bodies of water with poor access. Most float tubes and kick boats are propelled using kick fins or oars.

Liquid-crystal recorders

display the sonar signal on a screen made up of tiny squares, or pixels. For good resolution, the vertical pixel count should be at least 128. Some LCRs can be linked to turn the sonar device into a GPS instrument.

Flashers show the sonar signal on a calibrated dial or bar display. Unlike other sonar devices, flashers give you an instantaneous readout of targets, even at speeds over 60 mph. For this reason, flashers are the favorite in-dash sonar device for many expert fishermen.

Video graphs display the sonar signal on a cathode-ray tube, much like a television set. Videos are bulky, but give you better resolution than an LCR. Some video graphs have a color display, with different colors representing different-sized targets.

Sonar Devices & Other Electronic Aids

Before the age of electronic fishing, anglers had only a vague idea of water depth and bottom contour. And if they found a hot spot in a large body of water, they would have to be lucky to find it a second time.

Today, many anglers use navigational tools such as GPS (global positioning system) to return unerringly to their spots, and once they get there, they check the depth and scout for fish with sophisticated sonar.

Modern anglers also rely on other electronic aids, such as temperature gauges, trolling-speed indicators and marine radios. Together, these electronics take much of the guesswork out of the sport, enabling anglers to catch fish more consistently.

SONAR DEVICES. Commonly called depth finders or fish locators, sonar devices come in three basic types: liquid-crystal recorders (LCRs), video graphs and flashers.

All sonar devices operate on the same principle. The transducer, which can be attached to the boat's hull, transom or trolling motor, sends sound waves to the bottom, and the returning echos are recorded on a screen or, in the case of a flasher, displayed instantly on a dial. The screen or dial displays the bottom and any other objects above it, such as fish or weeds. With a little experience, the operator can also learn to distinguish different bottom types.

When fishing from a boat, it's ideal to have two depth finders, one in the bow and one near the stern. The latter is used whenever you're running the outboard motor. That way, you can see how deep the water is and avoid any shallow dangerous areas. In addition, you can reference your depth readings with a good lake map to find prime fishing spots without wasting a lot of time. The depth finder in the bow is used as your "underwater eyes" as you maneuver the boat with the bow-mount trolling motor.

OTHER ELECTRONIC AIDS. Fish often concentrate in specific temperature layers, around colder or warmer tributaries or in bays that are warmer than other parts of a lake. Temperature gauges help you locate these zones quickly. Some gauges monitor only surface temperature while others come with long cords that allow you to take the temperature at any depth.

Another electronic aid used by many fishermen is the trolling-speed indicator, which allows you to precisely monitor how fast you're trolling, so you can maintain the speed that fish prefer. And gaining in popularity are marine radios. They make it possible to exchange information with anglers several miles away. Most marine radios have weather bands to keep you informed of approaching storms.

Of all electronic aids, however, sonar devices are without question the most important to your fishing success. Perhaps the greatest difference between the expert and average angler lies in the expert's ability to accurately interpret the signals seen on the depth finder. These pages explain the basic types of depth finders and how to use them correctly.

How to Interpret Graph Readings

Hard bottom is indicated by a thick gray band (left bracket); soft bottom, a thin gray band (right bracket).

Weeds (arrows) appear as irregular shapes projecting off the bottom.

Baitfish schools (arrow) appear as an irregular clump not connected to the bottom.

Bottom-hugging fish (arrow) can be distinguished from the bottom by "air" beneath the signal.

Understanding "Hook Size" on a Graph

Many fishermen think a big hook on their LCR or video means a big fish. It could be, but it could also mean a small fish. Here's why.

Suppose two fish of equal size swim underneath your stationary boat. The first fish (number 1), is only a few feet down, where the cone is narrow. As a result, it passes through the cone quickly and makes only a short mark. The second fish (2), swims near the bottom, where the cone is wide. It spends more time in the cone, and consequently makes a much longer mark.

Here's another example: You're drifting or slow-trolling and pass over a bluegill (number 3) that is motionless or swimming slowly with the boat. It makes a long mark because it stays in the cone until the boat moves away. Then a good-sized bass (4) swims rapidly through the cone. It makes a shorter mark because it passes through the cone more quickly.

A more reliable indicator of fish size than arc length is arc thickness. The thickness depends on the strength of the reflected signal. And big fish reflect a much stronger signal than do little fish.

Maps & Navigational Equipment

Hydrographic maps, also called contour maps, are one of a fisherman's most valuable tools. They enable you to quickly find likely fish-holding structure that could otherwise be found only by hours of intensive scouting.

Although contour maps don't necessarily show every piece of structure in a given body of water, they reveal the largest, most prominent pieces. There will always be small points, inside turns and sunken islands that don't show up on the map.

Hydrographic maps show a body of water's structure with contour lines. (1) Closely spaced lines signify a sharp drop-off; (2) widely spaced lines, a gradual drop-off. Holes are indicated by (3) a series of concentric contour lines, with the greatest depth in the middle. Humps, or sunken islands, are also indicated by (4) a series of concentric contour lines, but the shallowest depth is in the middle. (5) Underwater points protrude out from the shore and (6) inside turns are shown by the sharp curve of the contour lines.

In addition to hydrographic maps, fishermen often make use of other map types. River charts, for example, show locks and dams, submerged wing-dams, riprap banks and mileage markers. Reservoir maps identify dams, stands of flooded timber, old roadbeds and the old river channel. GPS (global positioning system) maps show the precise latitude and longitude of lake features, which enables anglers to motor directly to a desired spot. And recreation maps include information valuable to anglers, such as location of public access sites and a list of fish species that are present in a particular body of water.

Maps are available through a wide variety of sources, including private companies, state or provincial natural-resource agencies, the U.S. Army Corps of Engineers and the Bureau of Reclamation.

Once a luxury enjoyed mainly by big-water boaters, GPS navigational units are rapidly gaining popularity on most types of fishing waters. Not only do they enable you to quickly find your spots, they make fishing safer by helping you navigate accurately in the fog and at night.

GPS also makes it easier to share fishing information. Rather than try to explain the location of a hard-to-find spot over the phone, for instance, an angler can give a friend the exact GPS coordinates.

GPS units rely on signals from U.S. military satellites, and they can be used anywhere on earth.

Many anglers are intimidated by the complexity of GPS devices, so they are hesitant to purchase one. One reason these navigation devices seem so complex is that they have

many advanced features that the average angler may never use. Most fishermen simply want to mark the location of a particular waypoint, such as a good fishing spot or a boat landing, so they can find it again later. Thankfully, the procedure for doing that on a GPS unit is quite simple.

After you use your GPS device for awhile and become comfortable with it, you can begin experimenting with some of the more complex features, such as setting up a navigation route that leads you to a series of waypoints.

Unlike old navigational devices like Loran-C, GPS is easier to operate, because you do not have to pre-program the unit to select certain signals. And it is more reliable, because it is not affected by weather. In addition, GPS units process navigation data more rapidly, usually within a second or two. Because the screen is updated so fast, there is less chance for steering error.

Full-size GPS units (top) have a separate antenna, or module (inset), that receives the satellite signals. They are powered by the boat's 12-volt electrical system. They have a large, easy-to-read screen. Hand-held GPS units (bottom) are powered by an internal battery and have a built-in antenna, so they are portable. They have the same features as a full-size GPS unit, but the screen is much smaller.

Trolling Equipment

Trolling has always been one of the most effective techniques for catching fish. Perhaps no other method allows you to present one or more lures to large numbers of fish spread out over a vast area.

For many fishermen, trolling involves nothing more than making a long cast behind the boat and maintaining a trolling speed and water depth appropriate for their lure choice. But modern innovations in trolling gear have revolutionized this age-old fishing method.

Anglers no longer have to guess how deep their lure is running or how fast it is going. They can set a downrigger to fish at a precise depth while a speed sensor can be attached to the downrigger cable to tell them exactly how fast the lure is moving at that depth. Some downriggers even feature bottom-tracking systems that raise and lower automatically to stay at a predetermined distance above the bottom. A transducer on the transom sends a signal to the downrigger, telling it when to change depth. Two or more downriggers can operate off the same sonar signal, all changing depths simultaneously.

And trollers are no longer limited to fishing straight behind the boat. By attaching their lines to side planers or trolling boards (opposite page), they can reach fish that might have moved off to the side when the boat passed over them.

Some planing devices go down as well as out. This enables deepwater anglers to cover a much wider swath of water than they otherwise would using only downriggers.

Downriggers (left) enable you to fish in deep water with relatively light tackle. An 8- to 12-pound lead weight, or cannonball, is lowered to the desired depth on a stainless steel cable. The fishing line is then attached to a release that trips when a fish strikes, allowing you to play the fish on a free line.

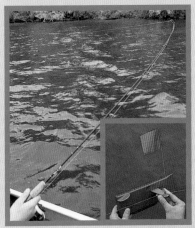

Side planers

(inset) attach to your line and pull it to the side as the boat moves forward. A strike trips a release, and the planer slides down the line until it hits a stop several feet from the lure.

Diving planes,

such as the Dipsey Diver®, track right, left or straight, depending on how you adjust the rudder. Tie your line to the front eye of the Dipsey Diver, and your lure to a 6- to 8-foot leader, which is attached to the rear eye. When a fish strikes, the diving plane flattens so you can reel in the fish without pulling against the plane.

Trolling boards

(1), plane to the side on a separate cord which is held by a planer mast (2). The fishing line is attached to the cord with a release (3). As the boat moves forward, the release slides down the cord to the desired point. A strike trips the release, and the angler fights the fish on a free line.

Clothing & Wading Gear

The right apparel keeps you comfortable in any weather and makes you less visible to gamefish. Here's what to look for:

CLOTHING COLOR. Wary species like trout or muskies flee at the slightest flash of color or movement. The secret to successfully catching fish is not alerting them to your presence before you've had a chance to make a cast to them or can get them to strike.

One of the best ways to avoid giving yourself away is to blend in with your surroundings. In most situations, drab colors such as blue or light brown give you the necessary camouflage. Avoid wearing bright colors, such as yellow or red, which can spook fish.

DRESSING FOR THE WEATHER. For the winter fisherman, dressing for the elements can be as important as choosing the right lure or live bait. Fly fishermen in the winter season, for instance, often spend hours wading icy water in frigid weather. Without the right clothing, they risk hypothermia. Likewise, ice fishermen must deal with temperatures that often dip below 0°F. When fishing in cold weather, dress in layers of synthetic materials that wick moisture away from the body, and wool or other insulating materials that keep you warm even when wet. Layers can be easily shed, if the weather changes.

In hot weather, be sure to keep your skin covered with thin, lightweight clothing to prevent sunburn. Long pants and long-sleeved shirts are recommended. Always use a waterproof sunblock with an SPF rating of 15 or higher on any exposed skin.

POLARIZED SUNGLASSES. Whenever you're fishing during daylight hours, polarized sunglasses are a must. They not only protect your eyes from flying hooks, they cut the glare off the water and allow you to identify fish-holding structure. If the wind is calm and the water is relatively clear, you may even spot shallow-water gamefish.

For overcast conditions, and early and late in the day, it's best you use glasses with amber or other light-colored lenses. Darker gray lenses are a popular choice on bright days. Whatever color lenses you decide to use, make sure they block harmful UV rays.

HATS. Even on overcast days, you need a hat with a brim to reduce glare and make it easier to spot gamefish. Hats made especially for fishing often have a brim that is dark on the underside to further reduce glare on the water.

The most popular type of hat is the baseball-style cap. Lightweight and comfortable, these caps come with visors of various lengths to shade your eyes. But they do not shade your ears and neck.

Some hats have a back flap that folds down to shade your

neck and ears. A full-brim hat sheds rain and helps protect the back of your head from hooks, a problem for some anglers when they're fly casting. Avoid brightly colored hats if you're fishing shallow clear water.

RAIN GEAR. It pays to carry a quality rain suit whenever you plan to spend a day on the water. That way, you're prepared for an unexpected storm.

A lightweight jacket made of a breathable material such as Gore-Tex® can be worn all day without overheating. Be ready to spend some money for such a rain suit, however, as breathable waterproof materials are quite expensive.

Although heavy and bulky, rubber rain gear provides the ultimate in rain protection. Worn over insulating layers, it will keep you dry and warm. Another advantage to rubber rain gear is that it's relatively inexpensive.

FLY-FISHING VESTS. A good vest should be lightweight, yet large enough to fit over a sweater or heavy shirt and hold your gear.

When choosing a vest, look for one with an assortment of pockets in various sizes for carrying accessories. The pockets should close securely with zippers or Velcro® to keep small items from falling out. The vest should also have a large zippered pocket in the back for storing lightweight rain gear.

Other handy features include a fly patch for drying flies before putting them in their box, and extended zipper tabs on the pockets, for easier opening with cold or gloved fingers.

WADING GEAR. Your choice of wading gear depends on the depth and temperature of the

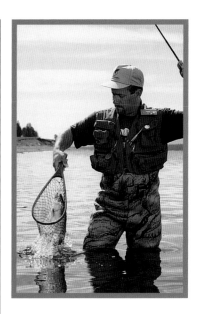

water you'll be in, how far you'll be walking and how much traction you'll need. Whatever gear you choose should fit well, keep you dry when wading and allow you to walk comfortably.

Wading gear comes in two common types: chest waders (above), which are best for wading in deep water; and hip boots, which are ideal for small, shallow streams or anywhere you are unlikely to wade deeper than mid-thigh.

Both types come in boot-foot and stocking-foot styles and are available in a variety of materials.

For warm weather, some anglers prefer wet wading. Instead of waders or hip boots, they wear shorts or lightweight, fast-drying pants, along with wading sandals.

WADING JACKETS. A good wading jacket is your best bet for extended foul-weather fishing because it combines the waterproof qualities of a raincoat with the short length and large pockets of a fly-fishing vest. Some jackets include neoprene cuffs to keep out water and a drawstring hood designed to fit over most hats.

Lures & Live Bait:
Making the Right Choice

Many fishermen choose their lures and live baits by trial and error. They keep changing until they find something that catches a fish. But choosing a lure or bait is not a random choice for expert fishermen. Instead, they select a lure or bait only after considering the following factors.

DEPTH. This is the prime concern in lure and bait selection. For example, fish in deep water will seldom chase a lure retrieved just below the surface. Try to estimate the most probable depth based on the season, time of day, weather, water clarity and past experience on the body of water.

In water shallower than 10 feet, anglers use surface lures, spinnerbaits, spinners or shallow-running crankbaits. Lightly weighted soft plastics will also work. In deeper water, use deep-running or sinking crank-baits, jigging lures or heavily weighted soft plastics. Live bait can be used in both shallow and deep water.

COVER. When fishing in thick weeds or brush, use any lure with a weedguard to prevent snagging. When fishing with live bait in and around cover, use a cone-shaped sinker and a weedless hook.

ACTIVITY LEVEL. The activity level of gamefish determines the size and action of the lure or live bait and the speed of the retrieve. Water temperature affects fish activity more than

any other factor. However, weather conditions, especially cold fronts, also play a major role.

After a cold front, or in cold water (when fish activity is at a minimum), live bait works well because it can be crawled along the bottom or suspended from a bobber. Lures such as jigging spoons and small jigs are also good cold-water choices.

WATER CLARITY AND LIGHT LEVELS. Most fishermen have different theories for selecting lure color. However, most agree that water clarity affects their choice of colors.

Many anglers insist that light-colored lures are better for fishing in clear water. But that does not explain the success of black or purple worms in clear waters. Fluorescent lures in yellow, chartreuse or orange seem to work best in murky water. Dark colors usually outproduce light colors on overcast days or at night.

When fishing at night or in a murky lake, use a noisy lure. Good choices include a topwater popper or chugger, a spinner-

bait with large blades, a buzzbait with a blade that ticks the shaft, or a crankbait with internal beads that rattle.

Beginning fishermen are often overwhelmed by the huge selection of lures and live-bait rigs at their local tackle shop. Many buy a large tackle box and fill each tray with a different lure. They never stick with one lure or live-bait rig long enough to learn how to use it properly.

Some beginners go to the opposite extreme. They catch a few fish on a particular lure or bait, then refuse to change. Their favorite may work well at times, but too often it catches little or nothing.

Top fishermen contend that you cannot catch fish unless you have confidence in your presentation, meaning your choice of lure or bait and how you retrieve it. When buying lures and live-bait rigs, select a few of each basic type, then learn how and when to use them. Catching fish is the quickest way to gain confidence in any presentation.

Spinner-type Lures

Standard spinner

Two aspects of spinner-type lures attribute to their success in both clear and murky water. In clear water, gamefish can spot the flash of the revolving blade from a distance. In murky water, they use their lateral-line sense to pinpoint the vibration from the turning blade.

Another reason for the success of these lures is the relative ease of using them. They will produce fish with a simple straight retrieve. And, when a fish strikes a spinner, it often hooks itself.

Spinner-type lures come in four basic designs. Standard spinners have a blade that rotates around a straight wire shaft. Most standard spinners have some type of weight behind the blade to make the lure heavy enough to cast. Weight-forward spinners resemble standard spinners, but the weight is ahead of the blade. Spinnerbaits have a shaft similar to an open safety pin. They have a lead head on the lower arm and a spinner blade on the upper arm. Buzzbaits resemble either standard spinners or spinnerbaits, but have a specially designed propeller.

Spinner-type lures will catch almost any kind of freshwater gamefish. These lures will work at any time of year, but they are especially effective when extremely cold or warm water makes fish lethargic and reluctant to chase anything moving too fast. Most spinner blades will turn even at very slow retrieve speeds.

Weight-forward spinner

Spinnerbait

Buzzbait

Different blades have different amounts of water resistance. A broad blade rotates at a greater angle to the shaft and thus has more resistance than a narrow one. A large blade has more resistance than a small one of the same shape.

The greater the resistance, the shallower the lure will run at a given speed. Generally, wide blades are best suited for slow retrieves and light current; narrow ones for fast retrieves and swift current.

Sensitive tackle will help you feel the beat of the spinner blade. If the beat stops, you may be retrieving too slowly, weeds may have fouled the lure or a fish may have struck it. When fishing a spinnerbait or buzzbait, use a stiff rod to drive the thick hooks into a fish's jaws.

When fishing spinner-type lures for panfish or trout, use 2- to 6-pound mono; for walleyes or smallmouths in open water, 6- to 10-pound mono; for bass in heavy cover, 12- to 25-pound mono; for casting muskie bucktails, 30- to 50-pound braided Dacron or one of the popular "superlines."

Plugs

Originally, the term *plug* referred to a lure carved from a block of wood. Many fishermen still consider wooden plugs the best, but most modern plugs are made of hollow plastic or hard foamed plastic.

Plastic plugs are less expensive and hold their finish better than wooden plugs. Plastic plugs of a given model are more consistent in shape, density and action than wooden ones. But wooden plugs sometimes have a better action than similar ones made of plastic. A balsa minnow, for example, wobbles more readily than a plastic minnow of the same size and shape.

Most plugs imitate baitfish, but some resemble animals like mice, frogs and crayfish. Other plugs attract fish by their action and flash, resembling nothing in particular. All plugs produce some sound that draws the attention of gamefish. It may be a high- or low-frequency vibration; a pop, gurgle or splash; or merely the sound of the hooks clinking on the hook

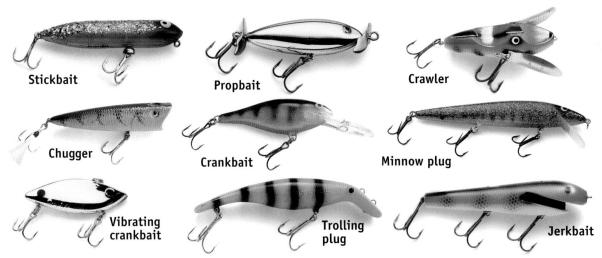

Stickbait

Propbait

Crawler

Chugger

Crankbait

Minnow plug

Vibrating crankbait

Trolling plug

Jerkbait

hangers. Some plugs also have chambers filled with shot that produce a loud rattle.

Some plugs are designed exclusively for surface fishing. Surface plugs work especially well when fish are spawning or feeding in shallow water. But they will sometimes draw fish up from deeper water.

Surface plugs are most effective at water temperatures of 60°F or warmer. The water must be relatively calm; otherwise, fish do not seem to notice the action. Surface plugs generally work best in early morning, at dusk or at night, although they may catch fish any time of day. They fall into the following categories:

Stickbait – These long, slender, floating plugs lack lips or propellers. They have no built-in wobble, so the fisherman must supply the action.

Propbait – Similar to stickbaits, these lures have a propeller at one or both ends.

Crawler – A large faceplate or wings on the sides make the lure crawl across the surface when retrieved steadily. Crawlers produce a plopping or gurgling sound.

Chugger – The indented face catches water when the plug is jerked across the surface, producing a popping or chugging

noise. Some chuggers have a slow, swimming action when retrieved steadily.

Subsurface plugs run at depths of 1 to 20 feet or more. These plugs are much more versatile than surface plugs. They work well in either calm or rough water and will catch fish at any time of day. You can select either shallow- or deep-running models, depending on the depth of the fish. Subsurface plugs fall into these categories:

Crankbait – Most crankbaits float at rest, but some sink and others are neutrally buoyant. All have a lip, which makes them dive and wiggle when retrieved.

Minnow plug – Like crankbaits, these plugs have lips and may float, sink or be neutrally buoyant. Designed to imitate thin-bodied baitfish, minnow plugs have a side-to-side wobble.

Vibrating crankbait – These thin-bodied plugs do not have lips. The attachment eye is on top of the head, resulting in a tight wiggle. Most vibrating crankbaits sink, but a few float while at rest.

Trolling plug – Designed primarily or exclusively for trolling, these plugs generally have a large flattened forehead that creates a wide, erratic wobble. Trolling plugs are difficult to cast because they are relatively light, and their

shape is too wind-resistant. Most trolling plugs float at rest.

Jerkbait – These large, elongated plugs are intended mainly for catching muskies and large pike. Most float at rest, dive when given a strong jerk, then float back to the surface. Many have metal tails that can be bent to change the action.

Plugs range in size from the tiny, inch-long models used for panfish to the huge, foot-long plugs intended for muskies. When selecting plugs, length is a more important consideration than weight. Following are plug lengths most commonly used for various types of gamefish.

Plug Length for Various Gamefish

SPECIES	PLUG LENGTH (inches)
Crappies	1 to 2
Small/medium trout	1 to 3
White bass	1/2 to 3
Smallmouth/ Spotted bass	2 to 3
Largemouth bass/ Pickerel	2 to 6
Walleyes	3 to 6
Salmon/ large trout	3 to 7
Northern pike, Muskies and Stripers	4 to 12

Jigs

Many expert fishermen consider jigs and jigging lures the most consistently productive of all artificial lures. They work for a wide variety of species under almost any conditions.

A jig is simply a piece of lead with a hook molded into it. A dressing of hair, feathers, tinsel or soft plastic generally conceals the hook. Other types of jigging lures include the jigging spoon, a very thick metal spoon; the vibrating blade, a thin metal minnow imitation; and the tailspin, a lead-bodied lure with a spinner at the rear.

Jigs and jigging lures can be fished slowly, so they work especially well in cold water. Low water temperature reduces the metabolic rate of fish, making them reluctant to chase fast-moving lures. But the slow jigging action will often tempt a strike. The rapid sink rate of most jigs and jigging lures makes them an excellent choice for reaching bottom in current or for fishing in deep water. Lake trout anglers, for example, regularly use these lures at depths of up to 100 feet with no extra weight added to the line. But jigs and jigging lures can also be effective in water only a few feet deep.

Most jigs and jigging lures have compact bodies, so they are ideal for casting into the wind or for casting long distances. The extra distance helps you take fish in clear water or in other situations where they are easily spooked.

Despite the effectiveness of jigs and jigging lures, many anglers have difficulty catching fish with them. The main problem is detecting the strike. Fish sel-

dom slam these lures as they do a crankbait or surface lure. Instead, they inhale the lure gently, usually as it settles toward bottom. If you are not alert or do not have a taut line as the lure sinks, you will not notice the strike.

Because strikes are often light, jigs and jigging lures should be fished with sensitive tackle. Most experts prefer a relatively stiff graphite rod, with just enough flexibility in the tip to cast the lure.

Ultralight to medium-power spinning or light baitcasting outfits work well in most cases. But heavier tackle is needed to handle lures over 3/4 ounce or to horse fish from heavy cover.

Use the lightest line practical for the species and fishing condi-

Standard jig

Jigging spoon

Vibrating blade

Tailspin

tions. If your line is too heavy, the lure will sink too slowly and will not stay at the desired depth when retrieved. Also, strikes will be more difficult to detect.

With ordinary monofilament, the twitch signaling a strike is hard to see. To detect strikes more easily, use fluorescent monofilament. Many jig fishermen wear polarized sunglasses to improve line visibility even more.

When selecting jigs and jigging lures, the main consideration is weight. Your selection must be a compromise based on the type of fish, water depth, current speed and wind velocity.

For panfish, most anglers prefer lures of no more than 1/8 ounce. Some panfish jigs, called micro jigs, weigh as little as 1/80 ounce. For mid-sized gamefish like walleyes and bass, 1/8- to 3/4-ounce lures normally work best. For larger gamefish like muskies, jigs of 3/4 ounce or more are usually the most productive.

The lure must be heavy enough to reach the desired depth, but not so heavy that it sinks too fast. Fish usually prefer a slowly falling lure to one plummeting toward bottom. As a general rule, allow 1/8 ounce for every 10 feet of water. For example, a lure of at least 1/4 ounce would be needed to reach bottom in water 20 feet deep.

In slow current, however, the same 1/4-ounce lure would only reach a depth of about 15 feet. As the current becomes faster, the weight of lure needed to reach bottom increases. Wind affects your lure choice much the same way as current. The wind pushes your boat across the surface, increasing water resistance on the line and lure. This makes it more difficult for the lure to reach the desired depth and stay there.

Soft Plastics

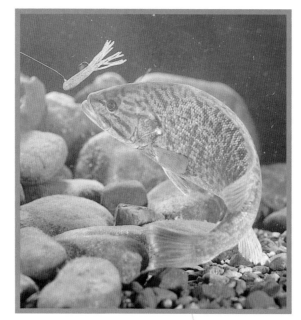

Fishermen have used soft-bodied lures since 1860, when the first rubber worm was patented. But most of the early lures lacked the lifelike action of modern soft plastics because the material was relatively hard by today's standards.

In 1949, an Ohio lure-maker began molding plastic worms from a new synthetic material, polyvinyl chloride resin. Bass fishermen who tested these lures soon reported fantastic results. Because the worms were so soft, they flexed with each twitch of the line, resulting in an irresistible action.

The popularity of soft plastics has skyrocketed since those early years. Most tackle stores now offer a wide selection of soft plastic worms, grubs, crayfish, shrimp, frogs, snakes, lizards, salamanders, salmon eggs and insect imitations. Today, fishermen use soft plastic lures for virtually all species of gamefish.

Soft plastics offer several major advantages over hard-bodied lures. A hard-bodied artificial does not have a texture like real food, so fish may immediately recognize it as a fake and eject it. If you do not set the hook instantly, you will probably miss the fish. But a soft plastic has a lifelike texture, so fish will mouth it an instant longer, giving you extra time to set the hook.

Many soft plastics can be rigged with the hook point buried inside where it cannot

Carolina rig with lizard

catch on obstructions. This way, a soft plastic can be retrieved through dense weeds or brush, or over rocks and logs with practically no chance of snagging. Yet the point will penetrate the soft material when you set the hook.

Another attribute of soft plastics is their ability to absorb scents. You can treat soft plastics with bottled fish attractants

or buy them with scents molded in. Scents quickly wash off hard-bodied lures, but soft plastic holds scent much longer.

Often, soft plastics look almost exactly like natural fish foods. Legs, feelers and even minute details like scales add to the realistic appearance. Many have translucent bodies that allow light to pass through, much as it passes through common foods like baitfish, worms, shrimp and insect larvae.

Modern soft plastics vary in hardness from almost jellylike to relatively firm. The softer lures look and feel more natural to fish. But the harder ones are more durable and stay on the hook better, especially when fished in snaggy cover. Most manufacturers use a plastic between these extremes.

To cast the smallest soft plastic lures, you will need light spinning tackle, light line, sinkers or a casting bubble. Or you can use fly tackle. To cast soft plastics less than 6 inches long, light spinning tackle and 4- to 8-pound mono usually work best. For larger lures with exposed hooks, most fishermen prefer spinning or baitcasting tackle with lines from 8- to 15-pound test. For larger soft plastic lures with hooks buried in the plastic, use baitcasting tackle with lines from 12- to 25-pound test.

Some manufacturers make powerful rods, called worm rods, specifically for driving the hook point through a soft plastic lure and into a fish's jaw. When working soft plastics through weeds or brush, use abrasion-resistant line.

Spoons

The flashy, wobbling motion of a spoon imitates that of a fleeing or crippled baitfish, triggering strikes from most species of gamefish. Spoons work best for large predators like northern pike, muskies, largemouth bass, salmon and trout. Because spoons appeal mainly to the sense of sight, they work best in relatively clear waters.

The long-standing popularity of spoons results not only from their nearly universal appeal to gamefish, but also from the relative ease of using them. Anglers normally fish spoons far enough above bottom so that snags are not a problem. And a fish usually hooks itself when it grabs a spoon.

Spoons are generally made of hard metal, either steel or brass. A few are made of tough plastic. Because one side is concave, a spoon catches water when retrieved and wobbles from side to side.

How a spoon wobbles depends on its shape and thickness. A long spoon usually has a wider side-to-side action than a short spoon. A deeply concave spoon catches more water and thus wobbles more widely than a flatter spoon. Thin spoons tend to wobble more than thick ones.

But thick spoons have some advantages. The extra weight makes them cast better, sink faster and run deeper than thin spoons.

Most spoons have a polished metal surface on at least one side. Sunlight reflecting off this surface makes the spoon visible for a long distance, especially in clear water. Some spoons have a hammered surface that scatters light in all directions, much the way the scales of a baitfish scatter light. High-quality spoons sometimes have a plated surface that reflects more light than the duller surface of cheaper spoons.

Spoons fall into three basic categories. Standard spoons include any non-weedless spoon heavy enough to cast. Trolling spoons are so thin that they are not practical for casting. Most standard and trolling spoons have a single or treble hook attached to one end with a split-ring. Weedless spoons usually have some type of weedguard to prevent the fixed single hook from fouling in weeds, brush or debris.

The main consideration in fishing a spoon is how fast you work it. A spoon will not wobble properly if fished too slowly or too fast. You must experiment to find the precise speed at which each spoon performs best.

Most anglers prefer light- to medium-power spinning or baitcasting tackle when fishing with spoons. Ultrasensitive rods are not necessary. Because fish tend to hook themselves on spoons, you need not be concerned about detecting strikes.

Spoons work best when fished with light monofilament. Heavy line restricts the wobble and is more visible to fish in clear water.

Standard spoon

Trolling spoon

Weedless spoon

Flies

Most traditional fly patterns are imitators, simulating natural foods eaten by gamefish. Practically all freshwater fish rely heavily on aquatic insects at some time in their life, explaining why so many flies used in fresh water are insect imitations. The diet of most adult fish, however, leans heavily toward crustaceans and baitfish, so a lot of flies mimic these food types.

Some imitators are painstakingly realistic, with antennae, jointed legs and other body parts that closely match those of the natural bait in every respect. But that degree of imitation is seldom necessary to fool a fish; in most cases, an impressionistic fly, one with the general look of the natural, will do the job equally well. When choosing an imitator, consider:

SIZE. Your fly should closely match the size of the natural. An imitation that is too large, even when presented well, is likely to spook the fish.

COLOR. You can't go wrong with a fly that's similar in hue to the natural. If you can't match the color, select a fly similar in shade. If the fish are taking a light-colored mayfly, for instance, don't use a dark-colored imitation.

SHAPE. A fly with the general profile of the natural may be all it takes to convince the fish to bite. When the fish are selective, however, pay closer attention to tail length, wing size and body shape.

ACTION. The overall look of a fly is normally more important than its action. But there are

Damselfly nymph – an imitator

Adams dry fly – a searching pattern

Royal Coachman dry fly – an attractor

times when action will trigger strikes. A fly with a marabou body, for example, may present a closer imitation of an undulating leech than does a fly with a hair body.

TEXTURE. Texture does not entice a fish to take a fly, but it may affect how long the fish holds on to the fly. A spun deer hair bug, for instance, feels more like real food than a hard-bodied bug, so a fish may mouth it for an instant longer before rejecting it, giving you more time to set the hook.

Often, you'll see insects hatching sporadically, but you won't be able to spot a predominant hatch. This is the time to try searching patterns, flies that represent a broad spectrum of insect life, rather than a specific insect form.

Some flies, called attractors, bear no resemblance to any kind of natural food. They rely on bright colors, flashy materials or sound to arouse a fish's curiosity or trigger a defensive strike.

Live Bait

Even in these times of high-tech artificial lures, over half of all freshwater gamefish caught in North America are taken using live bait. When fishing gets slow, even dedicated artificial-lure advocates know that it's time to turn to live bait. To discriminating gamefish, no artificial lure can duplicate the smell, action and texture of the real thing.

As experienced fishermen know, the best live baits are those you catch yourself – baits that can't be purchased at bait shops. Catching your own bait can be almost as rewarding as fishing with it. Whether you buy your bait or catch it yourself, live bait should be kept fresh and lively. Active, fresh bait is what catches fish. And you can save money by learning to keep your bait alive.

Many fishermen are stubborn when it comes to choosing baits and rigs. They stick with familiar combinations for hours on end, and grudgingly switch baits just about the time fish stop biting altogether. When testing a new live bait, give it a fair trial before switching to something else. You just might discover a new live-bait type that is destined to become your old favorite.

The following are brief descriptions of the most popular types of live baits:

BAITFISH. To most fishermen, the word minnow means any small fish used for bait. Technically, minnows are members of a family that includes 250 species in North America. Anglers use many of these for bait, including shiners, chubs, dace and even carp. The term *baitfish* includes not only minnows, but other fished used by anglers such as suckers, sculpins, madtoms, eels and small gamefish.

WORMS AND LEECHES. The earthworm is the most widely-used bait in North America and is one of the easiest natural baits to collect and keep. Hundreds of earthworm species are found throughout the continent. All have the same general shape but vary greatly in size and color. For this reason they can be used to catch a number of different fish species. Popular worms used for bait include nightcrawlers, garden worms, leaf worms, grunt worms, manure worms and gray and African nightcrawlers.

Leeches inhabit lakes, ponds, marshes and slow-moving streams throughout the country. All leeches have sucking disks at both ends. The mouth is located in the smaller disk at the head end. leeches use the large disk on the tail end only for clinging to objects. Fish eat many types of leeches, but only the ribbon leech is used widely as bait. A few anglers have found tiger leeches to be good panfish bait. Medicine and horse leeches are not as effective.

INSECTS. A land or terrestrial insect falls prey to fish when it drops or washes into a lake or stream. The most popular terrestrials used by anglers are crickets and grasshoppers.

Most insects eaten by fish live in the water. Called aquatic insects, they spend their egg and immature stages in the water and their adult stage on land. Immature insects, also called larvae, are wingless and

have tiny gills. They live on stream or lake bottoms, where they are a source of food for fish. Aquatic insects that are often used for bait include stoneflies, mayflies, caddisflies and hellgrammites.

SALAMANDERS AND FROGS. Generations of fishermen in the southeastern United States have used salamanders for bait. Salamanders are gaining popularity in other parts of the country. They are lively, durable baits that are especially attractive to large gamefish.

More than 100 species of salamanders live in North America. Nearly every species of salamander is used for bait. Members of the giant salamander family, the true waterdogs, live in water all of their lives and are the preferred bait species for many anglers.

Years ago, frogs were one of the most popular baits. Although they are still effective, frogs are not as widely used among today's fishermen. Frog populations in many regions have declined due to pesticides, disease and wetland drainage. Some states now restrict their harvest, but frogs can still be found in most areas. Leopard frogs, green frogs and bullfrogs are the most often used species.

CRUSTACEANS. Young fish feed heavily on water fleas and other microscopic crustaceans. Many adult fish regularly eat crayfish and other large crustaceans. This explains why crustaceans are effective as bait. The following crustaceans are used for bait by freshwater fishermen: crayfish, grass shrimp, scuds, mud shrimp, saltwater shrimp and freshwater shrimp.

OTHER NATURAL BAITS. Other popular baits used for catching fish include salmon eggs, clams, cut-bait and fish parts, and preserved baits.

SKILLS

As with all sports and outdoor activities, fishing requires that you have a good mastery of the basic skills before you can be successful. After all, it won't matter if you know what the best lure is or where the fish are biting if you can't make an accurate cast. And once you have a fish hooked, you still need to know how to fight and land it. Because these tasks may seem difficult to someone with limited knowledge of where to begin, this section details all of the important skills needed to get started fishing. You'll learn how to control the boat, make the perfect cast, set the hook, and play and land that fish of a lifetime. The angler in this photo is fighting a good-sized muskie on one of Ontario's top fisheries, Lake of the Woods.

Casting Techniques

1. Hold the line with your index finger to prevent line from flowing off the spool with the bail open.

I n casting, the two main considerations are distance and accuracy. As a rule, spinning gear gives you better distance; baitcasting gear, better accuracy.

The secret to becoming a proficient caster is learning to let the rod do the work. If you try to throw the lure rather than let the spring of the rod flick it out, you'll lose both distance and accuracy.

Your rod's power, action, length, guide size and guide placement greatly affect casting performance. If the rod is too powerful for the weight of the lure, it will not load enough on the backcast, and you'll have no choice but to throw the lure. If the rod is too light for the lure, it won't have enough power to propel the lure.

The lighter the lure, the more important it is to use a slow-action rod so the entire rod contributes casting power. The longer the rod, the more leverage for longer casts. Guides that are too small restrict line flow and create friction, which reduces casting distance. If the guides are spaced too far apart, the line slaps the rod between the guides during the cast, also causing excess friction.

The type and weight of your line also affect casting. The stiffer and heavier the line, the shorter your casts. Don't use line heavier than needed for the conditions. Be sure to fill the spool, but don't overfill it.

You can make long, accurate casts with most any modern reel, although there are a few specific considerations. Long-spool spinning reels, for instance, cast farther than those with shorter spools because the line level decreases very little from the start of the cast to the finish. When you try to make a long cast with a short-spool, narrow-arbor reel, the line begins slapping the spool toward the end of the cast, reducing casting distance.

1. Press the spool release and thumb the spool to prevent line from spinning off prematurely.

2. Bring the rod back briskly, stopping at the 10 o'clock position. The rod should bend back, or load, from the weight of the lure.

3. Stroke the rod forward with a smooth wrist motion, and, midway through the forward stroke, release the line from your index finger.

4. Feather the line with your index finger to stop the lure precisely on the target.

2. Bring the rod back briskly, stopping at the 10 o'clock position, just as you do in spincasting. For best accuracy, use a straight overhand motion.

3. Stroke the rod forward with a smooth wrist motion, and, midway through the forward stroke, lift your thumb to release the line.

4. Thumb the spool as needed during the cast to minimize backlashing and to stop the lure exactly where you want it.

How to Fly Cast

1. Let out the amount of line you want to cast in front of you. Stand facing your target with feet spread comfortably apart. Position your rod hand so the tip of the rod is pointing in the direction of the target, with rod, forearm and wrist aligned. Lower your rod tip and remove the slack from the line.

2. Raise your rod and begin to accelerate slowly and continuously until the entire fly line is off the water.

3. Apply a short, backward speed stroke, forcing a bend in the rod and propelling the line into the backcast.

4. Stop the rod crisply. A loop will form in the line as it moves overhead.

5. Pause as the back-cast unrolls behind you. When the line forms a small "J," begin your forward acceleration.

6. Make a short, fast forward stroke and immediately stop the rod (shown). Aim your cast about eye level above your target. Let the line settle to the water, while lowering the rod tip to the fishing position.

Setting the Hook

When a fish strikes your lure or bait, how you set the hook often determines the success in landing that fish. The style of bait, and the type of hook you are using will determine the best way to set the hook. The following are the most common ways to set the hook on a fish, along with popular situations in which to use this type of hook set.

SNAP-SET. The most popular style of setting the hook, the snap-set (opposite page) involves dropping the rod tip when a strike is detected, reeling up any slack that may be in the line and quickly snapping the rod upward. The snap-set is ideal for situations when a single hook is used. Bobber fishing and jig fishing are the best situations for the snap-set.

SWEEP-SET. When using baits with treble or multiple hooks, the sweep-set is the best way to go. When you feel a strike, simply sweep the rod away from the fish while keeping steady pressure on the line and reeling at a pace to keep any slack from forming. Another prime situation for using the sweep-set is when fishing with a slip-sinker or Carolina rig. If you use a snap-set when using these rigs, much of the power is used to lift the weight off the bottom and not transferred to the hook.

DOWN-SET. Used when fishing topwater baits, the down-set (below) is the best choice.

The "down-set" is the best choice when fishing topwater baits.

How to Snap-set when Fishing a Jig

Drop the rod tip when you detect a strike on your jig. Lean forward and point the rod at the fish. The fish should not feel resistance at this critical point.

Snap-set the hook immediately with a powerful upward sweep of the rod. Jerk hard enough so the hook penetrates the fish's jaw. If the first hook set does not feel solid, set the hook again.

It is similar in form to the sweep-set, but the rod tip is purposely pointed in a steep downward direction. Because of the fact that fish are near the surface when striking topwater baits, the downward motion allows you to get the most pressure on the fish and keeps the rod in position to prevent them from jumping after they're hooked.

Fly Rod Hook Sets.

Unlike other fly-fishing skills, setting the hook is almost impossible to practice without a fish at the far end of your fly line. A successful hook set is easiest if you have razor-sharp hooks on your flies. A dull hook has a much poorer chance of penetrating the mouth of a fish.

Timing is crucial when setting the hook with a fly rod. In general, you should set the hook as quickly as possible. The exception to this rule is when you are fishing a surface fly in slack water. In this situation, fish often feed in a more leisurely fashion and require a second or two in order to suck in the fly. When fishing surface flies, many anglers miss fish by setting the hook at the first visual sign of disturbance. Just as with conventional surface fishing, an angler should wait until he or she feels the weight of the fish before setting the hook. The exception would be when trout fishing in slow-moving waters; hesitate for one to two seconds after you see the trout hit. Set the hook too soon, and you'll pull the fly away from the trout; set the hook too late, and the trout may have already spit out your fly.

Setting the hook doesn't mean you should pull on it with great force. In the excitement of hooking a fish on a surface fly, many fishermen set the hook with too much zeal, resulting in broken monofilament leaders (tippets). The best hook sets are those made with a quick upward motion.

When fishing an upstream presentation, or when you have too much slack line on the water, strip in line with your line hand at the moment you set the hook. This removes most of the slack and improves your chances for a good hook set. Make sure to keep the line under the index finger of your rod hand as you set the hook, because this puts you in a good position to play the fish. You can usually bring your line in during the fight by simply stripping it in under your index finger. Large fish, however, may force you into a longer battle where you must use the fly reel.

After setting the hook with a fly rod, release pressure slightly on your index finger, and strip in an arm's length of line. After each pull (arrow), apply pressure with your rod hand index finger as you reach forward with your line hand for the next pull.

Playing & Landing Fish

After you have set the hook and a fish is on the line, a great deal of skill is required to land larger fish of any species. Provided you have chosen the right equipment for the situation, the number one rule to follow is to use the rod – along with the reel's drag – to tire out the fish. The combination of these factors, along with an angler's patience, will determine the outcome of the battle.

Playing Fish

Keep steady pressure on the fish whenever possible, reeling in line only when the fish allows. Never try to reel in a fish when it is swimming away from you. If you see your line coming toward the surface it is often an indication that the fish is going to jump. In this situation lower your rod tip toward the water and keep steady downward pressure on the line. Allowing the fish to jump often results in the fish "throwing" the hook.

Once the fish has tired itself out, slowly work it toward you by steadily pumping the rod upward and slowly dropping the tip to collect line. Be careful to never allow any slack in the line by always keeping a slight bend in the rod (above). Stop reeling in line when the fish is about 6 feet from the rod tip. Then, with the fish at the side of the boat, be ready for a sudden run by loosening your drag. If the fish runs under the boat, plunge the rod down into the water

Plunge the rod down into the water if the fish runs under the boat.

(opposite, bottom) and try getting to the other side of the boat by going either around the front or rear of the boat while keeping tension on the line.

Landing Fish

Many fish are lost near the boat after long, well-fought battles. The problem is often caused by the angler or boat partner not being prepared to land the fish, particularly a trophy fish. The following are the most common methods for landing fish:

Hand-landing is often the best method if you plan on releasing your catch, particularly on smaller fish. Most species of bass, for example, can be landed by firmly gripping the fish by the lower jaw. Most other species can be landed by firmly gripping the fish from the top side with your thumb on one side and fingers on the other near the back of the gill plate. Regardless of where you grasp a fish, always wet your hand first. That way, you won't remove the fish's protective slime layer.

Netting fish is often preferred by anglers who do not feel comfortable hand-landing fish, plan on keeping their catch, or are landing a very large fish. Netting is also a popular method when fishing for species with sharp teeth such as northern pike and muskies or from boats with high gunwales. It should be noted, however, that fish often endure additional stress when netted. This happens because the hooks often get tangled in the net, and it takes the angler a lot of time to free the fish from the tangle.

Gaffing has become mainly a saltwater technique for landing large fish that must be subdued once they near the boat. Larger freshwater species such as catfish, striped bass and salmon are occasionally brought to gaff, but the increased participation in catch-and-release fishing has greatly limited the use of gaffs.

Water-releasing has become a very popular technique for letting fish swim away unharmed after being caught. Water-releasing involves removing the hook from the fish while it remains in the water near the side of the boat. A pliers or hook remover aids in a quick release. With large fish like muskies, it pays to have the reel set on free spool in case the

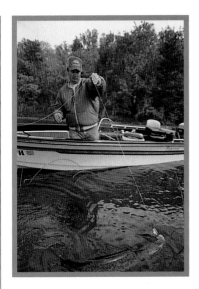

fish makes a sudden run away from the boat. That way, you can simply grab the line and slowly bring the fish back to boatside (above). If you don't have the reel set on free spool, the fish will pull the entire rod and reel into the lake.

You must be cautious water-releasing gamefish when you're using baits with multiple treble hooks. A sudden movement by the fish can lead to hooks getting embedded in your hand. For this reason, and in case you can't get a hook free from a fish's mouth without harming it, you should always carry a quality hook cutter.

How to Land a Fish from Shore

Keep a bend in the rod at all times. This keeps the line tight and helps the hook stay in the fish's mouth.

Get as close as you can to the water or, if possible, get into the water. Reach for the line to help steer the fish to you.

Keep the fish in the water to unhook it. That way, the fish won't be stressed, and it will swim away unharmed.

Releasing Fish

With fishing pressure on most bodies of water increasing, catch-and-release fishing is growing in popularity both as a fisheries management tool and as a voluntary measure among conservation-minded anglers. But the practice of catch-and-release is only effective if fish are properly handled before release.

In the past, anglers often kept everything they caught. Thankfully, times have changed.

As a rule, land fish as fast as possible. Allowing a fish to fight for an extended period will exhaust it and may cause a buildup of harmful lactic acids in its blood. The fish may swim away when released but it could die later from this buildup. To ensure that you don't needlessly tire a fish, choose a fishing line with a pound-test rating that allows you to put substantial pressure on the fish without breaking the line.

Tips for Handling and Releasing Fish

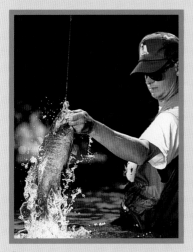

Grasp bass and other nontoothy fish vertically by the lower jaw (above). Never jaw-hold a fish at an angle because you could severely injure the fish's jaw.

Use a fine-mesh cradle instead of a net (inset) when landing large northern pike and muskies. A cradle restricts the fish's movement, preventing it from injuring itself.

Remove the hook with pliers while the fish is still in the water. Using a hook with the barb pinched down makes water-releasing very easy.

Hold a big fish horizontally with one hand in front of its tail and your other hand beneath its belly. Lifting a large fish vertically by the gills to measure or weigh it can cause the gill arch to tear.

Revive a fish by gently rocking it back and forth. The fish is ready to be released when it can swim free from your hands and remain upright on its own.

Release a fish with its head facing into moderate current of a river or stream. Strong gill movement indicates that the fish is ready to be released.

Another key to successfully releasing fish is keeping fish handling to a minimum. The best technique is to remove the hook from a fish's mouth without taking the fish out of the water. If you must hold a fish to unhook it, or if you want to take a quality photograph of your catch, wet your hands first to avoid removing the fish's protective slime layer.

Finally, try to limit the total amount of time a fish spends out of the water. If a hook is difficult to remove and you must hold the fish out of the water, periodically place it back in the water during the process. Don't attempt to rip out a hook that is deeply embedded in a fish's throat or stomach. Instead, simply cut the line and allow a fish's strong digestive acids to dissolve the metal hook.

Fish are ready to be released when they can swim free from your hands as you cradle them gently under the belly. If they can't right themselves or if they don't have strong gill movement, be patient and give them more time to recover. Tips for reviving fish and other tips on releasing fish are shown on this page.

Boat Control

The importance of precise boat control in fishing cannot be overemphasized. Many species of fish form tight schools, sometimes no more than a few feet across. Unless you can position your boat to work an exact spot, you will not catch fish consistently.

Another reason for precise boat control: many fish along a given piece of structure are likely to be at a similar depth. If you attempt to follow a specific contour, but your boat continually weaves from deep to shallow water, your bait will be in the fish zone only a small fraction of the time.

Boat-control Techniques

By mastering the following boat-control techniques, you can greatly improve your fishing success.

DRIFTING. This technique is most valuable in the following situations:

• On big water where trolling would be impossible because of heavy wave action.

• In shallow water where trolling over the fish would spook them.

• At the end of a backtrolling run, to fish your way back to the starting point for another run.

To completely cover a piece of structure such as a reef or flat, make parallel drifts over it.

Start each drift at a different spot so you are always fishing new water.

When drifting along a breakline after a backtrolling run, use your outboard or trolling motor to keep the boat on course. If you simply let the wind blow the boat, you will not follow the breakline, unless the wind happens to be blowing exactly parallel to it.

Drifting with the current is a widely used technique in rivers. Use a motor to control your drift, just as you would in a lake.

In a strong wind, you may have trouble presenting your lure or bait slowly enough to keep it in the zone where the fish are located. A sea anchor will slow your drift by as much as 90 percent. Other tricks for controlling your boat in the wind include filling your live well with water and positioning the heaviest fisherman in the bow seat. The extra weight in the front will keep the bow from swinging as much.

An outboard motor, even though it is not running, will help keep the boat drifting crosswise to the wind. Simply steer as you would if the motor were running and let the rudder control your drift. Keeping the

boat crosswise is especially important with two or more fishermen. It allows you to cover a wider swath and keeps the lines from tangling.

SLIPPING. This is another technique for slowing the speed of your drift in a strong wind or in fast current. One method of slipping is to point the bow into the wind or current and run the outboard in forward gear. Adjust your throttle so the boat drifts at the desired speed. You can easily move from one side to the other by pointing the bow slightly in the desired direction.

Another method is to turn your transom into the wind or current, then backtroll. The principle is exactly the same, but some fishermen feel they have more control this way.

If you locate a school of fish, you can use the slipping technique to hover over them. Simply open the throttle until the boat remains stationary.

FORWARD TROLLING. The technique of forward trolling with an outboard requires little explanation, but forward trolling with a bow-mounted electric motor is more complicated.

Using a bow-mount for forward trolling is equivalent to

using an outboard for backtrolling. You have good control because the boat is powered from the leading end. The principles of operating a bowmount are very similar to those discussed for backtrolling, but there are a few important differences.

On most boats, the depth-finder transducer is mounted on the lower edge of the transom. This works well for backtrolling because you get a depth reading directly below your motor, enabling you to adjust your course immediately as the depth changes. When forward trolling with a bow-mounted motor, however, the transom-mounted transducer may read a depth different from that below the motor. This prevents you from making the proper course adjustments, so you spend too much time fishing at the wrong depth. The best solution is to mount a transducer on the lower unit of your bow-mounted motor.

One drawback to forward trolling with a bow-mount is that your line tends to catch on the outboard, especially when a crosswind causes the line to angle under the boat. When you get a bite, you may have to run to the back of the boat to free the line from the outboard before setting the hook. You can solve this problem by tipping your outboard out of the water.

BACKTROLLING. The term backtrolling means trolling transom-first rather than bow-first. Backtrolling is a technique every walleye angler should learn. It offers the following advantages over forward trolling:

• You can troll much more slowly because the transom has more water resistance than the bow. In addition, most outboard motors are geared lower

How to Backtroll Along an Irregular Breakline

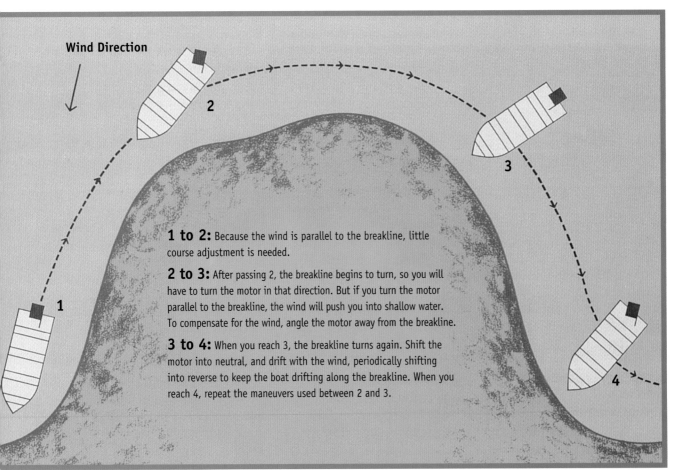

Wind Direction

1 to 2: Because the wind is parallel to the breakline, little course adjustment is needed.

2 to 3: After passing 2, the breakline begins to turn, so you will have to turn the motor in that direction. But if you turn the motor parallel to the breakline, the wind will push you into shallow water. To compensate for the wind, angle the motor away from the breakline.

3 to 4: When you reach 3, the breakline turns again. Shift the motor into neutral, and drift with the wind, periodically shifting into reverse to keep the boat drifting along the breakline. When you reach 4, repeat the maneuvers used between 2 and 3.

Point the transom into the wind and begin trolling in reverse. Watch your flasher closely, and when the depth changes, steer in the appropriate direction. In the above example, the angler is trolling from 1 to 4.

BOAT CONTROL

in reverse than in forward, so they troll more slowly at the same RPMs.

• A boat moving in reverse is easier to control and less likely to be blown off course than one moving forward. The principle is much the same in a front-wheel-drive automobile. Because the weight and power are at the leading end, it hugs the road better and is less affected by crosswinds than an automobile with rear-wheel-drive.

• Because the lines trail toward the bow rather than the stern, fishermen in the front seats will not get their lines tangled in the motor.

The most important rule of backtrolling is to move against the wind. If you backtroll with the wind, your bow will swing to the side and you will not be able to control the boat's direction. In most cases, the wind will be at an angle to the breakline, so you will not be able to troll directly into the wind and still follow the contour. But you can angle the transom into the wind and still maintain good control.

In a strong wind, you will need quite a bit of power to move the boat against the waves. In addition, you may need splash guards to prevent waves from breaking over the transom.

Most anglers prefer an outboard with a tiller handle for backtrolling. A tiller allows you to steer and operate the throttle with one hand while fishing with the other. If your outboard has power trim, you can slow your backtrolling speed by trimming the motor up. If the wind is light, a transom-mounted electric trolling motor works better than an outboard. It enables you to troll more quietly and move more slowly. And there are no exhaust fumes to blow into your face.

How to Work a Reef by Drifting

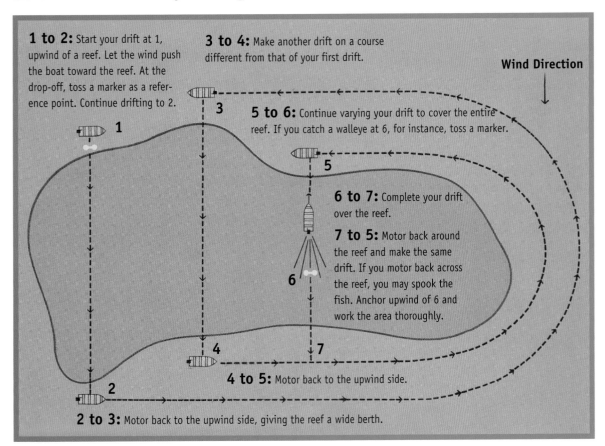

1 to 2: Start your drift at 1, upwind of a reef. Let the wind push the boat toward the reef. At the drop-off, toss a marker as a reference point. Continue drifting to 2.

3 to 4: Make another drift on a course different from that of your first drift.

Wind Direction

5 to 6: Continue varying your drift to cover the entire reef. If you catch a walleye at 6, for instance, toss a marker.

6 to 7: Complete your drift over the reef.

7 to 5: Motor back around the reef and make the same drift. If you motor back across the reef, you may spook the fish. Anchor upwind of 6 and work the area thoroughly.

4 to 5: Motor back to the upwind side.

2 to 3: Motor back to the upwind side, giving the reef a wide berth.

Locate fish on a reef by making a series of parallel drifts across the reef. By casting to each side of your drift path, you can cover a swath at least 100 feet wide on each drift. When you catch a fish, mark the spot. Instead of stopping to work the area, complete your drift and motor back around the reef. Anchor your boat far enough upwind of your marker so you do not disturb the fish, then fan-cast the area.

ANCHORING. This is the ultimate method of boat control because you can hold your boat in the exact position you want. Trolling and drifting are the best ways to locate walleyes, but once you find a school, you can work it more effectively by anchoring. And anchoring reduces the chance of spooking the fish.

To anchor securely, you must have a rope that is long enough and an anchor that is heavy enough and designed to bite into the bottom. If your anchor slips, it may drag through a school of walleyes and scatter them.

When fishing in a strong wind or fast current, tie your anchor rope to the bow. If you tie it to the stern, water may come over the transom. If you tie it to the side, water may slosh over the gunwale, and because the wind pushes against such a large area of the boat, the anchor may not hold. When anchored from the bow, the boat will ride better on the waves and is less likely to take on water.

Before anchoring, estimate how much rope you will need to hold the boat, then drop anchor at least that far upwind or upstream of the desired boat position. In strong wind or current, you may have to allow for some slippage before the anchor catches.

With the rope tied to the bow, even a slight wind or light current will cause the boat to swing back and forth. You can increase or decrease the amount of swing by using an electric motor. And you can hold the boat to one side or the other by turning your outboard to take advantage of the rudder. If you do not want the boat to swing, drop another anchor at the stern and leave only a small amount of slack.

To anchor sideways, simply turn the boat at a right angle to the wind or current, then drop two anchors simultaneously, one from the bow and the other from the stern. This way, the boat cannot swing from side to side and each angler has an equal chance of reaching the fish. Never anchor from the side in a strong wind or current because the boat could easily capsize.

Effective Anchoring Techniques

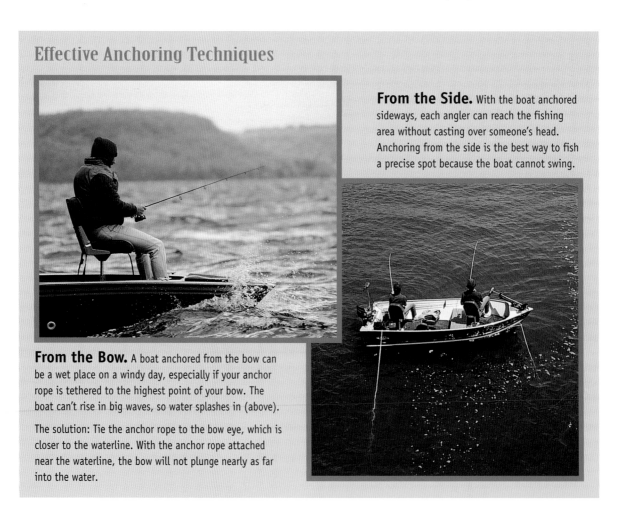

From the Side. With the boat anchored sideways, each angler can reach the fishing area without casting over someone's head. Anchoring from the side is the best way to fish a precise spot because the boat cannot swing.

From the Bow. A boat anchored from the bow can be a wet place on a windy day, especially if your anchor rope is tethered to the highest point of your bow. The boat can't rise in big waves, so water splashes in (above).

The solution: Tie the anchor rope to the bow eye, which is closer to the waterline. With the anchor rope attached near the waterline, the bow will not plunge nearly as far into the water.

Boat Control in the Wind

One of the most difficult boat handling situations that an angler will face is strong winds. Wind can keep you from fishing many areas of a lake and in some cases can keep you from getting out on the lake at all. On the other hand, wind can also be a blessing for fishermen as it limits light penetration into the water giving fish an advantage over their prey. Wind can also push baitfish against structure making them more accessible to fish species. It is also hard for baitfish to stay tightly schooled in strong wind and leaves them vulnerable to predation.

The ability to position your boat properly and fish the windy areas of the lake can produce the best fishing. When other anglers head for secluded coves or the lee side of the lake, try fishing the windy shores.

The other thing that wind can produce is current. Wind can push water between islands or over points and will often congregate fish that are taking advantage of food that is washed to them. These areas often hold active fish, particularly if the wind has been persistent and from the same direction for several days.

Tips for Fishing in Windy Conditions

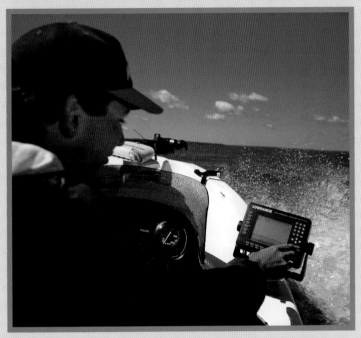

Look for walleyes on windblown shorelines near schools of baitfish that are blown into the area by the wind.

Position your boat into the wind when you're working a piece of structure or shoreline with a bow-mounted trolling motor. It is easier to control your speed and to keep the rear of the boat from blowing around.

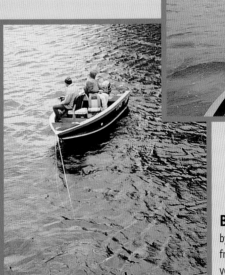

Backtroll with the wind by extending a sea anchor from your bow and running your motor in reverse. Without a sea anchor, the wind would swing your bow around, making precise boat control impossible.

how to CATCH FISH

After you've learned where a few gamefish species live and you've mastered the basic skills needed to catch them, you'll probably want to try your hand at more advanced tactics for other species. This section features all of the major North American gamefish species. Clearly written biology information is followed by in-depth detail on the best lures and techniques used to catch that species under many situations. The angler in this photo has learned how to catch largemouths from shore. His reward is a big fish from Missouri's Lake of the Ozarks.

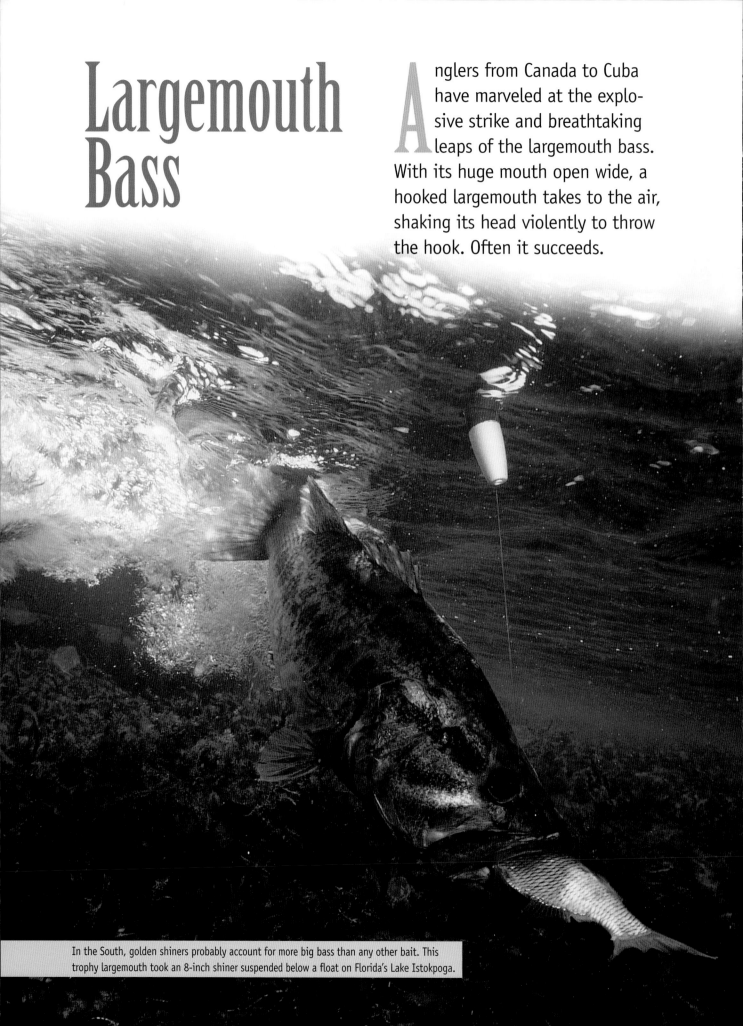

Largemouth Bass

Anglers from Canada to Cuba have marveled at the explosive strike and breathtaking leaps of the largemouth bass. With its huge mouth open wide, a hooked largemouth takes to the air, shaking its head violently to throw the hook. Often it succeeds.

In the South, golden shiners probably account for more big bass than any other bait. This trophy largemouth took an 8-inch shiner suspended below a float on Florida's Lake Istokpoga.

The largemouth has become the most widely distributed gamefish in North America, partly because of its reputation as a fighter, but primarily because of its remarkable ability to survive in almost any freshwater lake, pond or stream. It thrives in pine-fringed lakes of southern Canada, murky backwaters in Illinois and sprawling desert reservoirs in Mexico.

Black bass, bucketmouth and old linesides are but a few names for the largemouth bass, which is actually a member of the sunfish family. Like sunfish and crappies, bass fan out shallow, saucer-shaped nests in the spring, usually in water 2 to 4 feet deep. Most spawning grounds are in bays, cuts or channels protected from the wind. Rough water can easily scatter eggs or destroy nests on windward shores.

Largemouth bass spawn when water warms to the low- to mid-60s. Bass in Florida usually deposit their eggs in February, while largemouths in Minnesota may not spawn until mid-June. After dropping her eggs, the female leaves the male to guard the eggs and the young until they can fend for themselves. Nest-guarding males may strike at almost anything that swims their way. This explains why some states close the bass season or prohibit angling in certain spawning areas until the nesting season is over.

Typical bass foods are small fish, crayfish, frogs and insect larvae. The largemouth can adapt to almost any type of fresh water, because it eats a wide variety of foods.

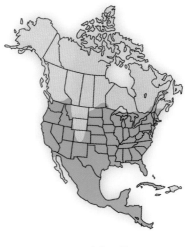

Largemouth Bass Range

Snakes, turtles, mice and even birds have been found in bass stomachs.

Largemouth bass shy away from bright sunlight and are most active under dim conditions. On sunny summer days, they feed at daybreak and dusk, spending midday along drop-offs close to feeding areas. Fishing is usually good on rainy or overcast days, but poor during and after a thunderstorm.

There are two subspecies of largemouth bass: the northern largemouth and the Florida largemouth. The two look nearly identical, but the Florida bass grows much faster. A trophy bass in Vermont might weigh 6 pounds, while 12-pound bass are not uncommon in Florida.

The world-record largemouth, 22 pounds, 4 ounces, was taken in Montgomery Lake, Georgia, in 1932. It is thought to be an intergrade between the two subspecies. Most experts believe the next world record will come from California, where several bass in the 20-pound class have been caught in recent years.

Largemouth bass have light greenish to brownish sides with a dark lateral band that may come and go. The jaw extends well beyond the rear of the eye. Florida bass have slightly smaller scales, compared to the size of the body, than northern largemouths. The scale count along the lateral line is 69 to 73 for a Florida; 59 to 65 for a northern.

Largemouth bass in a shallow slop bay.

Where to Catch Largemouth Bass

Largemouth bass spend most of their lives in water that is only 5 to 15 feet deep, but they will sometimes move into deep water to find food or to escape sunlight. Bass in the shallows are likely to hold near some kind of shady cover, especially if that cover is near deep water.

Natural and man-made features that attract largemouth vary greatly depending on the type of water. In general, however, fishermen should begin to look for largemouths around the following: emergent vegetation, such as bulrushes; floating-leaved vegetation, such as lily pads; submerged weeds, such as coontail; overhanging trees; stumps; brush; bridge pilings and boat docks.

The time of the year that bass are found on certain structure and cover types also varies. Following is a list of prime bass locations in natural and man-made lakes throughout the season.

Prime Locations in Natural Lakes:

• Shallow bays warm faster than the rest of the lake. Bass move in to feed and later, spawn. Mud-bottomed bays warm first; the dark bottom absorbs the sun's rays.

• Weedlines hold bass in summer and fall. Outside weedlines form where the water becomes too deep for adequate light penetration. Inside weedlines may also form from wave action or the water freezing to the bottom.

• Slop bays hold bass in summer because the thick layer of floating weeds keeps the water below relatively cool. These bays also furnish an abundant supply of food.

• Humps with a weedy or rocky bottom make excellent summertime bass hangouts. The weeds and rocks offer shade and the bass can easily retreat into the adjacent deep water.

• Points and inside turns along the breakline hold bass from early summer through winter. Gradually sloping structure is best in summer; sharp-sloping in late fall and winter.

• Shallow flats draw bass on warm, sunny days in late fall and winter. Shallow flats along protected shores are best, because they warm the fastest.

Prime Locations in Man-made Lakes:

• Main-lake points, particularly the ones near the old river channel, concentrate bass in summer and winter. Bass move up on the points to feed and rest in the adjacent deep water.

• River channel bends and intersections hold more bass in summer than straight sections of channel. Because the deep water in the river channel stays relatively warm in winter, it often holds large numbers of bass.

• Back ends of shallow creek arms, especially those with no flow, have the warmest water in spring. Like bays in natural lakes, they draw bass to feed and spawn. They also draw bass in fall, because they are the first spots to cool.

• Man-made features, such as submerged roadbeds, railroad grades, riprap banks and old building foundations, are important bass structure throughout the year. Reservoir maps help you pinpoint these features.

• Humps with timber or weeds are prime summertime bass spots, especially if they are located near the main river channel.

• Timbered flats are top feeding areas from spring to fall. The best flats are usually along a creek channel or river channel, where bass have easy access to deeper water.

Flooded brush makes excellent cover for largemouths. This bass was hooked by retrieving a spinnerbait through the brush on Oklahoma's Lake Eufala.

LARGEMOUTH BASS

How to Catch Largemouth

Because largemouth bass eat most any kind of food and live in most any kind of water, bass anglers must learn to be versatile. If you rely on only one method, such as topwater fishing, you may have excellent success in some situations, but practically none in others. You must adjust your tactics depending on time of year, type of water, type of forage and type of cover.

For instance, topwater lures are dynamite on warm summer mornings and evenings, when bass are gorging themselves in the shallows. But fishing topwaters would probably be a waste of time on a cold morning in late fall, when the fish are not nearly as active.

In very clear water, topwaters work best in low-light periods, but in murky water, they will catch bass all day long. Water clarity also affects your choice of lure color. Bright or fluorescent colors are a good choice in discolored water, while natural colors that mimic bass foods are almost always more effective in very clear water.

When bass are roaming open water in search of pelagic baitfish, such as gizzard shad, lures like crankbaits and spinnerbaits that run in the mid-depths will usually outproduce bottom-bouncing lures, like jigs and Texas-rigged plastic worms.

Perhaps the most important consideration in lure selection is cover type. If you're fishing in dense weeds or brush, for example, you need a lure that will track through the cover without continually fouling or snagging. Good choices include Texas-rigged worms, weedless jigs and spinnerbaits. In snag-free water, however, lures with open hooks work better because you'll hook a larger percentage of the fish that strike.

Lure selection is an important part of bass fishing, but it means very little unless you're familiar with the seasonal movement pattern of the fish on the particular body of water you're fishing. Until you discover this pattern, it pays to spend more time exploring the lake than cruising the aisles at the tackle store. If you can't find the fish, you can't catch them.

Fishing Spinnerbaits

Spinnerbaits are the best all-season lures for largemouth bass. They are especially effective in spring, when bass are in weedy shallows. Because of their safety-pin design, most are virtually snagless; the bent shaft runs interference for the upturned hook.

Polarized sunglasses are a must for fishing largemouth bass and other species of fish that relate to shallow-water cover. With an unpolarized view (top photo), the glare on the surface of the water prevents you from seeing fish and other underwater objects. However, the same scene viewed through a polarized lens (bottom photo) reveals a largemouth next to some rocks.

As a result, you can toss a spinnerbait into dense weedbeds, brush or timber without constantly hanging up. Spinnerbaits can also be counted down to fish along drop-offs, jigged along the bottom in water as deep as 20 feet and even run on the surface with the blade nearly breaking water. Most anglers use ¼- to 1-ounce spinnerbaits for largemouth.

Spinnerbaits come in two basic designs: single-spins, which have only one blade, and tandem-spins, which have two. A single-spin helicopters better, while a tandem-spin has more lift, making it a better choice for shallow-water presentations (below).

The style of blades on your spinnerbait also makes a difference. Colorado blades, for instance, have more water resistance than willow-leaf blades, so they spin better on a slow retrieve and ride higher in the water. Willow-leaf blades can be retrieved faster, so they work better for locating bass.

Spinnerbaits
include: (1) single-spin models, like the Classic Hart Throb; and (2) tandem-spins, like the Blue Fox Big Bass.

How to Fish a Spinnerbait for Largemouth Bass

Bulging. With your rod tip high, reel fast enough so that the blades almost, but not quite, break the surface and create a bulge. This retrieve will often draw bass up out of dense weedy or brushy cover.

Slow-rolling. When bass are buried in heavy cover and not particularly active, try reeling a spinnerbait slowly, bumping into weeds, branches and other objects. The change in action of the blades may trigger strikes.

Helicoptering. When bass are holding tight to vertical cover, like flooded trees, reel a single-spin spinnerbait up to the cover and let it sink vertically. As it sinks, the blades will spin, drawing the attention of bass.

Fishing Subsurface Plugs

This lure category includes a variety of hard-bodied baits that run from a few feet to as much as 30 feet beneath the surface.

Designed to be retrieved quite rapidly, these lures have a built-in wobble that makes them resemble swimming baitfish.

Most subsurface plugs used for largemouth bass are 3 to 6 inches in length. They include 4 major types:

MINNOW PLUGS. These long, thin-bodied lures have a small lip that gives them a tight wiggle. Some minnow plugs and crankbaits have long lips that make them run deep.

VIBRATING PLUGS. With the attachment eye on the back, these sinking plugs have tight vibrating action that fish can detect even in low-clarity water.

CRANKBAITS. A plastic or metal lip creates the wobble in these lures. Most crankbaits have a short, aerodynamic body.

TROLLING PLUGS. These hard-to-cast plugs are a good choice for covering expanses of water. Most have flattened foreheads that give them a wide, enticing wobble.

Tips for Fishing Subsurface Plugs

Bump the bottom with your plug or allow it to hit submerged branches and broad-leaved vegetation. This will change its action and may trigger strikes from bass.

Weight a subsurface plug to achieve the right buoyancy by applying strips of golfer's tape to the bottom. Seal in the tape with epoxy glue.

Subsurface plugs include: (1) minnow plugs, such as the Smithwick Suspending Pro Rogue; (2) vibrating plugs, such as the Bill Lewis Rat-L-Trap; (3) crankbaits, such as the Bomber Model A; and (4) trolling plugs, such as the Buck's Baits Spoonplug.

Topwater Fishing

Topwaters create a disturbance on the surface that bass mistake for a mouse, large insect or struggling baitfish.

There are 6 important types of topwater lures:

STICKBAITS. These lures have no action of their own, but a twitching retrieve, called walking-the-dog, makes them dart from side to side.

CHUGGERS. A scooped-out or flattened face makes these lures produce a chugging sound when you give them a sharp twitch.

CRAWLERS. A wide, cupped face plate or collapsible arms give these lures the crawling action.

PROPBAIT. Propellers on one or both ends throw water when you reel rapidly. The baits can also be fished with a twitch-and-pause retrieve.

FROGS AND RATS. Soft rubber or plastic-bodied frogs and rats have weedless hooks and can be retrieved over thick slop without fouling.

BUZZBAITS. The spinning buzzblade creates a lot of surface disturbance, and the safety-pin design makes these baits quite weedless.

Topwater lures include:
(1) stickbaits, such as Heddon Zara Spook;
(2) chuggers, such as the Rebel Pro Pop-R; (3) crawlers, such as the Fred Arbogast Jitterbug; (4) propbaits, such as the Smithwick Devil's Horse; (5) frogs, such as the Mann's The Frog; and (6) buzzbaits, such as the Strike King Jr. Buzz King.

Tips for Fishing Topwaters

Tie your line directly to the lure, rather than use a heavy clip or snap-swivel. The extra weight pulls the nose under, ruining the action.

Wait until you feel the fish before setting the hook. If you attempt to set as soon as you see a splash, you'll probably miss the fish.

Jigging

These lures are ideal for pin-point presentations to bass holding in tight spots. Although jigs and jigging lures work best in cool or cold water, they will catch bass most anytime.

JIGS. Lead-head jigs, usually called bass jigs, can be dressed with hair, feathers, rubber skirts, plastic tails or pork rind. Bass jigs used in heavy cover should have some type of weedguard.

JIGGING SPOONS. These heavy spoons are ideal for jigging verti-cally in very deep water. Because of their long, thin shape, they resemble a struggling baitfish when jigged erratically.

VIBRATING BLADES. Made of thin metal, these lures produce an intense vibration when jigged vertically. They can also be used like a crankbait.

TAILSPINS. The heavy lead body makes these lures sink rapid-ly, so they work well for jigging vertically in deep water. The spin-ner on the tail turns when the lure is pulled up and helicopters when it is dropped back. Tailspins also work well for long-distance casting to schooling bass.

Tip a bass jig with a plastic or pork trailer. A jig tipped with a plastic crayfish is called a jig-and-craw (above); with pork, a jig-and-pig.

Secure a pork trailer, so it can't slide up the shank and foul the hook, by first threading on a grub body.

1

2

3

4

Shake a bass jig and then let it rest in place to trigger a strike. Usually a largemouth will inhale the jig after it stops moving.

Jigging lures include: (1) rubber-skirted brushguard bass jigs, such as the S.W.A.T. Jig; (2) jigging spoons, such as the Hopkins Shorty; (3) vibrating blades, such as the Heddon Sonar; and (4) tailspins, such as Mann's Little George.

Fishing Weedless Spoons

Among the oldest of bass baits, weedless spoons are no less effective today than they were a half century ago.

Most weedless spoons have some type of wire, plastic or nylon bristle weedguard to keep the hook from fouling in dense weeds or brush. Some models are intended to run beneath the surface; others to skitter across the surface. Weedless spoons are often tipped with a pork or plastic trailer.

SUBSURFACE SPOONS. These metal spoons sink rapidly and can be fished through dense vegetation. Because of their heavy body, they can be cast long distances.

Some subsurface spoons have a spinner or propeller at the front end for extra attraction and additional lift.

SURFACE SPOONS. With their light plastic body, these spoons are easy to slide across the surface, so they work well for fishing over matted weeds. But they are not heavy enough for casting to distant targets.

Weedless spoons include: subsurface types, such as (1) the Normark Minnow Spoon and (2) Johnson Spinner Spoon, with a spinning head; and surface types, such as (3) the Heddon Moss Boss.

How to Fish Weedless Spoons for Bass

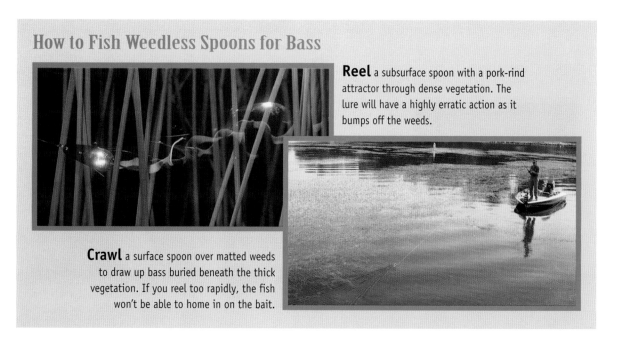

Reel a subsurface spoon with a pork-rind attractor through dense vegetation. The lure will have a highly erratic action as it bumps off the weeds.

Crawl a surface spoon over matted weeds to draw up bass buried beneath the thick vegetation. If you reel too rapidly, the fish won't be able to home in on the bait.

Fishing Soft Plastics

Soft plastics probably account for more largemouth bass than any other type of lure. In fact, plastic worms, which were introduced in the 1950s, soon began catching so many bass that one southern state introduced legislation to ban them! Today, soft plastics are available in three main types.

PLASTIC WORMS. While plastic worms are available in hundreds of shapes and sizes, the majority of largemouth fishermen rely on curlytail plastic worms from 6 to 8 inches in length. These worms are big enough to attract a good-sized bass and they have an enticing action when fished at a slow pace. Longer worms, those 10 inches or more, often result in a higher percentage of missed fish. Like other soft plastics, many of the worms manufactured today are scent-impregnated for added attraction.

CREATURES. This category includes a wide array of imitation crayfish, lizards, frogs, salamanders, eels, etc. Like plastic worms, these lures come in many shapes and sizes.

Soft plastics (below) include: (1) worms, such as the Berkley Power Worm, rigged Texas-style; (2) crayfish imitations, such as the Riverside Lures Floating Air Claw, used as a trailer on a Keen's Kritter; (3) tube baits, such as the Riverside Lures Pro Tube, rigged Texas-style; (4) grubs, such as the Berkley Power Skirtgrub, rigged on a Roll'r Rock Jig; (5) lizard imitations, such as the Riverside Lures Floating Air Lizard, on a Carolina rig; and (6) soft stickbaits, such as the Lunker City Slug-Go, rigged with an embedded hook.

How to Rig a Texas-style Worm

Thread a bullet sinker onto the line, then tie on a worm hook.

Insert the hook into the worm's head, then thread the first half inch of the worm onto the hook.

Push the hook through, give it a half twist and bury the point in the worm.

SOFT STICKBAITS. These baits have a straight, tapered body designed to swim erratically from side to side with a twitching retrieve. Most soft stickbaits range in size from 4 to 6 inches.

Because largemouth bass are usually found in or around some type of cover, most fishermen prefer to rig their soft plastics Texas-style (opposite page). When rigged Texas-style with a bullet sinker, soft plastics can be fished in the heaviest cover without hanging up because the hook point is buried in the lure. The disadvantage to this rigging is that during the hook set the hook point must pass through the worm before it penetrates into the mouth of the fish. As a result, your hooking percentage will be lower than if you used an exposed hook.

Another popular rigging method for soft plastics is a Carolina rig (below). This rig differs from a Texas rig in that the bullet sinker is positioned well up the line, rather than riding on the nose of the bait. This way, the bait sinks much more slowly and has a more enticing action. Depending on the density of cover, the hook point may or may not be buried in the bait.

Carolina rigging for largemouth bass.

How to Fish a Texas-rigged Worm

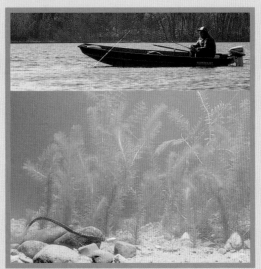

Crawl the worm along the bottom a few inches at a time, pausing for several seconds between each move. Work it through heavy cover such as weeds, brush or logs. The worm will rarely snag because the hook is concealed.

Watch your line closely at all times. If you see the line twitch slightly or it slowly moves to the side, point the rod tip in the direction of the worm and reel up any slack.

Set the hook immediately with a powerful sweeping motion. Driving the hook through the worm and into the mouth of a bass requires a stiff rod, low-stretch line and a hard hook set.

Getting Started

An observer at a professional bass tournament would hear a great deal of talk about finding the best pattern. When bass pros use this term, they are not referring to lure design. Instead, a pattern involves an elusive combination of two factors: bass location and the presentation needed to make fish bite. The pattern often changes from day to day and may even change several times a day.

The first step in unraveling a pattern is to locate the right type of fishing spot. Take into account the season, time of day and the weather. For example, on an overcast fall day, bass will most likely stay in the shallows.

On a bright day in summer, bass may feed in open shallows in early morning. But as the sun moves higher, they will move deeper or into shaded areas of the shallows.

When scouting for bass, most anglers use some type of fast-moving lure like a crankbait or spinnerbait. Hungry bass will strike almost anything, so this technique is the quickest way to locate an active school. Rig several rods with different types of lures. This enables you to switch quickly without taking the time to tie on a new lure.

Concentrate on features within the most likely depth range, but occasionally move to shallower or deeper water. If you catch a bass, carefully note the exact depth and the type of cover and structure. Work the area thoroughly,

but continue moving if you fail to catch another fish.

If you find an active school, try to avoid spooking the fish. Keep the boat at a distance and noise to a minimum. Without changing lures, work the school until the bass quit biting. Use a landing net for only the largest fish. Grab smaller bass by the lower jaw. Untangling a lure from a net takes too much time.

Presentation becomes more important after you have skimmed the active fish from the school. Switching to a lure with a different action, color or size often triggers a strike immediately. Select a lure based on the situation, and continue casting toward the fish. Experiment with various lures and retrieves to find the right combination.

Before you leave a good spot,

note its exact location on your contour map. List any landmarks on shore that can be used as reference points for finding the area quickly in the future. Some fishermen toss out a marker, then return later to see if the fish have resumed feeding. When a spot no longer produces, try to duplicate the pattern by looking for a similar location nearby. If you found bass on a sharp-breaking point with bulrushes on top, chances are you will find bass on similar points elsewhere. If these areas fail to produce, the pattern has probably changed.

If the weather remains stable, the patterns you find one day will probably be repeated about the same time on the next day. But a change in weather will probably result in a new set of patterns.

In some instances, several patterns exist at the same time. Bass sometimes bite equally well in deep and shallow water, and the type of lure makes little difference. On these rare days, almost anyone can catch fish.

Finding a pattern for deep-water bass can be difficult and time-consuming. These fish often ignore fast-moving lures, so you may have to use a slower presentation. When you hook a fish in deep water, try to land it quickly. Otherwise, its frantic struggling may spook other bass in the school.

At times, there is no definite pattern. You may catch a bass here and there, but seldom more than one in any spot. Keep moving and cover as many areas as possible, including those places where you caught fish earlier in the day. Record trip results in a log book. A well-kept log can help you to find successful patterns when conditions are similar in future years.

How Weather Affects Bass Fishing

Weather plays a greater role in the daily activity of large-mouth bass than any other factor. To improve your success, you should know how the following weather conditions affect bass fishing.

STABLE WEATHER. When weather conditions are stable or gradually changing, bass go through a routine of feeding and resting that is often predictable from one day to the next. For example, during an extended period of overcast weather, a school of bass may feed on a sharp-breaking point at midday, then drop back into deeper water. The school usually repeats this daily pattern, as long as weather conditions remain stable.

FRONTS. Largemouths feed heavily just before a strong cold front, often providing spectacular fishing for several hours. But once the front arrives, they eat very little until 1 or 2 days after the system passes. Catching bass under these conditions is difficult and requires special techniques with lighter lines and smaller lures.

WIND. Like warming trends, wind can either improve or ruin fishing. A steady wind will concentrate minute organisms near shore or along timber and brush lines. Baitfish feed in these areas, attracting bass and other predators. In spring, warm winds blowing from the same direction for several days can pile up warm water on the downwind shore. This warmer water holds more bass than other areas of the lake.

Waves washing into shore loosen soil and debris, creating a band of muddy water. Bass hang along the mud line, where they can avoid bright light, but still dart into clear water to grab food.

Calm conditions enable bass in clear water to see objects above them. Fishermen and boaters easily spook bass in shallow water. Wave action bends or refracts light rays, making it more difficult for largemouths to see movements on or above the surface.

RAIN. Rainy weather usually improves bass fishing. The overcast skies reduce light penetration, so bass are more comfortable in shallow water. In reservoirs, runoff flows into the back ends of coves. The murky water causes bass to move in and feed. The same situation occurs near stream inlets, drainage ditches or storm sewer pipes on many natural lakes.

Fishing success may decline during and after heavy rains. Runoff from torrential rains can muddy an entire body of water, causing fish to stop biting. Angling remains slow until the water clears, which may take several days or weeks.

Lightning and thunder drive largemouths into the depths. If the weather looks threatening, you should head for shore immediately. Your boat may be the highest point on the lake, making you vulnerable to a lightning strike.

Experienced fishermen can identify certain clouds and other atmospheric conditions that indicate coming changes in the weather. They know how bass react to these changes and plan their angling strategy accordingly.

Structure Fishing for Bass

Finding structure is the key to finding largemouth bass. Experts estimate that only 10 percent of a typical lake holds bass. And that 10 percent is usually around some type of structure. Fishermen who do not know how to find and fish structure have little chance for consistent success.

Structure simply means a change in the lake bottom. It could be a change in the depth or just a difference in the type of bottom material. Points, sunken islands, rock or gravel reefs, creek channels and shore-line breaks are typical structure in many waters.

Largemouths use structure as underwater highways. It provides easy access for bass moving from deep to shallow water. Structure also supplies bass with something to which they can relate. Given a choice, a bass will select a location near some type of recognizable feature.

The best bass structure has natural cover like weeds, flooded brush or timber, or man-made cover like riprap or brush shelters.

The quickest way to locate structure is to use an accurate contour map and a depth finder. With a little practice, you will learn to identify landmarks on shore for finding the general location of a good area. Then, by crisscrossing the area with your depth finder, you can pinpoint specific structure shown on the map. When you locate fish, note the exact depth. Chances are, bass on structure throughout the lake will be at the same depth.

Fishermen who spend a lot of time fishing one lake usually discover certain pieces of structure that routinely produce bass. In many cases, structure that seems identical produces nothing. Anglers have hired divers to inspect their secret spots, thinking there must be some difference that attracts bass. Often the diver finds nothing that could not be found in dozens of other areas. Bass sometimes choose spots for reasons we do not understand. The only solution for fishermen is to work many pieces of structure. Keep moving; try different depths and presentations until you find the right combination.

When fishing shallow structure, try spinnerbaits or shallow-running crankbaits — they cover a large area in a hurry.

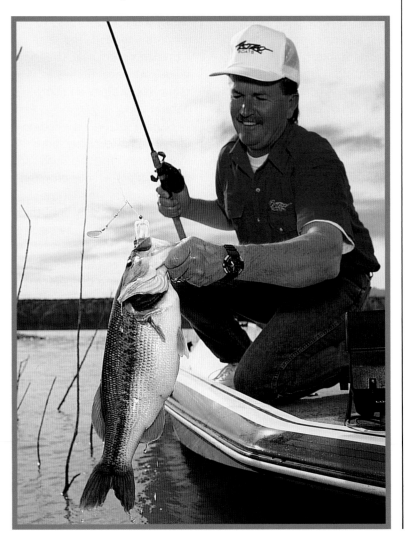

Fishing for Bass on Shallow Structure

Fishermen stand a much better chance of catching bass in shallow water than in deep water. Bass in the shallows are usually feeding and more likely to strike a lure.

But bass in the shallows pose two problems for anglers. The fish are often scattered. And they tend to spook easily, especially if the water is clear. To find bass on shallow structure, keep moving and use lures that can be cast and retrieved quickly so you can cover a lot of water. When you catch a fish, remember the exact location. You may want to return later for a few more casts.

When fishing in the shallows, avoid making unnecessary noises. Be especially careful not to drop anything on the bottom of the boat and do not run your outboard. Keep the boat as far away as possible and make long casts. If the water is very clear, watch the angle of the sun to avoid casting your shadow over the fish.

Almost any lure will work for fishing on shallow structure. The lure does not have to bump bottom to catch fish. A hungry bass in 6 feet of water will not hesitate to chase a buzz bait ripped across the surface, especially in warm water.

Most anglers prefer spinnerbaits or shallow-running crankbaits so they can cover a large area in a hurry. You may need a weedless lure if the structure has heavy weeds or brush. Carry a rod rigged with a plastic worm so you can work a brush clump or an isolated weedbed slowly and thoroughly. If a bass does take your lure in heavy cover, horse it back toward the boat to keep it from wrapping your line around weeds or limbs.

Fishing for Bass on Deep Structure

Before the advent of the depth finder, finding bass on deep structure was largely guesswork. Most fishermen worked shoreline structure because they could find it easily. Much of the deep, mid-lake structure was left unexplored.

The first anglers to buy depth finders enjoyed a fishing bonanza. Some schools of deep-water bass had never seen a lure. Fishing is not that easy today, but the angler who knows how to use a depth finder in conjunction with a lake map can consistently find bass on deep structure.

Prior to fishing any deep structure, explore the area thoroughly with your depth finder. Look for any variations on the structure, because these areas are most likely to hold bass. Make sure you understand the bottom configuration. This will make it easier to follow a contour and to keep your lure at a consistent depth.

When scouting a deep sunken island or flat, criss-cross the area several times. Toss a marker buoy onto the shallowest part of the sunken island or into the middle of the flat. The marker will serve as a reference point. Note the location of any projections or indentations along the edge of the structure, or any deep pockets on top.

To determine the shape of a submerged point, zigzag across it while edging farther into the lake. When you locate the tip of the point, throw out a marker. Then run the boat along each edge to find any irregularities.

Creek channels bordered by flooded timber are easy to follow. But channels without timber or brush can be difficult to trace. Watch your depth finder as you follow the edge. Drop enough markers to provide a picture of the channel configuration.

To find largemouths near a cliff wall, cruise slowly along the edge while watching the depth finder for signs of trees, brush or rock slides. Any type of projection different from the rest of the cliff will probably hold bass.

You can catch deep-water bass on deep-diving crankbaits, jigging spoons, heavy single-spin spinnerbaits, and heavy rubber-skirted bass jigs tipped with soft-plastic trailers or pork rind (below). Keep switching lure types until you get a strike. On some days, a quick-passing crankbait triggers a strike, while on other days you'll have more success by inching a jig across the bottom.

Fishing for Bass in Flooded Brush & Timber

When a bass feels the sting of a hook, its first reaction is to head for cover. And if that cover happens to be nearby trees or brush, the ensuing battle will test the skill of any angler.

Although it may be difficult to fight and land a bass in woody cover, fishermen who know how to work timber and brush rarely fail to catch bass.

Dams on large rivers have flooded vast expanses of timber and brush over the past few decades. After a reservoir fills, over 100 feet of water may cover the trees. In some impoundments, the entire basin is flooded timber with the exception of farm fields, roads and towns.

A low dam on a river will not cover an entire forest, but it will flood timber and brush in the backwaters. These trees also rot off in time. Waves pounding on stumps in shallow water wash soil away from the bases, exposing the root systems. The spaces between the roots make ideal bass cover. Stumps in shallow areas of reservoirs also have exposed roots under water.

Submerged trees may last indefinitely. Timber that protrudes above water eventually rots off at the water line, leaving only partially exposed trunks.

In some cases, the U.S. Army Corps of Engineers or other government agencies cuts the trees as a reservoir is filling. Once filled, the reservoir appears to be void of timber, but it has a forest of tree trunks several feet below the surface. Occasionally, loggers clear-cut most of the trees before a reservoir is created, leaving only stumps. Although tall timber may be hard to find, the chances of it holding bass are better than if the reservoir was filled with trees.

Some reservoir maps show the location of timber; some do not. If your map lacks such information, obtain a quad map, which shows the location of woodlands before the reservoir was filled. Chances are, the trees will still be there.

Flooded brush decays much faster than timber. You may find brush in deep water in some new reservoirs, but in older ones, brush grows mainly in the shallows. During prolonged periods of low water, brush flourishes along shore. When the water level returns to normal, the brush is submerged, providing excellent bass habitat.

Bass in natural lakes and

river backwaters seek cover in flooded brush, especially during spring and early summer when runoff raises water levels. The brush harbors foods such as minnows and insects.

Anglers who spend a lot of time fishing around timber know that certain types of trees are better than others. Generally, the largest trees or those with the most branches attract the most fish. Cedar trees, for example, with their dense network of branches, are consistent bass producers.

In southern lakes and sloughs, water-dwelling trees such as cypress provide homes for largemouths. Erosion along riverbanks often results in trees tumbling into the water. The branches offer cover and break the current.

In steep-walled reservoirs, rock slides carry trees and brush down the slope and into the water. The trees may provide the only cover along a cliff wall. In lakes and ponds that lack good shoreline cover, fishermen sometimes fell trees into the water, then cable the tree to the stump.

Spinnerbaits are an excellent choice for fishing in woody cover, as are Texas-rigged soft plastics and weedless bass jigs. If bass are feeding near the surface, try casting a topwater chugger or propbait.

Fishing for Bass in Weeds

Shallow Weeds

Bass fishermen in natural lakes catch more largemouths in shallow weeds than in any other type of cover. Shallow weeds include any type of emergent, floating-leaved or submerged plant in water 10 feet or less. The type of weed matters little to bass, as long as it provides adequate cover.

The best times to find bass in shallow vegetation are spring and early fall. In summer, weeds serve mainly as morning and evening feeding grounds. But some bass stay in the weeds all summer if the cover is dense enough to block out sunlight.

Shallow weeds near deep water usually hold the most bass. Given a choice, bass will choose a weedbed near a drop-off over one located in the middle of a large, shallow area.

Spinnerbaits, Texas-rigged soft plastics and weedless bass jigs are very effective for catching bass in shallow weeds. You can also try twitching a weedless plastic frog across matted surface weeds. Watching a bass explode from dense weeds to attack a topwater frog is one of the most exciting moments in bass fishing.

Deep Weeds

The secret to catching bass in deep weeds is to find a weedline. You can catch some largemouths in a wide expanse of deep weeds, but to improve your odds, concentrate on the edges.

Weedlines concentrate largemouths. When feeding, bass cruise along the edge or leave the weedline to move into shallow water. To rest, they sometimes retreat a short distance into the weeds.

Variations along the weedline hold the most fish. Bass recognize and use these specific spots as resting sites or ambush points. Look for a pocket or even a slight indentation along the edge. Largemouths also school around points of weeds that project farther out than the rest of the weedline.

Deep, weedy flats in clear lakes hold some bass, especially in summer. The fish hang just above the weeds while cruising the flat. Finding the bass may be difficult because they can be anywhere on the flat.

In a clear lake, weeds may grow to depths of 20 or 25 feet. But with a depth finder and a little practice, locating a deep weedline is not as difficult as you might expect. When you find a weedline, throw out one or more markers along the edge, keeping them just inside the weeds.

Use your trolling motor or drift along the weedline while casting a crankbait. Or troll a deep-running crankbait or Spoon Plug along the edge. Stay just outside the markers while letting out enough line so the lure ticks bottom. If you catch a bass while trolling or drifting, it is probably an active fish within a school. Mark the spot, then work it thoroughly. You may have to switch to a slower presentation to catch more fish.

Fishing for Bass on Man-made Structure

Fishing along man-made features like riprap banks and roadbeds is little different than working natural features such as shoreline breaks and weedlines. Bass may scatter over a long distance, so you must keep moving until you find them.

But when fishing around man-made features like docks and bridge pilings, you know exactly where to look. To catch bass holding tight to these features, cast beyond the spot where the fish are likely to be. Then retrieve the lure so it passes only inches away. When fishing a straight-edged feature like a house foundation, chances are that bass will be lined up near the base of the wall along the shady side. Many fishermen make the mistake of casting at right angles to the wall, then pulling the lure away. With this technique, the lure is in the strike zone for only an instant, so it would take dozens of casts to cover the wall completely. Instead, position your boat so you can cast parallel to the edge. Your lure will stay in the strike zone for most of the retrieve, enabling you to cover the edge quickly and thoroughly. This method also works well for fishing around natural structure and cover.

To work a specific spot like a

Anglers are more likely to find bass near a bridge over a deep channel than a bridge over a shallow expanse of water.

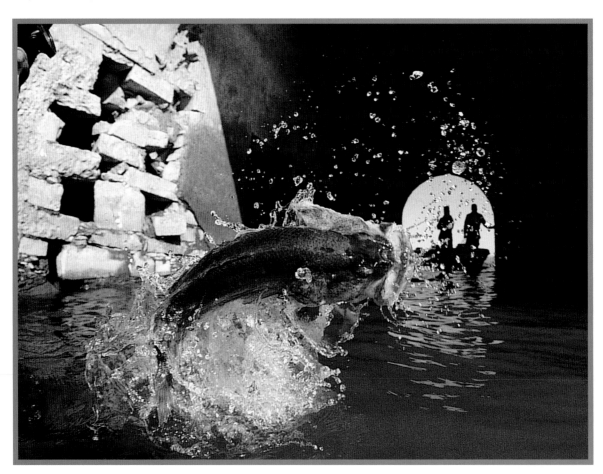

bridge piling, jig vertically around the perimeter while working different depths. Some anglers intentionally mis-tune a crankbait so it veers toward hard-to-reach locations like the spaces between dock posts.

Flippin' works well for placing a lure in spots that are difficult to reach by casting. It may be hard to cast into the area between two docked boats or to drop a lure next to the inside wall of a duck blind. But you can flip a jig easily into either spot.

To fish the shady spots under a dock, try a tactic called "skipping." Using a spinning outfit with 10-pound mono, cast a weedless worm with a sharp sidearm motion so it lands close to the dock, then skips underneath.

Bass prefer man-made features near some type of structure. Without deepwater refuge, the cover is of little value to bass. For example, you would be more likely to find bass near a bridge over a deep channel than a bridge over a shallow expanse of water.

Man-made features connected to a natural-movement path will also concentrate bass. Earthen dams are often built across dry washes to create farm ponds. After the reservoir is filled, bass moving along the dry wash channel encounter the dam and gather along both sides.

Features near heavy natural cover will not hold as many bass as those that are isolated. Bass pay little attention to a brush pile placed in a thick

weedbed. But the same brush pile placed on a weedless hump would be a bass magnet.

Finding submerged features can be difficult. Fishermen sometimes mark their favorite spots with plastic jugs, while some conservation agencies pinpoint fish attractors with buoys. But most underwater features lack visible signs. To find them, you must have reliable information.

Local anglers or bait shop operators may be able to help you find man-made features. If not, keep an eye on other fishermen, especially those anchored in unusual locations. When they leave, check out the spot. You may find a school of bass hanging around a brush shelter or car body.

Tips for Catching Bass from Man-made Structure

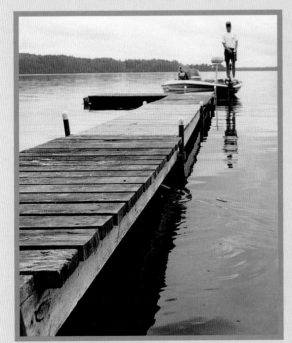

Cast your lure to the shaded side of a dock. Some fishermen prefer a 5½- or 6-foot spinning rod to skip the lure under the dock.

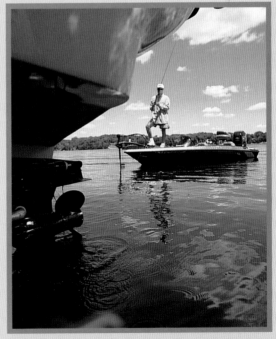

Flip a lure to the motor "washout" area when fishing a shallow-water dock. This area is often free of weeds and deeper than the surrounding area.

Catching Bass in Special Situations

For consistent bass-fishing success, you should know how to deal with special situations. Included in this chapter are some of the toughest fishing problems, along with some opportunities that many bass fishermen ignore.

Tough fishing conditions are not unusual. They begin in spring when bass complete spawning and the females refuse to bite. Heavy spring rains cause drastic fluctuations in water levels and clarity, both of which can slow fishing. In late spring and summer, cold fronts often pass through only a few days apart, bringing fishing to a standstill. By mid-summer, abundant food makes bass less inclined to bite. In late fall and winter, bass spend much of their time suspended in deep water where catching them can be difficult.

The difference between a good bass fisherman and an expert is the ability to solve these tough fishing problems. For example, when reservoirs become muddy after a heavy rainfall, most anglers give up. But the expert fisherman finds a creek arm with a clear stream flowing in and enjoys some of the best fishing of the year.

Successful anglers have another important skill: They know how to recognize and take advantage of fishing opportunities. Rivers and streams, for example, can provide quality angling in summer when fishing on lakes and reservoirs is slow. And fishermen who master night-fishing techniques often catch bass when daytime anglers fail.

Sometimes these opportunities last only a moment. An inexperienced fisherman will motor past a flock of diving gulls, paying little attention to the noisy birds. But the expert knows that gulls wheeling over the water often reveal a school of largemouths feeding on shad near the surface. He races to the spot and boats several bass before the school disappears.

Fishing for Suspended Bass

Finding suspended bass is easy; catching them is another matter. Fishermen scouting open water with depth finders sometimes spot bass far above bottom. But if the fish are in open water deeper than 20 feet, angling for them is probably a waste of time because they are not actively feeding.

Bass suspended near some type of cover are easier to catch. Fishermen on reservoirs often catch suspended bass by vertically jigging along sheer cliffs or in flooded timber at depths up to 50 feet. Begin by dropping a jigging spoon, vibrating blade or tailspin close to standing timber. Jig vertically, working the upper branches first. Gradually lower the lure, stopping to jig every few feet. Continue jigging all the way to bottom.

Bass often suspend below large schools of panfish in open water. The small fish usually hang from 5 to 10 feet below the surface with the bass several feet below them. On calm mornings and evenings, the panfish dimple the surface while feeding on tiny insects. Many anglers have seen the quiet water disturbed by the occasional swirls of bass grabbing small panfish. If you see this happening, try drawing bass to the surface with a topwater lure. Slowly walk the lure across the surface, creating a disturbance to attract suspended bass. Keep moving and cover as much water as possible. Some anglers use the countdown method if bass refuse surface lures. Cast into the vicinity of the bass, then count as the lure sinks. Begin your retrieve at different counts until you catch a bass. Then count the lure down to the same depth on succeeding casts.

Another effective technique for catching suspended bass is dangling live bait from a slip-bobber. As the bait sinks, the line slips through the bobber and stops at a sliding knot positioned at the desired depth. Adjust the knot so the bait hangs just above the fish.

Largemouths suspended in open water are more likely to strike if you use light line. A line weight of 6 to 8 pounds will subdue even the largest bass in water free of obstructions.

Fishing for Bass During Hot Weather

Most people begin their summer vacations about the time bass fishing takes its hot-weather nosedive. Even the best fishermen sometimes have trouble catching bass in midsummer.

There are many reasons for poor bass fishing during hot weather. Most significant is the abundant food supply. Baitfish hatched in spring reach a size attractive to bass in midsummer. Sunfish and perch, for example, have reached 1 to 2 inches, a size large enough to tempt bass. Largemouths pick off the young baitfish while cruising the edges of weedbeds. With natural food so easy to find, artificial lures have less appeal.

Midsummer finds sunlight penetration at its highest. With the sun directly overhead, bass must move deeper or find shade. Bridges, docks and other solid overhead cover may provide enough shade to keep the surface water several degrees cooler than the surrounding area. Slop or other matted vegetation may offer the only shade in shallow lakes that lack man-made cover such as docks. If the water temperature exceeds 80°F, bass look for cooler water in the depths, around springs or near coldwater tributaries. If they cannot find water cooler than 80°F, they become sluggish and eat very little.

Many anglers assume that largemouths do not feed during midsummer. But with the exception of shallow lakes in the

Deep South, bass eat more in midsummer than at any other time of the year. In one study of a northern lake, bass ate 222 percent more food per day during July and August than they ate in May and June.

These figures prove you can catch bass in summer. But you must be in the right place at the right time. When food is plentiful, it takes only a few minutes for a bass to eat its fill for the day.

If the weather is hot, clear and calm, these short feeding bursts take place at dusk, dawn or at night. Bass feed on the same shallow flats used at other times of the year. But you can also find active schools in deep water. If you catch bass at a certain time one day, they will probably feed about the same time the next day, unless the weather changes. Bass sometimes bite throughout the day if the weather if overcast, rainy or windy. The low-light conditions and slightly cooler surface

temperature cause bass to leave thick cover or to move shallower to feed.

Unless the water temperature exceeds 80°F, hot-weather fishing requires no special techniques. Use presentations and lures appropriate for the situation.

At temperatures above 80°F, small lures and slow retrieves work best. When fishing in slop, slowly reel a surface lure over the matted weeds. Or flip a 4-inch plastic worm into openings in the weeds. In deep water, try vertically jigging with a spoon, tailspin or jig-and-eel. If bass refuse these offerings, live bait may be the answer.

Fishing for Bass During Cold Fronts

Few anglers agree as to why bass fishing slows down after a cold front. But all agree that it does slow down. And if the cold front is severe, bass may not bite for several days.

Some fishermen blame the poor fishing on a rising barometer. But studies have failed to confirm that barometric pressure alone has any effect on fishing. Falling water temperature may have some impact. Even though the air temperature may change drastically, the water temperature changes little.

The most logical explanation is that extremely clear skies following a cold front allow more sunlight to reach the water. The strong light drives bass into deeper water or heavier cover. Divers have reported seeing bass buried in deep weeds with only their tails sticking out. The fish generally remain inactive for 1 to 2 days after the front passes. If bass do not have access to deep water, they bury in the thickest weeds in the shallows. If possible, you should avoid fishing in shallow bays following a cold front. These areas cool faster than the rest of the lake, making the effects of the front more noticeable to bass. Rivers and other murky waters continue to produce bass after a cold front. The turbid water allows little light penetration, despite the clear skies.

Catching bass holding tight to thick cover requires pinpoint casting. Most fishermen use small lures, slow retrieves and light lines to tempt lethargic bass.

Flippin' or simply dapping into heavy cover enables you to present a lure within a few inches of a bass. Jig the lure slowly, but pause occasionally so it hangs motionless. Sometimes a bass will stare at a lure for several minutes before striking. Live bait such as a nightcrawler may be the best solution for catching largemouths after a cold front. Bass examine their food closely, often ignoring everything but the real thing.

If a bass does bite, it often takes only a halfhearted nip at the lure or bait. Keep a tight line and watch carefully for the slightest twitch.

Fishing for Bass in Clear Water

Ultraclear water presents one of bass fishing's toughest

challenges. In some canyon reservoirs, strip pits and natural lakes, fishermen have observed bass cruising in water 20 feet deep. And when you can see the bass, the bass can see you.

Finding bass in clear water may be more difficult than finding them in murky water because the fish may go very deep to escape sunlight and warm temperatures. In canyon reservoirs, bass have been found at depths exceeding 100 feet. In murky lakes with heavy algae blooms, bass are confined to the shallows because the depths lack oxygen.

Not all bass go deep on sunny days. If there is brush and floating, matted weeds in the shallows, they may simply move into the shade. Overhanging cliffs, docks, bridges and other overhead cover also offer ample shade. These shallow-water fish are not easy to catch, however. They hold extremely close to the available cover so you must

be extremely accurate with your casts. Under this type of cover, bass will remain in the shallows all day.

When fishing in clear, shallow water, wear neutral-colored clothing, keep a low profile and avoid moving suddenly or casting your shadow over the fish. Although bass in shallow water tend to be spooky, they are still easier to catch than largemouths in deep water.

Largemouths in clear lakes bite best at dusk or dawn, and on windy or overcast days when light penetration is at a minimum. Fishermen on some crystal-clear lakes catch the majority of their bass at night, especially in summer. After the sun goes down bass in the depths move into shallower water, while bass in shallow water move out of heavy cover and cruise the weed edges looking for an easy meal.

Fast retrieves work best in clear water. A slow retrieve gives bass too much time to inspect your lure. Long casts help you avoid spooking the fish. To increase your casting distance, use spinning tackle with 4- to 10-pound monofilament. Avoid high-visibility line. Also avoid fluorescent or gaudy lures.

When possible, you can avoid fishing for clear-water bass by simply finding murky water from inflowing streams or from waves washing against a shoreline. The darker-colored water allows bass to escape bright sunlight and feed aggressively. Look for fish along the mud line where the murky and clear water meet.

Bright-colored lures are often the best choice when fishing for bass in low-clarity water.

Fish shallow water first in low-clarity lakes. The lack of light penetration limits deeper weed growth and oxygen levels in the deeper water areas. These anglers are fishing a slop bay on Wisconsin's Big Round Lake.

Fishing for Bass in Low-clarity Water

The fisherman who finds an area of low-clarity water in a clear lake may salvage an otherwise wasted trip. But more often, murky water means trouble.

Murky water results from muddy runoff, heavy blooms of algae or plankton, rough fish that root up the bottom or the roiling action of large waves. Many shallow, fertile bodies of water remain turbid year-round.

Low-clarity water confines bass to the shallows. In many low-clarity lakes and reservoirs, weed growth ends at about 6 feet and the water below 12 feet lacks oxygen. But turbidity filters out enough sunlight so bass are comfortable at depths of 4 to 8 feet.

Fishing surveys show that anglers catch bass at a significantly slower rate in extremely turbid water. To check water clarity, tie a white lure to your line, lower it into the water and note the depth at which it disappears. If you can see the lure at a depth of 1 foot or more, chances are you can catch bass.

Stay in the shallows when fishing low-clarity water. Little sunlight penetrates the cloudy water, so bass remain shallow all day. Target areas with fallen trees, weeds and brush. Keep in mind, however, that bass range farther from cover than they would in clear water. Cast large, noisy lures or those with a lot of flash. Many fishermen carry fine steel wool to polish their spinner blades, and add glitter or reflective tape to their lures.

You should also check out clear streams flowing into low-clarity lakes or reservoirs. These spots provide ideal conditions for bass, especially in summer. The fish find abundant food and cooler temperatures along the edge of the clear-water area that is created.

Fishing for Bass During Fluctuating Water Levels

When avid river fishermen meet to begin a day of fishing, the first question is, "What's the water doing?" They know that even a slight rise or fall can have a big impact on bass location.

Heavy rainfall or a lack of rain causes most water level fluctuations, but there may be other reasons. Irrigation pipes draw huge quantities of water from many rivers and reservoirs during summer. Flood-control reservoirs are drawn down in fall to make room for heavy spring runoff. The Corps of Engineers uses dams to control river levels for purposes of navigation.

A rise in water level causes any fish, including bass, to move shallower; a drop pushes them deeper. Fluctuations affect largemouths in shallow water more than bass in deep water. And a rapid rise or fall has a greater impact on fish movement than a gradual change.

Water levels change quickly in a river following a heavy rain. Bass respond immediately by moving into flooded vegetation near shore. Willows, for example, often become flooded when the water rises. The best way to catch bass in willows is to flip a jig-and-eel or plastic worm as close to the bank as possible and retrieve it through the branches. Flooded brush will hold bass as long as the water is rising or stable. Move your boat slowly just out from the edge and cast a spinnerbait into openings. Or cast parallel to the edge of the brush.

A slight drop in water levels will send bass scurrying to deep water, an instinctive response to avoid being trapped in an isolated pool. To be a successful angler you'll have to move with the fish.

It takes longer for the water level to change in lakes and reservoirs. A slow rise in water level will draw bass toward shore, although it may take several days. The fish remain shallow as long as the water is rising or stable, but they begin to filter into deeper water when the level starts to fall.

Changes in water level can be good or bad for fishing, depending on circumstances. A rise may draw inactive fish out of deeper water. They feed heavily because the flooded shallows offer a new food supply. But in some cases, rising water draws bass into shallow areas, where fishing is impossible.

Bass do not bite as well when falling water drives them deep. But falling water levels may concentrate fish in deep holes or other areas where they are easier to find. For example, if bass are scattered over a shallow flat near a creek channel, falling water would force all of the fish into the channel.

For up-to-date information on water levels, check water gauges, phone the Corps of Engineers or check water stage data in a local newspaper. Water gauges can be found on most large rivers and reservoirs. Look for gauges on bridge pilings or around a dam. Some gauges are marked in one-tenth-of-a-foot intervals, so changes can be detected more easily.

If this information is not available, establish your own reference point on a bridge piling, dock post or other object where a change would be easy to detect. Photographs taken at low water also help you record the exact location of structure and cover that is normally under water. Use a large tree or other object as a reference point when the level returns to normal.

Rising water may draw inactive fish out of deeper water. They feed heavily because the flooded shallows offer a new food supply.

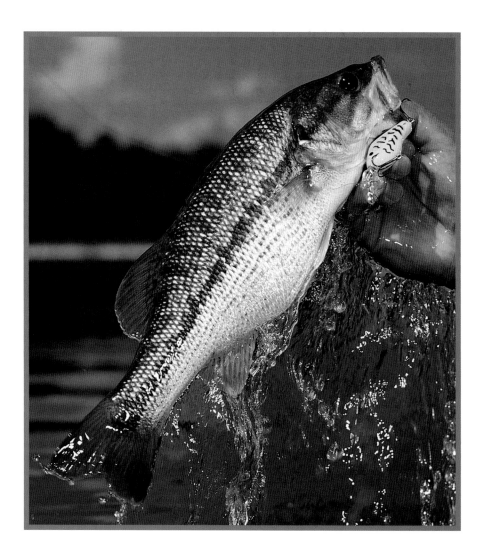

Fishing for Schooling Bass

When largemouths rip into schools of shad in open water, you can often catch your limit in minutes.

Anglers often encounter schooling bass, or schoolies, in late summer or fall while crossing open water on reservoirs. The frenzied feeding is most common in reservoirs with large populations of threadfin or gizzard shad.

Huge schools of shad roam the reservoir to feed on plankton. Schoolies, averaging 1 to 2 pounds each, follow the baitfish, periodically herding them to the surface. Feeding bass sometimes boil the surface for several minutes before the shad escape. To locate schooling bass, look for swirls on the surface and shad skipping across the water. Some anglers carry binoculars so they can watch for diving gulls. The birds swoop toward the surface to pick up shad injured by the feeding bass.

Reservoir fishermen frequently carry a spare rod rigged with a shad-like lure such as a vibrating plug, single-blade propbait or floating minnow plug. When the bass suddenly appear, they can begin casting immediately without taking time to re-rig.

When you spot schooling bass, quickly motor toward the fish, then cut the engine so the boat's momentum carries you toward the school. Use your electric motor to follow the school, staying just within casting range. When the bass sound, try vertical jigging or retrieve a deep-running crankbait through the area where the bass were surfacing.

When you start catching bass from a school, toss them into a live well; throwing them back may spook the school. You can easily keep schooling largemouths alive for the few minutes the frenzy is likely to last, and then throw them back.

Fishing for Spawning Bass

Fishermen continually debate the ethics of catching bass on their spawning beds. Most states allow fishing during the spawning period. But some anglers believe that catching spawners is detrimental to the long-term welfare of the bass population. Wherever such fishing is legal, many anglers voluntarily return their bass.

Both male and female bass will bite until spawning time arrives. But they refuse to strike lures while in the act of spawning. Afterward, fishermen catch mostly nest-guarding males. However, anglers in the Deep South often catch big females that appear to be guarding the nest along with the males.

Trophy largemouths bite best just before spawning. Look for them in slightly deeper water adjacent to their spring spawning grounds. More large bass are caught during the pre-spawn period than at any other time of the year. Large bass generally spawn before small ones, so fishermen seeking a trophy should start early in the season. If you catch nothing but small males, it probably means the females have finished spawning and dropped back to deeper water.

To locate spawning areas, cruise slowly through the shallows in a sheltered bay or along a shoreline protected from the wind. Wear polarized glasses to eliminate glare. They not only help you locate the nests, but they also make it easy to see the line twitch when a bass picks up your bait or lure.

Once you've located a nest, make a cast past it. Slowly retrieve your lure into the nest. Allow a jigging lure, like a Texas-rigged soft-plastic lizard or tube jig, to sit on the bottom in the nest. If the nest-guarding bass doesn't immediately grab the lure to take it out of the nest, gently shake the lure in place. Often this tempts the bass into picking up the lure. Once you see the jig disappear in the fish's mouth, or you see your line twitch, set the hook.

If you can't see individual beds because of waves or dark-colored water, simply retrieve a spinnerbait or shallow-running crankbait as close as possible to the edge of the weeds or through other cover types that may hold spawning fish. During this period, bass relate closely to cover and usually refuse to chase a lure into open water.

If spawning bass refuse to hit artificial lures, dangle live bait, such as a nightcrawler, golden shiner or waterdog, in front of nesting bass using a bobber rig. The fish are not interested in eating the bait, but they will pick it up and attempt to move it away if it comes too close to their eggs or fry.

How to Skip a Tube

Hold the rod tip low and make a sharp cast at the water's surface several feet in front of your target (1). The tube will bounce over the surface several times, covering a distance of 10 feet or more. If it touches down unmolested (2), jump it up sharply, and let it drop back to the bottom (3). After three or four jumps, crank in quickly and cast to another object.

Fishing for Bass in Streams

Stream fishermen contend that a bass living in current is a completely different animal than a bass in still water. It looks different, eats different foods and fights better for its size.

Largemouths in streams have sleeker bodies than bass in lakes. They seldom grow as large because they must expend energy just to fight the current. Crayfish, minnows, adult insects and insect larvae comprise a large part of their diet in most streams.

Fishing success on streams is more consistent than on most waters. Cold fronts have less effect on streams and bass continue to bite through summer. Flowing water does not become as warm as standing water and low oxygen levels are rarely a problem.

Fishermen who know how to read the water can easily spot likely holding areas. Bass rarely hold in fast current. They prefer slack water below some type of obstruction. Prime bass locations include eddies, logjams, deep pools and undercut banks.

They sometimes feed in a shallow riffle, but usually find a rock to break the current.

Experienced stream fishermen know of certain locations that routinely produce bass. A good example is a fallen tree in a deep pool. If a largemouth is removed, another fish about the same size will soon move in to take its place. Once you discover one of these spots, you will rarely fail to catch bass.

Wading is the best method of fishing a small stream, because it enables you to cover specific areas thoroughly. Most anglers use light spinning gear for casting small jigs, spinners or live bait. The most popular live bait rigs are the simplest: a nightcrawler with a #6 hook on a slip-sinker rig, a minnow with a #4 hook on a split-shot rig, and a crayfish with a #1 hook on a snag-resistant bottom-bouncer rig. Fly-fishing gear works better for drafting insect larvae and other small baits or for dropping lures or baits into hard-to-reach places.

When wading, cast upstream or across the current. Bass seldom strike a lure or bait retrieved against the current, because they are not accustomed to seeing food move in that direction. Work an eddy from the downstream side. Cast into the slack water behind a log or boulder and retrieve the lure or bait along the current margin. Then cover the slack water close to shore. Cast live bait upstream of an undercut bank. Take in line as the current washes the bait toward the overhang. Drift the bait as close to the bank as possible because bass seldom hang in the current. Drift your bait through a riffle by standing downstream of the fast water, then casting above it. Let the current tumble the bait along bottom. Cover the fast water thoroughly, then work the bait through the slack water along both edges of the current.

When fishing in large streams and rivers, use a shallow-draft boat and drift with the current. A trolling motor or outboard can be used to slow your drift, allowing more time to work good spots. Drop an anchor to hold the boat near deep pools that may hold several bass.

Fishing for Bass at Night

Asked to recall their first night-fishing adventure, most fishermen would tell of tangled lines, snagged lures and bass that got away. No doubt, fishing for largemouths at night poses some problems. But anglers who fish warm ponds, gin-clear waters or popular urban lakes know that night fishing is often the only way to catch bass. In the latter case, the heavy traffic of water-skiers and boaters drives bass deep during the day, but they move shallow to feed at night.

Bass seldom move far from their daytime haunts to reach nighttime feeding areas. Prime spots include distinct points along shoreline breaks; large, shallow flats extending from shore; and shallow mid-lake reefs. Bass move into the shallows and begin to feed just before dark.

To avoid spooking bass in these shallow areas, place markers during the day. Then sneak in to position your boat in the precise spot after dark.

Night fishing is generally best in summer, especially after a warm, still day with clear skies. On windy, overcast days, bass feed during the day so they may not feed again at night.

Most night fishermen use dark-colored lures that create turbulence or vibration. But some anglers swear by plastic worms. Try surface lures first to catch the active feeders. Bass can easily see the silhouette of topwater lures against the light background at the surface. Switch to deeper-running lures and work a break leading to deep water after giving surface lures a try. Some fishermen attach a snap to the line, so they can change lures easily without retying.

A slow, steady retrieve works best at night, because bass use their lateral line to home in on the lure. If you use an erratic retrieve, the fish may miss.

Moon phase may have some influence on night-fishing success. Most experts prefer to fish 2 to 3 days on either side of a new moon or a full moon.

In waters with heavy boat traffic, the biggest bass typically go on the prowl after the sun sets.

Smallmouth Bass

Wherever there is cool, clear water with a good supply of crayfish, anglers are likely to find smallmouth bass. And, whenever you hook a smallmouth, you're bound to see spectacular leaps and determination unrivaled among freshwater fish.

Prior to 1900, smallmouth bass were found mainly in the Great Lakes and in river systems in the east-central United States. But as the railroads moved west and north, smallmouth were stocked in many rivers, natural lakes and large reservoirs. Probably the most successful introduction was in the clear, rocky lakes of the southern Canadian Shield.

The smallmouth bass is a close cousin of the largemouth, though the species differ in many ways. Smallmouths, for example, prefer slightly cooler water. They are most active in water 67° to 72°F and spawn in water from the upper 50s to lower 60s. While smallmouth spawn in cooler water, they may deposit their eggs a few days later than largemouth. The reason is that shallow, weedy bays used by spawning largemouth

warm faster in spring than do the deeper, rocky sites preferred by smallmouth.

Where smallmouth and largemouth inhabit the same waters, smallmouth will usually be found a little deeper and are less likely to inhabit dense, weedy cover. Smallmouth prefer a firm, rocky bottom and, unlike largemouths, are seldom found on soft-bottomed structure.

Smallmouth respond to

Smallmouth bass have a jaw that extends only to the middle of the eye, rather than beyond the rear of the eye, as in the largemouth. The sides are greenish to brownish with dark vertical bars that come and go. Three dark bars radiate from the eye. Smallmouth commonly change color to match their surroundings.

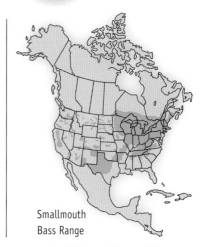

sunlight and weather changes in much the same way as largemouth (p. 74). They're most active under low-light conditions and during periods of stable weather.

Although crayfish are the smallmouth's favorite food, they also eat frogs and tadpoles, many kinds of small fish, worms and a variety of insects, including both immature and adult forms.

Smallmouth do not reach the size of largemouth bass. A 5-pound smallmouth is considered a trophy in most waters, though many 7- to 8-pounders are caught each year in Tennessee Valley Authority reservoirs in Kentucky, Tennessee and Alabama. The world record, caught in Dale Hollow Reservoir, Tennessee, in 1969, weighed 10 pounds, 14 ounces.

Smallmouth Bass Range

Dusk is an excellent time to catch smallmouths in shallow water. This good-sized fish took a small spinner on Arizona's Lake Apache.

Where to Catch Smallmouth in Lakes

Smallmouth bass lakes have one thing in common. They all have at least some rocky bottom to provide spawning habitat for bass. Cool, northern lakes have the largest smallmouth populations, although the biggest fish are caught in deep southern reservoirs such as those created by the Tennessee Valley Authority.

Most of a smallmouth's life is spent in 5 to 15 feet of water. They lurk in the shallows because most of their foods are there and because their eyes are not overly sensitive to bright sunlight. In southern reservoirs, midsummer heat may drive them into 30- to 40-foot depths dur-ing midday, though they return to the shallows to feed at dusk.

Smallmouth bass have well-defined territories. Once you find a good spot, you may have to change angling methods with the seasons, but you seldom have to move far to find the fish. Following is a list of prime smallmouth locations in natural and man-make lakes.

Prime Locations in Natural Lakes:

• Points attract smallmouth bass throughout the year. Look for long, gradually tapering sand-gravel points with bul-rushes, or points made up of golf-ball- to baseball-sized rock.

• Rocky shorelines surrounded by deep water are most produc-tive in summer and fall. The best humps taper gradually rather than plunge sharply into the depths.

• Weedlines hold smallmouth until the weeds die back in fall. Points and inside turns along the weedline, especially where there is a gravelly or rocky bot-tom, are key locations.

Prime Locations in Man-made Lakes:

• Rocky shorelines in pro-tected creek arms draw spawning smallmouth. The best shorelines taper slowly and have scattered boulders that afford protection for the nest.

• Main-lake points, especially those that have a rocky bottom and are near the main river channel, are good summertime feeding areas. After feeding, the fish can retreat to deep water.

• Submerged roadbeds attract smallmouth because of the hard substrate. Roadbeds are most productive in summer, but shal-low ones draw fish in spring and deep ones, in late fall.

Where to Catch Smallmouth in Rivers

Coolwater streams with moderate current and rocky bottoms are favorite smallmouth haunts. Rarely do they live in warm, muddy streams.

River smallmouths prowl rocky shoals to find food. They seldom are found over flat, sandy bottoms. Although they may feed in moderate current, smallmouth spend most of their time in slack water. They commonly lie in current breaks between fast and slow water. Eddies below points, rocks or bridge abutments are favorite hangouts. Often they gather just downstream of trees that have toppled into the water.

Unlike lake-dwelling smallmouth, those in rivers rarely form large schools. Instead, a fish picks out a quiet spot behind rocks or logs, where it lives with one or two other bass. When one is caught, another moves in to take its place. As a result, prime spots always hold bass, despite heavy fishing pressure. Following is a list of these high-percentage spots.

Prime Locations in Small Rivers:

• Boulders form eddies that make excellent feeding stations for smallmouth in summer and fall. The main eddy forms downstream of the boulder; a smaller one forms just upstream.

• Bars or points extending into the river deflect the current and create eddies that hold smallmouth in summer and fall. The fish tend to feed along the current line.

• Eddies that form alongside fast water below dams draw smallmouth from late spring into fall. Baitfish that gather in the eddies make easy targets for foraging smallmouth.

Prime Locations in Big Rivers:

• Wing dams, which are man-made current deflectors, draw smallmouth in summer and fall. The fish hold in the eddy just above the wing dam and often feed right on top of the wing dam.

• Deep cuts connecting the main channel with backwater areas are most productive in summer and fall. Look for the fish around fallen trees and other objects that break the current.

• Riprap is placed along highway or railroad embankments or on islands to prevent erosion. The riprap holds food and provides cover, so it draws smallmouth from spring through fall.

Riprap banks are great spots to find smallies.

River smallmouths often hold in the eddies behind boulders.

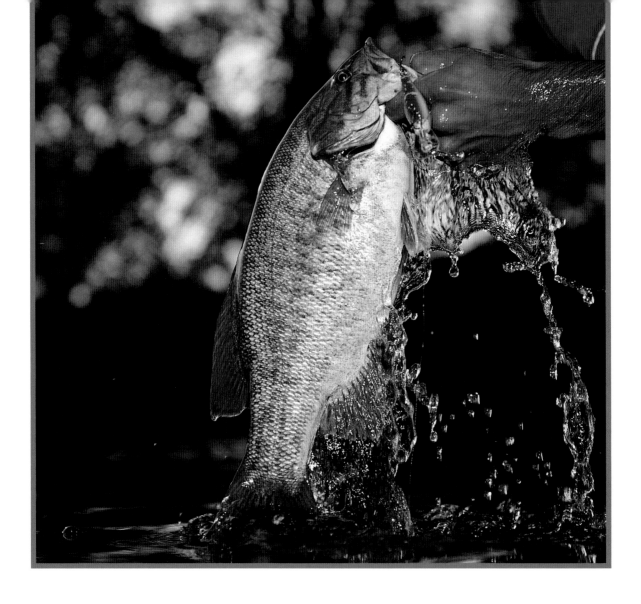

How to Catch Smallmouth

Many smallmouth-fishing techniques revolve around the fish's fondness for crayfish. Anglers use rubber-legged jigs, crankbaits and other artificials in brownish or orangish hues resembling the colors of live crayfish. And these lures are usually fished on the rocky bottoms where crayfish live.

But smallmouth also consume plenty of baitfish that are found in weedy or brushy cover or in open water. This explains why spinners, small minnow plugs, twister-tail jigs and other minnow imitations are also considered excellent smallmouth baits.

But smallmouth baits don't have to look like anything in particular; the fish will hit most anything that makes a lot of commotion. That's why topwater lures, such as stickbaits and propbaits, work so well for smallmouth.

As a rule, smallmouth are aggressive biters, especially where populations are high. It's not unusual to see two or three smallmouth chasing one that's been hooked, trying to steal the lure. The smaller fish are usually the most aggressive.

But there are times when smallmouth are finicky, and that's when live bait outperforms artificials. Besides crayfish, favorite live baits for smallmouth include leeches, nightcrawlers, hellgrammites and minnows, particularly shiners. Fish them the same way you would for walleyes, using slip-sinker or slip-bobber rigs. Or, just use a plain hook and a split shot.

Because of the smallmouth's legendary fighting ability, catch-and-release fishing is rapidly gaining in popularity. Without catch-and-release, heavily fished waters could not produce quality smallmouth fishing.

1

2

3

Fishing Subsurface Plugs

The same types of subsurface plugs used for largemouth work equally well for smallmouth, but smallmouth plugs are generally a little smaller, ranging in length from 2 to 3 inches. When smallmouth are feeding aggressively, however, they will take plugs up to 6 inches long.

Crankbaits are a good choice when you want to cover a lot of water in a hurry. The lip tends to deflect off of obstructions like logs and rocks, preventing hang-ups. Be sure to choose a crankbait suitable for the water depth you're fishing. Some models track only a few feet deep; others, more than 20.

Minnow plugs have a realistic look and enticing action that makes them a smallmouth favorite. You can fish them with a steady retrieve or twitch them on the surface. For the most wobble, tie on a minnow plug with a knot that clinches tightly to the attachment eye (such as the Trilene knot, p. 31) and slide the knot toward the bottom of the eye.

Vibrating plugs, when retrieved at high speed, emit a vibration that smallmouth find hard to resist. These lures sink, so you can count them down to any depth. But they are not as snag-resistant as crankbaits.

Subsurface plugs
include: (1) crankbaits, such as the Rebel Deep Wee R; (2) minnow plugs, such as the Normark Original Floating Rapala; and (3) vibrating plugs, such as the Normark Rattlin' Rapala.

Sub-surface Plug Tips for Smallmouth

Tune a sub-surface plug if it is not tracking straight. If the bait is running to the right, bend the attachment eye to the left, and vice versa.

Wait a few seconds after the plug lands before starting your retrieve. The splash may draw a smallmouth's attention, and it will strike the floating plug.

Jigging lures include: (1) curlytail jigs, such as the Berkley Power Grub on a mushroom-head jig; (2) creature-type jigs, such as the Gapen Ugly Bug; (3) bucktail jigs, such as the Wazp Genuine Bucktail Jig; (4) vibrating blades, such as the Cotton Cordell Gay Blade; and (5) tailspins, such as the Mann's Little George.

Jigging

Jig fishing requires a deft touch, but once you master it, you'll understand why it is considered one of the deadliest smallmouth techniques.

Smallmouth anglers use the same types of jigs and jigging lures used for largemouth, but one of the most effective is a mushroom-head jig tipped with a curlytail grub. Jig heads also work well for presenting live bait. Smallmouth will seldom ignore a lively leech, shiner or crawler tipped on a jig head.

Vibrating blades are popular smallmouth baits in man-made lakes throughout the South, but they are a good choice for vertically jigging in any type of water and will easily reach fish at depths of 40 feet or more. Jigging spoons and tailspins can be used for the same purpose.

Jig Tips for Smallmouth

Use bicolor jig heads to increase your odds of offering the right color. You can buy them or make your own by dipping heads in fluorescent paint.

Cut a piece of pork rind that is too big for smallmouth into smaller pieces about 2 inches long and 1/4 inch wide. Punch a hole in one end of each piece with an awl; the rind may be too tough to penetrate with a hook.

Fishing Soft Plastics

Plastic worms are normally considered a top largemouth bait, but there are times when worms and other soft plastics work just as well for smallmouth. When smallmouth are tucked into dense weeds, for example, a Texas-rigged worm is one of the few baits that will get at them without fouling. Worms used for smallmouth are usually 4 to 6 inches in length, a little shorter than those used for largemouth.

Soft-plastic crayfish and tube baits are good choices for tempting fussy smallmouth. The realistic legs and pincers wiggle enticingly, convincing stubborn fish to strike. These soft plastics should also be a little smaller than the ones used for largemouth.

Although Texas rigs are needed when smallmouth bass are in heavy cover, soft plastics fished on a mushroom-head jig work better when the fish are on a clean bottom, which is most often the case. The open hook will significantly improve your hooking percentage.

Topwater Fishing

If you like visual fishing and explosive strikes, try topwater fishing for smallmouth. The technique works best in spring, when smallmouth move into the shallows to spawn. But there are times when topwaters will "call up" smallmouth from water as deep as 20 feet.

Propbaits, stickbaits and chuggers are the most popular topwaters for smallmouth, but most any high-riding lure will work, including minnow plugs twitched on the surface and spinnerbaits held high enough so the blade almost breaks water.

The best retrieve depends on the mood of the fish. When they're active, a series of twitches with little or no hesitation between them may work best. But when they're finicky, you may have to pause 15 seconds or more between twitches.

Although a topwater strike may be explosive, a smallmouth sometimes just sips in the bait, barely disturbing the surface. Wait until you feel resistance before setting the hook. If you set when you see a splash, you'll probably pull the bait away from the fish.

Soft plastics include: (1) tube baits, such as the Berkley Power Tube, rigged on a tube jig; (2) worms, such as the Berkley Power worm, rigged on a mushroom-head jig; and (3) crayfish imitations, such as the Berkley Power Craw, rigged on a S.W.A.T. Jig.

Topwaters include: (1) propbaits, such as the Heddon Tiny Torpedo; (2) stickbaits, such as the Heddon Zara Puppy; and (3) chuggers, such as the Mann's Chug-N-Spit.

Fishing Spinners & Spinnerbaits

A flashing spinner blade appeals to the smallmouth's aggressive nature and predatory instincts. Smallmouth bass fishermen commonly use two different styles of spinners: standard (in-line) spinners, and spinnerbaits.

Standard spinners work well in shallow water with little weedy or snaggy cover. Simply cast them out and reel them in just fast enough to make the blade spin. When fishing a bank with a steep, sloping shoreline, cast parallel, rather than perpendicular, to the bank. A parallel cast keeps the lure in productive water longer. A spinner with a size 2 or 3 blade is most effective for smallmouth fishing.

Spinnerbaits are a better choice in weedy or brushy cover because they are resistant to fouling. Most anglers use 1/8- to 1/4-ounce spinnerbaits for smallmouth, but night fishermen often use large spinner-baits weighing up to 1 ounce. Because cruising smallmouth look up for their food, spinner-baits should be retrieved fast enough to keep them running no more than a foot beneath the surface. If you don't get a strike within the first 10 feet, quickly reel in and cast again.

Fly Fishing

Not only is fly fishing one of the most exciting ways to catch small-mouth, it's also one of the most effective. Some flies are nearly perfect imitations of smallmouth foods; others attract smallmouth by the flash or surface commotion they produce. Most smallmouth flies range from size 2 to 6.

Bass bugs, which have bodies made of cork, plastic or clipped deer hair, are fished on the

Spinners include: (1) standard spinners, such as the Blue Fox Vibrax Minnow Spin; and (2) spinnerbaits, such as the Hart Sniper.

Spinner-fishing Tips for Smallmouth

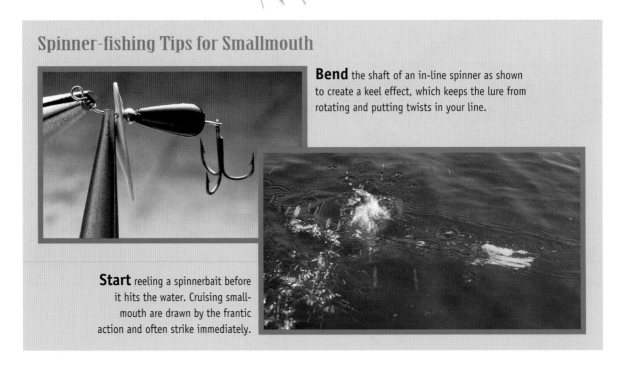

Bend the shaft of an in-line spinner as shown to create a keel effect, which keeps the lure from rotating and putting twists in your line.

Start reeling a spinnerbait before it hits the water. Cruising small-mouth are drawn by the frantic action and often strike immediately.

surface, usually with a twitch-and-pause retrieve.

Crayfish flies have lifelike claws made of hair or feathers. Leech flies have a long tail made of marabou or a chamois strip. Many are weighted so they can be fished on the bottom.

Smallmouth anglers also use big streamers that resemble shiners or other minnows, nymphs that look like hellgrammites or immature dragonflies and even dry flies, usually mayfly or stonefly imitations.

Use a fly with a mono weedguard when fishing in snaggy cover. If you tie your own flies, you can easily make a weedguard by tying in a piece of 20-pound mono.

The big, wind-resistant flies used for smallmouth require a weight-forward or bass-bug-taper line, preferably 6-weight to 8-weight.

Lower the rod tip when smallmouth jump to prevent them from breaking the tippet.

Work a bass bug with your rod tip only a few inches above the water's surface to better control the fly and increase your hooking percentage.

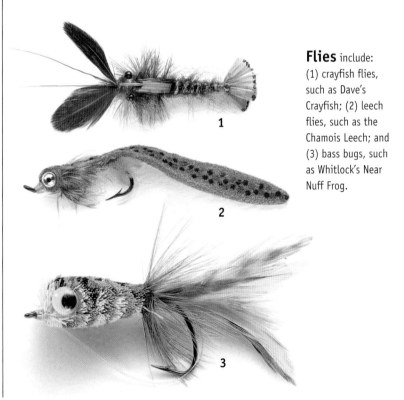

Flies include: (1) crayfish flies, such as Dave's Crayfish; (2) leech flies, such as the Chamois Leech; and (3) bass bugs, such as Whitlock's Near Nuff Frog.

Striped bass from the Cooper River, South Carolina.

Striped Bass & White Bass

When a school of striped bass or white bass churns the surface in pursuit of baitfish, there is no faster fishing. They instantly strike any lure cast into their midst. And these members of the Temperate Bass family rank among the strongest-fighting gamefish.

White bass, often called silver bass or sand bass, are found exclusively in fresh water, mainly in big rivers and lakes connected to them, and in large reservoirs. Striped bass, also called rockfish or stripers, are native to the Atlantic coastal waters of North America and, in the late 1800s, were stocked along the Pacific Coast. The fish migrate up major coastal rivers during their spring spawning runs.

When South Carolina's Santee and Cooper rivers were dammed in

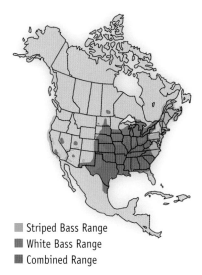

■ Striped Bass Range
■ White Bass Range
■ Combined Range

1941, striped bass were trapped above the dam. By 1950, stripers were thriving in the newly created reservoir and fishermen were enjoying an exciting new sport-fish. The success of stripers in Santee-Cooper led to stocking programs in many other states and to development of the white-rock or wiper, a white bass/striper hybrid that has been introduced in many southern reservoirs.

Stripers and white bass have similar lifestyles. Both species migrate up rivers and streams in spring, spawning when the water temperature reaches about 58°F. Similarly, they both prefer large bodies of water that have an abundance of gizzard or threadfin shad, their primary food. They are rarely linked to structure or cover; instead, they roam wide expanses of open water following schools of baitfish.

The pack-feeding behavior of stripers and white bass makes them an easy target for anglers. When foraging bass tear into a school of shad, the baitfish flip out of the water in an attempt to escape, often drawing flocks of sea gulls. Savvy fishermen look for the gulls diving into the water, quickly motor to the edge of the melee, and then cast into the swirling water.

White bass rarely exceed 3 pounds, while stripers often weigh more than 30. The record white bass, caught in Lake Orange, Virginia, in 1989, weighed 6 pounds, 13 ounces. The largest striper taken from inland waters, 67 pounds, 8 ounces, was caught in O'Neill Forebay, California, in 1992. The record hybrid, 27 pounds, 5 ounces, came from Greers Ferry Lake, Arkansas, in 1997.

Striped bass have silvery sides with 7 or 8 dark horizontal stripes that are not broken. The stripes extend all the way to the tail. The body is more elongated than that of a white bass, and there are two patches of teeth on the tongue, rather than one.

White bass have silvery sides with unbroken black stripes above the lateral line. The stripes below the lateral line are faint and irregular. The stripes usually stop short of the tail. The tongue has a single patch of teeth at the base.

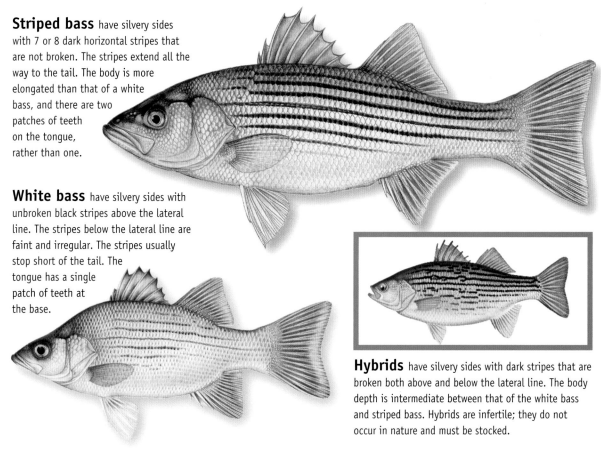

Hybrids have silvery sides with dark stripes that are broken both above and below the lateral line. The body depth is intermediate between that of the white bass and striped bass. Hybrids are infertile; they do not occur in nature and must be stocked.

Stripers and white bass thrive in Kentucky's Lake Cumberland (above) and other southern reservoirs.

Where to Catch Stripers & White Bass

Stripers and white bass are constantly on the move. A school of hungry bass may appear out of nowhere, providing fantastic fishing for several minutes, and then disappear just as quickly.

Huge schools of stripers and white bass migrate upstream in spring, stopping in pools and eddies along the way. They move upriver until a dam, waterfall or other obstruction blocks their progress.

After spawning, both species retreat downstream where they scatter into the open water of lakes or reservoirs. They spend most of the summer in water from 20 to 40 feet deep. At daybreak and dusk, they move onto shallow sand flats to chase schools of shad or shiners.

By late summer or fall, young-of-the-year shad have grown large enough to interest the bass, and the pack-feeding behavior mentioned earlier begins. Stripers and white bass may slash into a school of shad at any time of day.

In the North, late fall and winter fishing is slow because feeding diminishes greatly in water cooler than 50°F. But ice fishing for white bass can be outstanding if you can locate the spots where large schools winter. In the South, fishing for both white bass and stripers remains good through the winter months. In winter, the fish spend less time roaming open water and are more likely to tuck into heavy cover, such as flooded timber. Following is a list of the top locations for finding and catching stripers and white bass throughout the year.

Prime Striper & White Bass Locations:

• Dams stop the spring spawning migration of stripers and white bass. The fish congregate in eddies or slack water near the fast current, where they feed on shad, shiners and other small baitfish.

• Back ends of creek arms attract spawning stripers and white bass in reservoirs. The fish are drawn into the back ends by warm water and flow from inlet streams.

• Edges of sand flats are excellent striper and white bass spots in summer and fall. The fish rest in the deep water and move up on the flat to chase shad and other baitfish early and late in the day.

• Main-lake points, especially those with extended, sandy lips, concentrate stripers and white bass in summer and fall. Often, the fish move onto the points to feed in early morning.

• Warmwater discharges from power plants attract huge schools of shad during winter. The shad, in turn, draw stripers and white bass, offering fast fishing for anglers willing to brave the elements.

• Deep water along the dam face holds shad, stripers and white bass during the winter months. The zone just above the dam usually has the reservoir's deepest, warmest water.

How to Catch Stripers & White Bass

The techniques for catching white and striped bass are similar, but stripers demand tougher equipment and bigger baits. For white bass, use a light- to medium-power spinning outfit with 4- to 8-pound-test line; for stripers, a medium-heavy to heavy power spinning or baitcasting outfit with 15- to 40-pound-test.

Both species are easiest to catch during the spring spawning

When white bass are schooled up, you can easily catch a few dozen of them in an hour or two. This fast-paced surface action took place on Elephant Butte Lake, New Mexico.

period. When thousands of fish are concentrated in the tailwaters of a dam or the back end of a creek arm, they strike most any bait tossed their way.

Once the fish complete spawning and scatter into open water, finding and catching them becomes a lot tougher. That's when trolling techniques work best, because they enable anglers to cover wide expanses of water. Once a school is located, some fishermen stop and jig spoons or lead-head jigs straight below the boat.

In waters with good populations of threadfin or gizzard shad, fishing picks up again in fall as the fish begin tearing into large shad schools on the surface. Then, anglers switch to a technique called jump-fishing (opposite).

In the North, white bass are sometimes taken by ice fishing. The fish congregate in huge, very tight schools, and, if you can locate one, you can expect some fast action.

Jump-fishing lures for stripers include: (1) plugs, such as the Normark Super Shad Rap; (2) popping plugs, such as the Cordell Pencil Popper; and (3) jigs, such as the Northland Bucktail Jig, tipped with a curlytail grub. Jump-fishing lures for white bass include: (4) topwaters, such as the Heddon Tiny Torpedo; (5) tailspins, such as the Mann's Little George; and (6) jigs, such as the Mister Twister Sassy Shad.

Jump-fishing

When you spot a flock of gulls circling and diving into the water, there's a good chance that they've located a school of stripers or white bass tearing into a mass of shad. During the onslaught, many of the shad are injured, providing the bass with an easy meal.

Should you see such a feeding frenzy, get to the spot in a hurry. But don't motor right up to the school with your outboard or you'll spook the school. Instead, stop well short of the school and quickly move up to the school using your electric trolling motor (below). If you're careful not to get too close to the fish and spook them, the action may last for an hour or more. If you're not, they'll be gone within seconds and you'll have to look for another school.

Some fishermen rig one rod with a topwater and another with a jig or diving plug. Then, if one presentation fails to produce, they can quickly switch to the other rig and avoid wasting time.

White bass anglers often rig two or more jigs on the same line. When a bass grabs one jig, other bass give chase in an attempt to steal it. They spot the other jig and you haul in a pair of fish.

Jump-fishing Tips

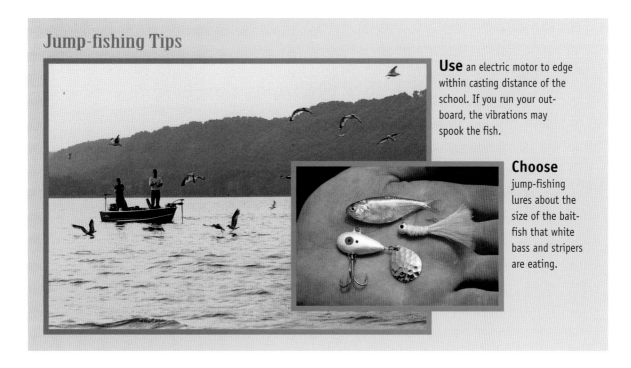

Use an electric motor to edge within casting distance of the school. If you run your outboard, the vibrations may spook the fish.

Choose jump-fishing lures about the size of the baitfish that white bass and stripers are eating.

Trolling

The trolling methods used for white bass are simple; just toss a small crankbait, vibrating plug or jig behind the boat and troll through an area known to produce white bass.

But trolling for stripers gets a lot more complicated. Anglers use downriggers and side planers to spread their lines vertically and horizontally, maximizing their coverage. In spring and fall, when the water is cool, most trolling is done in the upper 25 feet. In summer, however, you may have to get your lines into 40 to 60 feet of water. That's when downriggers are a must.

Most striper fishermen troll very slowly, using a bow-mount electric motor to avoid spooking the fish. If you can find a source of live shad or net your own, they make excellent bait. Hook shad through the nostrils with a size 2/0 hook. If shad are not available, use a bucktail or horsehead jig tipped with a curlytail grub.

Once you locate a school of white bass and stripers, switch to a technique that gives you more thorough coverage, like jigging. Continue to work the spot until the school disperses, then resume trolling.

Trolling lures for white bass include: (1) crankbaits, such as the Storm ThinFin; and (2) vibrating plugs, such as the Cordell Super Spot. Trolling lures for striped bass include: (3) horsehead jigs, such as the Hyper Striper Stump Jumper; and (4) minnow baits, such as the Cotton Cordell Red Fin.

Trolling Tips

Choose gizzard shad (bottom) instead of threadfin shad (top) whenever possible. Gizzard shad work better for bait because they are hardier and grow to a larger size. You can distinguish between the two by differences in coloration. The gizzard shad has a blackish margin on the tail; the threadfin, yellowish. To keep shad lively while trolling, push the hook through the shad's nostrils. Use a 2- to 3-ounce egg sinker about 4 feet above the hook to get the shad down deep.

Make a spreader rig by bending a piece of stiff wire as shown. A spreader enables you to troll three jigs at a time on a single line and keeps them tracking far enough apart so they don't tangle.

Topwater Fishing

The commotion made by a topwater lure appeals to the aggressive feeding instincts of stripers and white bass. Topwaters work best around spawning time, when the hungry predators are chasing baitfish in the shallows. But they can be effective anytime the fish are feeding in shallow water, particularly early and late in the day.

Small stickbaits and prop-baits, from 2 to 3 inches long, are the best choice for white bass. Fish a stickbait with a walking-the-dog retrieve; a propbait, with a brisk, steady retrieve.

Stripers find it hard to resist large, noisy popping plugs. Some of these plugs are nearly a foot long. When you see a fish swirl on the surface, cast the plug several feet past the swirl, then retrieve it with a series of powerful jerks for maximum splash.

Floating minnow plugs worked on the surface also account for good numbers of stripers. Just cast the lure out and retrieve it slowly enough that it makes a noticeable wake.

Other Striper & White Bass Techniques

The aggressive nature of stripers and white bass means that they're vulnerable to a wide variety of presentations.

Casting with lead-head jigs has long been a popular method. The fish seem to prefer jigs fished with a straight retrieve rather than an erratic jigging action, but it pays to mix up your retrieves to see what works best on a given day.

Vertically jigging with lead-heads or jigging spoons is a favorite deep-water method,

but it also works well for jump-fishing (p. 119). While one angler casts to the surface feeders, another vertically jigs for fish that remain on the bottom.

Balloon fishing with live shad is one of the most effective methods for trophy stripers. A balloon tied to the line with an overhand knot will keep a large shad afloat, yet the shad can easily tow the balloon around, covering all the water around your boat. When a striper bites, line slips through the balloon, causing it to bob erratically.

Striper fishermen also troll or drift using a live or cut shad or herring on a tandem-hook harness. White bass anglers sometime tip their jigs with strips of white-bass belly meat (right) when fishing gets tough.

Fly fishing for white bass and stripers is gaining in popularity. Any bright-colored streamer will catch white bass. For stripers, try bulky streamer patterns tied with materials that "breathe" in the water.

Topwater lures for white bass include: (1) stickbaits, such as the Heddon Zara Puppy; and (2) propbaits, such as the Cotton Cordell Crazy Shad. Topwaters for striped bass include: (3) floating minnow plugs, such as Cotton Cordell Redfin; and (4) popping plugs, such as Cotton Cordell Pencil Popper.

White bass fishermen attach a 1/4-inch by 11/4-inch-long strip of belly meat to the jig when fishing is slow.

Sunfish

The near-universal popularity of sunfish is easy to understand. For a youngster just learning to fish, they are one of the easiest fish to catch. For an expert, catching big sunfish is as much of a challenge as catching big bass or pike. For an angler interested in sport, sunfish put up a great fight on light tackle. And for those who enjoy eating fish, their sweet-tasting meat is unsurpassed as table fare.

The sunfish family includes crappies, black bass and true sunfish (genus Lepomis). When anglers use the term "sunfish," they are referring to the latter. The largest and most important to fishermen are the bluegill, redear and pumpkinseed. In the South, sunfish are often collectively referred to as bream (pronounced "brim"). Many types of true sunfish do not grow large enough to interest anglers.

Hybridization is common among sunfish species. Practically every kind of sunfish will crossbreed with every other kind that inhabits the same waters. The result is numerous varieties of sunfish that even experts have trouble identifying.

Sunfish begin to spawn in spring, at water temperatures from the upper 60s to low 70s. The male builds a nest on a sand or gravel bottom, at depths from 6 inches to 3 feet. The nests, which are round, light-colored depressions, are often very close together, forming a spawning colony.

After depositing her eggs, which may number more than 200,000, the female abandons the nest. The male stays on to guard the eggs and, later, the fry. The male is very aggressive and will attack anything that comes near the nest, including a fisherman's bait.

Sunfish may spawn several times over the course of the summer. Multiple spawning attempts are more common in the South than in the North. In the South, the fish commonly spawn around the full moon.

Sunfish have a varied diet consisting mainly of larval and adult insects, crustaceans, mollusks and, sometimes, small fish. They rely heavily on sight and scent to find their food.

Despite heavy fishing pressure, sunfish often overpopulate a body of water because they produce too many young. This results in high competition for food and a low growth rate. Under these conditions, none of the fish attain large size. The biggest sunfish are caught in southern waters and, throughout the North, in lakes and ponds with relatively low sunfish populations.

Bluegill Range

Bluegills are named for the distinctive powder-blue coloring on the lower part of the gill cover. They have a black gill-cover lobe, or ear, and a dark spot at the rear base of the dorsal fin. The world record, 4 pounds, 12 ounces, was caught in Ketona Lake, Alabama, in 1950.

Redears get their name from the red or orange margin on the gill-cover lobe. The sides are greenish with red or orange flecks. Commonly called shellcrackers, redears are fond of snails. The world record, 5 pounds, 7 ounces, was taken in Diversion Canal, South Carolina, in 1998.

Pumpkinseeds have gold-colored sides with a lacework of blue or green and orange or red flecks. The orange or red spot on the gill-cover lobe is smaller than that on the redear. The world record, 1 pound, 6 ounces, was caught in Oswego Pond, New York, in 1985.

- Pumpkinseed Range
- Redear Range
- Combined Range

Where to Catch Sunfish

Sunfish can survive in most any kind of warmwater environment, including ponds, strip pits, natural lakes, man-made lakes and rivers of any size. The fish are rarely found in coldwater lakes or streams, except in shallow weedy bays or backwaters where the water is much warmer.

Many anglers prefer to fish for sunfish around spawning time, when they're heavily concentrated and aggressively feeding. As a rule, the fish bite best at water temperatures above 60°F, but you can catch them any time of the year. Some north-country fishermen would argue that sunfish bite best just after freeze-up.

Sunfish do most of their feeding in daylight hours. Peak fishing times are early and late in the day, but you can catch some fish all day long. Weather is not much of a factor in fishing for sunfish, although a strong cold front may slow the action.

Following are some of the best places to find sunfish in their most important habitats: natural lakes, man-made lakes and rivers.

Prime Locations in Natural Lakes:

• Shallow, weedy bays with sand-gravel shorelines make good spawning areas. Sunfish return to these areas in fall and stay through early winter.

• Points with stands of bulrushes or other emergent vegetation are sometimes used for spawning and may hold sunfish into early summer.

• Extended lips of points, especially those with plenty of submerged vegetation, are good sunfish producers from late spring into fall.

• Weedy humps are prime summertime sunfish locations. The bigger fish usually hold along the deep edge of the weedline.

Prime Locations in Man-made Lakes:

• Back ends of creek arms warm earliest in spring and draw sunfish in to spawn. The best creek arms are fed by clear creeks.

• Creek channel edges are excellent summertime locations. The fish find cover among the flooded timber and can easily retreat to deep water in the channel.

• Main-lake points that slope gradually into deep water hold sunfish in summer and fall. Sunfish often suspend in open water just off the points.

• Deep holes at the lower end of creek arms hold large numbers of sunfish in winter. The holes serve as staging areas for fish that will swim up the arms to spawn in spring.

Prime River Locations:

• Brush piles offer cover and give sunfish a spot where they can get out of the current. New brush piles with plenty of small twigs are best.

• Weedy backwaters of medium- to large-size rivers hold sunfish year-round. They offer food, cover and a place to escape the current.

• Eddies that form below obstructions such as points, boulders and logjams provide the slack-water habitat that river-dwelling sunfish require.

Sunfish prefer to spawn in shallow, weedy bays with sand-gravel shorelines.

Pumpkinseed feeding in a lily pad bay.

A waxworm-teardrop jig combo is very effective for catching sunfish.

Sunfish lures include: (1) jigs, such as the Double 00 Flu-Flu; (2) teardrops, such as the JB Squiggie tipped with a Berkley Power Wiggler; and (3) spinners, such as the Johnson Crazytail Beetle Spin.

Slip-bobbers make changing your fishing depth quick and easy.

How to Catch Sunfish

Bobber fishing with live bait, such as worms, small leeches, grasshoppers, crickets, grass shrimp and waxworms, accounts for more sunfish than any other method. However, tiny jigs and other small artificials fished with ultralight tackle can be equally effective. And when sunfish are concentrated in the shallows, particularly at spawning time, fly fishing with poppers or wet flies may be the best technique of all.

When fishing with a bobber rig (left), use 2- to 6-pound mono with a size 8 long-shank hook. About 10 inches from the hook, add enough split-shot so the bobber barely floats.

Normally, the bait should be 6 to 18 inches off the bottom. Alternately jiggle the bobber and then let it rest. Most bites come after the bait stops moving.

Good electronics are a big help in sunfish fishing. You can easily spot large schools adjacent to cover or suspended in open water. Then, all you have to do is put your bait at the right depth and you'll have instant action.

Fishing for Spawning Sunfish

Spawning time offers the fastest sunfish action of the year. The fish concentrate in shallow areas where fishermen can easily find them. Nest-guarding males attack baits or lures that come too close, and females feed through the spawning period.

Your chances of finding heavy concentrations of fish are best early in the spawning season. Sometimes individual fish will nest several times over the course of the summer. Many experts believe that sunfish spawn only within a few days of a full or new moon.

In murky waters, sunfish may nest as shallow as 6 inches. But in clear lakes, anglers sometimes catch spawning sunfish in water 15 feet deep. Big sunfish usually nest deeper than small ones.

Sunfish often return to the same spawning grounds year after year. The same fish may spawn several times over the course of the season. Once you find a spawning area, carefully note its location so you can find it again. Many southern fishermen claim they can locate spawning sunfish by smell. The fish, especially bluegills and redears, emit a musky, fish-like odor.

You can prolong your fishing by moving to new waters as the spawning season progresses. Sunfish nest earliest in shallow, murky lakes because they warm the fastest. When they complete spawning in these waters, others are just beginning in deep, clear lakes. Sunfish spawn earlier in the South than in the North. In Florida, bluegills begin spawning in February compared to May and June in Wisconsin.

Avoid spooking fish when you approach beds in shallow

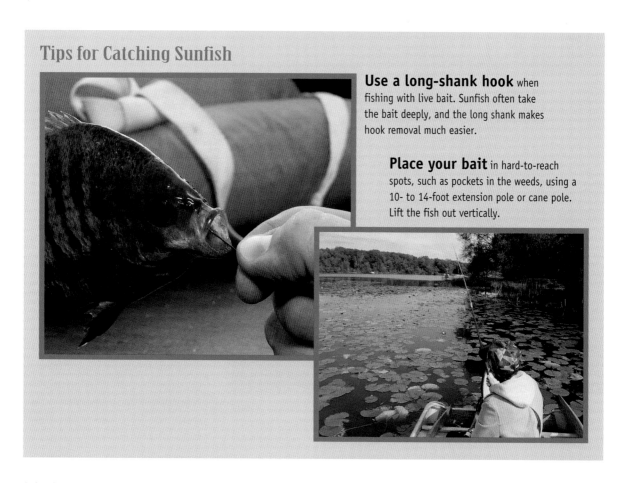

Tips for Catching Sunfish

Use a long-shank hook when fishing with live bait. Sunfish often take the bait deeply, and the long shank makes hook removal much easier.

Place your bait in hard-to-reach spots, such as pockets in the weeds, using a 10- to 14-foot extension pole or cane pole. Lift the fish out vertically.

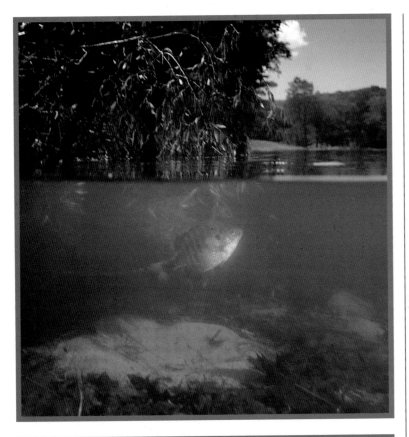

water. Move slowly, keep a low profile and do not make unnecessary noise. Cast beyond, then retrieve your lure or bait into the nest area.

Some anglers motor slowly through likely spawning areas, then mark the nests by poking sticks into the bottom or tossing out small Styrofoam® markers. The activity may spook the fish, but they usually return within 15 minutes. Fishermen then sneak back to work the nests.

When fishing for spawners, set the hook the instant you feel a bite. Males instinctively grab any object that invades the nest, then carry it away. If you wait for the fish to swallow the bait, it may be too late.

Fishing for Sunfish in Trees & Brush

Submerged trees or brush provide prime sunfish habitat in almost every type of fresh water. In spring, sunfish spawn in or near timber and brush in shallow water. Later in the year, they find cover and food around trees and brush in deeper water.

All types of sunfish relate to timber and brush, but these cover types are especially attractive to bluegills, redears and warmouth.

Any woody cover will hold sunfish. But some trees hold more fish than others. Cedars and oaks, for example, offer excellent cover. They have a dense network of branches and they rot more slowly than most other trees.

When scouting for sunfish, look for trees that indicate bottom type. Pine trees, for instance, grow mainly on sandy soil, so they may reveal the locations of spawning areas.

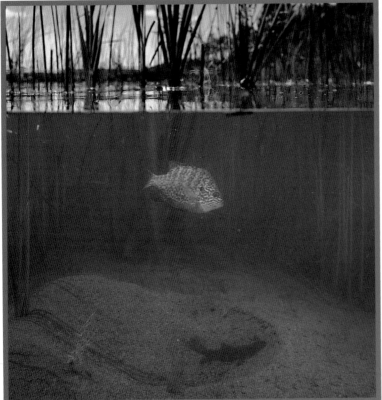

Find spawning sunfish near overhanging cover, like willow branches (top), which offers protection from birds and other predators. But sunfish will not nest in heavy shade. Also look for fish in pockets of emergent plants (bottom) or along the edges of bulrushes, buttonbush and cattails.

Trees and brush near some type of structure generally hold more sunfish than a flat expanse with similar cover. For example, a fallen tree on a point will usually attract more sunfish than a fallen tree along a straight shoreline with uniform depth. A change in the height of trees often provides a clue to bottom structure. A stand of trees growing higher than the surrounding timber may pinpoint the location of a drop-off.

Snags pose a constant problem when fishing in timber and brush. To offset this problem, try the following strategies. Rig your rod and reel with 12- to 15-pound line and a heavy sinker. The extra weight enables you to bounce the sinker to free a snagged lure. Or use 4-pound mono and a tiny lure like a 1/32-ounce jig. Cast over submerged brush or tree limbs, then retrieve slowly, allowing the jig to occasionally bump the branches. If you snag a branch, do not shake it violently while trying to free the lure. This will scare the fish away. Instead, break the line, tie on a new hook and resume fishing.

Fishing for Sunfish in Weeds

Weeds are prime sunfish habitat. Small sunfish hide among the leaves to escape predators. Larger fish seek the shade of overhead vegetation. Sunfish also feed on aquatic insects attracted to the weeds.

Matted weeds, or slop, block out sunlight. Sunfish find shade and cooler temperatures below the dense layer of vegetation. Slop usually consists of lily pads mixed with coontail or milfoil, and some type of filamentous algae. In the South, water hyacinth forms dense mats that cover entire lakes.

The best sunfish waters have light to moderate weed growth. If a lake has dense weeds throughout, too many sunfish survive so they become stunted.

Aquatic plants with large, wide leaves offer better cover than weeds with sparse, thin leaves. Look for sunfish in shallow weedbeds in spring. Small fish often remain in weedy shallows all summer, but larger fish prefer weeds close to deep water.

The biggest sunfish usually

Fallen trees near deep water usually hold sunfish, especially if they have a lot of branches. Shallow brush can provide cover in early season and during periods of high water. Sunfish use deeper brush patches in summer and winter.

To catch sunfish in weeds, most fishermen use a light rod, a small bobber and live bait.

hang along the edges of weedbeds. Weedlines form where the water becomes too deep for plants to get enough sunlight, or where the bottom changes to a different material.

Like trees, aquatic weeds provide a clue to sunfish location by indicating the bottom type. Bulrushes, for example, grow mainly on sandy bottoms, while lily pads grow in mud. A fisherman searching for spawning sunfish would have better luck near a bulrush bed, because most species of sunfish prefer to nest on a hard bottom.

To catch sunfish in weeds, most fishermen use a light rod, a small bobber and live bait. Some prefer a long pole to reach small pockets and to lift fish straight up before they can tangle the line around plant stems. Accomplished fly fishermen can place a popper or bug in a tiny opening by casting from a distance.

Fishing for Sunfish Around Man-made Features

In lakes that lack natural cover and structure, man-made features are excellent sunfish spots. Docks, piers, boathouses, duck blinds and swimming platforms offer shade and overhead cover. Other features like bridges, submerged roadbeds, riprap banks and even anchored boats hold fish. Where there is an abundance of natural sunfish habitat, man-made features attract fewer fish.

Many anglers place brush piles or other homemade attractors near docks or favorite fishing spots. An attractor can make a good spot even better.

Man-made features in the shallows draw large sunfish in spring and fall, especially if

Where to Find Sunfish Around Man-made Structures

Anchored boats, rafts and other floating objects may provide the only shade in areas that have flat, barren bottoms. Sunfish will form loose schools just below a boat that has been moored for several days.

Fish attractors vary from crib shelters to bundles of brush. These crib shelters will be hauled to a desired location, then sunk with blocks.

Docks in water 10 to 15 feet deep with some weeds or brush nearby may draw large sunfish. But docks in shallow water attract only small fish.

deep water is nearby. But only small fish remain when the water warms. Man-made objects in 10 to 15 feet of water will hold big fish during the summer months.

Most anglers suspend their bait near submerged man-made objects. But you need special techniques to reach sunfish under platform-like features. If the water is calm, try skipping a lure under a dock, much like you would skip a rock across the water. Or use a long pole to poke your bait under a swimming platform.

Fishing for Sunfish on Deep Structure

Sunfish experts know that the biggest fish are usually found where the depth drops rapidly or the bottom type suddenly changes.

Any type of structure may hold sunfish, but the best struc-ture has ample cover like brush, trees or weeds.

In early morning and late afternoon, sunfish feed in shallows adjacent to shoreline breaks and creek channels, or on the tops of points and humps. In midday, they retreat to deeper water. During summer, bluegills may go as deep as 25 feet and redears to 35 feet. Other sunfish species seldom go deeper than 15 feet.

When you locate sunfish on structure, carefully note the depth. Chances are, others will be at the same depth. Sunfish on structure rarely hang more than a foot or two off bottom. But they sometimes move away from struc-ture and suspend in open water.

To catch sunfish on struc-ture, most fishermen use live bait. Crickets, grasshoppers, small nightcrawlers, leeches and insect larvae are among the favorites. Attach split-shot

about a foot above the bait, and fish it on a 1/8- or 1/4-ounce slip-sinker rig. Or suspend the bait a few inches off bottom with a bobber. Some anglers tip a 1/16- or 1/32-ounce jig with live bait. You can add split-shot just ahead of the jig so it sinks faster.

Fishing for Sunfish in Special Situations

Veteran sunfish anglers con-stantly watch for unusual fish-ing opportunities. For example, a hatch of mayflies or other aquatic insects can concentrate sunfish in the shallows and start a feeding spree. Grasshoppers or other land insects fall or are blown into the water, causing sunfish to snug up to the bank and wait for an easy meal.

Fishermen sometimes fail to recognize good sunfish spots. Heated discharges from power plants often draw sunfish during coldwater periods. Beaver ponds and piles of fresh beaver cuttings are commonly overlooked.

Many streams offer excellent fishing, especially for redbreast, green and longear sunfish. Look for slack-water areas off the main channel. Canals and drainage ditches connected to sunfish waters may hold large numbers of fish.

Ponds provide top-quality fishing in some regions, especially in central and southern states where winterkill is not a problem. Several state-record sunfish have been caught in ponds, including a 2-pound green sunfish in Illinois and a 4-pound, 3½-ounce bluegill in Kentucky.

Many ponds, however, contain only stunted sunfish. To combat this problem, some pond owners install sunfish feeders. Most of these devices dispense food pellets; others are platforms that hold the carcass of a dead animal so maggots continually fall into the water. Sunfish that learn to use these feeders grow larger than others in the pond.

Fly Fishing

If you like fast action, try casting a popper onto a sunfish spawning bed on a warm spring evening.

Bluegills are the most surface-oriented of the sunfish. Besides poppers, they will also slurp in sponge bugs, dry flies and terrestrials. Redears, or shellcrackers, which feed mainly on snails, are less likely than bluegills to take surface offerings.

Most any small wet fly or nymph fished near the bottom will catch all types of sunfish.

Flies for sunfish

include: (1) poppers, such as the Pan Pop; (2) sponge bugs, such as the Creepy Cricket; (3) nymphs, such as the Hare's Ear; (4) wet flies, such as the Wooly Worm; and (5) dry flies, such as the Black Gnat.

Fly-fishing Tips for Sunfish

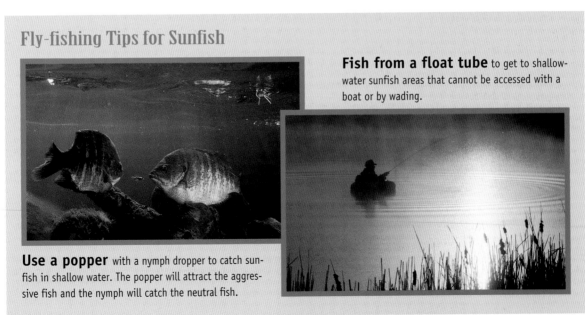

Fish from a float tube to get to shallow-water sunfish areas that cannot be accessed with a boat or by wading.

Use a popper with a nymph dropper to catch sunfish in shallow water. The popper will attract the aggressive fish and the nymph will catch the neutral fish.

Ice Fishing for Sunfish

Ice fishermen catch more sunfish than any other type of panfish. Anglers have little trouble finding sunfish; the challenge is locating the keepers.

Big sunfish bite best in early winter when the ice is only 2 to 3 inches thick and again just before ice-out.

Sunfish school by size. Large fish generally stay within a foot of bottom, while small sunfish may suspend several feet. If you begin catching small fish, try a different depth or move to another area. Once you find a good spot, look for landmarks to pinpoint the location. Chances are, it will produce fish next season.

Just after freeze-up, look for sunfish in weedy areas less than 8 feet deep. Holes in weedy bays are prime early-season locations. Later in the winter, sunfish move to deeper water along drop-offs, but seldom stray far from cover. If the water has enough oxygen, the fish may be as deep as 25 feet. Most species of sunfish require higher oxygen levels than crappies or yellow perch.

How to Catch Sunfish Through the Ice

Sunfish generally inspect baits or lures closely, ignoring anything of the wrong size or color. For greatest consistency, use light line, small baits and delicate bobbers. Four-pound monofilament will handle any sunfish. Heavier line usually results in fewer bites.

Most ice fishermen prefer insect larvae for sunfish. Thread them on a #8 or #10 hook, or on a small jig, spoon or teardrop. Favorite lure colors include orange, yellow and chartreuse. When hooking insect larvae, tear the skin slightly so the juices ooze into the water. The scent attracts sunfish.

Spring-bobbers work better than standard floats for signalling sunfish bites, which may be very subtle. A sunfish sometimes grabs the bait without moving the wire. But when you lift the rod, the wire bends from the weight of the fish. Other times, fish will push the bait upward, relieving tension on the wire. Another advantage of a spring-bobber: you can easily change depth without stopping to adjust a float.

Early morning and late afternoon offer the best angling, although sunfish bite throughout the day. They seldom bite after dark.

Hook several grubs on a small teardrop jig or hook for sunfish.

Crappies

T he popularity of crappie fishing has skyrocketed in recent years. Outdoor magazines are now devoting more space to the sport, and there are even crappie-fishing tournaments with huge purses.

Crappies can be one of the easiest fish to catch, but they are one of the hardest to find consistently. Their nomadic habits mean that they seldom stay in one place for more than a few days at a time. They are quite predictable around spawning time, however, explaining why most anglers focus on that period.

Although crappies begin congregating in shallow bays shortly after ice-out, they are moving in to feed on baitfish drawn by the warm water, not to spawn, as many anglers believe.

135

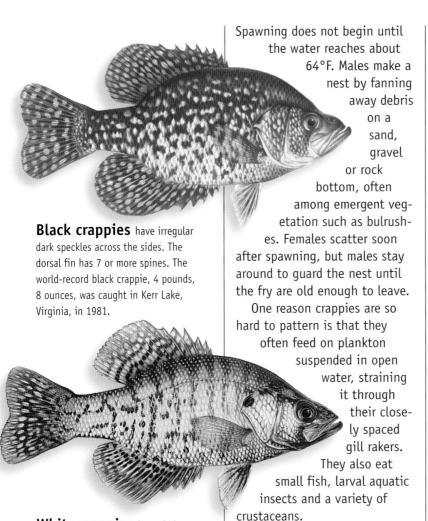

Black crappies have irregular dark speckles across the sides. The dorsal fin has 7 or more spines. The world-record black crappie, 4 pounds, 8 ounces, was caught in Kerr Lake, Virginia, in 1981.

White crappies have dark speckles set in vertical bars. Dorsal spines number 5 or 6. The body is more elongated than that of a black crappie and the forehead has a sharper depression. World record: 5 pounds, 3 ounces; Enid Dam, Mississippi; 1957.

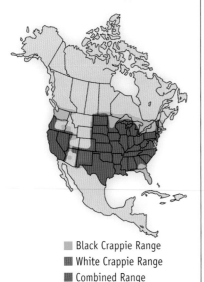

■ Black Crappie Range
■ White Crappie Range
■ Combined Range

Spawning does not begin until the water reaches about 64°F. Males make a nest by fanning away debris on a sand, gravel or rock bottom, often among emergent vegetation such as bulrushes. Females scatter soon after spawning, but males stay around to guard the nest until the fry are old enough to leave.

One reason crappies are so hard to pattern is that they often feed on plankton suspended in open water, straining it through their closely spaced gill rakers. They also eat small fish, larval aquatic insects and a variety of crustaceans.

Crappie populations are cyclical. The fish can be extremely abundant for a few years, but then the population begins to thin out and fishing becomes difficult. No one knows for sure why this happens.

There are two species of crappies: black and white. Black crappies are more abundant in the North; white crappies prevail in the South. However, their ranges overlap considerably. White crappies are often found in turbid lakes; black crappies require clearer water.

Crappies are one of the prettiest fish in fresh water. Anglers have given them more than 50 colorful names including calico bass, specks, strawberry bass, papermouths and bachelor perch.

Where to Catch Crappies

Crappies are found in nearly every state and in many waters of southern Canada. They live in most warmwater lakes and in the slow-moving stretches of warmwater rivers. Black crappies favor hard bottoms with plenty of weedy cover. White crappies are found on hard or soft bottoms with lots of woody cover, particularly sunken brush. In waters where cover is scarce, both black and white crappies often use man-made fish attractors such as sunken coniferous trees.

Although crappies are usually found near some type of structure or cover, they sometimes roam open water in search of food. Finding them can be difficult because they may suspend over the deepest part of a lake.

Crappies feed both day and night, although the prime feeding time is usually around dusk. In clear lakes, they often bite best at night. Crappies can be caught any time of the year, but feeding slows considerably at water temperatures below 50°F.

Like bluegills, crappies tend to overpopulate many waters, causing the fish to become stunted. Anglers seeking big crappies should fish waters where the population is relatively low. Following are some of the best spots to find crappies in natural lakes, man-made lakes and rivers.

Prime Locations in Natural Lakes:

• Shallow bays with dark bottoms warm much earlier in spring than the main lake,

Crappies often use brush piles for cover.

drawing baitfish, which, in turn, draw hungry crappies.

• Emergent vegetation, particularly bulrush, makes ideal spawning cover for crappies. Look for the old, brown bulrushes, not the new-growth green ones.

• Rock piles and weedy sunken islands with deep water nearby are good summertime locations. Crappies can find baitfish around the rocky or weedy cover.

• Deep holes hold crappies in late fall and winter. Most of the weeds in shallower water have died off, and the deep water is a few degrees warmer.

Prime Locations in Man-made Lakes:

• Entrances to creek arms hold crappies in late winter and early spring, before spawning time. Look for the fish near the creek channel or off deep points.

• Back ends of creek arms with brushy cover draw spawning crappies. Some fish also spawn on brushy points in creek arms.

• Edges of creek channels or the main river channel attract crappies in summer. The fish usually hold in the flooded timber.

• Deep stretches of the main river channel or deep creek channels concentrate crappies in late fall and winter. Deep points also draw fish.

Prime River Locations:

• Brushy sloughs are important crappie spawning locations. Look for the fish along sand-gravel, rather than mud, banks.

• Deep backwaters hold crappies most of the year. The best backwaters have plenty of cover, such as weeds, stumps, fallen trees or brush piles.

• Eddies in the main river channel give crappies a place to escape the current. Large eddies below points and dams are prime crappie locations.

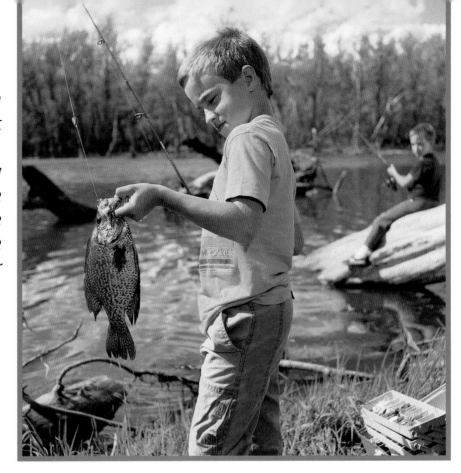

In the spring, crappies can often be caught close to shore. These young anglers were fishing on the banks of the Mississippi River in Minnesota.

How to Catch Crappies

Lures for crappies
include: (1) jigs, such as the Blue Fox Foxee Jig; (2) crankbaits, such as the Normark Mini Fat Rap; (3) minnow plugs, such as the Rebel Floating Minnow; (4) spoons, such as the Eppinger Dardevle; and (5) spinnerbaits, such as the Blue Fox Big Crappie.

Crappie anglers rely heavily on minnows or lures that resemble them. Minnows are usually fished on a slip-bobber rig set to keep the bait slightly above the depth of the fish. Most anglers hook minnows behind the dorsal fin for bobber fishing

and through the lips, head or eye sockets for casting or trolling.

Lure choice depends on the depth of the crappies. Jigs and small, deep-diving crankbaits are best in water deeper than 10 feet. In shallower water, try small spinners or spinnerbaits, minnow plugs or spoons.

A slow, erratic retrieve is normally best, although crappies

Tips for Catching Crappies

Hook minnows according to angling technique. For bobber fishing, hook the minnow behind the dorsal fin (top). When trolling, hook it through the lips (middle). For jigging, hook the minnow in the head or through the eye sockets (bottom).

Set a slip-bobber so your bait rides just above the weeds. Let the bobber drift. A strong wind will lift the bait too far above the weeds, so you must add more weight or lower the bait by readjusting the bobber stop.

occasionally strike fast-moving lures. Twitching the lure, then allowing it to settle back, may entice stubborn crappies to bite. They usually grab the lure as it sinks. The countdown method (below) works well for casting jigs or other sinking lures to suspended crappies.

Light tackle with 2- to 6-pound-test line is adequate for most crappie fishing. When fishing in stumps or brush piles, however, you'll need 10- to 17-pound line to avoid constant break-offs. When using a float, make sure you balance it with enough weight so the fish feel little resistance when they take the bait.

When crappies are in the shallows, fly fishing with bright-colored wet flies and small streamers ranks among the most effective techniques. Crappies seldom feed on the surface, so poppers are not a good choice.

The crappie nickname, paper-mouth, comes from the paper-thin membrane around the mouth. Once you hook a crappie, do not set the hook again or try to horse the fish in, because the hook may tear out of its mouth.

Fly Fishing

Wet flies and small streamers rank among the deadliest of all

The countdown method for suspended crappies works by casting a jig, then counting as it sinks. With 6-pound line, a 1/32-ounce jig drops about 1 foot in 1 second; a 1/8-ounce jig, about 2 feet. Begin your retrieve at different counts until you find crappies. With a 1/8-ounce jig, retrieve #1 (started at 3 seconds) and retrieve #2 (6 seconds) pass too far above the fish. But retrieve #3 (9 seconds) draws a strike. If you know where fish are located, count down to 1 to 2 feet above that depth.

Flies for crappies

include: (1) wet flies, such as the Yellow Sally; and (2) streamers, such as the Muddler Minnow.

crappie lures, especially in spring, when spawners move into the shallows.

If you can see spawning crappies in the shallows, cast to the darker-colored fish, which are the males. They're considerably more aggressive than the females.

Once crappies leave the shallows, they can be difficult to find, and fly fishing is not nearly as effective.

Fishing for Spawning Crappies

A stealthy approach is the key to catching spawning crappies. Even the slightest disturbance will scatter the fish off their beds. Many fishermen make the mistake of anchoring their boats in spawning areas.

To catch spawning crappies, you must place your bait near the fish, sometimes within inches. Crappies seldom leave their beds to chase food. Instead, they hover motionless near cover, waiting for baitfish to swim past. Fishermen who toss out a minnow, then wait for crappies to come to them, have little chance of success.

The depth of your bait or lure can be critical. Spawning crappies rarely feed on bottom, nor will they swim upward more than a few inches. Experiment with different depths to find the exact level.

In clear lakes, look for crappies by poling or drifting through a spawning area on a calm day. You may scare off the fish by approaching too closely, but if you mark the spot and return a few minutes later, the fish will be there.

Use light spinning gear and small minnows for spawning

Locate spawning crappies among emergent vegetation such as bulrushes.

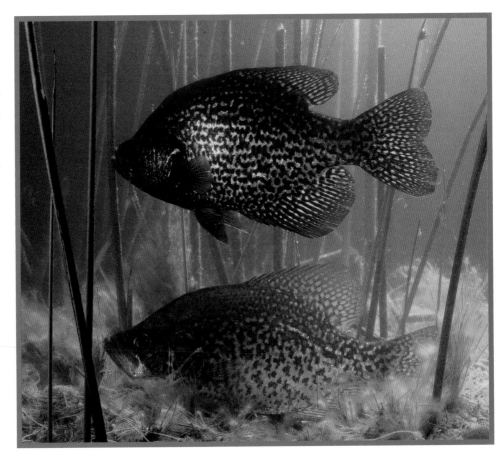

crappies. Suspend the baitfish below a small float, then cast beyond the spawning area and inch the bait toward the fish. Or simply dangle the minnow in front of a crappie with only a split-shot for weight.

A long pole works better than any other gear when you can see crappies. It enables you to place the bait in exactly the right spot without disturbing the fish. In southern reservoirs, fishermen use long poles to work brushy shorelines of coves. The brush is often too thick to work with standard gear, but with a long pole, you can drop your bait into small openings without getting snagged.

Fly fishing works well for crappies spawning in light cover. Cast a minnow-like streamer beyond the fish, allow it to sink a few seconds, then retrieve slowly. Experiment to determine the right depth and whether a steady or erratic retrieve works best.

Fishing for Crappies in Timber & Brush

Reservoir fishermen catch the vast majority of their crappies around various types of woody cover. Natural lakes generally have less timber and brush than reservoirs. But where anglers find such cover, they usually catch fish.

Baitfish move into timber and brush to find cover and to pick tiny organisms off the branches. Schools of crappies then move in to feed on the minnows. The cover also offers the crappies shade and protection from predators.

Shallow timber and brush provide excellent springtime cover. You can generally find crappies in water less than 6 feet deep.

The wood absorbs heat from the sun and transfers it into the water, drawing fish from the surrounding area. Crappies also use this cover in fall.

During summer, crappies use woody cover in deeper water, usually 10 to 20 feet. In winter, open-water anglers catch crappies in stands of flooded timber, often as deep as 35 feet.

Most crappie fishermen use 12- to 20-pound monofilament and light-wire hooks when fishing in dense brush. Some use line as heavy as 30-pound test. Crappies do not notice the line because the branches break up its outline.

Many anglers prefer a tiny jig and a float when fishing in brushy cover where snags pose a constant problem. Adjust the float to keep the jig just above the branches, then retrieve with short twitches. The dancing jig will lure crappies out of cover.

Short casts work best in timber and brush. They enable you to place your bait or artificial lure accurately, and to control the path of your retrieve to avoid snags.

Flooded brush draws crappies, especially in the spring. Rising water floods scrub vegetation in reservoirs, along streambanks and in river backwaters. Deep brush piles hold crappies in the summer.

Weedlines offer excellent crappie fishing, especially at twilight or on overcast days when crappies cruise the edge of the weeds in search of food. In bright sunlight, they seek shade and cover in the weeds, but usually no more than a few feet from the edge. Weedlines provide protection from large predators, as well as ambush sites where crappies can lie motionless, then dart out to grab passing baitfish.

Fishing for Crappies in Weeds

Anglers who fish natural lakes know that if they find the right kinds of weeds, they will probably find crappies. Weeds are not as important in most reservoirs, but coontail and milfoil provide good crappie cover in some man-made lakes.

In spring, crappies generally seek out some type of emergent or floating-leaved vegetation. But in summer and fall, they prefer submerged weeds. Wide-leaved varieties usually hold more crappies than narrow-leaved types. The fish prefer cabbage, but they will use narrow-leaved plants when other types are not available.

When weeds begin to die back in fall, look for crappies around plants that are still green. This vegetation offers better cover than weeds that have deteriorated. In clear lakes, you may be able to see the tops of green weeds. But in murky or deep water, you will have to snag the plants with your rod and reel.

Unlike most other panfish, crappies seldom use dense weedbeds. They prefer sparser vegetation. This allows you to use light tackle, and to retrieve jigs and other open-hooked lures without constantly snagging weeds.

Fishing for Crappies on Deep Structure

Crappies roam widely throughout most waters, using structure as underwater navigation routes. In reservoirs, for instance, crappies follow creek channels from deep water to shallow feeding areas.

Veteran crappie fishermen know which structure to fish at different times of the day and year. The upstream end of a creek channel holds few fish in midday, but often teems with crappies in the evening. A deep hump that comes alive with crappies in summer will be devoid of fish in early spring.

Many fishermen make the mistake of anchoring near structure and waiting for crappies to come to them. If they wait long enough, they may catch some fish. But you can greatly improve your odds by moving along structure until you find crappies.

Trolling with jigs works well for finding crapples on structure. Work the breakline slowly with a 1/8- or 1/4-ounce jig, or use a jig-minnow combination. Lift the jig about a foot off bottom, let it sink, then repeat. Crappies usually lie in a narrow band along the breakline, so once you find the fish, you must keep the boat at the exact depth.

When you locate a school, hover over the area with an electric trolling motor. If you throw an anchor near the school, crappies will scatter. Top areas to locate crappies on deep structure include:

• Rock piles that top off at 12 to 20 feet hold crappies in summer. Algae on the rocks harbors tiny insect larvae that attract baitfish, which then draw crappies.

• Inside turns along a breakline hold more crappies than straight edges. Wind concentrates food in pockets formed by inside turns.

• Humps with moderately dense weed growth on top are good summertime crappie spots. Bald humps seldom hold crappies.

• Points with large underwater shelves protruding from the end hold more crappies than points that plunge sharply from shore.

Fishing for Crappies on Man-made Features

Crappies use man-made features more than any other panfish. Features like fish attractors, bridges and docks are especially important in waters that lack natural cover. In studies on two Tennessee Valley Authority reservoirs, an acre of water with artificial brush piles attracted 4.8 times more crappies than areas without the brush. And crappies in the brushy areas were substantially larger.

Features near deep water attract the most crappies. A fish attractor in water shallower than 10 feet may draw crappies in morning and evening, but seldom holds fish at midday.

Fishermen catch crappies around a variety of man-made objects. Bridges, piers, docks and submerged features like roadbeds, building foundations and fencelines will hold fish at some time of the year.

Fish attractors, especially brush piles, produce crappies more consistently than other man-made features. Fisheries agencies often place brush piles in reservoirs where trees and other cover were removed before the lake was formed. Many fishermen make their own brush piles, then sink them off the end of a dock or along a drop-off. Other attractors include hay bales, tires, stakebeds and crib shelters.

Because of the crappie's roving nature, attractors that hold fish one day may be worthless the next. In lakes with many submerged brush piles, fishermen often establish milk runs, moving from one pile to the next until they find fish.

Most anglers use a bobber and minnow when fishing a brush pile. The fish generally hold in a small area, so still-fishing produces more fish

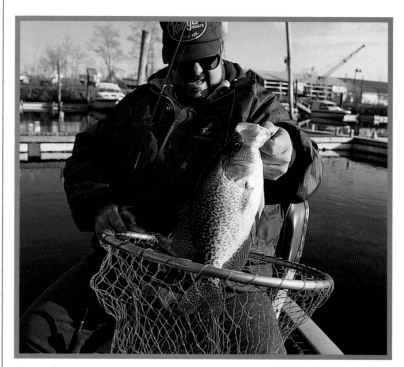

Crappies often hang around marina dock posts in late fall. This 2-pound "slab" hit within inches of a dock post on the Connecticut River.

Suspended crappies can be difficult to locate because they follow and feed on schools of roaming minnows.

than casting or trolling. But the angler who can work a small jig over the brushtops without snagging will usually catch more crappies than the still-fisherman.

Fishing for Suspended Crappies

Crappies have a greater tendency to suspend than any other panfish. Fishermen commonly find the fish hanging in midwater, sometimes far from structure or cover. They will suspend in any season but mainly during summer.

Schools of crappies suspend to feed on plankton or on small baitfish that gather to eat the minute organisms. Most types of plankton are sensitive to light.

They move shallower in the evening and deeper at midday.

When crappies are hanging over open water, you may waste a lot of time searching for them. A depth finder will improve your odds dramatically. Many fishermen troll or drift along a breakline, periodically changing depths until they find the fish.

Tips for Suspended Crappies

Horizontal layering usually takes place just off a weedline at the same depth as the base of the weeds. Crappies (arrow) may move away from the weeds and form a horizontal layer in open water. If the fish are deeper than 6 or 8 feet, the best way to catch these fish is by trolling. Begin by tying on a 1/32- to 1/16-ounce jig, then tip the jig with a twistertail or tube body. Make a long cast behind the boat, and use your trolling motor to slowly troll over the fish. Every 5 seconds or so, sweep your rod forward about a foot to make the jig change speeds. If you don't get a strike with your first pass over the fish, turn around and let out a bit more line. Don't expect to feel a distinct "thump" when a crappie strikes. Instead, you'll simply notice some weight on the end of your line. When this occurs, gently sweep the rod forward to set the hook.

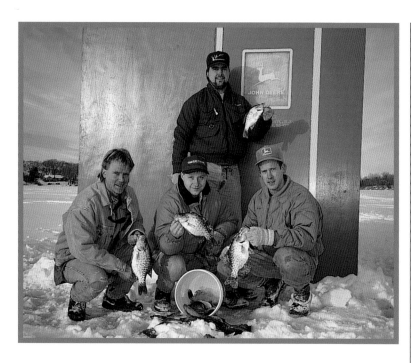

Ice Fishing for Crappies

Crappies inhabit deeper water than most other panfish. In midwinter, they may be found at depths of 30 feet or more. They usually hang near structure, but may suspend just off structure or in open water. Crappies suspend farther off bottom than other panfish, sometimes rising 15 to 20 feet.

Early and late winter offer the best crappie action. Look for the fish around their usual springtime haunts in water 15 feet or shallower. They prefer a weedy area near the top of a drop-off. Just after freeze-up, fishermen catch crappies in water as shallow as 3 feet.

Crappies are more sensitive to light than other panfish, so cloudy weather usually means better fishing.

They often go on a feeding binge one to two hours before a snowstorm. But the clear, bright skies following a cold front usually slow fishing. Crappies form dense, suspended schools in deeper water and refuse to bite.

Many crappie experts use portable depth finders to locate likely spots. The units save time because you can sound through the ice rather than drill holes to check the depth. You can also spot suspended crappies by sounding through the ice.

If you do not have a depth finder, continually adjust the depth of your bait until you find fish. At times, crappies pack into extremely tight schools. To catch these fish, you must find the exact spot.

Tactics for Winter Crappies

A small minnow dangled below a tiny bobber undoubtedly accounts for more wintertime crappies than any other technique. An active 1½- to 2-inch minnow usually works best. When fishing is slow, some anglers switch to larval baits like Eurolarvae, waxworms, goldenrod grubs and mayfly nymphs, often sold as mayfly wigglers.

Most fishermen use larvae to tip small jigs or teardrops. Crappies do not rely on scent as much as sunfish, but the larvae often seem to help. Jigs with soft plastic molded around the hook also work well. Crappies evidently mistake the plastic for real food.

Fishermen sometimes have trouble hooking crappies because they mouth the bait before they swallow it. When your bobber goes under, wait a few seconds to set the hook. If you miss the fish, wait longer the next time. If you still cannot hook the fish, switch to a small bait or try a jigging lure.

Glow-in-the-dark lures produce lots of winter crappies in low-light conditions. Tip them with either Eurolarvae or small crappie minnows. For maximum attraction, many nighttime crappie experts employ a standard camera flash to intensify a lure's glow and make it last longer.

Yellow Perch

Yellow perch rank among the tastiest of freshwater fish, so it's not surprising that they're so popular. Closely related to walleyes and saugers, perch live in many of the same waters, but they are rarely abundant where water clarity is very low. Their largest populations are in clear, northern lakes with moderate weed growth, but perch have been stocked in many southern waters.

Like walleyes and sauger, perch are coolwater fish, preferring water temperatures from the mid-60s to low 70s. But they feed throughout the year and, in the North, are a favorite of ice fishermen.

Yellow perch spawn soon after the ice goes out in spring, usually when the water reaches about 45°F. They lay their eggs in jellylike bands that cling to rocks, plants and debris on the bottom. Staggering numbers of young are

Yellow perch have yellow to yellow-green sides with 6 to 9 vertical bars. In some waters, their bodies are tinted gray or brown. Spawning males have more intense colors with orange or bright red lower fins.

hatched, much to the benefit of predators such as largemouth bass, northern pike and walleyes.

Important perch foods include immature aquatic insects, crayfish, snails, small fish and fish eggs. Adult perch do most of their feeding on or near the bottom and are not as likely to suspend as sunfish or crappies. Because of their poor night vision, perch feed only during the day.

In many waters, perch become too abundant and, as a result, never reach a size large enough to interest fishermen. A 7- to 8-inch perch is acceptable to most anglers, but perch often grow much larger. The world record, 4 pounds, 3 ounces, was caught in the Delaware River, New Jersey, in 1865.

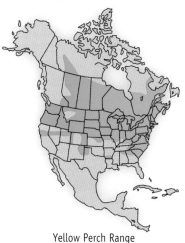

Yellow Perch Range

Where to Find Yellow Perch

Finding small yellow perch can be as easy as dangling a worm off most any dock. But the angler looking for jumbo perch faces more of a challenge.

Spring

Yellow perch begin moving out of deep wintering areas toward shallower water in early spring. In the southern part of their range and along the Atlantic Coast, spawning migrations begin as early as late February. Perch in northern lakes start their spawning runs in mid-April or early May.

Perch often migrate long distances, sometimes 20 miles or more, to reach their spawning grounds. In the Great Lakes, most perch spend their entire lives in large, warmwater bays. These fish edge out of deep water near rock reefs and islands onto reef edges. Others move into the mouths of tributaries or into man-made drainage ditches.

Perch are very selective as to where they spawn. They prefer

sand, gravel or rock bottoms with scattered weeds or brush. In most lakes and reservoirs, they spawn in shallow, protected bays in water 5 to 12 feet deep. Generally, the larger the lake, the deeper they spawn. In the western basin of Lake Erie, perch spawn on off-shore reefs in 10 to 20 feet of water, and occasionally as deep as 30 feet.

Yellow perch in Chesapeake Bay and other East Coast estuaries winter in brackish water at the mouths of large tributaries. The fish move upstream after a series of balmy spring days or a warm rain. Many perch spawn just below small dams on the upper ends of the streams. Others deposit their eggs in quiet, brush-choked areas where the stream may be only 2 to 3 feet deep.

Summer

After spawning, yellow perch in most natural lakes and reservoirs linger several weeks in their spawning bays. Look for the fish in 15 to 25 feet of water. Some remain all summer unless the water becomes too warm, forcing them to find deeper, cooler water.

Jumbo perch prefer water temperatures between 65° and 70°F. Look for them in the thermocline, usually where it intersects with bottom. Some fish suspend in the thermocline over open water. Perch will also suspend in or above the thermocline to feed on plankton, baitfish or mayflies moving toward the surface to hatch.

In the Great Lakes, perch move toward open water in the bays, often gathering around rocky shoals and islands. The best reefs are isolated from other structure and have numerous projections or points. During the day, the fish feed along the points in 20 to 30 feet of water. Toward evening, they move onto the points in water as shallow as 6 feet. Great Lakes anglers also catch large yellow perch around breakwaters, pilings and docks. The best fishing spots are in 15 to 25 feet of water, with rock or sand bottoms and some vegetation.

Yellow perch in estuaries remain in the tributaries through summer. They school in deep holes at the mouths of secondary streams, or around piers, bridges and old pilings.

Fall & Winter

In fall, perch in deep lakes and reservoirs move into the shallows around rocky shorelines and reefs. Great Lakes fishermen record huge catches around concrete piers in only 6 to 8 feet of water. In East Coast estuaries, some fish move up secondary streams in fall. Others remain in their deep, summer locations. During winter, anglers catch few perch in waters that remain ice-free. But ice fishing is popular on many northern lakes.

Daily Movements

Schools of perch begin feeding in midmorning, once the sun has moved high enough to brighten the depths. They may continue to feed off and on throughout the day. As twilight approaches, the schools move shallower and begin to break up. Schools re-form the following morning.

Cold fronts affect yellow perch less than they do most other panfish. Even during periods of extreme cold, anglers find and catch perch in the same areas they fished during mild weather.

Use a thin strip of belly meat from a perch or a minnow head instead of a whole minnow when perch are striking short. The belly meat or minnow head provides necessary scent and your hooking percentage will be much higher.

How to Catch Yellow Perch

The gluttonous feeding habits of yellow perch make them an easy target for anglers. You can catch them any time of year; in fact, some of the most impressive catches are made by ice fishermen.

Live bait fished near the bottom accounts for the majority of yellow perch. You can fish the bait on a plain size 4 to 6 hook, usually with a slip-sinker or split-shot rig, or use it to tip a lead-head jig or a jigging spoon.

Perch are found in many of the same spots that hold walleyes. Look for them in shallow bays and on shallow flats in early spring and on points, weedy or rocky humps and irregular breaklines the rest of the year.

Most yellow-perch anglers rely on light spinning tackle with 4- to 6-pound mono. The fish are not strong fighters, and the light tackle helps cast the small baits and lures.

Fishing for Perch in Open Water

After spawning, large yellow perch abandon shallow cover and head for open water. They school around rock or sand-gravel reefs and sparse weedbeds. At times, they can be caught over soft, mucky bottoms, especially when mayflies or other aquatic insects are emerging from the mud.

Perch in open water normally stay near bottom at depths of 20 to 35 feet, but they may feed on reefs that top out at 10 to 15 feet. In some lakes, they suspend while feeding on plankton or schools of small baitfish.

To locate open-water perch, drift or troll slowly using a fluorescent spinner baited with a worm, minnow or strip of perch belly meat. The spinner will often catch fish that ignore other offerings. Troll just fast enough to make the blade turn.

When you find perch, a slip-bobber rig, tandem-hook rig or other still-fishing technique may work better. Many fishermen prefer small jigs.

Anglers have devised some novel methods to concentrate perch. Some tie colored plastic flags to the anchor rope. Others lower pieces of metal on a rope, so they clang on the rocks. Chumming with small pieces of baitfish will attract perch and may excite them enough to trigger a feeding burst. A jigging lure spliced into the line just above the hook will also draw perch toward the bait.

Ice Fishing for Perch

Ice fishing for yellow perch (right) peaks just before ice-out when they cruise shallow flats and rock piles. In early winter, anglers on natural lakes catch many perch in the back ends of bays or off shoreline points in water only 4 to 8 feet deep. By midwinter, most perch have moved to deep water, generally from 20 to 40 feet. They gather along breaklines just off sand or mud flats, often near the base of a drop-off.

Midmorning to midafternoon offers the fastest action. Changing weather conditions have little effect on perch fishing.

Most perch fishermen rate minnows as the best bait. Using a #6 hook, pierce the minnow's back just below the dorsal fin. Use a bobber to suspend the baitfish about 6 inches off bottom.

Perch fishermen often tip artificials with Eurolarvae, waxworms, minnow heads or perch eyes. However, check your local regulations before using perch eyes for bait, as some states do not allow this practice.

The best types of artificials include small jigs, small jigging spoons, and the Normark Jigging Rapala (below). Favorite lure colors include silver, gold, red, yellow and chartreuse.

Catfish

Although catfish do not get a lot of press, they rank near the top of the popular gamefish list. Only bass and panfish have a larger following. If you have ever battled a very large cat or dined on fresh catfish fillets, you can easily understand why these bewhiskered fish have so many fans.

Flathead and blue catfish commonly exceed 50 pounds and many topping 100 pounds have been taken, but most were not officially documented. Channel catfish weighing more than 20 pounds are scarce, though some big rivers produce much larger ones. White catfish, the smallest kind, rarely exceed 5 pounds.

Channels and flatheads are the most common catfish species. Blue catfish populations have declined in many areas, but huge blues are still caught

This trophy channel cat came from the Red River in Manitoba.

in parts of the central and southern United States. White catfish are confined mainly to the East and West Coasts.

Catfish thrive in medium- to large-size warmwater rivers, or in lakes connected to rivers. Most warmwater impoundments have good catfish populations. Catfish can tolerate extremely muddy water and even moderately high levels of pollution. Unlike bullheads, they can't live in waters prone to winterkill.

The highly varied diet of catfish consists mainly of fish, fish eggs, insect larvae, mollusks, crustaceans and aquatic plants. They also eat dead and rotting organic material.

All species of catfish have an acute sense of smell, and their whiskers, or barbels, are equipped with taste buds. They can easily find food in muddy water or after dark by probing the bottom with their barbels as they swim along. Their well-developed senses of smell and taste explain the effectiveness of stinkbaits.

Catfish start to spawn in late spring when the water temperature reaches about 70°F. They have a curious habit of spawning in enclosed areas such as sunken barrels, hollow logs, muskrat runs and other holes in riverbanks.

Following are world records for each of the catfish species:
• Channel – 58 pounds; Santee-Cooper Reservoir, South Carolina; 1964
• Flathead – 123 pounds, 9 ounces; Elk City Reservoir, Kansas; 1998
• Blue – 111 pounds; Wheeler Reservoir, Alabama; 1996
• White – 21 pounds, 8 ounces; Gorton Pond, Connecticut; 2001

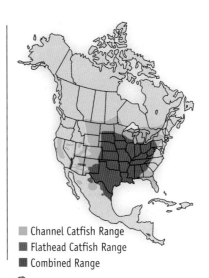

■ Channel Catfish Range
▥ Flathead Catfish Range
▥ Combined Range

Channel catfish.

Sometimes called blue channel cats, these fish have dark bluish gray to silvery sides, often with

dark spots that tend to disappear as the fish grow larger. The tail is deeply forked and the anal fin is shorter and more rounded than that of the blue catfish.

Flathead catfish. Often called the mud cat or yellow cat, this species has a flattened head, tiny eyes, a squarish tail and a protruding lower jaw that make it easy to distinguish from other catfish.

Blue catfish. Closely resembling the channel cat, the blue cat has bluish to grayish sides that are not spotted. Like the channel cat, the blue has a deeply forked tail, but the anal fin is longer and has a straighter bottom edge.

White catfish.

The white barbels distinguish this from the other species, whose whiskers are black or dark brown.

The sides are gray-blue to blue-black and are sometimes mottled. The tail is moderately forked and the anal fin is shorter and more rounded than that of a channel or blue cat.

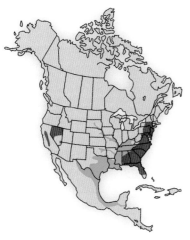

■ Blue Catfish Range
▥ White Catfish Range
▥ Combined Range

Catfish are often found in river pools containing flooded brush, stumps and fallen trees.

Where to Find Catfish

Catfish evolved in the currents of our rivers and streams, and, in these waters, they usually reach their greatest numbers and largest size. Catfish adapt better than most freshwater species, however, and their natural ranges have been greatly expanded by stocking programs. Today they exist in waters of all shapes and sizes, from tiny farm ponds and creeks to the Great Lakes and the Mississippi River. Every state except Alaska is home to at least one of the "big three" species – channel, flathead and blue.

The types of waters where catfish are not found are relatively few. They rarely thrive in cold, fast-running streams where trout are abundant. Nor do they do well in the cold, oligotrophic lakes of the Far North. Mesotrophic lakes with large walleye populations may support good channel cat and/or bullhead populations, but blues and flatheads usually are absent or scarce, and channel cat numbers never reach their full potential. With the exception of white cats, all our freshwater catfish are intolerant of brackish and salt water.

Almost everywhere else, thriving populations of catfish are found. Big fertile rivers. Bayous. Large, man-made impoundments. Oxbow lakes. Creeks. City water-supply lakes. Sloughs. Irrigation canals. Ponds. Smallmouth streams. State wildlife agency lakes. River backwaters. Strip pits. Overflows. Clear water, muddy water, warm water, cool water and everything in between – if it's not too polluted, catfish of one form or another are likely to call it home.

Catfish have an affinity for woody cover. You'll find them on brushy flats, in flooded timber and around "snags" – trees or parts of trees that wash into river pools.

In small rivers, finding catfish is not much of a problem. You simply look for the deep holes, especially the ones with plenty of snags. In big rivers and reservoirs, however, catfish are harder to find because they move a lot more. Like most other gamefish, they follow the forage. They also move to find comfortable water temperatures.

In late fall, for instance, cats migrate great distances to reach warmwater discharges of power plants. In the warmer water, they feed all winter.

Big-river cats also migrate to reach deep wintering holes. Often, thousands of fish can be found in a hole of only a few acres. These wintering catfish are dormant and seldom bite; divers have been known to grab them and carry them to the surface.

Water stage plays a major role in catfish movement. When the water is low, they tend to move into deep holes and stay put. When it's rising, they are drawn into shallow creek arms and backwaters.

Catfish avoid sluggish or stagnant water. They sometimes feed in fast current, but more often, you'll find them in the slower water alongside it. Blue cats prefer faster water than do channels or flatheads, often holding in swift chutes or pools with moderate current.

Catfish bite best at night, but can be caught during the day, especially after a heavy rain when river levels are rising. Then, even midday fishing can be good. Catfishing slacks off when the water temperature drops below 55°F. At temperatures below 40°F, they rarely feed.

Typical catfish waters? There's no such thing. Our adaptable catfish have a remarkable ability to thrive wherever they may be.

Prime Catfish Spots

Holes are one of the best locations to catch catfish in these types of rivers. The most productive ones are found on an outside bend of the river and have structure present on the upstream side, such as timber or large boulders.

Current seams (arrow) form where fast and slow water meet. Catfish hold in the slow water and dart into the fast water to feed.

Grooves are slack-water areas found between two open gates of a dam. Catfish hold in the slow water and dart out into the current to feed.

Riprap banks, especially long, irregular ones, are great catfish hideouts. Cats use cavities between rocks to spawn, but good stretches are used year-round.

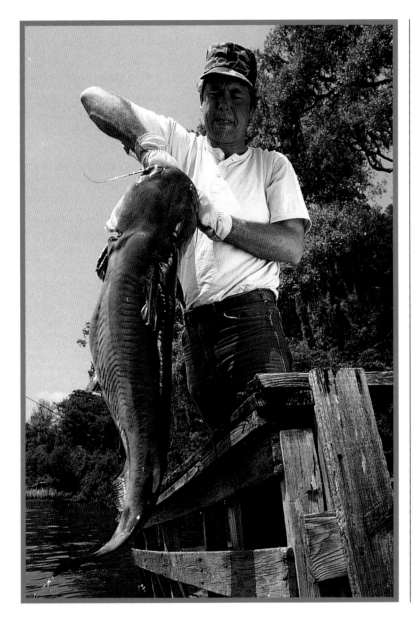

How to Catch Catfish

Choosing Cat Baits

Although you may occasionally catch a catfish on a jig, spinner, crankbait or other artificial lure, the vast majority of cats are taken on natural or prepared baits. And there are times when cats take baits suspended from a float, but bottom rigs account for by far the most of them.

The list of catfish baits is nearly endless. You can catch cats on soap, congealed chicken blood, entrails of small animals, freshwater clams that have rotted in the sun for a day or two, dead birds, mice, frogs, worms, crayfish, grasshoppers, Limburger cheese, doughballs and any number of homemade or commercially produced stinkbaits. Live or dead fish, especially those with high oil content such as gizzard shad and smelt, are effective because they give off a scent that carries a long distance.

Any kind of catfish may grab

Popular Catfish Baits

Big lively sucker minnows are the best choice for trophy flatheads.

Worms work great for smaller cats.

any one of these baits, but flat-heads are most likely to take live baitfish; channels, dead or prepared baits. Blues and whites are intermediate in their bait preferences.

By understanding each species' food preferences and habits, you can narrow the choices to a select few. First, determine what catfish feed on in the body of water you'll fish. Local fisheries biologists, bait shops and anglers can help in this regard, so seek their advice. As a rule, the most abundant forage in a body of water is also the best to use as bait.

If you want a few channel cats for the frying pan, your bait selection can run the gamut from nightcrawlers to crayfish. But to catch a heavy-weight river blue catfish, you'd be smarter to use a good-sized chunk of shad or skipjack herring.

If you're a serious catter, someday you'll go home reeking of stinkbait. Catfish love stinkbait like kids love candy, and every dedicated catter has his favorite version – a malodorous

brew of blood, guts, cheese, rotten fish and who knows what – he swears is head and shoulders above the rest. There are more stinkbait recipes than you can possibly imagine.

Commercial baits cover a wide array of bait considered "stinkbaits," including blood bait, dip baits, sponge baits, tube baits, doughbaits and chunk baits in a zillion varieties. All catch cats, but only if you understand the advantages and disadvantages of each.

Don't plan on catching lots of trophy cats using these baits. Small channel and blue cats are most likely to be caught on stinkbaits. Young fish of these species scavenge more than heavyweight adults. As they grow in size, their diet becomes less varied, consisting mostly of live baitfish, crayfish and other abundant forage.

Rigs for Catching Catfish

The best catfishing rigs usually are the simplest. With fewer components, there's less chance something will fail. Simple rigs also are easier to make and easier to cast, plus there's less weight to

interfere with natural-looking bait presentations.

The simplest rig of all is nothing more than a baited hook at the end of your line. It works well in a surprising variety of catfishing situations. Most of the time, though, you'll have to use a weight to get your bait on or near the bottom. In fact, rigs with weights as heavy as 16 ounces are used by catfishermen at certain times.

The following section illustrates the most common bottom and float rigs used by catfishermen, as well as some variations for special situations.

Bottom Rigs

Since most catfish are found on or near the bottom, bottom-fishing rigs are by far the most common used by catfishermen. These can be put into two categories: slip-sinker rigs and fixed-sinker rigs.

SLIP-SINKER RIGS. These are favored by many catfishermen, because they allow the fish to run with a bait without feeling any tension. The simplest slip-sinker rig consists of a hook, an

Cut-bait is the #1 choice for big blues and channels.

Tube baits are most effective on small blues and channels.

Bottom Rigs

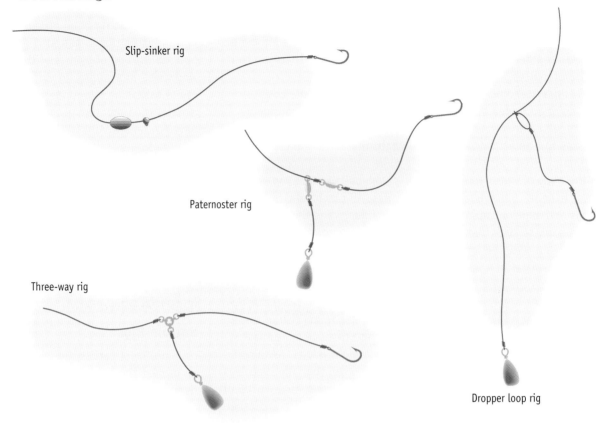

Slip-sinker rig

Paternoster rig

Three-way rig

Dropper loop rig

egg sinker, and a split-shot for a stop (above). To improve on this rig, add a swivel between the sinker and the hook. By substituting a bell or walking sinker for the egg sinker, you create a rig less likely to roll along the bottom and snag when fishing in current. You can dispense with the swivel altogether and let the sinker ride snug against the baited hook. Few catfishermen use this simplified version, but it works great in heavy current where a long leader is likely to get snagged.

Another variation of a slip-sinker rig involves adding an additional swivel above the main-line swivel, then adding a 6-inch dropper line and a bell or bank sinker (above). English fishermen refer to this as a paternoster rig; it allows the bait to ride higher off the bottom than an in-line rig.

FIXED-SINKER RIGS. With these rigs, your bait rides higher than it would with a slip rig. They also anchor your bait better in strong current and are popular with catfishermen who fish tailrace waters. This is a versatile presentation, useful for both still-fishing and drift-fishing.

Three-way rigs, also called the Wolf River rigs in some parts of the country, is probably the most popular of this style. To make this rig, tie the main line to one eye of a three-way swivel, and add drop lines 12 and 24 inches long to the other two eyes. Tie a hook to the longer drop line and a sinker (bell, pyramid or bank) to the other. If you fish in very snaggy conditions, the sinker drop line should be a lighter pound test than the main line. This way, if the sinker gets hung up, the lighter dropper line breaks, and you can salvage the rest of the rig. If a three-way swivel is unavailable, use a barrel swivel instead. Tie the main line to one eye and the two drop lines to the other.

A fixed-sinker rig that works well for small cats and bullheads involves placing the hook in front of the sinker so that light bites can be detected better. This is called the dropper loop rig (above). To make this rig, simply tie a bell or bank sinker to the end of your line, then tie in a dropper loop knot (p. 33) 12 to 18 inches in front of the sinker. Then add a 6-inch section of line with a hook to the loop. In areas without hook restrictions, you can add

Drift rig with split-shot

Drift rig with dropper

Float Rigs

Float rig using slip-bobber with egg sinker

Float rig using slip-bobber

multiple loops and hooks farther up the line.

Drift rigs, those commonly used by steelhead fishermen, are good catfish rigs in certain situations, such as in small streams with light current, or when drift-fishing relatively shallow water. To make this rig, simply tie on a hook, and add split-shot 12 to 18 inches up the line (above). In snaggy areas, modify this rig by adding a barrel swivel, then attach a 6-inch dropper to one of the eyes. Add the appropriate amount of split shot to the dropper. If the shot gets hung up, apply pressure and the shot pulls off the dropper, saving the hook and swivel.

Float Rigs

These rigs are great for drifting baits through river cat hideouts, or targeting suspended catfish. The simplest consist of nothing more than a fixed bobber above a hook and perhaps a split shot or two. A more versatile version employs a slip-bobber (above). Tie a bobber stop on the line, then add a bead and a slip-bobber. Attach a hook and add two or three split shot to sink the bait and stand up the slip-bobber. Adjust the stop knot so the slip-bobber suspends the bait at the desired depth. With this rig, the bobber slips down to the split shot to allow casting, then slips up to the bobber stop to hold the bait at the correct depth.

A variation of this rig performs well when fishing large live baitfish for flatheads, or big pieces of cut-bait for blue and channel cats. Affix the bob-

ber stop, then run a bead, slip-bobber and an egg sinker up the line. You'll need a big float to hold up this rig (above). The size of the sinker is determined by the size of the bait. Big baits require heavy sinkers, often up to 4 or 5 ounces for a sizable bluegill or sucker.

Tie a barrel swivel beneath the sinker, at the end of the main line. Then, to the bottom eye of the swivel, affix a 10- to 20-inch leader and a large hook. For flatheads, impale a large baitfish just behind the dorsal fin. For large blues and channels, use a large chunk of cut-bait, such as shad or skipjack herring.

Specialty Rigs

Creative catfishermen have come up with countless variations of standard cat rigs. Of

Specialty Rigs

Baitwalker rig

Float-paternoster rig

Bottom-bouncer rig

course, they can't all be shown, but below are some of the well-known specialty rigs that have produced more than just a few nice cats.

Take the paternoster rig mentioned in the slip-sinker section, add a slip-bobber, and you have a float-paternoster rig (above). This rig works great for fishing a large live bait in shallow water. Slide a slip-bobber on the line before tying the rig. The sinker lies on the bottom while the baitfish struggles against the float. Leave a foot or two of slack line between the sinker and the float; this gives the bait extra room to think it's escaping. The dropper line to the sinker should be light enough to break off if the sinker gets snagged.

Baitwalkers and bottom bouncers (above) are thought of by many fishermen as walleye rigs, but they have applications to catfishing as well. Simply attach a leader of 12 to 36 inches to the eye of the swivel, and add a hook. Baitwalkers can be fished in fast current. The foot of the sinker is virtually snag-free, and the safety-pin shape keeps the bait near the bottom. This rig works best when cast directly downstream.

Bottom bouncers are a similar design, but the wire continues through the weight, which causes the sinker to ride up and over snags. Bottom bouncers are great for drift-fishing live or cut-bait over snaggy areas where other sinkers would surely hang. To rig, tie the main line to the front eye, and attach the leader to the swivel on top.

Rods, Reels & Lines

Choosing rods, reels and line for catfishing is like buying a vehicle. Numerous styles of each are available, everything from simple and inexpensive to fancy, high-dollar designs with all the bells and whistles. Not everyone wants the same thing.

Catfishermen use a wider variety of rods and reels than any group of sport fishermen – everything from tiny spinning outfits that fit under a car seat to long surf-casting rods with huge reels.

If you spend most of your time dabbling for bullheads in farm ponds, a light spinning or spin-casting outfit with small-diameter line works great. If channel cats are your quarry, and you fish waters where 5- to 10-pounders sometimes surface, a 6- to 7-foot, medium-action bass-fishing combo is more than adequate. If snagging is your thing, and you're hoping to bring in one of the 100-pounders lurking in a dam tailrace, better go equipped with a 10- to 16-foot heavy-duty saltwater baitcasting rig spooled with 40- or 50-pound line.

It all boils down to using common sense when shopping. Look at the options available, then buy the best combination you can afford for the conditions and catfish you encounter. For example, when fishing around snags and rocks, you'll need 20- to 50-pound-test line. This way, you can turn a big catfish before it can wrap your line around an obstruction and break free. In the strong current of a tailrace, you may need up to a pound of weight to keep the bait on bottom and prevent it from drifting.

Techniques for Catching Cats

Still-fishing

A sit-and-wait game. The angler presents a bait on or near the bottom, then waits for a catfish to find it. Catfish have keen senses, and there are times when moving a bait around is counterproductive because it's difficult for feeding cats to find. The juices and scent of a bait disperse through the water and are detected by the catfish's senses of smell and taste. The cat then uses those senses to zero in on the prospective dinner. If the bait is taken away too fast, however, all bets are off. That's why, in many cases, it's best to let a bait sit for a while before moving it. Still-fishing lets you do just that.

Still-fishing from a Boat

The obvious advantage of still-fishing from a boat is mobility. Bank-bound anglers are limited in their choice of fishing areas, while boat anglers are limited only by the size of their fuel tank.

You'll need at least one and preferably two anchors for this type of catfishing. One is better than none, but with a single anchor, your boat is likely to swing in the breeze or current, tangling lines and requiring you to frequently move your rigs. Using two anchors, one on each end of the boat, keeps the boat stationary so your rigs can be spread out and cover more water.

For this method to be effective, the angler must determine areas where catfish are likely to be feeding. A cat's superb senses allow it to zero in on a bait several yards away, but a bait placed too far outside their realm of sensory ability goes undetected. Try to pinpoint prime fishing areas, then narrow your fishing zones down to a few best spots.

For example, a riprap bank is an ideal place to find catfish. But riprap may extend for hundreds of yards, and cats won't be equally dispersed along its entire length. Look for features that concentrate catfish – a large snag within the rocks, rocks of a different size (big boulders within a long stretch of smaller rocks) or points.

Likewise, when fishing along an inundated creek channel, look for some nuance of structural difference that may attract catfish – a pocket or point on the channel edge, a stump field

Trophy flatheads, like this fish from the White River in Arkansas, are often caught after dark.

or cluster of timber, a deeper hole along the outside bend. Position your boat for best access to the structure you've chosen, then cast your bait to that spot and wait for a bite.

When using multiple lines, it's best to have rod holders strategically placed around the boat to hold the rods, and the reels should be equipped with free-spool clickers. This way, the lines are spread out, and a fish can take a bait without pulling a rod in the water. When using a reel without a clicker, keep your combo in your hand, with a finger on the line to detect bites. Rods leaned against the side of the boat can get yanked into the drink by even small catfish. If half an hour passes without a bite, move to another location and set up again. Likewise, if catfish are biting and the action suddenly stops, it's best to move.

Still-fishing from Shore

Most catfishermen, up to 70 percent in some areas, fish from shore. Some do so simply because it's convenient, while others do it out of necessity. For most catters, though, fishing from shore is simply "the way it's done." You and a buddy build a fire on the riverbank, bait up a few rigs, and prop your rods on forked sticks. A cat will bite sooner or later, and the action starts. But if not, it's an enjoyable outing anyway.

If the action part of the outing is as important as the aesthetics, be sure to pick a bankfishing site within casting distance of prime catfishing areas. This might be a clearing on shore near the outside bend of a river or a gravel bar adjacent to a deep hole on a small stream. The best areas have flat, brush-free banks where casting is easy.

Ideally, you should be able to walk from one good fishing site to another without any problems. If catching fish is your top priority, don't sit in one spot hour after hour if nothing's happening. Fish for 15 to 30 minutes, and if nothing is biting, move to the next spot. It's typical to find a good hole, catch several cats, then find the action tapers off. This is why frequent moves can increase your catch rate.

Of course, leapfrogging isn't to everyone's liking. And in some areas, it's impossible due to the lack of good bankfishing sites. If this is the case, cast your bait to the best-looking spot you can reach, then prepare to wait out your quarry. Place your rod in a rod holder, put the reel in free-spool, flip on the bait clicker, and relax

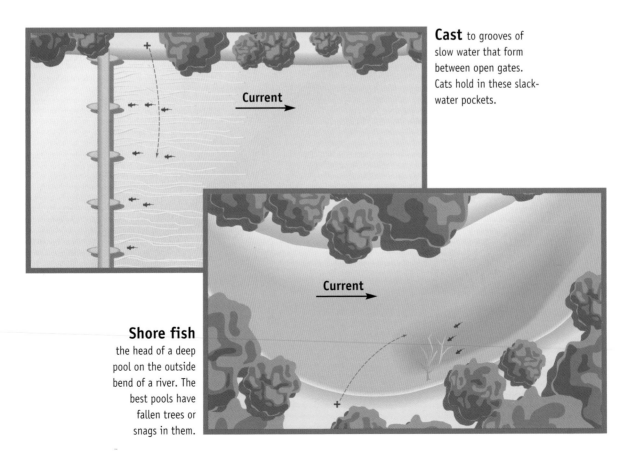

Cast to grooves of slow water that form between open gates. Cats hold in these slack-water pockets.

Current

Shore fish the head of a deep pool on the outside bend of a river. The best pools have fallen trees or snags in them.

Current

until the action starts. This method may not put lots of catfish on your stringer, but it's a great way to target trophy fish.

Tailwater areas below dams rank among the best for shore-fishing enthusiasts. The U.S. Army Corps of Engineers, the Tennessee Valley Authority and other agencies provide riverside walkways, fishing piers and other shoreline facilities to accommodate visiting anglers. Blue, flathead and channel catfish concentrate in huge numbers in dam tailwaters, especially during their upstream runs in spring. Because of this, your odds of catching a trophy cat are above average.

Tailwater anglers usually fish with 10- to 14-foot fiberglass rods and sinkers that weigh up to 8 ounces, which allow for the long casts necessary to reach prime catfish areas from shore, and get to the bottom fast in the strong current. Bottom rigs of any sort work, but most anglers opt for a three-way rig, or a slip-sinker rig with either a bell or egg sinker.

One of the best places to consistently catch catfish below a dam is the slack-water areas between open gates known as grooves (p. 153). To fish these, cast your rig into a groove and leave it there for about 15 minutes. If there are no takers, lift your rod tip high to pick the weight up, and let the current wash it downstream a few feet. Then let the weight down again, and repeat the process. By doing this, an angler can cover a long stretch of bottom from a single spot on shore.

When there's good water flow through or over a dam, the roiling waters directly below generally provide the best catfishing,

but don't overlook other prime tailwater areas. These include scour holes at the end of wing dams, the downstream side of underwater boulders, retaining walls, riprap, spillways and lock-wall edges.

Although tailraces are the most popular spots to fish cats from shore, there are others that can provide good catfishing as well. Fishing piers are becoming more numerous across the country, and are often built on prime catfishing waters. The best part about piers is they offer fishing opportunities for everyone. Most are wheelchair accessible, and provide safe, convenient locations to take the whole family catfishing. Look for buoys around piers that mark sunken fish structures, such as old Christmas trees and brush piles. These often hold numbers of catfish.

The confluence of two rivers is another good spot to try for catfish. Keep your rig near current-breaking structure such as the current seams and sand or gravel bars that form when two rivers meet.

No matter where you fish from shore, be sure you have the right equipment. Never use tackle that is too light; remember, cats generally aren't line shy, so use as heavy a line as your equipment can handle. The chance of hooking a trophy fish is always there, and a big cat can be tougher to land from shore than from a boat. A net is best for landing large fish, but if you're fishing alone, beaching the fish may be necessary. And finally, bring lots of terminal tackle – you're going to lose a lot of it to snags – that's just a fact of shore fishing.

Carry two anchors to position a boat sideways in a good hole. This way rods are spread out to cover more water and avoid tangles.

Use a clip-on float to detect bites. With the rod in a holder, pull line down and attach float so it falls off when reeling (top). When a cat bites, the float rises.

Tie light line between the sinker and swivel of a three-way rig. Then, if you get snagged, the sinker breaks off and you salvage the hook and swivel.

A large flat adjacent to a creek channel that is sparsely covered with snags holds fish almost year-round, and is easier to drift than an irregular bottom.

Drift-Fishing

Drift-fishing doesn't fit the traditional "sit-and-wait" approach used by most catfish anglers. But think about this: If you anchor a bait on bottom with a sinker, you must rely on the catfish's acute senses to find the bait. Drift-fishing, however, helps you help the cats find the bait. It's an active approach that often means more catfish on waters where it can be used.

Two basic methods of drift-fishing are commonly employed in catfishing – drift-fishing in a boat, and drift-fishing baits beneath a bobber.

Drift-fishing in a Boat

This is a commonly used cat-fishing technique in late winter and early spring. As winter passes and water warms, catfish leave cold-weather haunts and scatter, making them difficult to pinpoint. The same thing occurs any time water in a lake or river is quickly rising or falling. Drift-fishing allows the angler to cover more water and find these widely scattered fish.

Drift-fishing doesn't need to be complicated. Fish from the same boat you already use when catfishing. Use the same rods, reels, line and other tackle already in service. Use one rod or a dozen, but determine beforehand if there are any restrictions. In some areas, you can fish with as many poles as you dare to; in others, the number is limited.

If the wind's blowing, you can get by without a trolling motor, but unless you're on an exceptionally large body of water where you can make an extremely long drift, you're not likely to catch as many catfish. Wind drifting is typically a one-way, time-consuming affair – make a drift, take up the rods, motor back up, reset the rods, drift again. An electric trolling motor, on the other hand, allows constant fishing without fuss. It also permits you to vary your speed and control direction, important factors when trying to get fussy catfish to bite.

If you'll be using several rods, and most drift-fishermen do, you'll want some way to hold them at the ready. A few sturdy clamp-on rod holders fitted around the transom work OK in some situations. But it's better to use permanently mounted models that won't be torn off the first time a big cat hits. These are available in many different styles. Purchase those that work best on your boat, then place them at strategic positions in a semicircle around the forward or rear half of the craft.

When rods are in place, a drift-fishing boat looks like a big spider moving across the water with legs pointing in all directions. Start by using a variety of baits rigged at different depths. For instance, if you're using six poles, rig two with pieces of cut-bait, two with chunk-type stinkbaits and the other two with minnows. Set two baits so they drift just above the bottom, two at mid-depths, and two just a few feet beneath the surface. This lets you test different baits and depths until you find the cat-fish's preference that particular day. Once it's established that catfish are favoring a certain depth or bait, then rig and set the rest of the rods accordingly.

A float rig (opposite page) is ideal for fishing near the bottom while drifting. The main line is run through the eye of a pencil weight, a type of bottom-bouncer sinker constructed from a long plastic or nylon tube filled with lead. A ball-bearing swivel is tied below the

CATFISH

weight to keep it from sliding down. A 24- to 36-inch leader is then tied to the lower eye of the swivel. A small bobber or float is affixed in the middle of the leader, and a wide gap hook is tied at the end. The float suspends the baited hook above bottom to help prevent snags.

For mid-depth and near-surface presentations, use a trolling-sinker rig (right). These sinkers are overlooked by many catfishermen, but they are extremely useful when drifting for catfish. Keeled or torpedo-shaped models track well with little side-to-side action. Planing versions have wings that cause the sinker to dive and achieve more depth. Bead-chain swivels are molded into most to prevent line twist. To rig, simply tie your main line to the front eye of the sinker, then attach your hook to the rear eye with a 2- to 3-foot leader. Vary the sinker size according to water depth and drifting speed.

Savvy anglers experiment with different drift speeds until they determine what is most effective. In muddy or heavily stained water, you might have to drift-fish very slowly for catfish to find your bait. In a clearwater lake, fast-moving baits may be very effective. The key word here is "experiment." Try to figure how catfish are likely to react in the type of water you're fishing, then adapt your tactics to conform with those expectations. But if your game plan doesn't produce within a short time, try something different.

Once you determine the speed catfish seem to favor, do

Float rig (top), and trolling-sinker rig.

your best to maintain that speed without variation until you no longer catch fish. One mistake anglers often make is drifting at the same motor thrust traveling against the wind as when headed with the wind. On an otherwise still lake, you travel faster with the wind than against it, assuming you never reposition your electric-motor throttle. Therefore, in order to maintain your ideal trolling speed, you must adjust the throttle up or down depending on which way you are traveling. On extremely windy days, you may even have to run the trolling motor in reverse to keep from drifting too fast.

The same is true when in current. When traveling against the flow, you must increase the throttle to maintain the same speed you had when traveling downstream. Fail to do so, and your speed changes drastically. So will the number of catfish you'll catch.

These factors may explain why, on a particular day, you'll catch catfish when drifting in one direction and not in the other.

It's important to use a good depth finder for drift-fishing.

Catfish may be roaming, but they'll still be near structure or along the thermocline. By first looking at a contour map and a quick check of prominent bottom changes with sonar, you could be catching catfish instead of wandering aimlessly.

Drift-fishing with Bobbers

When wading or bank-fishing a river, you can drift your bait beneath a bobber. This is the best way to thoroughly work eddies of swirling water behind fallen trees, boulders and other current breaks.

Use a large, round slip-bobber in heavy current when fishing with heavy baits. A smaller cigar-shaped bobber works fine in slow current, or when using small baits.

Position the bobber stop so your bait hangs a foot or two above the bottom. Add just enough weight to hold the bait down and stand the bobber up, then let the rig drift naturally in the current, guiding it alongside catfish-holding structure.

Keep a tight line at all times. A slack line bows downstream ahead of the bait. This leaves you in a bad position for setting the hook when a catfish hits because all the energy of the hook set is used taking in the slack.

Feed line as the bait moves downstream. If the rig hangs up, your bobber will tip over or stop. Lift it a bit to get the bait moving again. If nothing happens after you've worked an area thoroughly, move your bobber stop up the line and drift through deeper. Or move downstream to another spot and try again.

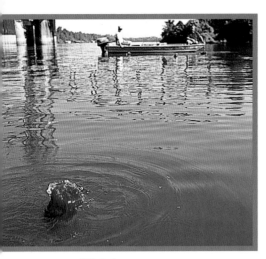

Watch for any jugs that bob erratically or go under. Pursue the jug once it starts moving away.

Trotlining. Use a burlap bag full of rocks to weight the end of the line. This type of trotline is best when fishing perpendicular to shore in heavy current.

Jug Fishing

Most anglers think of catfish as bottom feeders, but there are times when cats suspend in midwater to feed on sunfish and other baitfish.

Free-floating jugs are often rigged with a 50-pound monofilament dropper line that has 4 to 6 size 2/0 hooks equally spaced to cover the entire depth spectrum. A 2- to 3-ounce sinker holds the dropper line in a vertical position. The line should almost, but not quite, reach bottom.

Jug fishing is simple. Just put your favorite bait on the hooks and then release the jugs upwind of the area you want to fish. Or let them drift down a river. You can let your boat drift with the jugs or let them drift on their own, coming back to check them later. When you see a jug dancing, pick it up and pull in your cat.

Trotlining

Trotlining is an age-old method of catching fish. While a few anglers declare the method unsporting, it is legal in many states and regularly practiced on numerous prime catfishing waters throughout the United States.

A trotline is simply a stout line placed horizontally across an expanse of water. Tied at regular intervals along the main line are short lines with baited hooks. For some now forgotten reason, these short lines were once called trots, hence the name trotline. The main line is made of heavy-duty nylon cord, often 600-pound test or more. The trots are made of 100- to 200-pound-test nylon and are 1 to 2 feet long. Most trotlines are 25 to 125 yards long with 20 to 100 hooks.

Ready-made trotlines are available at many tackle shops, but beware of cheap products with poor quality components that could break under the strain of a heavy fish. Most serious trotliners custom-make all the lines.

Most trotliners set lines during the day, then bait them right at dark. (If the lines are baited during the day, gar, turtles and other pests strip the hooks.) The lines are then run periodically throughout the night and again right at dawn. Lines should always be removed when you're done fishing, so there's no chance of another angler or animal getting tangled in the hooks.

Use special care when running the lines. Most trotliners work in pairs, for camaraderie and division of labor. Each person should keep a knife handy, either on their belt or strapped to a leg, to cut the line if someone is accidentally hooked. More than one trotliner has drowned after getting snagged by a hook and pulled under by a trotline weight.

Limblining is often the best way to present live bait or cut-bait to catfish located near heavy shoreline cover.

Noodling is a high-risk sport, and participants should be aware that death or serious injury can result from carelessness.

Limblining

In its simplest form, a limbline is nothing more than a baited hook and line tied to a stout yet springy limb overhanging the water. When a catfish bites, the limb's flexibility keeps the fish from breaking the line.

The line for limblines should be at least 25-pound test, preferably braided Dacron. A 2/0 to 4/0 steel hook is tied to the line, then a weight should be added just above the hook when using large baitfish, or if there is a strong current. Limblining works best at night, so use a piece of cloth or reflective tape to mark each set so it can be easily found at night.

Willow limbs are the best tie-offs for limblines because they're long, flexible and easy to find. But green branches of any sort work, as long as they are strong and pliable.

Limblining laws vary considerably from state to state, so check the regulations before trying it. Be certain to remove all lines at the end of a night's fishing, because an abandoned line can be dangerous to wildlife and to other fishermen passing by.

Noodling

The term "noodling" is derived from the word noodle, meaning a very stupid or silly person; a fool. This is not surprising since noodling is the technique of hand-grabbing a catfish. No hooks, lines, fishing poles or reels are used.

To noodle, one simply must be brave enough, or foolish enough, to reach into an underwater hole and extract a catfish. The best holes in which to noodle catfish are old muskrat or beaver bank dens, crevices beneath rocks, hollow logs and undercut banks. Cats occupy such nooks at various times throughout the year but are most often holed up during the spawning season in late spring and early summer.

Most noodlers enter shallow water – never as deep as the noodler is tall – take a good breath, then plunge beneath the surface and probe likely catfish hideouts. A short cane pole can be inserted to determine if anyone is home. If a catfish is, and it's spawning season, the fish attacks the pole, rattling it. The noodler then surfaces for air, and prepares to capture the cat.

What happens next is not for the faint of heart. When the noodler places his hand into the hole of spawning cat, the fish may nip, bite or, if the fish is large enough, actually engulf the noodler's hand. Once the cat has grabbed on, it may spin, causing the sandpaperlike teeth to scrape and shred the noodler's skin. At this point, the noodler's goal is to get to the surface with the cat in tow.

Check local regulations before noodling. And above all be careful; a huge cat can drown a man, even in shallow water.

Special Situations

Thick Cover

On waters with little fishing pressure, thick cover might not hold any more large catfish than other, more easy-to-fish areas. But on heavily fished waters, there seems to be a definite correlation between big cats and woody tangles.

There are two reasons for this. First, catfish don't get big by frequenting heavily fished haunts. Most heavyweights get big by living in out-of-the-way places where most anglers don't dare to venture. That's why they haven't been caught already.

Second, big catfish instinctively prefer the protection of heavy cover. Outsized cats are extremely wary and angler-shy, which contributes to their natural tendency to hide in the most concealed places possible.

Not every patch of thick cover holds big cats. The best provide easy movement between shallow and deep water. Look for brush piles, fallen trees, inundated willows and buckbrush, flooded timber and other dense woody cover along channel drop-offs, underwater humps and holes, the edges of shallow flats and other fast-breaking structure. Other hideouts hold big cats, too, but these are among the best.

One hot spot to investigate is an outside river bend containing several downed trees. Outside bends generally have deep pockets of water adjacent to a channel break. Add the thick cover of branchy underwater treetops and you have an ideal cat hideout.

Heavy line and tackle are a must for this type of fishing. You don't want to let a hooked fish fiddle around in the cover. Get it out of there, as quick as you can, and let it do its fighting in open water. Use at least 20-pound-test line on a quality baitcasting reel, and a long, stout rod. Strong, abrasion-resistant line is a necessity when horsing big battlewise cats out of these hideaways. A long rod is best in this situation and accomplishes two things: more leverage than a short rod to muscle a fish out of thick brush, and better accuracy to place a rig into dense thickets where casting is virtually impossible.

Be sure to set your drag just barely below your line's breaking point. You don't want a big brush-pile cat peeling off any more line than necessary, or you'll be hung up in an instant.

The best rig to use for fishing thick cover is a plain hook, unweighted. The size of the hook is determined by what type of bait you use. Weighted rigs can be used in certain situations, such as heavy current, but for the most part, they get tangled in cover more often than not.

Another effective way to fish thick cover is with a slip-bobber rig. This way, there's less chance of getting snagged, and you can fish in and around cover effectively by controlling the drift of the rig in the current or wind.

Any standard catfish bait can be used, but cut-bait is hard to beat because it won't tangle up like live minnows. Thread a chunk about 2 inches square on a 3/0 hook, and unless the current is strong, don't use any weight.

Get within rod's reach of the cover, and work slowly and precisely, moving your rig over, under and through the cover until you can ease it down into an opening. You can catch a few nice cats along the edge of the cover, but most are buried in it and strike only when the bait is right on their nose.

When a fish does strike, react immediately; set the hook hard and reel like crazy. This battle requires heavy tackle and brawn, not finesse.

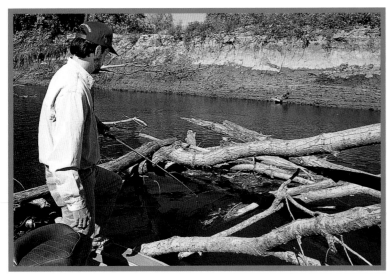

Use a sturdy rod rigged with heavy line to catch cats out of heavy timber. Pull the line so the bait is snug against the rod tip, then work the bait into cover and drop it.

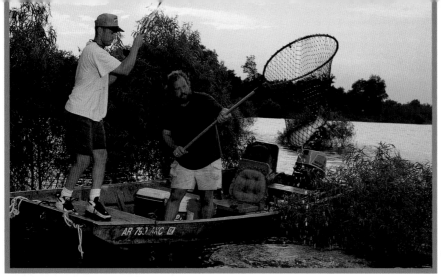

The Mississippi River in Arkansas holds good numbers of catfish. When the water is high, fish close to the flooded trees and bushes.

Fluctuating Water Levels

Rising and falling water in a river or lake can have a dramatic influence on catfish activity. Under some conditions, cats move about like nomads, stuffing their guts to the point of bursting. In other situations, they settle in around current-breaking structure and wait for the food to come to them. There are no hard-and-fast rules, but it pays to know what catfish are likely to do when water levels fluctuate.

During a fast rise or fall, such as several inches a day, small catfish in rivers tend to concentrate in areas where they can escape the excessively heavy flow – scour holes, channel edges, inundated lakes and backwaters. Although sedentary, these catfish actively feed, and higher fish densities usually mean better catches for savvy cat fans who know where their quarry is likely to be holed up. To locate fish-holding structure, use a flasher or liquid-crystal graph, then fish them using the appropriate drift-fishing or still-fishing techniques.

Big catfish don't behave like their smaller brethren in this situation. Being more powerful, they're not as affected by the fast-moving water. As a river starts to rise or fall, they go on a feeding spree that may carry them upstream and downstream through their home area several times in just a few hours. Many enter smaller tributaries and gorge on the smorgasbord of food items washed downstream. Others simply roam, and eat whatever happens by.

Except during flood conditions, this is a great time for bankfishing. Big cats are moving more, increasing the chance of one finding your bait. Use a three-way rig with a heavy sinker to keep the bait stationary yet visible off the bottom. And be sure you're properly equipped. This is one of the best times to hook a trophy-class flathead or blue.

Water-level fluctuations in big lakes and reservoirs tend to be less severe, thus they seldom have the dramatic influence on cat behavior found in rivers. Heavy rainfall, however, often triggers feeding frenzies that send catfish scurrying about in search of newly available food items.

In river-connected oxbows, the influence of rising and falling water is more noticeable. A fast rise scatters catfish. They seldom stay concentrated and hold around cover. Most suspend and randomly move around.

Drift-fishing with multiple rigs is the best option to locate and catch these fish during a fast rise. Set your rods so your baits run at different depths, then troll slowly, making large zigzagging sweeps. Troll over structure between normal resting and feeding areas. If you're patient and cover lots of water, sooner or later you'll catch fish.

A fast drop in water level moves catfish to deep-water haunts until the water level stabilizes. Many fish suspend, holding tight to cover in a lake's midsection.

These catfish can be reluctant to bite. Still-fishing rigs work best on them, and you'll have to present your bait very close before they'll take it. Smaller baits work best in this situation – nightcrawlers, grape-sized chunks of cut-bait, small minnows, etc.

Fishing runout areas – the cuts connecting oxbow lakes and their parent rivers – also can be outstanding during a fast fall. Baitfish concentrate near these runouts, and catfish follow for an easy meal. A slip-bobber rig is the best choice here. Cast above the runout and guide the rig past brush and other current-breaking cover.

Cold Water

Many anglers think catfish are inactive in cold water. That's only partially true. Blue and channel catfish feed actively throughout winter in most waters. Flathead catfish, on the other hand, become lethargic in cold water. Food habit studies indicate very little winter feeding. They become essentially inactive when water temperatures drop below 45°F and rarely take a bait unless it's placed right under their nose.

To catch channel cats and blues consistently in cold water, it helps to understand their winter feeding patterns.

One such pattern involves winter-killed shad. Gizzard and threadfin shad, two primary catfish forage items, are intolerant of severe cold. When the water temperature dips below 45°F, both species become cold-stressed. If the cold persists and the water temperature continues dropping, many of the shad die. This is a yearly event on many first-rate cat waters.

When the die-off starts, catfish flock around shad schools like buzzards around a roadkill. They gorge themselves on these dead and dying baitfish to the point of bursting. This pattern may last a day or a month, depending on the weather. But while it lasts, fishing for big blues and channels is at its best.

To capitalize on this cold-weather pattern, use sonar to pinpoint schooling shad, then throw a cast net over the school to collect your bait. Large shad can be sliced for cut-bait, but small whole shad (an inch or

two long) work best. Hook two or three on a single hook, running the hook through the eyes and leaving the barb exposed (above). Now lower your rig through the school of baitfish to the bottom, reel it up about a foot, and hang on. If the feeding frenzy is in full swing, mere seconds pass before a fish strikes and the fight begins.

Be sure to keep plenty of shad ready for rigging. Where one cat is caught, there usually are dozens. Don't be caught without bait when the bite's on.

Freshwater mussels are another of the catfish's favorite winter foods. These mollusks live in dense colonies or *beds*. In winter, blue cats and channels congregate around these beds where they feed day after day with little expenditure of energy. Beds are usually near shore in 3 to 6 feet of water. They can be pinpointed during low-water periods or found by moving parallel to shore and probing the bottom with a cane pole. Catfish return to the same beds each season, so once a bed is found, memorize its location or mark it on a map.

A slip-sinker rig is ideal for fishing around mussel beds. Use mussel flesh for bait, or small chunks of cut shad or herring. Although the catfish may be

feeding mainly on mussels, they won't pass up a piece of cut-bait that's properly presented.

Cast to the shell beds you've found, and let your bait sit on the bottom undisturbed for up to 15 minutes. If no bite is forthcoming, move to another spot and try again. If you catch a cat, fish the water for several yards in either direction. It's likely others are feeding in the area as well.

The coldest weeks of winter may bring on a period of reduced feeding activity as the water temperature reaches its lowest extreme. As the water nears freezing, a catfish's metabolism drops dramatically, and very little food is needed to maintain a healthy state. This does not mean, however, that catfish cease to feed altogether. The low level of metabolism simply permits the fish to survive if food supplies are scarce, and anything that can be eaten without an undue expenditure of energy, including the angler's bait, is still gobbled up.

During this period, you may have to use sonar to pinpoint individual fish, then lower a bait very close to them in order to entice a strike. Most of these cats lie right on the bottom, sometimes partially covered by silt and mud. In rivers and ponds, look for them congregated in the deepest holes. There may be hundreds in a spot no larger than an acre. In reservoirs, look for winter schools around creek and river channel drop-offs, power-plant discharges, humps and inundated lakes and ponds. Cut-bait fished using a vertical presentation is ideal in all these situations.

Deep Water

To master deep-water catfishing, you need to first understand why cats move to deep water. In midsummer, many lakes stratify into three layers, because they are too deep for wave action to thoroughly mix the water. The warmest, oxygen-rich water stays on top: the cold, dense oxygen-free water settles on the bottom, and a middle layer of cool, oxygen-rich water called the thermocline forms in between. The thermocline is the zone of water where the temperature drops very fast. Of the three layers, the thermocline best satisfies the fishes' needs for dissolved oxygen and water temperature, and is also where the baitfish are. Rivers, on the other hand, never stratify because the water is constantly moving and stays mixed from top to bottom.

The depth and thickness of the thermocline varies from one body of water to another. In smaller lakes, it may be 10 feet down and only a foot thick; in extremely large, deep lakes, it may be 30 feet down and several feet thick. Regardless of its location and size, the thermocline is where most sizable catfish are during periods of temperature extremes.

A submersible temperature gauge shows you, by degree, exactly where the thermocline is. Or, you can use a liquid-crystal graph to locate the correct depth. On many locators, the thermocline shows up as a foggy band across the screen. Sensitive units pick up this layer because the water is more dense at the thermocline. Even if the thermocline doesn't show up on your locator, you'll still notice the bulk of the fish are suspended in a distinct band of water (the thermocline).

If you have a depth sounder, try to locate cover or structure in the thermocline where catfish might concentrate – a channel drop-off, an underwater hump, the edge of an inundated pond, deep weedbeds or perhaps a cluster of tall stumps beneath the surface. If you don't have a depth sounder, look for topside features that may continue underwater to the desired depth – bridge or dock pilings, long, steeply sloping points, rocky ledges, toppled trees or the outside edge of a weedbed.

A bell sinker bottom rig is the best choice for taking bottom-feeding catfish in areas where the thermocline touches the lakebed. Add your favorite bait – worms, chicken liver and cut-bait are excellent choices – then cast the rig and let it sit on the bottom.

If catfish are suspended, try fishing bait under a slip-bobber rig. This way, you can fish your bait at the same level as the thermocline, merely by adjusting the bobber stop to the proper depth.

Another good way to catch suspended cats is by drift-fishing. Keep your baits near the thermocline and cover lots of water, either by drifting with the wind or using an electric trolling motor. Once you find fish, work the area thoroughly, as cats often school up around large pods of baitfish.

Inundated creek and river channels are among the most common types of structure where deepwater cats are found. Use a flasher or graph to help pinpoint fish concentrated in these areas. Among the specific spots to check in the main body of a lake are those where feeder creeks merge with river channels. Check the water on the two points created by the juncture of the two streams, and for several yards in all directions, up the feeder stream, and up and down the river channel.

Secondary creek channels can also be prolific catfish producers. Look for those in or near the thermocline that offer sharp breaklines and ledges or drop-offs.

Deepwater catfish, especially blues and channels, are often found in loose schools. When you find one, others are likely to be nearby. You'll increase your catch rate if you make a concerted effort to work your bait thoroughly around each piece of cover.

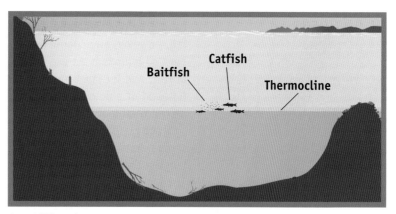

Stratification of a lake or reservoir occurs during extended periods of hot weather and causes most fish, including catfish, to change locations according to temperature and oxygen levels. A key location is near the thermocline, especially near schools of baitfish.

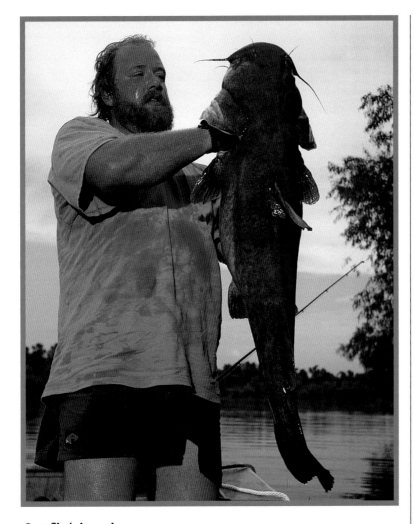

Catfishing is extremely popular in the South. This big flathead was caught in the Mississippi River in Arkansas.

Fishing for Trophy Catfish

How big is a trophy catfish? That depends on several things – where you fish, the type of catfish you're seeking, maybe even how big a catfish you've caught before. Generally speaking, however, any channel cat over 20 pounds is an exceptional fish, and for most anglers, a flathead or blue over 50 would be the trophy of a lifetime.

Trophy catfish inhabit many waters, but few anglers challenge them with rod and reel on a regular basis. Few know how to do it, and fewer still possess the persistence to be successful. Trophy-class catfish may be older than the anglers who seek them, and with each passing year, they become more elusive. Catching these monsters may be the greatest challenge in freshwater fishing. It is possible, though, and you can soon catch a trophy if you keep the following things in mind.

First, don't bother fishing for trophy catfish unless you have lots of patience. Catching one doesn't happen every day, even for those familiar with their daily habits. As one avid catfish angler put it, "Fishin' for giant cats is like trophy muskie fishing, only lonelier." You may spend days or weeks trying to pinpoint a single trophy fish. And as the hours pass, the doubts begin to grow, and you start wondering if it's worth it.

That's why many anglers give up trophy catfishing even before they land their first big fish; they don't have enough patience.

Learn to bide your time without getting frustrated. Bring a comfortable seat, plenty of cold drinks and snacks, a can of bug spray, and a buddy to talk to. It could be a long night. Maybe several long nights. But sooner or later, the patient catter reaps his reward.

Persistence is equally important, says Randle Hall, a trophy cat guide from Corinth, Texas.

"Anyone can learn the tactics necessary for catching cats," he notes. "You learn that you have to change the places you fish and what you fish and how you fish from day to day as weather and other conditions dictate. But to catch a trophy-class fish, you have to keep bait in the water where the big ones swim. Learn all you can about a lake or river where you know those big fish are. Then stay at it, day after day, learning more. Catfishermen who do that have the best chance of catching a trophy, maybe even a world record."

Invest in good heavy tackle, and maintain it in good condition. Joe Drose of Cross, South Carolina, one of the world's top trophy catfish guides, has this to say about catching trophy cats.

"The tactics and rigs you use probably aren't as important as the preparation," he says. "Any time you're fishing water where big catfish live, there's a chance Godzilla's gonna bite. You have to be ready for him every time you go out there, or he'll find a way to get the best of you.

"You should only fish with good tackle – high-quality rods, reels, line and so forth. And pay attention to details all the time. For instance, be sure to change your fishing line regularly, and check it every time you catch a fish to see if it's scarred up and needs to be replaced. I figure lots and lots of folks have hooked world-record-class catfish, but they simply weren't prepared to land them. A guy will think, 'Gee, I should have changed that leader.' But he doesn't do it. He throws it out there anyway. And wham! The next world record hits. It rolls and wraps up in the line and suddenly that leader snaps where it's scarred. The fish is gone, and the guy is heartbroken. If only he'd taken a minute to replace that leader, he might have caught the fish of a lifetime.

"Bottom line is, you've got to be prepared before you hook that fish, and know exactly what to do after you hook it. If not, you don't stand a chance."

Be picky about the bait you use, too. Trophy-class cats rarely are caught using chicken liver, stinkbaits, catalpa worms, cheese and other things that small cats frequently eat. Baitfish are your best bet – live ones for flatheads, and either live or cut-bait for big channels and blues.

Trophy cat seekers also should know how to properly play and land a big fish. Heavyweight cats don't give up easily, and even if you hook one, that's no guarantee you'll get it on the dry side of a boat.

Don't fight a fish with the reel. Play it with your arms and the rod. Point the rod straight up, and allow the bend of the rod to tire the fish. Hold your ground while the catfish is fighting; then, when it eases up, lower your rod tip toward the water, reeling on the drop. Be patient, and don't apply unneeded pressure.

Be sure your drag is set at a point just below the breaking strength of your line. Then, when a cat makes a run, the drag gives line. You may spend many days fishing before you finally hook a giant cat. If you get spooled or your line snaps, all that work was for nothing.

Keep a big, sturdy landing net handy, too. It's nearly impossible to land a giant catfish with your hands. Get it in a net, or risk losing it. Avoid nets with thin-walled aluminum handles; they'll buckle under the weight of a big cat.

If you know you're going to keep a big cat, a gaff hook is great for handling a fish that might be too large for a net.

When you finally land your first trophy catfish, take great pride in the fact that you've managed to triumph over one of freshwater fishing's finest trophies. Catch your second and third, and you enter a fraternity of elite anglers.

Bait for Catching Trophy Cats

Cut-bait works best for blue and channel catfish. Use big chunks of shad, herring and other oily baitfish.

Live bait is the most productive bait for catching trophy flathead catfish. For big fish, the larger, the better. Suckers, chubs and other fish 10 to 14 inches long are best.

Bullheads

All you need is an old lawn chair, a cane pole and a can of angleworms to fill a gunnysack with bullheads.

Prime time for bullhead fishing is late spring and summer, after the water temperature has reached at least 60°F. Bullheads may feed anytime during the day, but become more active toward evening when they cruise the shallows for insect larvae, snails, worms, fish eggs and small fish. Bullheads also eat a variety of aquatic plants. Like catfish, bullheads rely on an acute sense of smell, plus taste buds in their barbels, to find food. This explains why they bite so well after dark.

Bullhead fishermen generally use two or three small worms on a long-shank hook. The long hook provides additional leverage for removing the barb from a bullhead's mouth. Because bullheads have poor eyesight, the exposed shank does not keep them from biting. Most anglers attach a small rubber-core sinker and fish the worms on the bottom. Some add a bobber and dangle the bait just off the bottom.

Slow-moving rivers, shallow lakes or ponds are favorite bullhead spots. Black bullheads tolerate the muddiest water; browns and yellows prefer clearer water with more weeds.

Because bullheads are so resilient, populations often become stunted from overcrowding. In freeze-out lakes, bullheads often outlast other fish species, because they require only minute amounts of oxygen. Bullheads have been known to survive in lakes that freeze almost to the bottom by simply burrowing several inches into the soft ooze.

Bullheads are delicious if caught in spring and early summer, but as the water warms, their flesh softens and may develop a muddy taste. Fishermen should be extremely careful when handling or cleaning bullheads, because their pectoral spines are coated with a weak venom and can inflict a painful wound. Always grab a bullhead as shown below to avoid the sharp dorsal and pectoral spines (arrows).

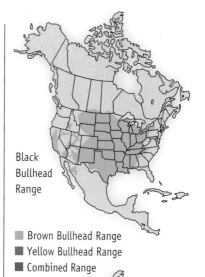

Black Bullhead Range

■ Brown Bullhead Range
▦ Yellow Bullhead Range
▓ Combined Range

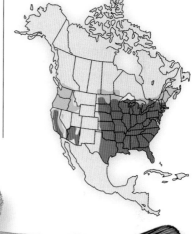

Black bullheads have greenish to gold sides that are not mottled. The barbels are grayish to black. The tail has a slight notch and there is usually a pale bar at the base. The anal fin is rounded and the pectoral spines are weakly barbed. The world-record black bullhead, 7 pounds, 7 ounces, was caught in Mill Pond, New York, in 1993.

Brown bullheads have yellowish to brownish sides, usually with distinct mottling. The barbels are dark brown to black. The tail, which is square or slightly notched, does not have a pale bar at the base. The anal fin is rounded and the pectoral spines are strongly barbed. The world record, 6 pounds, 1 ounce, was taken in Sugarloaf Pond, New York, in 1998.

Yellow bullheads have yellow to yellow-brown sides with no mottling. The chin barbels are whitish to pinkish; the upper barbels, brown. The anal fin has a straight lower edge and the tail is rounded. The world-record yellow bullhead weighed 4 pounds, 4 ounces. It was caught in Mormon Lake, Arizona, in 1984.

Walleyes & Saugers

Walleyes and saugers are creatures of darkness. Like deer, owls and many other animals that are active at night, they have a layer of pigment, called the tapetum lucidum, in the retina of the eye. This light-sensitive layer enables them to see well even in murky or dimly lit water, a fact important to fishermen. The sauger has a larger tapetum than the walleye, making its eyes even more light-sensitive.

Walleyes and saugers may inhabit the same waters, though saugers are primarily a river species. When found in the same waters, saugers usually go deeper than walleyes, because of their light-sensitive eyes.

The two species are quite similar in appearance, but they can be easily distinguished by the white tip on the lower part of the walleye's tail and the rows of black spots on the sauger's dorsal fin. Walleyes and saugers sometimes hybridize to produce saugeyes.

Classified as coolwater fish, walleyes and saugers are usually found in water from 60° to 70°F in summer. Spawning begins in spring when the water warms to the mid- to upper 40s, which means early March in the South to mid-May in northern climates. Saugers spawn about a week later than walleyes. Fishing is good just before spawning but is very difficult once spawning begins. The action picks up again about 10 days after spawning has been completed.

Although some walleyes survive longer than 20 years, most live 10 years or less. In the South, walleyes may reach 2 pounds in only 3 to 4 years and fishermen annually catch 15- to 20-pounders. In northern waters, where growth is slower, it takes about 6 years for a walleye to reach 2 pounds and an 8-pound fish is considered a trophy.

Saugers are shorter-lived, rarely surviving past 13 years. Southern saugers grow to a weight of 2 pounds in about 4 years; in the North, it may take 7 years to reach that size. But northern saugers are longer lived and reach a larger size.

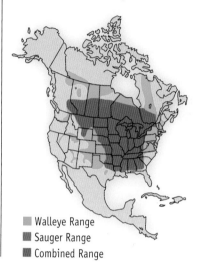

- ■ Walleye Range
- ■ Sauger Range
- ■ Combined Range

Walleye. The sides are olive-green with gold flecks and the belly varies from white to yellow-gold. The spiny (front) dorsal fin is not spotted, but has a black blotch at the rear. There is a white tip on the lower lobe of the tail. World record: 22 pounds, 11 ounces; Greer's Ferry, Arkansas; 1982.

Sauger. The sides are yellowish brown to gray with darker brown blotches. The spiny dorsal fin has several rows of distinct black spots. The pectoral fin has a black spot at the base. The tail may have a thin white band at the bottom but, unlike that of the walleye, has no white tip. World record: 8 pounds, 12 ounces; Lake Sakakawea, North Dakota; 1971.

Walleyes frequently inhabit rocky humps.

Where to Find Walleyes & Saugers

Walleyes and saugers are highly mobile. Tagging studies have shown that they may swim more than 100 miles to reach a desired spawning area. They also move vertically in response to changes in light penetration, water temperature and oxygen content.

In spring, the fish remain in warm shallows for several weeks after spawning, usually in water no more than 20 feet deep. They can stay in the shallows all day, because the low angle of the sun's rays has little effect on their light-sensitive eyes.

As summer approaches, the shallows become too warm and the sun rises higher in the sky, forcing the fish to retreat to cooler depths. However, they may move shallower to feed in morning and evening. Walleyes rarely go deeper than 30 feet, but saugers may go as deep as 50.

In fall, the fish move shallower as the surface begins to cool. Once again, the sun is low on the horizon, so the fish can feed in shallow water all day. But the fall turnover scatters the fish and may push them deeper. By the time the surface temperature drops into the 40s, they may be as deep as 50 feet.

Oxygen content also affects walleye and sauger location. In summer, many fertile lakes lack oxygen in the depths, so the fish are forced to remain in the shallows, sometimes in depths of 10 feet or less.

Following is a list of some of the best spots in natural lakes, man-made lakes and big rivers to catch walleyes and saugers.

Prime Locations in Natural Lakes:

• Bulrush beds on shallow points and reefs draw walleyes and saugers in spring and late fall. Fish hold along the edges.

• Gravel-rubble shorelines (below), especially those exposed to the wind, make excellent spawning habitat.

• Gradually sloping points close to the spawning grounds attract post-spawn walleyes and saugers.

• Deep reefs and humps, particularly those connected to other structure by a saddle, are good midsummer spots.

• Sharp-dropping points in the main lake produce walleyes and saugers from late summer to late fall.

• Irregular breaklines hold more walleyes and saugers in summer and fall than a breakline with few points or inside turns.

Prime Locations in Man-made Lakes:

• Rocky main-lake points are prime locations in summer. Points with an extended lip where the fish can feed are better than points that drop off rapidly.

• Deep pools in tributary streams concentrate pre-spawn walleyes and saugers and often produce some of the year's biggest fish.

• Sharp-sloping points near the old river channel draw fish in fall. After feeding on the points, the fish can move to deep water in the river channel to rest.

• Riprapped embankments make good spawning habitat and will often hold fish into early summer.

Prime Locations in Big Rivers:

• Tailwaters (below) of major dams hold walleyes and saugers from late fall through spawning time in early spring. The fish concentrate in eddies alongside the fast current.

• Wing dams make ideal feeding areas from late spring through fall. Walleyes often feed right on top of the wing dam; saugers, in deeper water off the front or back slope.

• Rocky shorelines with light current attract walleyes and saugers in summer and fall. Rocky bottoms produce more food than sandy or muddy bottoms.

Gravel-rubble shoreline of a natural lake provides excellent spawning habitat.

Tailwater eddies below a dam hold walleyes during the fall and winter.

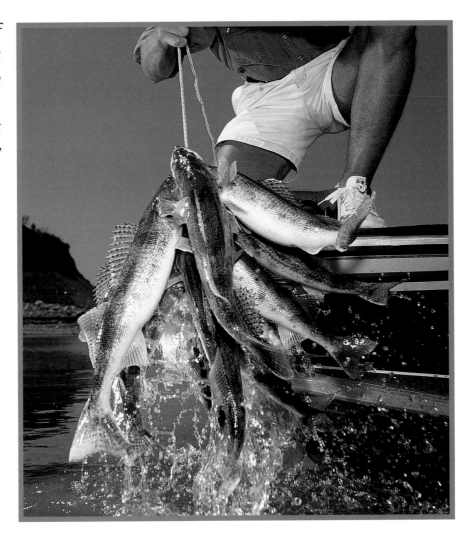

This stringer of big saugers was taken on Lake Sakakawea, North Dakota's largest body of water.

How to Catch Walleyes & Saugers

Walleyes and saugers are known for their finicky feeding habits. Although there are times when they will slam most any artificial lure you throw at them, they normally have to be teased and tempted, often with some type of live bait. In fact, live-bait presentations account for the majority of walleyes and saugers taken.

The techniques for catching walleyes and saugers are nearly identical, the difference being that saugers are normally caught in deeper water.

Live bait can be fished on a slip-sinker or slip-bobber rig, pulled behind a spinner, tipped on a jig or simply fished with a plain hook and split shot. But whatever technique you choose, location is of the utmost importance.

Walleyes and saugers are schooling fish, often clustering tightly on small structural elements, like points, inside turns and patches of rocky bottom. Consequently, your presentation must be precise in order to keep your bait in the strike zone.

This explains why boat control is such an important part of walleye and sauger fishing. You must be able to work a spot very slowly while keeping your bait at a consistent depth. Such control normally requires an electric trolling motor.

But the fish are not always linked to exact spots. They sometimes scatter over large flats or even suspend in open water. At these times, you need to cover more water, so the most productive methods are trolling with plugs or spinner rigs.

Side planers and downriggers, used mainly in trout and salmon fishing, are gaining popularity among walleye enthusiasts. These devices enable you to cover more water than you otherwise would, and to precisely control your fishing depth.

Electronics play a huge role in walleye fishing. Without a good graph, for instance, you'd find those tight schools of fish only by accident. On big water, it would be nearly impossible to return to a productive spot without a GPS unit.

Fishing Spinners

Trolling with a spinner and live bait is one of the oldest walleye techniques, and it is just as effective today as ever. Spinners work equally well for saugers, but are used less frequently.

Most fishermen rely on spinner rigs with size 2 to 4 blades. In clear water, silver, gold or brass blades usually work best. In murky water, choose fluorescent orange or chartreuse. A rig with a single size 4 to 6 hook works best for minnows or leeches; a double- or triple-hook rig is a better choice for crawlers, because it will catch the short strikers.

Spinner rigs must be weighted to get them to the bottom. You can add a sinker to the line a few feet ahead of the rig, but many anglers prefer to use a three-way-swivel or bottom-bouncer rig to keep the spinner off the bottom. A 1/2-ounce sinker will get you down to a depth of about 10 feet. Add about 1/2 ounce more weight for each additional 5 feet.

A different type of spinner, called a weight-forward spinner, is very popular on the Great Lakes. Fishermen usually put a nightcrawler on the spinner so that no more than an inch of the worm trails behind the hook. To locate walleyes with a weight-forward spinner, you simply cast it out, count it down to different depths, and retrieve it fast enough to keep the blade turning.

Store your spinner rigs on a Tackle Tamer. Insert the hook through the eyelet and wind the leader on snugly. Use the Velcro tab to secure the free end to prevent the rig from coming loose and tangling.

Spinners include: (1) single-hook rigs, such as the Northland Rainbow Spinner; (2) triple-hook rigs, such as the Northland Sting'r Hook Harness; (3) floating rigs, such as the Northland Float'n Spin Harness; and (4) weight-forward spinners, such as the Storm Hot'N Tot Pygmy.

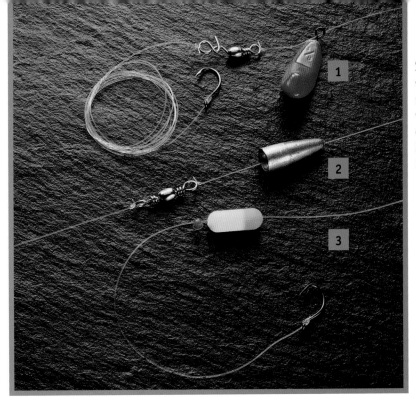

Slip-sinker rigs are available with (1) walking sinkers, for clean or rock bottom; or (2) bullet sinkers, for weedy bottom. Rigs with a float ahead of the hook (3) lift your bait above a blanket of weeds or reach fish that are holding a little off the bottom.

Fishing with Slip-sinkers

Walleyes and saugers are notorious for picking up the bait and then dropping it as soon as they feel resistance. A slip-sinker rig eliminates this resistance, allowing the fish to swim away on a free line after grabbing the bait.

All you need to tie a basic slip-sinker rig are a hook, sinker and stop. When you pull the rig ahead, the stop catches the sinker and moves it along. But when a fish bites, it pulls the line the opposite way and the sinker stays put.

The sinker is probably the most important component. It must be heavy enough to get the rig to the bottom. As a rule, you'll need 1/8 ounce of weight for every 10 feet of depth.

Most anglers use an egg sinker or walking sinker, but a bullet sinker works better in weedy cover.

The length of the leader must also be considered. When walleyes and saugers are near bottom, there is no need for a long leader. An 18- to 36-inch leader works well in this situation. But when the fish are suspended, you may need a leader over 10 feet long.

How to Fish a Slip-sinker Rig

Hook a minnow through the lips; a leech, just above the sucker and a nightcrawler, through the tip of the head and out the side, about 1/4 inch from the tip. Lower the rig until the sinker touches the bottom. Continually adjust the amount of line you have out as the depth changes. Hold the line with your index finger as you troll or drift; keep the bail open. Release the line when you feel the slightest tug (1). Let line flow freely off the spool until the fish stops running (2). Point the rod at the fish and quickly reel up slack until you feel some resistance. Then set the hook with a sharp snap of the wrist (3).

Slip-bobber Fishing

When walleye or sauger fishing gets tough, you can often tempt the fish to bite by dangling the bait right in their face. The best way to do this is to suspend it from a slip-bobber rig. This type of rig is also effective when walleyes and saugers are suspended at a certain depth, or when they are holding on a small piece of structure like an isolated rock pile.

A slip-bobber works better than a fixed bobber for fishing in deep water. With a fixed bobber set at more than a few feet, you would not be able to cast the rig.

You can make a slip-bobber rig by knotting a piece of string or rubber band on the line at the desired fishing depth. Thread on a small bead and then the bobber. Add split shot for balance. Tie on a size 4 to 6 hook and bait with a leech, crawler or minnow. For night fishing, use a lighted float powered by a tiny lithium battery (right).

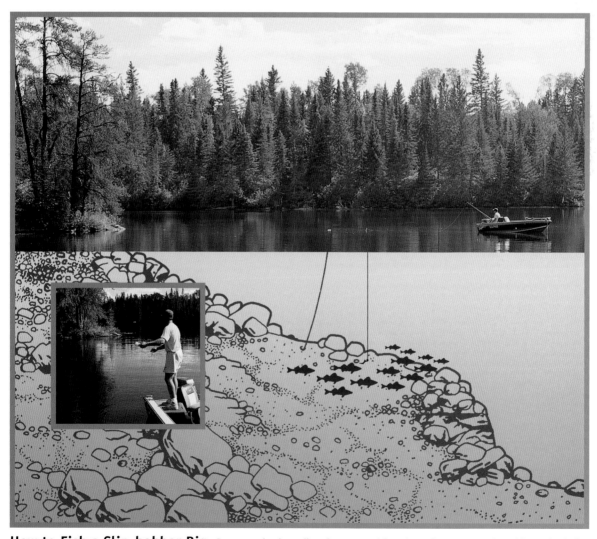

How to Fish a Slip-bobber Rig. Drop a marker buoy (inset) on a promising piece of structure or alongside a school of walleyes that you spotted on your graph. Position your boat within casting distance of your marker, then toss out a slip-bobber rig set to the right depth. Even negative fish have a hard time ignoring a bait dangled right in their face.

Jigging

A jig is the ideal lure for walleyes and saugers. It sinks quickly into the depths they inhabit and it is designed to be worked slowly to tempt fussy biters. Most walleye and sauger fishermen tip their jigs with live bait for extra attraction, regardless of whether the jig already has a soft plastic, feather or hair dressing.

How you work a jig depends on the mood of the fish. When the water is cold and the fish sluggish, a very slow, gentle jigging action usually works best. But when the water warms and the fish become more aggressive, try a more intense jigging action.

The usual way to work a jig is to cast it out, let it sink to the bottom, then retrieve it with a series of twitches and pauses. After each twitch, you must keep the line taut while the jig sinks back to the bottom. The fish usually strike when the jig is sinking, and if your line is not taut, you won't feel a thing. Sometimes you'll feel a distinct tap when a fish strikes; other times, the jig may just stop sinking prematurely or you may just feel a little extra resistance. Whenever you feel anything different, set the hook.

A sensitive, fast-action rod is a must for jig fishing. It helps you feel even the lightest tap and gives you an immediate hook set, so the fish can't spit the jig before you respond.

Jigs include: (1) bucktail jigs, such as the Wazp Genuine Bucktail Jig; (2) combination soft plastic and feather jigs, such as the Lindy Little Joe Fuzz-E-Grub; (3) curlytail jigs, such as Gopher Tackle Connie Jig with Riverside Lures Grub; (4) propeller jigs, such as the Northland Whistler Jig; and (5) stinger-hook jigs, such as the Northland Fire-Ball Jig, which has a small treble hook designed to catch short strikers.

Tip a jig with a minnow by (1) pushing the hook through the lips, from the bottom up. To keep a minnow on the jig longer, (2) hook it through the eye sockets. The most secure method of attaching a minnow is to (3) insert the hook point into the mouth and then push it out the top of the head. Hook a leech (4) through the sucker end.

Trolling with Plugs

Trolling has long been an effective way to catch walleyes and saugers, but with the advent of walleye tournament fishing, the popularity of this technique has skyrocketed. Trolling is the best way to locate fish in unfamiliar waters, because it enables you to cover a lot of water in a hurry.

In years past, trolling simply meant tossing out a lure behind a moving boat. But modern trollers use a variety of devices, such as side planers and down-riggers, that greatly increase their efficiency. Side planers spread your lines horizontally, while downriggers precisely position them vertically.

Deeper-running plugs have also improved the troller's success. Some crankbaits now dive to a depth of 30 feet with no added weight. Experienced trollers know which plugs to select when they want to fish a particular depth.

Low-stretch, thin-diameter braided lines have been a big help, as well. These lines have less water resistance, so plugs run deeper than with ordinary lines. And because they don't stretch, you'll get much better hook sets.

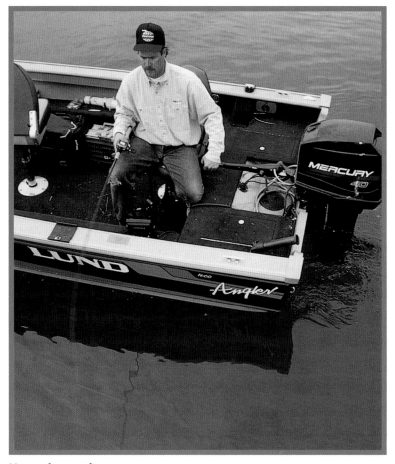

Vary the action and speed of the plug by periodically sweeping the rod tip forward, then dropping it back. The change often triggers a strike from a fish that has been following the plug. Reel in a few turns when you feel the plug bumping bottom; let out more line if you haven't felt it bump for a while. Continue to adjust your depth as you troll along. When a fish strikes, it usually hooks itself.

Trolling plugs include: (1) crankbaits, such as the Normark Shad Rap; and (2) minnow baits, such as the Storm Thunderstick.

1

2

Trolling with Downriggers, Diving Planers & Planer Boards

In deep clearwater lakes, anglers often troll using downriggers or diving planers to reach walleyes that are roaming the depths in search of food. This specialized equipment is not only easy to use but very effective for precisely presenting spoons, crankbaits and spinners to a desired depth.

DOWNRIGGERS. Downriggers range from portable clamp-on units to electronic retrieval systems capable of raising and lowering downrigger balls by the push of a button. There are also those that "jig" the lure up and down to add to the lure action, and bottom-tracking systems with auto depth setting, to maintain a consistent distance off of the bottom. These electric or winch-style winding systems hold the wire cable that lowers the downrigger balls, which usually weigh 2

to 10 pounds, down to depths in excess of 100 feet.

To use a downrigger for walleyes, simply let out the lure 40 to 60 feet behind the moving boat, insert the monofilament fishing line into a clip-release mechanism, and lower the ball while at the same time letting out the line from the reel.

When the desired depth is reached, secure the downrigger ball, engage the reel and put the rod in the rod holder. Finally, reel in enough of the line so there is a substantial bend in the rod, but not so much that it causes the line to release from the clip.

When a fish strikes, the line will release from the clip and the loaded rod will assist with the hook set. The best rods for this purpose are durable and have light or medium actions.

While most release clips have tension adjustments, walleyes often do not strike the line hard enough to release the line from

the clip. To solve this problem, many anglers use a #12 rubber band between their line and the release clip (above). Walleyes should be able to easily break the rubber band to indicate strikes.

Whenever possible, walleye anglers should use 10- to 12-pound mono, which won't be damaged when a fish releases it from the jaws of the clip.

Downriggers enable anglers to target schools of suspended walleyes that rarely see fishing lures. These unpressured, aggressive fish are often some of the biggest the lake or reservoir has to offer.

DIVING PLANERS. Another consistent way to send a walleye lure to a desired depth is to use a diving planer, which attaches fairly close to the lure (5 to 10 feet) and can send it down to a maximum depth of 60 feet.

Some diving planers, like the Dipsy Diver, plane down and off to the side of the boat. Twisting an adjustable dial on the planer causes it to change the diving angle from left or right. The more it is set to run to the side, the shallower it runs. A trip mechanism with an adjustable tension setting releases when a fish strikes to free the tension of the disc against the water, allowing anglers to fight the fish directly.

Diving planers have considerable water resistance and must be fished on heavy line and tackle. Most anglers prefer monofilament lines with breaking strengths from 14 to 30 pounds and 7- to 8-foot soft-action salmon-type rods, which are generally set in rod holders because of the enormous amount of drag caused by the pulling planer.

Spoons, spinners and shallow-running crankbaits run well with diving planers. Lures that won't cause the planer to run other than the way it was designed are the best choice. Deep-diving crankbaits often pull on the planer, causing it to run in an undesirable manner.

Compared to downriggers, diving planers are less precise in their ability to take lures to a particular depth. However, diving planers are inexpensive and therefore the number-one choice of many anglers faced with deepwater walleyes.

PLANER BOARDS. Lifelong jig fishermen cringe at the thought of connecting their line to a board and dragging crankbaits around the lake with their outboards attempting to trigger walleyes into striking. But for anglers wanting to catch fish on days and in places that wouldn't produce very many walleyes using other techniques, learning how to fish with planer boards is a good idea.

Planer boards allow anglers to expand their coverage area at multiple depths. They not only work well to reach walleyes in clearwater areas where fish are spooky or on large flats, but also work very well to catch walleyes suspended in open water.

IN-LINE BOARDS. The angler's line is attached to a clip on the board, sending the line off to the side of the boat. This enables the angler to cover a wider area and run lures through water undisturbed by the boat.

By design, the boards either angle left or right when trolled (above). They attach to the line by a release clip, a pinch or twist clip that attaches to 10- to 12-pound line without damaging it, even when a walleye strikes. Most walleye anglers prefer to attach the clip tight to the line so it doesn't release when a fish strikes. If a board does release, anglers will have to go back to retrieve it, often in waves or at night. Some manufacturers make lights that easily attach to the flag portion of the boards so they can easily be found at night.

Mono, lead core and superlines are the most popular lines when using planer boards. Because of their thin diameter, superlines often pull free from most board release clips when a walleye strikes. Wrap the line twice around the clip to keep the board attached to the line, eliminating the need to relocate the board at night or in waves. A bouncing, bobbing or dipping board usually means there is a fish on. To land the fish, slowly reel in the line until the board reaches the boat. Detach the board, and continue fighting and landing the fish. While planer boards are most often used to catch walleyes on large flats, they are equally effective on suspended fish. When trolling with side planers, a turn in either direction causes the inside or outside lures to run at different depths and speeds, which often triggers fish. With sinkers attached to the lines, lures and live-bait rigs can be run off of planer boards to reach fish suspending 40 to 50 feet beneath the surface.

Anglers also use planers to run their baits into shallow areas where walleyes would normally spook from boat traffic. Slowly trolling live bait shallow 15 to 20 yards behind the planer board is a good method to catch walleyes in 2 to 5 feet of water.

SKI-TYPE BOARDS. Big double and triple ski-type boards are towed on 200-pound-test lines attached to a mast-and-reel system at the bow of the boat. These big ski-type boards aren't used by walleye anglers as much as are the smaller in-line type boards. However, the larger boards work well for pulling heavy lead core and for trolling multiple lines.

Effectively being able to cover lots of water with planer boards takes practice. When beginning to learn, never make sharp turns. Long, gradual turns will prevent multiple lines from crossing and tangling.

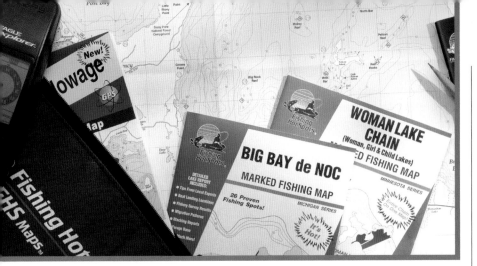

Purchasing quality lake maps, like these from *Fishing Hot Spots*, is the first step to finding fish-holding structure.

Getting Started

Discovering the right combination of location and presentation is called "finding the pattern." The ability to find the pattern quickly is what separates the expert from the average walleye fisherman.

The first step in finding the pattern is to use your knowledge of walleye behavior and seasonal movements to make an educated guess at where the fish will be. Examine a lake map and identify the most likely areas. Then, choose a presentation suited to the habitat and the mood of the walleyes. Take into account the type of water, time of year, cloud cover, wind speed and direction, and time of day.

If the pattern you choose does not pay off in a half hour or so, analyze all the available information, then try something different. For example, if you are marking walleyes on your flasher or graph, but cannot make them bite, it makes little sense to move to another spot. Instead, try a different bait or troll at a slightly slower speed. Or try adding a spinner or other attractor to trigger the fish. Often, a minor change in presentation makes a big difference.

To better understand the principles of finding the pattern, consider how an experienced walleye fisherman would handle this hypothetical situation:

The body of water is a typical mesotrophic walleye lake with water clarity of about 8 feet. It is early in the season and the walleyes completed spawning only a week ago. The skies are overcast and there is a breeze from the southeast.

Checking his lake map, the angler finds two gradually sloping points along the northwest shore. One is about 1/4 mile from a spawning creek, the other about 3/4 mile. Both appear to be likely spots, considering the season and the wind direction.

After motoring to the point closest to the creek, he checks the structure with his flasher. But the signal is weak, indicating a mucky bottom. Without wasting time fishing this unlikely spot, he motors to the other point. This one looks much better; the flasher shows a double echo. A few bulrushes are beginning to poke out of the water on the shallow portion of the point, indicating a firm, sandy bottom.

Taking into account the cold water and the likelihood of walleyes being scattered at this time of year, he decides to troll around the point using a shiner minnow on a slip-sinker rig. Starting his trolling run at 8 feet, he works his way out to 15 feet, then back in again. On the second pass around the point, he feels a light pickup at 12 feet, but the fish drops the bait. Several more passes result in one more pickup, but again the fish does not hold on.

Reasoning that there is a school of walleyes holding on the point but not actively feeding, he decides to try a slower presentation. He anchors the boat far enough off the point that he will not spook the fish, but can still reach them. He rigs up a slip-bobber, hooks on a leech, sets the depth at 11 feet, then casts to the precise spot where the fish bit.

Almost immediately, the bobber goes under. He sets the hook and reels in a 2-pound walleye. In only 45 minutes, he has his limit of 1- to 3-pound fish.

If the fisherman had not understood the elements discussed earlier, he would have gone home empty-handed. For example, without an understanding of seasonal movement patterns and the effects of weather, he would never have found the spot in the first place. Without a sensitive rod, he would not have felt the light pickups that told him that fish were present. And without the versatility to try a different presentation, he might have struggled for a fish or two, but probably no more.

The pages that follow will detail the most common walleye-fishing situations you are likely to encounter on typical walleye waters. If you practice the suggested tactics, you'll be well on your way to catching walleyes consistently.

Fishing in Timber & Brush

In many rivers and reservoirs, timber and brush provide the only shallow-water cover. Weeds are scarce or nonexistent, so walleyes rely on timber and brush to provide a supply of food and a shady resting spot.

You can find some walleyes around almost any kind of submerged timber, including flooded trees, stumps, logs on the bottom, and trees toppled into the water from an eroded bank. But your chances of finding good numbers of walleyes will be better if you know what type of timber to look for.

The best timber is near deep water. A timbered flat along the edge of a creek channel, for instance, will hold more walleyes than a timbered flat with no deep water nearby. A tree toppled into deep water off a steep riverbank will attract more walleyes than a tree toppled onto a shallow sandbar. Toppled trees with the small branches intact are better than old trees with only large limbs remaining. Walleyes can find baitfish and insects among the small branches.

Timber may hold walleyes anytime from the prespawn period until late fall. But brush holds walleyes mainly in spring, when high water floods willows and bushes along the bank.

Walleyes move into the brush when the water level begins to rise. As long as the water continues to rise or stabilizes, they remain in the brush. But when the water begins to drop even the slightest bit, they move to deeper water. This movement may be an instinctive reaction, to avoid being trapped in an isolated pool.

Anglers who specialize in fishing timber and brush prefer cone-sinker rigs with weedless hooks, brushguard jigs, or $1/16$- to $1/8$-ounce jigs with fine-wire hooks. Such a hook improves your hooking percentage, and if it does snag, it will usually bend enough to pull free. Other good lures and rigs include spinnerbaits, jigging spoons, slip-bobber rigs, and crankbaits and minnow plugs with clipped trebles.

If you are afraid to drop your bait or lure into the thickest tangle of sticks and logs, you will catch only the most aggressive walleyes, which are also the smallest ones. The bigger walleyes usually hang out where the cover is densest, so you will have to risk losing a few rigs to catch them.

Fishing in Weeds

In years past, few walleye anglers ever considered fishing in the weeds. They were told at an early age that walleyes always preferred a hard, clean bottom, so that is where they fished. But largemouth bass fishermen knew differently because they often pulled walleyes from the weeds using spinnerbaits, crankbaits and plastic worms.

Even today, the average walleye angler seldom fishes in the weeds. Many do not realize that walleyes spend a significant amount of time in the weeds; others think that walleyes in the weeds cannot be caught.

Walleyes move into weeds to find food, shade or cooler temperatures. Many types of baitfish use the weeds for cover, so a walleye cruising through the tangle can easily grab a meal.

On a bright day, walleyes can often find adequate shade and cool temperatures in a weedbed, instead of retreating to deep water. The temperature in the weeds may be five degrees cooler than elsewhere in the shallows.

If walleyes are raised in rearing ponds during their first summer of life, they become accustomed to living in weeds. It is possible that these walleyes, after being stocked into a lake, have a greater tendency to live in the weeds than walleyes reared naturally in the lake. If a lake also has natural reproduction, there may be separate populations of weed-dwelling and reef-dwelling walleyes.

Weeds produce oxygen, but it is unlikely that walleyes would move into weeds for that reason. Only in rare cases would oxygen levels in shallow water reach levels low enough to affect walleyes, even in waters where there are no weeds.

Eutrophic lakes are most likely to have populations of weed walleyes. Because the depths lose oxygen during the summer, walleyes may have no choice but to remain in the epilimnion where weeds offer the only shade. But you may find weed walleyes in mesotrophic and even in oligotrophic lakes. And walleyes in big rivers frequently feed in weedy backwaters, or in weedbeds in slack pools or along current margins. Occasionally, you will find reservoir walleyes in weeds, but fluctuating water levels prevent most types of weeds from taking root.

Not all weeds attract walleyes. The best weedbeds are in or near deep water. Seldom will you find the fish on a shallow, weedy flat with no deep water nearby. Broadleaf weeds generally hold more walleyes than narrowleaf varieties; submergent weeds more than emergent or floating-leaved types.

You can find walleyes in weeds almost any time of year. But weed fishing is usually best in summer and fall, the times when young-of-the-year baitfish are seeking cover from predators.

Fishing along the edge of the weeds is easy. Simply cast or troll a slip-sinker rig or a jig along the weedline, keeping it as close to the weeds as possible. But when walleyes are actually in the weeds or suspended above them, fishing is much more difficult.

What seems like a bite often turns out to be a weed. If you hook a strand of sandgrass, for instance, tiny branchlets break off as your hook slides along the stem, creating a jerking sensation. On the other hand, what feels like a weed may be a walleye.

If you attempt to fish with live bait, the bait will often come off the hook when you pull free of a weed. And regardless of what technique you use, you will continually have to remove bits of weed from your hook.

Different types of weeds demand different fishing techniques. You can retrieve a lure through some types of weeds without fouling, but other types will catch on the hooks. To fish effectively in weeds, you need to experiment with different tactics to find the one most suited for the situation.

Tactics for Weed Walleyes

You can rip a jig through tall broadleaf weeds by making a sharp sweep with your rod tip when you feel resistance. Any type of jig weighing from 1/16- to 1/8-ounce will work, but many anglers prefer pyramid jigs because weeds slide over

Tips for Catching Weed Walleyes

Use a bullet sinker when fishing a slip-sinker rig through the weeds. The tapered sinker will not pick up bits of weeds as much as a standard sinker will.

Present a minnow on a weedless jig. The soft brushguard keeps the hook free of vegetation, yet the lure still hooks a high percentage of biters.

the head instead of catching on the eye. In dense weeds, keep the jig riding above them rather than trying to rip through them. Another good option is to select a weedless jig with the attachment eye at the nose, which lets the lure slip through weeds easily.

It's best to work the edges of a bed of long, stringy weeds. These weeds grow in clumps and walleyes often hold in the open water nearby. A jig fished in the weeds would foul continuously.

With a mono-leader type spinner, you have the choice of using a minnow, leech or nightcrawler. Troll at a slow speed, keeping the rig just above the weedtops. If you feel the rig touching weeds, lift your rod tip. A floating spinner will keep the bait riding higher.

Another effective tactic is retrieving a spinnerbait through dense weeds, letting it helicopter to bottom when it comes to a deeper pocket. Use a standard spinnerbait with a minnow or plastic curlytail in place of the rubber skirt.

If the walleyes aren't aggres-

sive, try casting a slip-bobber rig into a pocket in tall broadleaf weeds. Adjust the bobber stop so the bait dangles just above bottom. Slip-bobbers also work well for fishing above a blanket of sandgrass or alongside beds of coontail, milfoil or other long, stringy weeds.

Another good choice for finicky fish is the floating slip-sinker rig. Instead of a standard walking sinker, use a cone sinker, which will slip through the weeds easily. Attach a float ahead of your bait, or hook your bait to a floating jig head so your bait rides above the weeds. Troll or retrieve the rig over sandgrass or other low-growing weeds.

If the weeds don't grow to the surface you can cast a shallow-running crankbait or minnow plug over a weedy flat or point, keeping the plug just above the weedtops. Trolling over the weeds may spook the walleyes, so you're better off casting. Switch to a deep-running crankbait or minnow plug for trolling along the deep weedline.

Fishing in Rocks

A bottom of jagged and broken rocks is one of the best places to find walleyes. But it is one of the most difficult places to fish, especially when using live-bait rigs.

Some types of artificial lures work well over rocky bottoms. Small jigs, floating crankbaits and weight-forward spinners are among the best choices. Select a crankbait that will run just above the rocks. If the lure should hit a rock, the lip will usually keep it from snagging. With a weight-forward spinner, reel just fast enough to keep it off bottom. By tipping it with a nightcrawler, you can increase its buoyancy and fish it more slowly.

With an ordinary slip-sinker rig, the rocks seem to reach out and grab the sinker. You can reduce the frustration and catch a lot more walleyes by using the following techniques:

• Suspend your bait from a slip-bobber. Position your bobber stop so the bait hangs just above the rocks.

• When trolling, lower your rig to the bottom, then reel in a foot or two so the sinker does not drag on the rocks. Occasionally drop your rod tip back until the sinker touches the rocks, to make sure the depth has not changed.

• Float your bait off bottom with a floating jig head or some other type of floating rig, or use an inflated nightcrawler. For extra flotation, hook the crawler through the middle and inject both ends with air. A floating rig will keep your hook out of the rocks but will not prevent your sinker from snagging.

• Use a snag-resistant slip-sinker such as the Lindy No-Snagg. Available in weights from $1/8$ to 1 ounce, these tube-shaped sinkers are designed to avoid snags in both rocks and brush.

• Keep your line as close to vertical as possible when fishing on a rocky bottom. When trolling with a light sinker, you must let out a lot of line to reach bottom. Because your line is at a low angle, your sinker can easily wedge between the rocks (below). With a heavier sinker, you can use a much shorter line. The line is at a greater angle to the bottom, so the sinker usually climbs over the rocks instead of wedging between them.

light sinker

heavier sinker

Fishing in Low-clarity Water

Most walleye fishermen would be surprised to learn that low-clarity waters frequently support more walleyes than clear waters. Low-clarity waters are usually high in the nutrients needed for a healthy food chain. And because low-clarity waters filter out sunlight, walleyes can spend more time in the food-rich shallows. Low-clarity water usually results from one or more of the following:

• Suspended mud or clay resulting from carp, bullheads or other rough fish stirring up the bottom, from wave action in a shallow basin, or from erosion of nearby farmlands.

• A heavy algae bloom caused by highly fertile water. The water may be very clear in spring and fall, but greenish or brownish in summer.

• Bog stain caused by decomposition of tree leaves and aquatic vegetation.

Walleye fishing in low-clarity waters tends to be more consistent than in clear waters. The fish seem less affected by weather changes, particularly cold fronts. Because the walleyes stay relatively shallow most of the time, they are easier to find.

Your fishing strategy in these waters depends on the visibility. If it is less than a foot, artificial lures usually work better than live bait. It is easier for walleyes to detect the sound, vibration and brighter color of an artificial. If you prefer live bait, add a fluorescent spinner or other colorful attractor.

Walleyes in waters where visibility is less than a foot generally bite best in midday. Fishing from 10 a.m. to 4 p.m. is usually better than at dawn or dusk. Night fishing is likely to be poor. Calm, sunny days are better than cloudy, windy days.

The best lures for these waters usually produce sound or vibration. Crankbaits and vibrating plugs with rattle chambers, vibrating blades, and spinners are good choices. Surprisingly, jigs work well even though they produce comparatively little vibration. Fluorescent orange and phosphorescent (glow-in-the-dark) jig heads are good choices. Untipped jigs are just as effective as jigs tipped with live bait. Walleyes in low-clarity waters are conditioned to strike at any glimpse of movement or anytime they detect vibration with their lateral-line system. Live bait does not add to the visibility or vibration and may result in short strikes.

If the visibility is from 1 to 3 feet, live bait is probably a better all-around choice than artificial lures. But a spinner or other attractor on your live-bait rig will produce more fish.

Fishing in morning and late afternoon is usually better than fishing at midday, but the walleyes will start biting later and stop earlier than in clearer water. Cloudy or windy days are usually better than calm, sunny days. If the visibility exceeds 3 feet, strategies for low-clarity water are not needed.

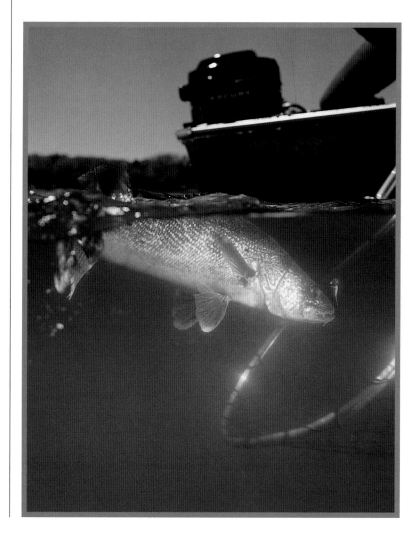

Fishing During the Spawning Season

Most waters in the northern states and Canada are closed to walleye fishing around spawning time. Portions of the Great Lakes, some rivers and reservoirs in the North and most waters in the South are open continuously.

The spawning period offers some of the year's best fishing, and some of the worst. If the weather stays warm for a few days, walleyes usually bite well. A rise in water temperature of only a degree or two can trigger a burst of feeding. But a cold front, even if it is not severe, has the opposite effect.

As a rule, walleyes bite better in the afternoon than in the morning, especially early in the spawning season. If the water temperature rises gradually through the day, as it often does, fishing peaks at about 3 or 4 p.m.

In rivers, fishing during the spawning period is best in years when the water level is low and stable. Walleyes concentrate in pools and eddies, so they are easy to find. In high water, they scatter into flooded vegetation where finding and catching them is difficult.

How to Catch Pre-spawn Walleyes

In the early stages of the spawning period, you can usually find walleyes in deep water in the vicinity of their spawning area. In most cases, they will be at depths of 15 to 30 feet.

Because the water temperature is cold, walleyes are not feeding aggressively. You can often catch them by jigging vertically with a jig and minnow, or a vibrating blade. Vertical jigging will usually take more fish than casting and retrieving because you can feel the subtle strikes more easily. If you are missing too many fish, attach a stinger hook to your jig.

Later in the pre-spawn period, walleyes begin to feed more actively. They mill about near the spawning area, sometimes moving into water only 2 to 3 feet deep, even during the day. Anglers often make the mistake of fishing too deep, especially if the water is discolored from runoff.

A jig still works well, but because the fish are more aggressive, you may not have to tip it with a minnow. If you can get by without one, you will probably miss fewer short strikers. Another effective technique is casting or long-line trolling with a shallow-running crankbait or minnow plug. You can also use a small minnow on a split-shot rig.

Timing is the most important consideration for anglers who fish at spawning time. Although females will not bite once they start to spawn, all of them do not spawn at the same time.

Those that have not started to spawn can still be caught. But as the spawning period progresses, fishing for females becomes a waste of time.

In years when the water warms slowly, however, females that spawned early resume feeding before the spawning period is over. Fishing gradually picks up as more females recover. When females are in the midst of spawning, you can find others that have not started to spawn by moving to a body of water where the timing of the spawning run is different. Or you can work different spawning areas in the same body of water. In some lakes, for instance, one segment of the population spawns in a tributary stream, another along the shoreline and yet another on an offshore reef. Stream spawning begins first; shoreline spawning a week or more later; and reef spawning another week or more after shoreline spawning. So even if the stream fish are in the middle of spawning, many of the reef fish have not started to spawn.

Approximate Date of Spawning Peak at Different Latitudes

Latitude	Date
55°	May 17
52½°	May 13
50°	May 8
47½°	April 30
45°	April 20
42½°	April 12
40°	April 4
37½°	March 27
35°	March 19

At a given latitude, the peak may be a week earlier in shallow bodies of water; a week later in deep ones. The peak may be 10 days sooner in an early spring; 10 days later in a late one.

Fishing in Ultraclear Water

Anglers who live on ultra-clear walleye lakes often complain that the waters are fished out. But when they voice these complaints to conservation agencies, they often learn that good numbers of walleyes were caught in test nets.

Walleyes in ultraclear lakes, where the clarity is 10 feet or more, are much harder to catch than those in low-clarity waters. The fish may feed at depths of 5 feet or less at night, then retreat to water over 40 feet deep in midday. And in water this clear, they are easily spooked by any unusual sound or sudden movement.

On calm, sunny days, walleyes in these waters feed most heavily around dusk and dawn, or at night. On windy or overcast days, they also feed at dusk and dawn, but some feeding takes place during midday.

The secret to catching walleyes in clear lakes is to keep noise and movement to an absolute minimum, especially when fishing in water less than 20 feet deep. You can often double or triple the number of strikes by using 4-pound-test line instead of 8-pound test. Use clear or low-visibility line instead of fluorescent line.

To prevent spooking the walleyes, keep your boat as far from the fishing area as possible. Anchor and use long casts to reach the fish instead of hovering in place and fishing vertically. When trolling with a floating minnow plug, let out a lot of line in order to reach bottom. Some anglers use an electric trolling motor instead of the outboard to avoid spooking fish. You can also use a planer board when trolling in the shallows. Let out 50 to 100 feet of line, attach it to the board, then let out more line. The board will pull your line as much as 50 feet to the side of the boat's wake so you do not spook the fish.

When fishing with live-bait rigs in ultraclear water, it usually pays to use a plain hook and as little hardware as possible. Most anglers prefer a slip-sinker, split-shot or slip-bobber rig. By still-fishing with a slip-bobber, you can avoid continually casting or trolling over the walleyes.

The best artificials are those with a natural look. Dark colors generally work better than bright or fluorescent colors. Minnow plugs outperform crankbaits because they more closely resemble the baitfish prevalent in these waters. Black-and-silver, black-and-gold, and perch finishes work best. Jigs also produce well, especially when tipped with a minnow. Black, purple and brown jigs are usually most effective.

In the clearest lakes, you may have no choice but to fish at night, especially during periods of sunny weather. Use the same baits, lures and techniques that you would during the day, but fish in much shallower water. Some fishermen prefer wading to fishing from a boat because they can move quietly along the shore without spooking the walleyes.

Clear lakes usually have lush growths of submerged weeds. And the weeds grow in much deeper water than in other lakes. If the weeds are dense, you may find walleyes in relatively shallow water, even if the weather is sunny. Or they may move deeper and hold in the area where weed density tapers off. Anyone who spends much time fishing in clear lakes should become familiar with the techniques for catching walleyes in weeds.

Fishing for Suspended Walleyes

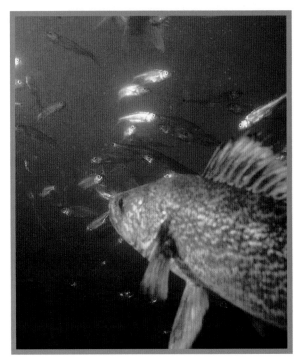

Walleyes may suspend off bottom for any of the following reasons:

TEMPERATURE. In a clear lake, walleyes retreat to deeper water after feeding to avoid sunlight. But in low- to moderate-clarity water, they often move laterally rather than vertically, especially if the water is stratified into temperature layers. By moving laterally, they can avoid drastic temperature changes.

Walleyes that feed on reefs, for instance, often suspend in nearby open water when feeding is completed. They usually move less than 100 yards. Many fishermen make the mistake of assuming that the walleyes have moved deeper, so they waste a great deal of time searching barren water.

OXYGEN. If the deep water lacks sufficient oxygen in summer, and there is a shortage of shallow-water structure, walleyes may have no choice but to suspend.

TOXIC GASES. Walleyes often suspend on calm, sunny days in summer. In many instances, the fish are suspending to avoid high levels of toxic gases near bottom. Calm, sunny weather allows maximum sunlight penetration. Sunlight promotes decomposition of organic bottom sediments, which produces levels of carbon dioxide, hydrogen sulfide and methane gas that could be toxic to walleyes.

To escape, walleyes suspend above the layer of toxic gases. If the bottom is rich in organic materials, they may move up as much as 10 feet.

In windy weather, water circulation prevents toxic gases from accumulating, so walleyes need not suspend to avoid the gases.

FOOD. The walleye's favorite foods are not necessarily linked to the bottom. Open-water baitfish like shad and ciscoes, for example, can be found at almost any depth. On calm mornings or evenings, you may see baitfish schools dimpling the surface. Walleyes will ignore their oxygen and temperature preferences for an easy meal, so they pursue the baitfish in open water or hang just below the surface schools. Walleyes may suspend to feed on immature insects, particularly emerging mayfly nymphs.

How to Catch Suspended Walleyes

Finding and catching suspended walleyes can be a difficult assignment. Walleyes suspended off structure are there to rest, not to feed. Walleyes suspended in pursuit of baitfish are willing to bite, but they may not notice your bait among the clouds of natural food.

To catch suspended walleyes, you must present the right bait or lure at precisely the right depth. Finding this depth requires either a graph or flasher or a lot of experimentation.

One of the simplest ways to catch suspended walleyes is to use a slip-bobber rig. Set your bobber stop at the appropriate depth, bait up with a leech, nightcrawler or minnow, and wait for a bite. This technique works especially well for walleyes that are not actively feeding.

If the walleyes are within a few feet of bottom, you can float your bait up to them rather than lowering it down. Most anglers use a slip-sinker rig with some type of floating jig head or a float that attaches to the leader.

You can also catch walleyes that are within a few feet of bottom by jigging vertically with a vibrating blade or tailspin. While drifting with the wind, jig with long sweeps of the rod; keep the line taut as the lure sinks to bottom.

You can catch walleyes suspended at any depth by casting or trolling with vibrating plugs, jigs, vibrating blades and weight-forward spinners. To locate walleyes with these lures, use the countdown technique. Many fishermen prefer to tip their jigs and spinners with live bait.

Fishing After a Cold Front

The toughest time to catch walleyes is after a severe cold front. Normally, crisp temperatures and ultraclear skies follow passage of the front. Walleyes respond by tightly hugging the bottom or burying themselves in dense weedbeds. They feed sporadically if at all. When they do eat, the feeding period will be short. Depending on the severity of the cold front, it may take up to 3 days for the fish to resume normal activity.

Post-cold front conditions present problems for even the best fishermen, but the following tactics may improve your success:

• Do your fishing very early or very late in the day, or at night. Your odds of finding active walleyes are best during low-light periods. Dangle a minnow or leech from a lighted slip-bobber. A stationary bait may tempt inactive walleyes to bite, and you can easily see the bobber.

• Fish 5 to 10 feet deeper than you normally would at a given time of day. Increased light penetration from the clear skies drives the walleyes into deeper, darker water.

• Try fishing in the weeds. Some walleyes will seek cover in shallow vegetation rather than move to deep structure. Weed walleyes resume normal activity before the walleyes in deeper water.

• Use live bait. A small bait will usually work better than a large one. Walleyes in a lethargic state are not likely to chase a fast-moving artificial. A good way to present live bait to cold-front walleyes is with a slip-sinker rig using a leader no more than 18 inches long. A lethargic walleye will not swim upward to grab your bait; a short leader keeps your bait near bottom.

• Use a lighter-than-normal jig, and tip it with live bait. A lighter jig takes more time to sink, so it forces you to retrieve very slowly and gives the fish extra time to strike. Fish slowly. Walleyes may even ignore live bait if it is moving too fast. Anchoring is often more effective than trolling or drifting.

• Attach a stinger hook if the fish are striking short. A half-interested walleye will often take a nip at the tail of a minnow or crawler, then let go before you can set the hook. With a stinger, you will hook a good percentage of these fish.

• Use light, clear line. Post-cold front walleyes are particularly line-shy. Some fishermen use monofilament as light as 4-pound test.

• If you are fishing on a relatively clear lake with no success, try a lake with darker water or a river.

• In large, shallow lakes with silty bottoms, the strong winds accompanying a cold front stir up the bottom. For several days after the front, the water may be so turbid that you have to fish shallower than normal if the walleyes are to see your bait. In most cases, midday fishing is best.

River Fishing

The secret to catching river walleyes is knowing how current and fluctuating water levels affect their behavior, and adjusting your tactics accordingly.

CURRENT. Walleyes will tolerate a slight current, but seldom will you find them in fast water, unless there is some type of cover to serve as a current break. You can find river walleyes in slack pools, in eddies or downstream from some type of current break like an island, a bridge pier or a large boulder. But many anglers make the mistake of fishing only the downstream side of obstructions. Current deflecting off the face of a wingdam or other current break creates a slack pocket on the upstream side (right), providing an ideal spot for a walleye to grab drifting food.

Current edges are to a river what structure is to a lake. Walleyes will hold along the margin between slack and moving water. This way, they can rest in the still water and occasionally dart into the current to get a meal.

FLUCTUATING WATER LEVELS. Most good river fishermen prefer low, stable water for walleye fishing. Under these conditions, the water is at its clearest, and the walleyes are concentrated in well-known spots.

Rising water causes walleyes to move shallower. They often feed near the base of flooded willows or brush, sometimes in water only a foot deep. If current in the main channel becomes too swift, the fish move into backwater lakes, oxbows, sloughs or cuts where there is practically no current. Or they may swim into the mouths of feeder creeks that are normally dry.

Walleyes continue to feed as long as the water level is rising or stable. But when it begins to fall, they immediately sense the change and move to deeper water to avoid getting trapped in a dead-water pool. Once they move deeper, feeding slows and fishing becomes much tougher.

Fishing Tactics

More river walleyes are taken on jigs than on any other lure. In still water, you can easily reach bottom in 15 feet of

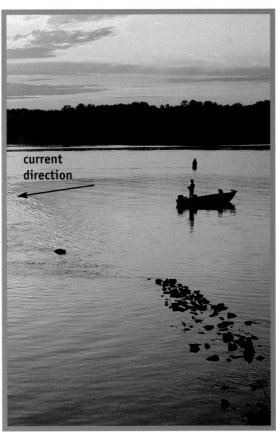

current direction

water with a 1/8-ounce jig, but you will need a 1/4-ounce jig to reach the same depth in moderate current. Most anglers prefer round-head or bullet-head jigs for fishing in current because these types have less water resistance than others.

Jigs are normally fished by casting from an anchored position just upstream of a pool or eddy, by casting to pools and eddies while slipping downstream, by vertically jigging while drifting with the current or by jig trolling downstream.

Trolling against the current with crankbaits, minnow plugs and vibrating plugs accounts for a tremendous number of river walleyes. If the current is not too swift, you can often catch fish by trolling along the edges of the main channel. Other productive trolling areas include long riprap banks, edges of long sandbars and islands, and rocky shorelines. Use lead-core line or heavy sinkers to keep your plugs ticking bottom.

Another productive plug-fishing technique is casting to a riprap or rocky shoreline while the boat drifts with the current. River walleyes often lie tight to the bank, especially if the water is rising.

If the bottom is relatively clean, you can lower a slip-sinker rig to bottom and drift live bait with the current. Let out just enough line to reach bottom. If the water is discolored, a fluorescent spinner ahead of your bait can make a big difference.

Ice Fishing

Ice fishermen account for a major share of the big walleyes taken in many lakes. Where baitfish populations are high, anglers rarely catch the well-fed trophies in summer. The big fish start getting caught in late fall when predation begins to reduce the baitfish crop. They continue biting into the winter.

The best time to catch walleyes is just after the ice becomes thick enough for safe fishing. In shallow lakes, walleyes continue to bite for 3 to 4 weeks. The action usually slows as the fish gradually become more dormant. Fishing picks up again in late winter, especially after the snow begins to thaw.

In deeper lakes, walleyes also bite best at first ice, but good fishing usually continues later into the winter. So, if you plan to fish in mid- to late winter, your odds are generally better on a deep lake than a shallow one.

Because walleyes feed most heavily in dim light, fishing is generally better at dawn and dusk than at midday, and better on dark overcast days than on sunny days.

Wintertime walleyes in clear lakes generally inhabit deeper water than those in low-clarity lakes. Look for them in water from 10 to 15 feet deep at first ice; from 20 to 40 feet in midwinter; and again from 10 to 15 feet in late winter. In low-clarity lakes, they usually stay at depths of 5 to 15 feet through the entire winter.

If you know a good spot to catch walleyes in the summer, there's a good chance you will find them there in the winter. Prime wintertime spots include rock piles, sunken islands, shoreline points, underwater points and inside turns. The shoreline structure normally holds the most walleyes in the early and late season; the mid-lake structure in the midwinter. In lakes with little structure, walleyes sometimes relate to weedbeds or submerged timber.

In most waters, walleyes stay within a foot of the bottom in winter. They seldom suspend, except in fertile lakes.

Fishing Tips

Dangling a live minnow beneath a float probably accounts for more walleyes than any other ice-fishing technique. But when walleyes are feeding aggressively, you can often catch more on a jigging lure tipped with a minnow head or small dead minnow (below) than on a live minnow. You can

switch holes more easily, and after catching a fish, you can drop your lure back down immediately without taking the time to put on another live minnow.

Many anglers make the mistake of arriving at their spot in the afternoon, just when the walleyes move in, then drilling holes. The noise is sure to drive the walleyes out of the area. Instead, get to your spot and drill your holes at least an hour before they normally start to move in. Drill several holes so you can quickly move from hole to hole to find the fish.

Tip-ups work great for winter walleyes. They allow an angler to use more than one line at a time.

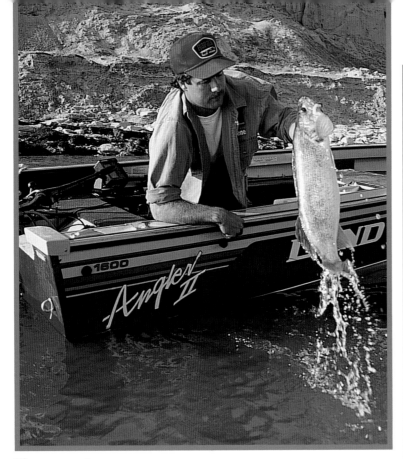

If you want a chance at a trophy walleye, you have to spend time on waters known for producing big fish. This monster was caught and then released in Lake Sakakawea, North Dakota.

Trophy Walleyes

Few bodies of water contain large numbers of big walleyes. In a moderately fished lake, for instance, the combination of natural mortality and angling catch reduces the number of fish of a given age by about 50 percent each year. Thus, if a population contained 1,000 1-year-old walleyes, 500 would remain at age 2, 250 at age 3, and only 2 at age 10.

Adding to the challenge is the fact that big walleyes are much warier than small ones. Their exceedingly cautious nature explains why they live so long. If a big walleye sees or hears anything unusual, it stops feeding and heads for deeper water. Trophy hunters know that the poorest time to catch a big walleye is on the weekend when the lake is overrun with water skiers and pleasure boaters.

If you fish long enough, you may catch a trophy walleye using the same strategy you would employ for average-sized walleyes. But you can greatly boost your odds by selecting waters likely to produce big fish, carefully choosing your fishing times and using techniques suited to trophy walleyes.

Selecting Trophy Waters

Reservoirs in the Southeast produce some giant walleyes because of the fast growth rate. But walleyes in the North are more abundant and have a much longer life span. Even though the top-end weights are not quite as high, northern waters produce many more walleyes of 10 pounds or more.

If you want to catch a big walleye, but do not know where to go, base your choice on the following:

• Water area – All other factors being equal, a large body of water is more likely to support big walleyes than a small one. A 500-acre natural lake may hold a few 10-pound walleyes, but on a per-acre basis, a 5000-acre lake would hold a lot more.

• Size of walleye population – Waters that produce lots of small walleyes generally yield few trophies. Competition for food and living space makes it more difficult for the fish to grow to a large size. And waters where walleyes are plentiful usually attract large numbers of anglers. Heavy fishing pressure reduces the average size of the walleyes and cuts your odds of boating a trophy.

• Usable forage – A body of water may be full of forage fish, but if they are not of a size acceptable to walleyes, they do not contribute to the trophy potential. In fact, a large population of unusable forage is detrimental. The productivity of any body of water is limited, so the larger the population of oversized forage, the smaller the crop of usable forage.

For example, many lakes in the North contain large populations of ciscoes. But in most cases, the cisco crop consists mainly of fish over 10 inches in length, too big for the vast majority of walleyes. These lakes produce few trophies. A few northern lakes, however, have populations of dwarf ciscoes, a strain that never grows longer than 7 inches. These lakes have much greater potential for big walleyes.

When to Catch Trophy Walleyes

Anglers catch by far the most trophy walleyes during the following three periods: just before spawning; in early summer, when the big females have completely recuperated from spawning; and in late fall, when the fish are feeding heavily in preparation for winter.

During the pre-spawn period, large numbers of big females crowd into a relatively small area. Although they are not feeding heavily, you may be able to catch a fish or two because of the sheer numbers present. Good fishing lasts until spawning begins.

About 2 weeks after spawning, the big females start to bite again, but they are still scattered and can be very difficult to find. You may catch an occasional large walleye, but seldom more than one. Your chances of finding a concentration of big walleyes are much better after they have settled into their typical summer locations. The best fishing begins about 5 to 6 weeks after spawning and generally lasts 2 to 3 weeks.

Late-fall fishing is extremely unpredictable, but if you can find the walleyes, a high percentage of them will be big. The preponderance of large walleyes in late fall can be explained by the fact that most of them are females. To nourish their developing eggs, females must consume more food than males, up to six times more according to some feeding studies.

In waters that stratify, the depths are warmer than the shallows once the fall turnover is completed. Big walleyes may swim into shallow water for short feeding sprees, but at other times may be found as deep as 50 feet. Although difficult to find, they form tight schools, so you may be able to catch several from the same area.

Techniques for Trophy Walleyes

Catching a walleye over 10 pounds is a once-in-a-lifetime accomplishment for most anglers. But some fishermen catch several that size each year. If you spend a lot of time fishing waters known for trophy walleyes, but seldom land a big one, you are probably making one or more of the following mistakes:

• You may be fishing at the wrong depth. In most waters, big walleyes feed in the shallows during low-light periods, especially in spring and fall. But at most other times, they prefer relatively deep water, deeper than the areas where you typically find smaller walleyes.

Often, big walleyes use the same structure as the smaller ones, but hang 10 to 15 feet deeper. This behavior can be attributed to a walleye's increasing sensitivity to light as it grows older. In addition, bigger walleyes prefer cooler water, and they can usually find it by moving deeper.

In deep northern lakes, however, the shallow water stays cool enough for big walleyes through the summer. If the walleyes can find boulders or other shallow-water cover to provide shade, they may spend the summer at depths of 10 feet or less. In these lakes, most anglers fish too deep.

• You may be using baits and lures too small to interest trophy walleyes. If you have ever cleaned a big walleye, you were probably surprised to find one

Big walleyes eat big baitfish.

or more 6- to 8-inch baitfish in its stomach. Big baits draw far fewer strikes than small ones, and most anglers are not willing to fish all day for one or two opportunities.

• You may be fishing at the wrong time of day. If the water is very clear, or if there is a great deal of boat traffic, big walleyes will feed almost exclusively at night.

• Your presentation may be too sloppy. Big walleyes are extremely cautious. They are much more likely to take a bait attached to a size 6 hook and a 6-pound-test leader than one attached to a 1/0 hook and 15-pound leader. In clear water, some trophy specialists use a 4-pound leader.

Another common mistake is making too much noise. Unless the fish are in water deeper than 20 feet, you should not troll over them with your outboard motor. Avoid dropping anything in the boat and do not attempt to anchor on top of the fish. Set your anchor at a distance and let the wind drift your boat into position.

Pike & Muskies

These top-rung predators are regarded by many anglers as the ultimate gamefish – powerful fighters that will test even the most skilled fisherman. With their long, powerful body, huge head and razor-sharp teeth, it's easy to understand why these fish have such a fearsome reputation. It is not uncommon for a pike or muskie to strike a bass or walleye struggling on a fisherman's line.

In North America, three members of the pike family are of interest to fishermen. They include the northern pike, muskellunge and chain pickerel. Grass and redfin pickerel are caught occasionally, but they rarely exceed 12 inches in length.

Lakes with shallow, weedy bays or connecting marshes have the highest pike populations, but the fish can adapt to most any kind of water. Muskies are less adaptable; they require clearer water and a higher oxygen content.

Pike spawn soon after ice-out, beginning when the water reaches about 40°F. They scatter their eggs onto dense vegetation in shallow bays or marshes. Muskies spawn several weeks later, at a water temperature of 49° to 59°F in slightly deeper water.

Pike and muskies are opportunists, feeding on whatever prey they can find. They may eat muskrats, mice, turtles, salamanders, small ducks and other birds, but most of their food is fish, preferably cylindrical-bodied fish that slide down easily. They commonly take fish one-half their own body length.

Willing biters, pike often follow a lure, hitting it repeatedly until hooked. Because pike are so easily caught, the large ones can be readily skimmed off a population. Today, most pike weighing over 20 pounds are taken in remote northern lakes and rivers where fishing pressure is light. Muskies are much harder to catch, commonly following a lure all the way to the boat and then turning away at the last second. This explains why muskies often reach 35 pounds or more, even in heavily fished waters.

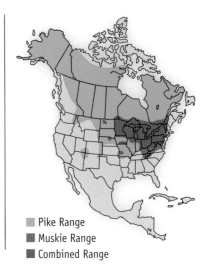

■ Pike Range
▨ Muskie Range
▨ Combined Range

Northern pike have greenish sides with rows of cream-colored, bean-shaped spots. The tips of the tail are usually rounded. The world-record northern pike, 55 pounds, 1 ounce, was caught in Lake of Grefeern, West Germany, in 1986. Pike are also called jacks, pickerel or snakes.

Muskellunge have a lighter background color than pike, usually with dark spots or bars, but sometimes with no markings. The tips of the tail are pointed, rather than rounded. The world-record muskellunge, 69 pounds, 11 ounces, was caught in Chippewa Flowage, Wisconsin, in 1949. Muskellunge are commonly referred to as muskies, and are also called lunge, maskinonge and dozens of other local names.

It's hard to beat the thrill of hooking and landing a big pike from shore. This trophy came from a shallow bay of Selwyn Lake, which is located along the boundary of Saskatchewan and the Northwest Territories.

Where & When to Find Pike & Muskies

Locating small northern pike is not much of a challenge. They spend nearly all of their time in shallow, weedy water from 2 to 15 feet deep. But finding big pike is not as simple. They are found along with the small ones in spring, but when the shallows warm in summer, they scatter into 20- to 40-foot depths where they can be hard to locate. Good-sized muskies also spend more time in deep water than do small ones, but the tendency is not as strong as it is in pike.

Summertime pike fishing is difficult if the water gets too warm. If pike cannot find water cooler than 75°F, they feed very little. Pike feed actively through the winter months, however, and are a frequent target of ice fishermen.

Muskies prefer warmer water than pike and are seldom found in waters that don't reach at least 68°F in summer. This explains why their range does not extend as far north. Muskies are much less active than pike in winter and are rarely caught by ice anglers.

Pike bite best during daylight hours; the action begins to slow at sunset and night fishing is seldom worthwhile. Fishing is usually better on overcast days than on sunny ones. Muskies are much more likely to feed at night.

Anglers in clear lakes have discovered that night fishing with big, noisy surface lures is a deadly muskie technique. Like northerns, muskies seem to bite best under cloudy skies.

Tagging studies have shown that pike are highly mobile, going wherever they must to find food. Muskies move about much less, so when you spot a big one, remember the location and fish it again at a later date. Following is a list of prime northern pike and muskie locations in natural lakes, man-made lakes and rivers.

Prime Locations in Natural Lakes:

• Weedy bays make good spawning areas. Pike prefer to spawn in shallower bays than do muskies.

• Weedy humps, especially those covered with cabbage, hold pike and muskies in summer.

• Weedy saddles connecting two pieces of structure, like a point and an island, are good spots in summer.

• Narrows usually have currents that attract baitfish. They hold pike and muskies in summer and fall.

• Rock reefs near deep water produce pike and muskies from summer through early fall.

• Stream mouths draw bait-

fish, which, in turn, attract pike and muskies through the open-water season.

Prime Locations in Man-made Lakes:

• Shallow coves in creek arms warm early in spring and attract spawning pike and muskies.

• Points (above) projecting into creek channels hold pike and muskies that have just finished spawning.

• Timber-covered humps in the main lake, especially those near the main river channel, hold fish in fall.

Prime River Locations:

• Backwater lakes make good spawning areas in big rivers. The fish may stay in deep backwaters all year.

• Weedbeds are excellent pike and muskie producers from late spring until the weeds turn brown in fall.

• Deep pools with light current are good year-round pike and muskie locations in smaller rivers.

Pike & Muskie Tackle

Even young pike do not hesitate to attack other fish of nearly their own size. This small pike is grabbing a shiner about one-half its own length.

Whether you prefer live bait or artificial lures, one basic rule applies in pike and muskie fishing: use big bait if you want to catch big fish. A good guideline is to select a bait about one-fourth the length of the fish you expect to catch. Go a little smaller in early spring or under cold-front conditions.

It's a good idea to carry a selection of lures that run at different depths, from the surface down to 30 feet. That way, you'll be ready regardless of whether the fish are shallow, deep or somewhere in between.

Many pike and muskie anglers make the mistake of using rods, reels and lines that are too light. When they finally get the strike they've been waiting for, they fail to hook the fish because their rod was too flimsy to drive the hooks into the fish's bony mouth. Or, they hook the fish and then lose it because of a broken line.

A medium-heavy power baitcasting outfit spooled with 12- to 25-pound monofilament or braided line is ideal for most northern pike fishing. For muskies, use a heavy-power baitcasting rod with 30- to 50-pound line.

Whatever outfit you choose, be sure to attach a wire leader. The fishes' sharp teeth will easily shear off monofilament or braided line.

Fishing Bucktails & Spinnerbaits

Pike and muskies find it hard to resist the vibration and flash of a big spinner blade. Large in-line spinners are usually called bucktails, because of the deer-hair tail dressing. But the dressing may also consist of feathers or some kind of synthetic material. Spinnerbaits are more weedless, because of their upturned single hook and safety-pin shaft.

Bucktails and spinnerbaits are normally fished by casting, especially when you're working specific targets, such as a dense clump of weeds or a downed tree. But they can also be trolled to cover large flats or weedlines.

In spring, try a spinner from 3 to 5 inches long. Later, when the water warms, try a 6- to 10-incher. You can regulate the depth at which the bait tracks by changing your retrieve speed and rod angle. When you want the bait to run deeper, slow down your retrieve and keep your rod tip low. For even more depth, let it sink for a few seconds before you start reeling. To keep the bait shallow, reel faster and hold your rod tip high. With a little practice, you can make the blades "bulge" the surface, creating a wake that attracts fish.

For extra attraction, tip a spinnerbait with a live minnow or a plastic grub. Don't use minnows or grubs more than 4 inches long or you'll get too many short strikes.

Spinners include: (1) bucktails, such as the Windels Original Harasser; and (2) spinnerbaits, such as the M/G Muskie Tandem.

Bulge a spinnerbait by holding your rod tip high and reeling fast enough so the blades almost, but not quite, break the surface. Bulging works best when the fish are active.

Fishing Topwaters

Not only is topwater fishing one of the most exciting ways to catch pike and muskies, there are times when it is one of the most effective.

When the fish are buried in dense weeds, for example, most other lures would foul in the vegetation. But the noise and surface disturbance from a topwater will draw the fish out of the weeds.

Topwaters work best from late spring through early fall, when water temperatures are warmest. They are much less effective in cold water.

Fishermen use a variety of topwaters for northern pike and muskies. Buzzbaits have a double- or triple-winged blade on a straight or safety-pin shaft. Stickbaits are long, slender plugs with no built-in action; they dart from side to side when you give the rod a series of sharp downward twitches. Propbaits have a propeller at one or both ends. Crawlers have a cupped face or arms that produce a wide wobble and a gurgling sound.

Fishing Subsurface Plugs

It's no wonder that subsurface plugs work so well for pike and muskies – their wobble and vibration mimic that produced by a swimming baitfish, the primary pike-muskie food.

The trick to fishing with subsurface plugs is to select one that runs at the depth you want to fish. If you're casting to a weedbed that tops off at 3 feet, for instance, it makes no sense to use a bait that runs at 10 feet; you'll spend all your time picking weeds off the hooks. Conversely, if the fish are holding at the base of a deep weedline, a shallow runner would not get down far

Topwaters include: (1) buzzbaits, such as the Blue Fox Double Buzzer; (2) stickbaits, such as Poe's Giant Jackpot; (3) propbaits, such as the Gooch's Tallywacker; and (4) crawlers, such as the Hi-Fin Creeper.

Subsurface plugs include: (1) crankbaits, such as the Storm Mag Wart; (2) minnow plugs, such as the Bomber Long A Magnum; (3) trolling plugs, such as the Believer; and (4) vibrating plugs, such as the Normark Rattl'n Rapala.

206

enough to draw a strike.

There are four basic types of subsurface plugs. Crankbaits have a broad front lip, which gives them a strong wobble. Minnow plugs have a narrower lip and slimmer body, so their wobble is less intense but more natural. Trolling plugs have an extra-wide wobble, because of their broad, flattened head. Vibrating plugs have no lip and the attachment eye is on the flattened back, giving them a very fast, tight wiggle.

Jerkbait Fishing

As their name suggests, jerkbaits are designed to be fished with a series of jerks of the rod, which imparts an erratic darting action much like that of an injured baitfish.

The majority of jerkbaits are floaters, although many anglers add weight to the hooks or body of the lure to get it down a little deeper.

Jerkbaits are normally fished with a series of sharp, downward twitches of the rod to achieve a side-to-side or up-and-down action. Fishermen normally use short, stiff rods so the rod tip does not hit the water on the downward stroke.

Jerkbaits vary widely in shape, size and action, but most of them fall into two categories. Gliders, which dart from side to side, and divers, which dart downward. Divers generally run deepest and, because they have little lateral movement, will track through sparse weeds better than a lure with broad side-to-side movement.

Fishing Spoons

These traditional pike-muskie baits are no less effective today than they were decades ago. One reason spoons work so well is that they're versatile. In most cases, you troll or retrieve them at a steady pace, but you can also use an erratic stop-and-go retrieve, jig them vertically in deep water or skitter them across the surface.

The main decision you must make when selecting spoons is thickness of the metal. Choose a thick spoon for distance casting; a thin one for maximum wobble.

If you'll be fishing in dense weeds or other heavy cover, select a weedless spoon. Add a pork strip or soft-plastic curlytail for extra attraction. Most of these baits have only a single hook; to improve your hooking percentage, make sure it is needle-sharp.

When fishing with spoons, attach them to a flexible, braided-wire leader. This way, they will have an enticing wobble. A thick wire leader restricts their action too much.

Jerkbaits include: (1) divers, such as the Suick Muskie Thriller; and (2) gliders, such as the Fudally Reef Hawg. The former has a metal tail fin that can be bent up or down to change the angle at which the lure dives.

Spoons include: (1) open-hook models, such as the Eppinger Dardevle; and (2) weedless models, such as the Johnson Silver Minnow tipped with an Uncle Josh pork strip.

Jigging

Most anglers do not associate jigs with pike and muskie fishing. Yet there are times when jigs will outproduce all other artificials.

A slow-moving jig is hard to beat in early spring or late fall, when cool water temperatures make the fish lethargic and unwilling to chase lures like bucktails and topwaters. Jigs are also effective after a cold front or in very clear water.

The most important considerations in jig selection are weight and head shape. If your jig is too light, you'll have a hard time keeping it close to the bottom, especially in a strong wind. Pike and muskies often strike a jig as it's sinking. If the jig is too heavy, it will sink faster than it should, giving the fish less time to make the decision to strike. Jigs for pike-muskie fishing normally weigh $3/8$ to $7/8$ ounce.

An ordinary roundhead jig is adequate for fishing on a clean bottom, but in weedy cover you'll need a brushguard jig. A swimmer head will keep the jig riding above the weeds. In late fall, when muskies are found on deep rock piles, pyramid jigs dragged along the bottom are most effective.

Jigs include: (1) round-head jigs, such as the Jack's Casting Shad Head, rigged with a Renosky Shad; (2) pyramid-head jigs, such as the G. Mahs Stand-Up Jig, rigged with a Mann's Jelly-Hoo; (3) brushguard jigs, such as the Jacobson Skirted Stalker, rigged with a Mojo Twin Tail; and (4) swimmer-head jigs, such as the Jack's Swimmer Head, rigged with a Kalin's Leapin' Lizard.

Fly Fishing

A big pike or muskie can test the skill of even the most accomplished fly fisherman. Luckily, the fish tend to make relatively short runs, so if you take your time and don't try to horse them in, you'll be able to tire them out and land them.

Pike and muskies are most vulnerable to fly fishing in spring. Warming water draws them into shallow weedy bays where they are easily taken on divers, poppers, sliders and large streamers. When the fish go deep in summer, you'll need weighted flies and sinking lines to reach them.

Depending on the size fish you expect to catch, select flies ranging from size 2 to 4/0. If you'll be fishing in weeds, brush or logs, be sure your fly has a mono or wire weedguard.

You'll need a 7- to 10-weight rod and a weight-forward line to cast these heavy, wind-resistant flies. Most anglers use a 6- to 9-foot leader with an 8- to 14-pound-test tippet and a 12- to 30-pound shock tippet made of multi-strand coated wire.

Flies include: (1) sliders, such as the Umpqua Swimming Baitfish; (2) divers, such as the Dahlberg's Mega Diver; (3) streamers, such as the Lefty's Deceiver; and (4) poppers, such as the Skipping Bug.

Live-bait Fishing

Only a few decades ago, live baitfish accounted for about three-fourths of all pike and muskies caught by anglers. That percentage is considerably lower today, but there are times when the fish are interested in nothing but baitfish.

When the bite is off because of cold water or for any other reason, baitfish will still produce. The majority of anglers use live baitfish, primarily suckers, chubs and shiners from 5 inches to more than a foot long. But dead baitfish, especially oily, smelly ones like smelt or ciscoes, are used a great deal by pike fishermen. They appeal to the pike's keen sense of smell more than do live baitfish.

You can fish your bait on a bobber rig or just cast it out and let it lie on the bottom. You can also cast it unweighted and give it a jerky retrieve to imitate a dying baitfish. Or, you can slow-troll it along the edge of a weedbed, using enough weight to keep it near the bottom.

Baitfish can be rigged with just a single hook, usually size 1/0 to 6/0, pushed through the nose. Be sure to attach the hook to a wire leader. You can also use baitfish on a quick-strike rig with one double or treble hook near the pectoral fin and the other near the dorsal. This way, you're able to set the hook immediately when a fish bites. Not only do you increase your hooking percentage, the fish don't have a chance to swallow the hook, so you can release them alive.

How to Bobber-fish for Pike & Muskies

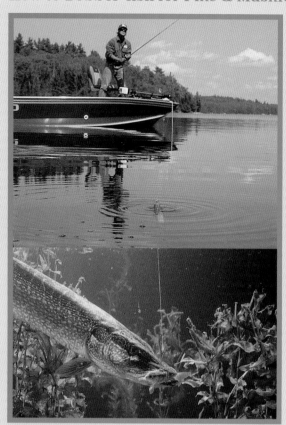

Feed line when your float goes under. In most cases, a pike or muskie grabs the bait sideways and starts swimming away. If it feels resistance, it may drop the bait. Pike and muskie often swim for a distance, then stop to turn the bait and swallow it headfirst.

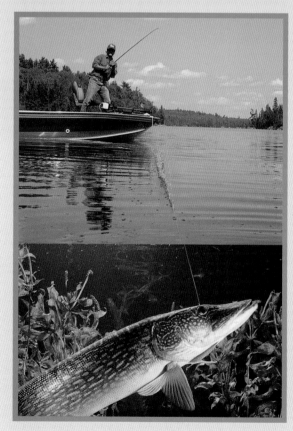

Set the hook when the fish starts moving again. Be sure that you've reeled up enough slack so you can feel the weight of the fish before setting. The time you must wait from the moment a pike or muskie takes your bait to the hook set varies from 30 seconds to 30 minutes, depending on the size of the baitfish.

How to Use the Figure-eight Technique

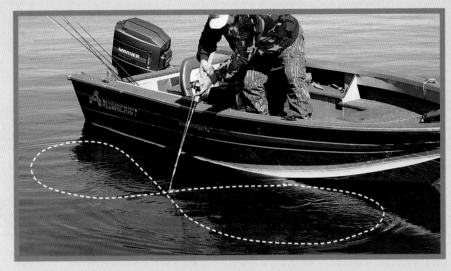

Reel the lure to within about a foot of the rod tip and, with the tip well beneath the surface, begin making large figure-eight patterns. Often the quick change of direction will entice the fish to strike.

Getting Started

When a northern pike or muskie decides to take your bait, nothing will change its mind. These fish have been known to ram the boat when an angler lifts a lure from the water.

But pike and muskies are not always willing biters. In fact, muskies may well be the toughest of all gamefish to catch. Even if you locate one, getting it to hit is another matter. They're notorious followers; some days you'll see a dozen for every one that strikes. Because of this trait, fishermen should learn the figure-eight maneuver (above).

Pike and muskies have bony mouths, so sharp hooks are a must. But hooks large enough for these fish are usually quite dull when you buy them. It pays to carry a good sharpening device that will handle big hooks.

Always carry jaw spreaders, needlenose pliers and sidecutters for clipping off hooks. You

can hand-land small pike and muskies, but for big ones, you may need a large net or cradle.

Most experienced anglers release big pike and muskies to fight again. But some fishermen make the mistake of bringing these fish into the boat where they may thrash around uncontrollably and injure themselves. A better option is to net or cradle the big fish, then keep the net or cradle in the water as you remove the hooks. As long as the fish is in the water, it won't be harmed.

Many pike and muskie anglers who fish with partners unhook these large fish without the use of a net or cradle. Working as a team, one angler grabs the tail of the played-out fish at boatside to prevent it from thrashing. The other angler frees the hooks with longnose pliers (above).

The strong catch-and-release ethic among dedicated muskie anglers has had a major impact in preserviing quality muskie fishing. Carry a camera to document your catch. If you want fish to eat, take small northern pike.

Fishing in Weeds

Knowing what kinds of weeds to fish and when to fish them is perhaps the biggest challenge facing pike and muskie anglers. You've probably read that the fish prefer certain kinds of weeds and avoid other kinds. Unfortunately, it's not quite that simple.

Broad-leaved species of cabbage, for example, are widely considered to be the top pike and muskie producers. But that doesn't mean you'll automatically find fish when you find the right kind of cabbage.

A cabbage bed in a shallow bay, for instance, produces well in spring because the fish are still in the shallows after spawning and the water is cool enough for them to be comfortable. By summer, however, most of the larger fish have moved to deeper, cooler water, leaving only a few small stragglers. By fall, cool temperatures in the shallows kill the cabbage. Once it turns brown and the leaves start to deteriorate, it provides little cover and no longer produces oxygen, so the remaining fish move out.

The same kind of cabbage on a deep hump, on the other hand, holds no fish in spring. The water is too cold and the weeds are not fully developed. But as the cabbage grows lush in summer, it draws a lot of fish. Some remain into fall because the weeds do not turn brown as early as those in the shallows.

Ideally, pike-muskie weeds should have broad leaves to provide plenty of shade, they should be tall enough to give cover to fish cruising just beneath the surface, and they should be spaced widely enough to allow the fish to maneuver easily. However, if there are no weeds of this type growing in the areas the fish are using, they'll select some other type.

Emergent weeds, such as bulrushes, don't fit this description, but they draw plenty of pike and muskies in spring, when the fish are still in their spawning bays, and in fall, when submerged weeds start to die.

Floating-leaved weeds, such as lily pads, also hold pike and muskies in spring, and may continue to hold them in summer, assuming the beds do not become choked with other weeds. The dense overhead canopy keeps the water a few degrees cooler than surrounding water warmed by the sun.

Deep submergent weeds, such as coontail, attract pike and muskies from midsummer through fall. Often these weeds form a dense blanket several feet thick, so the fish cruise just above them or along the edges. Deep submergents remain green longer than other plants.

Different weed types dictate different lures and fishing methods. To fish emergents and floating-leaved weeds, use weedless lures, such as spinnerbaits, weedless spoons and brushguard jigs. For working the tops of submergent weeds, use topwaters, spinnerbaits and swimmer-head jigs. You can also fish weedtops with shallow-running crankbaits, minnow plugs, jerkbaits and bucktails; use deeper-running models to work deep weedlines. To fish a pocket, use a brushguard jig or weedless spoon, or helicopter a spinnerbait into it.

For tight pockets, toss out a minnow on a slip-bobber setup, or rig a minnow on a weedless hook and freeline it through the weeds. When the fish are scattered over large weed flats, try trolling with spinnerbaits.

Weed fishing requires heavier-than-normal line, not only to horse fish from heavy cover, but to reduce the chances that abrasion from stems and leaves will weaken the line. Use either braided Dacron or extra tough mono. A longer-than-normal rod comes in handy for guiding your lure through the weeds.

In the summer, try trolling subsurface lures at speeds from 3 to 8 mph. for pike and muskies scattered over large weed flats or strung out along a weedline. You can cover the water in a hurry, and the fast-moving lures trigger lots of strikes.

Fishing in Woody Cover

Standing timber, stumps, sunken logs, fallen trees and brush are important pike-muskie cover, particularly in rivers and man-made lakes, where water-level fluctuations may limit growth of aquatic plants. Newly flooded reservoirs have better woody cover than old ones; in time, the small branches rot away and the wood deteriorates.

In most cases, the best woody cover is adjacent to deep water. Isolated clumps of trees, which often indicate an underwater hump, are some of the best pike-muskie hangouts. Timbered points that extend into the old river channel are also good producers. The fish can feed in or along the edge of the timber, then easily retreat to deep water in the channel.

Another important type of woody cover is the man-made fish attractor. Some of these devices are constructed much like a log cabin, with several layers of interlocking logs. Others are merely piles of branches lashed together and weighted with cement blocks. Most often, these structures are placed in areas with little other cover.

To fish protruding treetops, brush piles, newly fallen trees or any other shallow woody cover that still has fine branches, use a spinnerbait, weedless spoon or topwater lure. Brushguard jigs, regular jigs with light-wire hooks and crankbaits with the leading barbs of the trebles removed work well in deeper woody cover without many fine branches.

If you're convinced that a specific piece of woody cover is holding fish, but they're ignoring artificials, lower a quick-strike bobber rig with a live baitfish into or alongside the cover. When a fish bites, set the hook immediately and horse it out of the wood before it swims around a branch or log.

Sturdy tackle and heavier-than-normal line is a must when fishing the wood. Some reservoir anglers use line up to 50-pound test to pull fish out of the tangle. Heavy line also enables you to straighten hooks so you can free snagged lures. A lure retriever comes in handy too.

Brushy flats alongside a creek channel or the old river channel make excellent feeding areas for pike and muskies. You'll find most of the fish along the outside edge, where the flat drops into the channel.

Fishing After a Cold Front

Cold fronts top the list of excuses used by muskie anglers. It takes a severe cold front to slow the pike action, but even a mild cold front can shut down the muskies.

As a cold front approaches, the fish "turn on." They continue to feed heavily until the front passes. Then, the colder temperature, often coupled with clear skies and a strong northwest wind, causes the fish to move off the structure or bury themselves in weedy or woody cover. Feeding activity subsides as insect hatches stop and baitfish move out of the shallows.

The effects of a cold front are most noticeable on clear lakes, especially in spring when the fish are in shallow water. River fish are not immune to cold fronts, but show less response than lake fish.

You can increase your chances of catching cold-front pike and muskies by using the following tactics:

• Concentrate your efforts from late afternoon until just after dark, the time when the water temperature normally peaks. This may be the only time of day when the fish feed.

• Fish 5 to 10 feet deeper than normal. The clear skies allow sunlight to penetrate deeper.

• Stick with your prime spots, returning to them every couple of hours. Don't waste time exploring new water.

• Use live bait or smaller-than-normal lures and slow presentations.

• Present your lure or bait as close to the cover as possible. Cold-front fish are not chasers. A lure that bumps the cover may "wake them up."

• Try trolling just off structure where you've found fish before. This is the best way to catch fish that the cold front has pushed out of the weeds.

Behavior of pike and muskies changes dramatically with the passage of a cold front. Before the front, the fish (orange) are moving about and feeding along the edges of a weedbed and on top of the weeds. Anglers are often successful at catching these fish by using traditional lures and retrieves. But after the front passes, the fish (blue) are much less active. They bury in the weeds, suspend off to the side of them or move deeper. Because the location and mood of the fish has changed, you need to alter your methods to be successful.

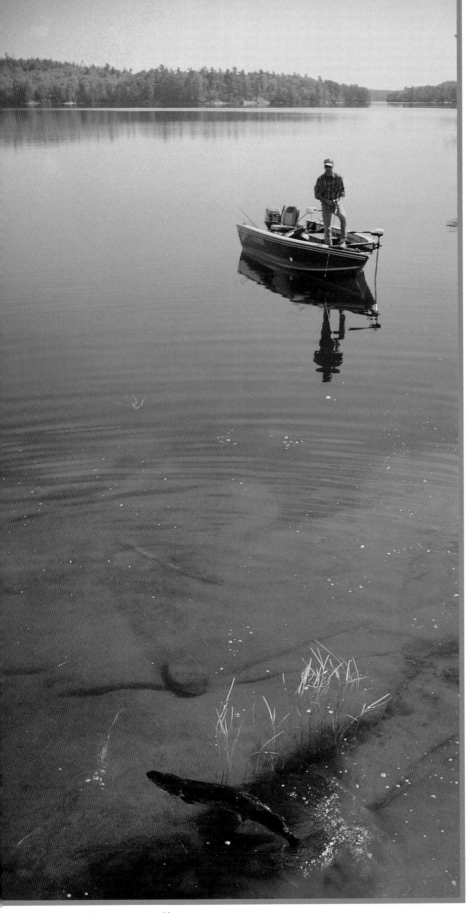

Keep your distance when casting to pike or muskies in clear water; they're much spookier than their murky-water relatives. Wearing bright clothes or casting your shadow over the fish could also spook them.

Fishing in Clear Water

The sight-feeding habits of pike and muskies explain why they flourish in clear lakes - and why they're better able to scrutinize lures and spot sloppy presentations than are their murky-water relatives.

Deep, clear, oligotrophic lakes and early-stage mesotrophic lakes can be especially tough. Because the depths are well oxygenated, the fish have no trouble descending below the thermocline to pursue coldwater baitfish such as ciscoes. Instead of being tightly linked to cover, where they're easy to find, the fish spend much of their time suspended in open water.

Clearwater fish are spookier too. They're more likely to spot your boat, see your shadow or notice a heavy line or leader.

But clear lakes produce some trophy-sized pike and muskies, so it pays to learn how to fish these waters. To improve your success, consider the following:

Overcast, windy days are much better than sunny, calm ones.

Pike and muskies tend to feed earlier and later in the day than in lower-clarity waters. Muskies may bite best at night.

Try these lakes in spring and fall, when the fish are in the shallows, rather than in summer, when they're suspended.

Select lures in natural colors, such as white, black, brown and gray. A small amount of fluorescent color, such as an orange spinner blade, may help, but the entire lure should not be fluorescent.

Use lures that give you a little extra depth. Examples include deep-diving crankbaits, weighted jerkbaits and heavy bucktails.

Small-diameter lines also get your lures a little deeper and are less likely to spook the fish.

If you think you know where the fish are, but they won't bite, try live bait.

Fishing in Low-clarity Water

Pike and muskies thrive in some lakes where the visibility is only a few inches. They become accustomed to feeding in the discolored water, apparently using their lateral-line system more than vision.

Low clarity may be caused by an algae bloom, suspended silt or clay, or bog stain (opposite page). If the water is permanently discolored, the fish feed on a fairly regular schedule. But if the discoloration is temporary, usually the result of a heavy rain, vision feeders have trouble finding food - and anglers' lures. Fishing remains slow until the water starts to clear.

Most low-clarity lakes are shallow and eutrophic. They warm sooner than most other lakes in spring and offer good early-season fishing. Normally, these lakes have little oxygen below the thermocline in summer, so the fish are confined to relatively shallow water. In fact, you'll commonly find them at depths of 15 feet or less all year, and sometimes in only a foot or two.

Panfish are the major food in many of these lakes, so pike and muskies spend much of their time cruising the weedy cover where the small fish live. But in extremely murky lakes, sunlight cannot penetrate deep enough to promote growth of rooted vegetation, so pike and muskies use other types of cover, such as rocks and logs.

Unlike clear lakes, where the fish usually bite best early and late in the day or at night, low-clarity lakes are better during the middle of the day. The

"night bite" is apt to be slow. Calm, sunny weather generally shuts down the fishing in clear lakes, but not in murky ones.

Because the fish rely so heavily on their lateral-line sense to find food, large, noisy lures, including topwaters, rattling plugs and big-bladed spinnerbaits and bucktails, are excellent choices. Bright and fluorescent colors are usually more productive than drab ones.

Whatever lure you select, use a steady, rather than erratic, retrieve. This way, the fish can home in on the lure more easily. Always make a figure eight, or at least an L-turn, at the end of the retrieve, in case a fish is following.

Finesse is not much of an issue in these lakes. You don't have to worry about the fish seeing your boat or shadow, and you can get by with heavy lines and leaders. But don't go so heavy that your casting and lure presentation suffers.

Tips for Fishing Low-clarity Waters

Select a topwater with an intense action when fishing low-clarity waters. Pike and muskies are most likely to notice lures that kick up a lot of water, and the commotion won't spook them.

Rocky points or any exposed rocks on the bottom hold pike and muskies, especially in lakes with little weedy or woody cover. It takes only a few boulders to attract fish.

Fishing for Suspended Northern Pike & Muskies

Radio-tagging studies have proven that pike and muskies suspend more often than most anglers realize. This behavior is most common in deep, clear lakes and reservoirs with high populations of pelagic (open-water) baitfish. In some lakes, big muskies suspend after spawning, then move to shallow structure once the weeds develop.

Many anglers hesitate to fish for suspended pike and muskies; they believe their movements are random and discovering a pattern is impossible. But in most cases, the fish suspend near some type of structure or a school of baitfish, so locating them is not as much of a guessing game as you might think.

Trolling is the quickest way to find suspended fish. In natural lakes, motor along the edge of weedy shoreline breaks, points and humps; in reservoirs, along the edge of old river or creek channels. Always S-troll, steering toward the structure, then away from it.

If you have no idea of the right depth, start trolling in the thermocline. Watch your depth finder closely for marks indicating fish or schools of baitfish, then set the depth of your lines accordingly. As a rule, pike hang a little deeper than muskies because they prefer cooler water. Some anglers pinpoint individual fish or baitfish schools on their graph, enter its position in a GPS unit, then troll through the spot.

When you're trolling through fish but can't trigger a strike, try motoring at double or even triple your normal speed. Or, try ripping the lure forward, then quickly dropping it back. The abrupt change of action often makes a difference.

You can get down as much as 30 feet with deep-diving crankbaits and minnow plugs, and another 5 to 10 feet with each ounce of lead added to your line. Trolling with downriggers or wire line will get you even deeper and give you more precise depth control.

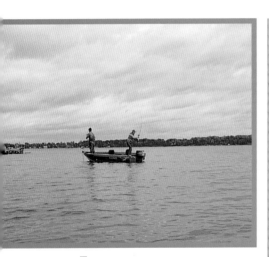

Try an occasional cast toward deep water when working a weedline. Or, have your partner cast out while you cast in. This way, you'll find out whether the fish are hugging the weeds or suspended over deep water.

Night Fishing for Muskies

Until recently, night fishing for Esocids was thought to be a waste of time; anglers believed the fish fed only in daylight hours. This is usually a safe assumption in regard to pike, but night fishing for muskies produces some impressive catches, especially on clear lakes or lakes with heavy daytime boat traffic. Hybrids have an intermediate tendency to bite after dark.

Night-fishing action peaks in midsummer, when the surface temperature is warmest. Night stalkers prefer hot, calm, muggy weather, along with a full moon. Night fishing after a cold front is not as productive, although muskies may bite for an hour or so after dark.

At night, you'll find muskies on the same structure as in daylight hours, but much shallower. It's not unusual to catch them in water less than 2 feet deep.

Following a calm day with steadily rising temperatures, try topwater baits or bucktails; on a windy night or after a day of falling temperatures, try a crankbait or other subsurface lure. The fish aren't likely to notice a topwater when the surface is choppy.

Select lures that can be retrieved slowly and steadily, yet make a lot of noise or produce strong vibrations. If you use a lure with an erratic action, fish won't be able to home in on it and they'll often miss it. Many anglers prefer black lures, but color is less important than size; larger lures make larger silhouettes.

Be sure to set out markers in daylight so you can easily find your spots after dark. Carry a strong spotlight so you can see

the markers from a distance. If you motor over the fish in an attempt to find your spot, they'll move away.

Some anglers make the mistake of setting a lantern in their boat in an attempt to see better. Although a bright light illuminates the area around the boat, it impairs distance vision, so you won't be able to see casting targets or surface strikes. With no light, your eyes will adjust to the darkness in 15 minutes or so.

When you see or hear a fish "blow up" on your lure, resist the urge to set the hook. Sometimes, they'll slash at it 3 or 4 times before they get it. Don't set the hook until you feel the weight of the fish.

It pays to keep your boat orderly when fishing at night. Close your tackle box and stash any excess gear to prevent unnecessary tangles. Always carry an extra rod in case of a bad snarl or backlash.

Wear a headlamp covered with green cellophane when night fishing. The light enables you to see most follows, yet it won't spook the fish. Another option: draw your lure through the area illuminated by your green bow light.

Clamp a shop light to the gunwale after replacing the bulb with a 60-watt, 12-volt RV bulb. Turn the light on only when you want to land a fish. Otherwise, it may spook any fish following your lure.

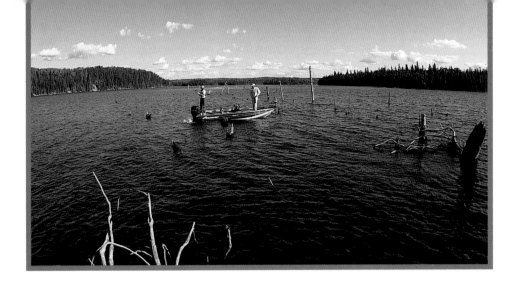

Fishing in Fluctuating Water

The challenge in fishing pike or muskies in rivers and reservoirs is knowing where to find them and how to fish them at different water stages. After a heavy rain, for example, a river may rise several feet overnight, and the normally clear water looks more like heavily creamed coffee. The fast current forces the fish out of their usual haunts and into newly created eddies along the bank. If the rising water spills over the bank into adjacent lowlands, the fish will move into the flooded area to escape the current.

The muddy water requires lures that are highly visible and produce a lot of noise or vibration. Good choices include bulky bucktails and spinnerbaits with large Colorado blades, big rattling plugs and noisy topwaters.

As a rule, the fish continue to feed as long as the water is rising. One theory is that the rising water washes in food for smaller fish, activating them and, in turn, stimulating pursuit by predators. Feeding usually slows when the water starts to drop and the fish move to deeper structure.

Water-level changes need not be severe to cause problems for anglers. Often, a rise or drop of only a few inches displaces the fish, and an even smaller drop may slow the bite. As a rule, the faster the water drops, the poorer the fishing.

In big rivers, falling water forces pike and muskies out of shallow backwaters and into the main channel. In smaller rivers, the fish move into the deepest pools. Fish confined in pools are extremely vulnerable. As their food supply dwindles, they grow hungrier and thus easier to catch.

In reservoirs, rising water brings the fish closer to shore and farther back into the creek arms. You'll find them on shallow, timbered flats, along the bases of rocky bluffs and way up into secondary and tertiary creek arms. When the water drops, they move back to the river or creek channels.

River and reservoir anglers pay close attention to water-level gauges, noting not only the reading at the moment, but also whether the water is rising or falling. Along many big rivers, you can get water-level and flow information from local Army Corps of Engineers offices.

Where to Find Pike & Muskies in Low Waters

Pools below rapids. These spots draw a wide variety of baitfish and gamefish in low water, so they make ideal pike-muskie feeding areas.

Extremely low water in reservoirs, usually the result of fall drawdowns, drives pike and muskies out of shallow portions of the main lake and the creek arms and into the old river channel and deep creek channels.

Ice Fishing for Northern Pike

Even before ice forms on lakes and river backwaters, pike go on a feeding binge that continues for several weeks after freeze-up. Some of the year's fastest action takes place during this period.

Pike feed more actively than most other gamefish in winter. Muskies feed very little once the water temperature falls below 40°F, but ice fishermen occasionally catch one by accident.

In early winter, look for pike in shallow, weedy bays, especially around large patches of green weeds. Before freeze-up, try to locate weedy areas likely to produce once the ice forms. You can also find green weeds by peering down holes in the thin ice.

By midwinter, most pike have moved out of the bays into deeper water, although small pike sometimes stay in the bays all winter. Larger pike may stay around too, if the bay has deep enough water. Weedy cover becomes less important in midwinter; most pike hold along the edges of deep points, humps or rock piles.

Pike activity slows in midwinter, but they may be more concentrated. If you find the right spot, you'll catch plenty of fish. If your lake is prone to

oxygen sags in winter, you'll probably find the pike right under the ice, where the oxygen level is highest. Pike return to the shallow bays in late winter and feed heavily until ice-out.

River pike spend most of the winter in weedy bays and backwaters. They remain in these slack-water areas as long as the oxygen level holds up. Once it starts to sag, however, they move closer to the current, often to the mouth of the backwater or bay or into the main river. When the ice begins to thaw in late winter, pike return to their early-winter spots.

Tip-ups account for the vast majority of winter pike. Where it's legal to use more than one line, groups of anglers commonly set out a spread of tip-ups large enough to cover an entire bay or sunken island. While watching their tip-ups, anglers

often jig with another line.

Tip-up fishermen generally use live baitfish from 5 inches to more than a foot long, but dead smelt and ciscoes are gaining in popularity. Some anglers feel that dead bait works better when pike are inactive and don't want to chase a lively minnow.

Spool tip-ups with 25- to 40-pound Dacron line or nylon-coated tip-up line. The latter doesn't soak up water, so it won't freeze on above-water reels. Rig baitfish as you would for bobber fishing using a 20- to 30-pound braided-wire leader and a single hook, treble hook or quick-strike rig.

Jigging offers some definite advantages over tip-up fishing. Because you can move around more easily, you can keep trying new holes until you find fish. And jigging will sometimes trigger strikes from pike that refuse a stationary bait.

Select a fairly stiff jigging rod about 3 1/2 feet long and a spinning or baitcasting reel with 8- to 12-pound mono. Any good-sized jigging lure will catch pike. Flashy or bright colors such as silver, red-and-white and chartreuse generally work best. When the fish are aggressive, try large lures; when they're finicky, use smaller ones. You can also jig with a dead baitfish on a quick-strike rig.

Place tip-ups at a variety of depths along a breakline to find active northern pike. Suspend sucker or shiner minnows above the weeds to prevent fouling. In deep water, or in areas without weeds, keep the minnows near the bottom.

Trophy Fishing

As northern pike and, to some extent, muskies grow larger, they prefer cooler water. This usually means they'll be found deeper than the smaller members of their breed. This deep-water pattern is strongest in summer. At other times of the year, the fish can find cool enough water in the shallows.

Many trophy fishermen have discovered that they could catch larger muskies by trolling rather than by casting, mainly because trolling allows them to keep their lure in deep water more of the time.

Because large northern pike have a stronger penchant for cold water than do muskies, they're often found at even greater depths in summer, as there is adequate food and oxygen. Pike also satisfy their need for cold water by congregating in spring holes.

Until recently, most writers have linked pike and muskies to shallow, weedy water. Paintings often show the fish lurking in dense weeds or rocketing skyward out of a thick weedbed. The scarcity of big pike in summer is usually attributed to sore mouths resulting from the loss of teeth. In reality, however, pike and muskies in most waters feed heavily in summer. They just don't spend much time in the places most anglers expect to find them.

Fishing the shallows makes sense in spring and fall, when the water is cool, although the fish may go deep in late fall. But in summer, the odds are with the angler who works deeper water.

Not to say that you'll never catch a big pike or muskie in the shallows in summer, but in most waters, it's an oddity. Muskie anglers who ply shallow weedbeds catch a few respectable fish, but most admit that the going gets tough when warm weather sets in.

Shallow weedbeds that do

Thanks to fishing organizations such as Muskies, Inc., most avid muskie anglers practice catch-and-release.

attract big pike and muskies in summer have one thing in common: deep water nearby. Evidently the fish rest in the depths, then move into the weeds to feed. Seldom will you find trophy-caliber pike or muskies in a shallow weedbed far from deep water.

Just how deep is deep? It all depends on the type of water. In a shallow, eutrophic lake, for instance, the depths lack oxygen in summer, so the fish can't go below the thermocline. If there is adequate oxygen, however, the thermocline is no barrier. In Ontario's gigantic Lake Nipigon, for example, pike have been netted in water more than 100 feet deep.

When the fish go deep, locating them can be a problem. Some relate to deep humps or points; others roam open water, if that's where the food is. In deep, oligotrophic lakes, for example, trophy-sized pike and muskies feed heavily on ciscoes and whitefish, both of which often suspend over deep water.

Anglers equipped with good electronics can graph the fish, then troll for them using lead-core or wire line, or downriggers.

Some deep-diving crankbaits can reach depths of 30 feet or more if you use small-diameter mono from 12- to 20-pound test. But fish suspended in open water are rarely enthusiastic biters. And the spot where you catch them one day may not produce the next.

Muskies on shallow structure don't roam as much as those in open water. Should a big muskie follow your lure, but refuse to strike, note the location; the fish will probably stay in the general vicinity. Trophy hunters sometimes work on the same muskie for months before they finally catch it. Big pike are much less likely to hang out in a specific area.

Most trophy specialists recommend big lures for catching big fish, but there are times when you'll do better on smaller lures. In lakes where small perch are the main forage, for instance, a 6-inch lure may be more effective than a 12-incher. Smaller-than-normal lures also work better in early spring, after a cold front or at other times when the fish are not feeding actively.

Many trophy hunters swear by huge live baitfish, usually suckers from 14 to 20 inches long. But baitfish this large are hard to find, so you'll probably have to catch your own.

With these big baits, you may have to wait 10 minutes or more to set the hook. If you follow the recommended procedure of letting the fish swim off, stop to swallow the bait and then swim off again before you set, chances are the fish will be deeply hooked. A quick-strike rig (below) solves this problem. You'll be able to set the hook right away and greatly reduce deep-hooking losses.

As a rule, your best chances for big fish are in big waters – large lakes and river systems. Just as goldfish attain only a small fraction of their size potential in an aquarium, pike and muskies seldom reach maximum size in small lakes or streams. And even if they did, the odds of their succumbing to a well-placed lure are considerably higher.

One notable exception to the big water/big fish rule: Even small lakes with a good supply of salmonid (salmon family) forage often produce gigantic pike and sometimes muskies. Western trout lakes with good populations of kokanee salmon, for instance, yield astounding numbers of 20- to 30-pound pike because of the coldwater, high-fat food. Some of these lakes are only a few hundred acres in size.

Of course, the best way to boost your chances of connecting with a trophy is to fish in waters that have a lot of them. After all, you can't catch what isn't there.

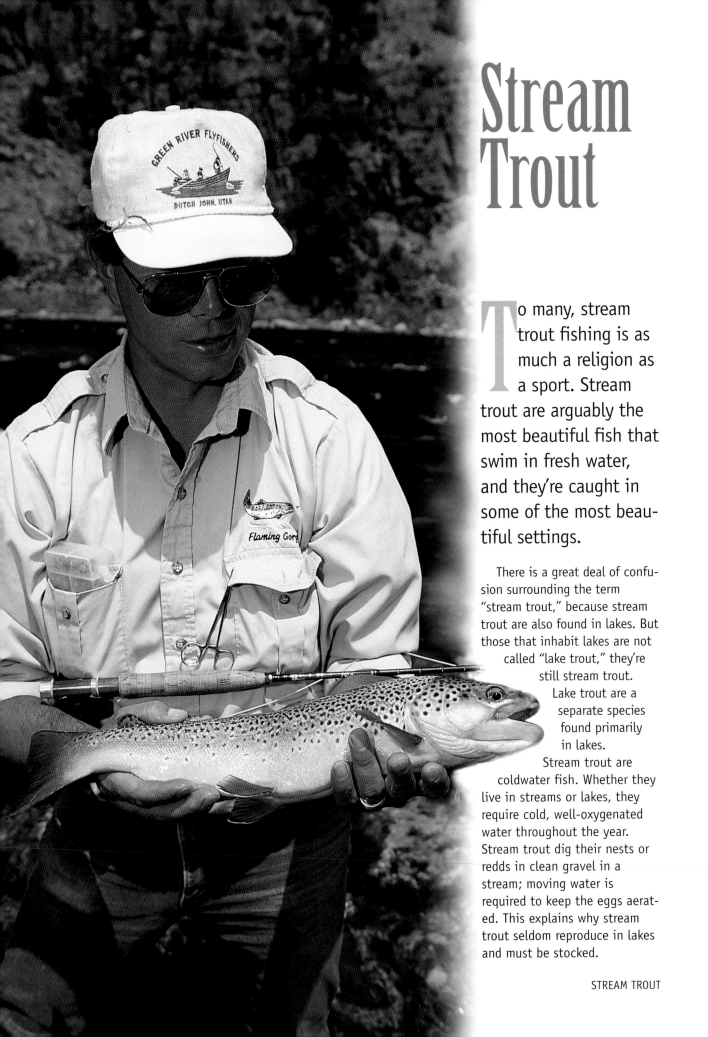

Stream Trout

To many, stream trout fishing is as much a religion as a sport. Stream trout are arguably the most beautiful fish that swim in fresh water, and they're caught in some of the most beautiful settings.

There is a great deal of confusion surrounding the term "stream trout," because stream trout are also found in lakes. But those that inhabit lakes are not called "lake trout," they're still stream trout.

Lake trout are a separate species found primarily in lakes.

Stream trout are coldwater fish. Whether they live in streams or lakes, they require cold, well-oxygenated water throughout the year. Stream trout dig their nests or redds in clean gravel in a stream; moving water is required to keep the eggs aerated. This explains why stream trout seldom reproduce in lakes and must be stocked.

Fishermen pursue four major stream trout species in North America. Brook trout are considered the easiest to catch. They favor water of about 54°F, and are rarely found where the water temperature exceeds 65°F. As a result, they usually live in the upper reaches of streams or near the mouths of tributaries. Rainbows prefer water of about 55°F, but are found in waters up to 70°F. They prefer relatively swift water. Cutthroats are found mainly in the West; they prefer the same water temperatures as rainbows. Brown trout, considered the most difficult to catch, favor water of about 65°F but can tolerate temperatures as warm as 75°F. They sometimes live in warmer, slower-moving streams unsuitable to other trout.

Stream trout rely heavily on insects for food, but small fish make up a large part of the diet of lake-dwelling stream trout. Small fish are also the major food for trout in warmer, marginal-quality streams. These waters have fewer trout, but are more likely to produce a trophy.

Trout are known for their wariness, and it's easy to understand why. In addition to man, many kinds of birds, mammals, crustaceans and other fish prey upon them. When alarmed, they immediately take cover beneath overhanging vegetation, undercut banks or fallen trees. Or they hide behind a boulder or in a deep pool.

Large trout hooked in small streams are difficult to land. Fast, powerful swimmers, big trout instinctively dash for cover when hooked, often wrapping your line around a snag and breaking free.

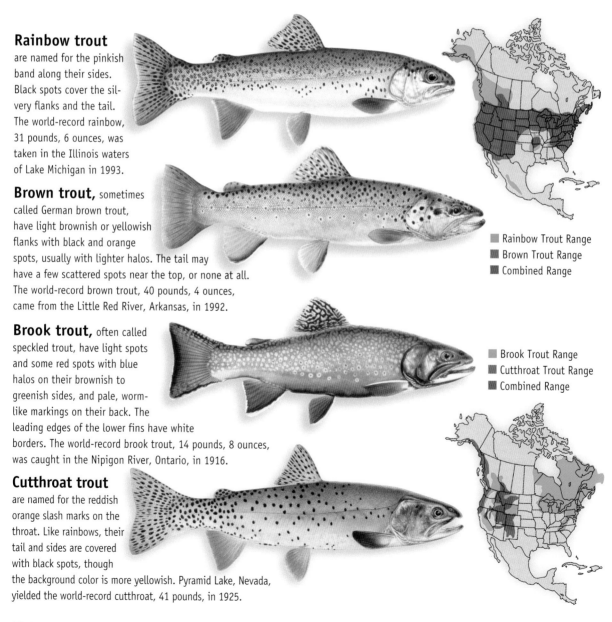

Rainbow trout are named for the pinkish band along their sides. Black spots cover the silvery flanks and the tail. The world-record rainbow, 31 pounds, 6 ounces, was taken in the Illinois waters of Lake Michigan in 1993.

Brown trout, sometimes called German brown trout, have light brownish or yellowish flanks with black and orange spots, usually with lighter halos. The tail may have a few scattered spots near the top, or none at all. The world-record brown trout, 40 pounds, 4 ounces, came from the Little Red River, Arkansas, in 1992.

Brook trout, often called speckled trout, have light spots and some red spots with blue halos on their brownish to greenish sides, and pale, worm-like markings on their back. The leading edges of the lower fins have white borders. The world-record brook trout, 14 pounds, 8 ounces, was caught in the Nipigon River, Ontario, in 1916.

Cutthroat trout are named for the reddish orange slash marks on the throat. Like rainbows, their tail and sides are covered with black spots, though the background color is more yellowish. Pyramid Lake, Nevada, yielded the world-record cutthroat, 41 pounds, in 1925.

■ Rainbow Trout Range
■ Brown Trout Range
■ Combined Range

■ Brook Trout Range
■ Cutthroat Trout Range
■ Combined Range

Where to Catch Stream Trout in Rivers & Streams

Most anglers would be amazed by the number of trout living in a typical coldwater stream. But the fish are seldom seen because they spend most of the day in cover. They show themselves only when they leave cover to find food.

As a rule, trout feed most heavily when the light is dim. Insect activity usually peaks during evening hours, leaving the stream teeming with prime trout food. So it's not surprising that many anglers prefer to fish late in the day.

During an insect hatch, trout may go on a feeding binge and catching them is easy. But not all insects hatch at the same time. The best strategy is to monitor the hatches on your stream and plan your fishing accordingly.

Water temperature also affects feeding activity. In spring, trout are most active in the afternoon when the water is warmest. Later in summer, they feed in the early morning when the water is coolest.

The largest trout are usually caught during peak feeding times. They keep smaller ones away from the best feeding spots. Small trout are forced to feed in areas that aren't quite as good.

Rising water may be a good indication that trout are feeding. Rains wash insects and other foods off streambanks and overhanging trees. As the stream rises and the current grows stronger, insect larvae and other morsels are dislodged from bottom. Trout begin feeding when the swirling water carries food past their lies.

The best feeding lies are places where the natural flow of water gathers food. Examples are eddies, deep holes below rapids or waterfalls and shallow riffles. On warm, sunny days, trout may hold under shaded streambanks, eating food that falls or washes into the water.

When not feeding, trout seek shade and cover in resting areas beneath undercut banks and logs, below large rocks or in deep pools. Even when resting, however, a trout will dart from cover to grab food as it drifts by.

Trout location may change during the year, depending upon water temperature. A stream with springs scattered along its course stays cold enough for trout all summer. But if spring-flow is confined to one section, the remainder of the stream may become too warm, concentrating the trout in water cooled by the springs.

Following is a list of some of the most important spots to find stream trout in moving water.

Prime Locations in Streams:

• Riffles are excellent morning and evening feeding areas for trout. Riffles hold an abundance of insect life, but trout are hesitant to feed in riffles during the day, because they would be exposed to predators in the shallow water.

• Runs are deep, narrow, moderately fast-moving areas between riffles and pools. Runs hold good-sized trout most anytime, as long as they have adequate cover.

• Eddies form both upstream and downstream of a boulder. Unfortunately, many anglers don't realize this, and they work only the downstream side. Eddies also form downstream of points, sharp bends, islands and obstacles such as bridge pilings.

• Pocket water is shallow with many scattered boulders. The water may seem too shallow for trout, but the deep pockets that form below the boulders make excellent trout cover.

• Deep pools make good mid-day resting areas for medium- to large-sized trout. Pools are easy to recognize because their surface is smoother and the water looks darker than other areas of the stream.

• Undercuts usually form along outside bends from the force of the current cutting into the bank. They provide shade and overhead protection from predators and are most likely to hold trout in midday.

• Plunge pools at the base of a falls often hold the largest trout. The force of the cascading water scours out a deep hole and creates an eddy that enables trout to escape the fast current.

Current pattern determines distribution of trout in a stream. Trout will not waste energy constantly fighting the current, so they take cover in protected areas such as (1) eddies below boulders, (2) eddies that form beneath undercut banks on outside bends and (3) eddies that form below gravel bars.

STREAM TROUT

Where to Catch Stream Trout in Lakes

Stream trout thrive in a variety of coldwater lakes, from tiny ponds to immense bodies of water such as lakes Superior and Michigan. Because the fish require such cold water, however, most lakes do not have suitable habitat.

Most huge, deep bodies of water can support trout because their volume is so immense that the water never gets too warm. Lakes located at high altitudes or in the Far North also stay cool enough for trout all year. Most other small lakes and ponds, however, will not support trout unless they are spring-fed, because their water gets too warm in summer.

Two-story lakes have warmwater fish in their warm upper layer and trout in the depths. These lake are low enough in fertility that the depths contain adequate oxygen throughout the year.

In some lakes, trout populations are continually replenished by reproduction in tributary streams. However, stream trout cannot reproduce in most lakes and reservoirs, so they must be stocked.

Much of the year, trout remain near shore, feeding on minnows, insects and crustaceans. They sometimes school around food-rich inlets or near rock bars, sunken islands and points extending from shore. Their location, however, depends more on water temperature than on structure or bottom type.

During summer, trout may be forced deeper as the lake warms. They often squeeze into the narrow band of the thermocline because water below this point has too little oxygen. Although the surface water is warm, trout rise to feed on insects in early morning and late evening.

Compared to most gamefish, lake-dwelling trout are easy to catch. As a result, their numbers can be quickly reduced if fishing pressure is heavy. The best angling is in lightly fished waters where trout can grow for several years before they are caught.

Following is a list of some of the best locations to catch stream trout in lakes.

Prime Lake Locations:

• Gradually sloping shorelines hold the most trout in deep, very cold lakes. The sun has a chance to warm the water along the shore, concentrating food and attracting trout.

• Rocky points, especially long, gradually sloping ones, are prime feeding areas in many trout lakes. Trout move up on the points in morning and evening to

This fly fisherman is casting for rainbow trout along a gradual shoreline of Lake Cholila, Argentina.

feed on hatching insects and forage for bottom organisms.

• Stream mouths are consistent trout producers in most types of trout lakes, because the inflowing water carries a variety of insect life.

• The thermocline may be the only suitable summertime habitat in some two-story lakes.

The surface waters are too warm and the depths lack oxygen, so trout are forced into a narrow layer, usually at a depth range of 20 to 30 feet.

• Weedbeds provide the shallow-water cover that trout require. Trout are hesitant to leave weedy cover, because they become easy targets for preda-

tory birds. The weeds also harbor insects, crustaceans and other foods.

• Shallow bays hold trout in early spring. Water in the bays warms much faster than that in the main lake, drawing minnows and starting insect hatches. When the bays warm, trout move back to the main lake.

Rainbow trout in lakes often search for insects on gradually sloping rocky points.

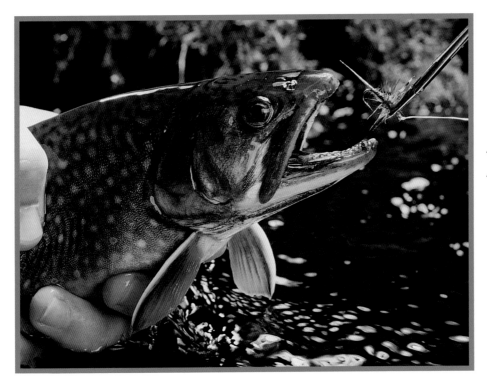

This brook trout, which was fooled with an Adams dry fly, came from one of New York's most famous trout streams, the Beaverkill.

How to Catch Stream Trout

Stream trout survive by being wary. Any sudden movement, shadow, noise or vibration will send them darting for cover. And once spooked, no amount of coaxing will get a trout to bite. If it is obvious that a trout has been disturbed, move on to another spot, because it may be a while before the fish resumes feeding. Because trout are so skittish, you must take extra care when approaching a trout's lie and presenting your lure.

When approaching the stream, for example, keep movement to a minimum. Study the water carefully to locate possible trout lies. Plan your fishing strategy before making the first cast. Wear drab colors, keep low and avoid open backgrounds. Because light rays bend at the water surface, trout can see all but the lowest objects along the streambank.

When wading, try to avoid scuffing the bottom, making large ripples or casting a shadow over the suspected lie of a trout.

Fly Fishing for Trout

Why fly-fish? After all, you can catch trout and salmon by spinning or baitcasting, both of which are easier to learn.

Fly fishing is by far the oldest of these methods, with a history stretching back at least six centuries. So the modern fly angler, equipped with a lightweight graphite rod rather than a buggy-whip wooden pole, has the satisfaction of carrying on a long and colorful tradition.

But nostalgia, no matter how strong, can't account for the survival of this old-time method into the space age, or for the manifest increase in its popularity in recent years. Despite its ancient origins, fly fishing remains a versatile and productive way to outwit wary salmonids.

Many of the most common foods of trout can be imitated only with flies; even the tiniest spinning and casting lures are much too bulky. Aquatic insects, such as mayflies and caddisflies, make up most of the diet of stream trout. Imitations of these delicate creatures are much too light to be cast with ordinary spinning or baitcasting techniques.

In fact, any trout food can be imitated successfully with flies. With a 6- or 7-weight fly line and a rod to match, you can fish anything from the tiniest midge imitations, not much bigger than a gnat, on up to streamers that simulate minnows several inches long.

The most frantic angling for stream trout comes during cloudlike insect hatches. yet it can also be the most frustrating. The fish may be rising all around you, but if you're limited to casting hardware, you're almost certainly out of luck. When rising to a hatch, trout generally refuse all imitations of other types of food.

Some of the biggest trout feed almost entirely on baitfish. In lakes, spoons and minnow plugs usually work better for these fish than streamer flies, which don't have much action in the still water. But in streams the current gives streamers an erratic, undulating movement more lifelike than the steady wobbling of hardware. And generally you can mimic the size, shape, and color of particular baitfish more closely with flies than with plugs or spoons.

Many famous trout streams have flies-only regulations. Although spinning and baitcasting equipment is sometimes allowed, such tackle makes it difficult to present a fly realistically enough for the educated trout found in these waters. For casting flies softly and maneuvering them like living creatures through a maze of currents, fly-fishing tackle nearly always works best.

Some anglers hesitate to try fly fishing because matching the hatch seems too complicated. But you don't have to know the insects by their species names, or carry scores of different fly patterns. In nearly all cases, an approximate imitation will do the job. Actually, a hatch is not so much a problem as an opportunity. Seeing exactly what the fish are feeding on is a big advantage; in most other kinds of fishing, all you can do is guess.

It's true that learning to fly-fish takes time and effort. To become really skilled may require several seasons of experience on the water. But it's also true that you can start enjoying this traditional way of angling, and start catching fish, after only a couple of brief practice sessions.

As in any other kind of fishing, the learning is part of the fun. Actually, it's a process that never ends, even if you fish a lifetime. The tips on the following pages will get you started right.

Choosing Equipment for Fly Fishing

If you're new to fly fishing for trout, you don't need to spend thousands of dollars getting rigged up with several different fly rod and reel combos suited for every situation imaginable. Instead, consider where you'll be fishing, what size trout swim in those waters, and what size fly you'll need to cast.

Although there are times when the biggest trout in the stream will take the smallest fly in your box, those times are the exception. Smaller trout tend to be insect eaters; big trout, fish eaters. So fly size and weight of tackle tend to increase with the size of the trout. To simplify your equipment choice, think about whether you'll be catching more light trout (fish weighing less than a couple of pounds) than heavy trout (fish weighing 5 pounds or more).

LIGHT TROUT. Small stream enthusiasts rely on short rods, light lines and tiny flies for the skillful presentation these fish demand. For them, a rod that's capable of delivering a fly with pinpoint accuracy at 20 to 30 feet is more important than one that will cast an entire line. Specifically, use a 1- to 5-weight fly rod, double-taper or weight-forward fly line, 7½- to 12-foot leaders, and tippets from 1-pound test (8X) to 4-pound test (5X).

HEAVY TROUT. You'll need heavier tackle for casting big, wind-resistant flies and powering good-sized trout out of fast current or dense cover. Big trout are usually found in big water, and this type of tackle also helps make the long casts necessary to reach the fish and to punch the line into a strong wind. Specifically, use a 7- to 9-weight fly rod, double-taper or weight-forward fly line, 7½- to 9-foot leaders, and tippets from 5-pound test (4X) to 15-pound test (0X).

If you want to buy a single outfit that will work for most trout fishing, consider a 9-foot, 6-weight rod, with balanced reel and line. Although it may not be ideal for casting the tiniest mayfly patterns or the biggest streamers, it will do the job in most trout-fishing situations.

Treat your fly with a paste dressing so it floats high. Be sure the fly is dry before applying the dressing. If not, dry it with a desiccant powder.

Adams

Cast up and across the stream. Allow the fly to float downstream naturally with the current. As the fly drifts, strip in any slack line.

Fishing with Dry Flies

Nothing is more suspenseful than watching a big trout or salmon rise slowly to a floating fly, perhaps to reject it at the last moment or perhaps to engulf it and give you a battle demanding all your finesse.

Despite the intimidating technical discussions in books and magazines, dry-fly angling is generally the easiest way to fool a trout with a fly. It offers these advantages:

• You can read surface currents easily.

• If the trout are rising, you can see where they are and often what they're feeding on as well.

• You know exactly where your fly is and whether it's working as it should.

• You can detect strikes by sight.

Dry flies are designed to imitate the adult stages of various aquatic insects. The classic dry, with a stiff tail and hackle and a pair of upright wings, is a good approximation of a mayfly. Stonefly imitations are similar but larger, with a single hair wing angled backward. Caddis patterns are small, like mayfly imitations, but have wings lying tentlike along the body; they are sometimes tied without hackle. Midge flies, almost microscopic,

Avoid drag. If the fly floats faster or slower than the current, it leaves a wake (left) that gives it an unnatural appearance.

If trout ignore a drag-free drift, try skating your dry fly across the surface.

have hackle but no wings.

When selecting a dry fly on the stream, most anglers attempt to match the hatch. Recognize, however, that trout often feed selectively; and the particular insect you notice first, the biggest or most abundant species, may not be the one they want. Examine the rises and the naturals adrift on the stream to determine what the fish actually are taking. If you don't have a fly that duplicates it in size, shape and color, settle for matching the size. An artificial slightly smaller than the real thing usually works better than one that's bigger.

Traditionally, dry-fly anglers have fished in an upstream direction. The fly drifts toward you, so you strip in line and can easily pick up the short length remaining on the water when you're ready for the next cast.

Cast diagonally upstream, rather than straight up, so your leader and line won't drift over the fish and spook it. To reach difficult lies, you may want to cast across stream or downstream.

Regardless of the direction you cast, always drop your fly well upstream of the fish and let it drift into position. Remember, the rises of a fish are misleading; they do not indicate the spot where the trout actually lies.

On the drift, you must avoid drag. If the current pulls your line so the fly is dragged across the surface, the trout will refuse it and may even stop rising. Keep some slack in your leader at all times, and also in your line if needed. Once the line is on the water, you can mend it to maintain slack. When you fish in a downstream direction, simply pay out your line as fast

as the current takes it.

At times, the drag-free drift may be less productive than skating a dry fly across the surface (above). You do this by making a short cast downstream, then holding your rod tip high and shaking it gently from side to side while stripping in line. The fly will skip erratically on the water like a caddisfly attempting flight. The action is very different from the steady slide across the surface resulting from drag (left).

Dry flies often catch trout and salmon when they aren't rising, and even when no insects are hatching at all. Under these conditions you drift your fly naturally to the spots where fish are most likely to lie, or skate it over them. An effective tactic is to make several casts to a single spot, creating the illusion of a hatch.

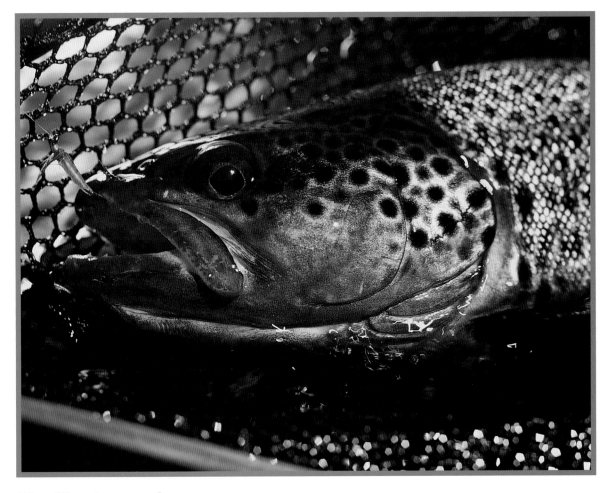

Wet flies have soft, absorbent hackle for quick sinking and a lifelike action that represents a drowned adult insect.

Light Cahill

Fishing with Wet Flies

The standard wet fly has almost become a museum piece. A century ago, it was the only artificial fly in use in America; today the angler who wants a sunken fly is far more likely to tie on a streamer or nymph, which more closely resemble important trout foods such as baitfish and larval insects. Yet there are excellent reasons for using the wet fly even now, none of them sentimental.

Traditional wet-fly techniques are the simplest and most effortless in fly fishing. There's less casting than with dry flies, so you cover the water more quickly Also, wets are effective in fast, broken currents that would quickly drown any dry. Wet flies are generally much smaller and less air-resistant than streamers, so they're easier to cast. And your presentation and retrieve need not be as precise as in fishing with nymphs.

Wet flies have soft, absorbent hackle for quick sinking and lifelike action. The standard wet has a feather wing; dull-tinted patterns of this type are thought to represent drowned adult insects. Featherwing wets with gaudy

How to Fish with the Wet-fly Drift

Cast across stream, then let the fly swing in the current. Follow the drifting line with your rod, keeping the tip up to absorb the shock of strikes. Mend the line as it swings. Slight drag won't turn the trout off, but a wet fly dragged rapidly won't get many strikes. Retrieve the fly in twitches after it swings below you. Trout usually strike at the end of the drift, as the line is straightening below you. After retrieving, lengthen each subsequent cast by 1 to 3 feet until you've thoroughly covered all the water you can reach from your position. Then, take a step or two downstream and repeat the process.

colors and metallic tinsels may suggest tiny baitfish, but serve mainly as attractors useful for brook trout and Atlantic salmon. Some wet patterns, called hackle flies, lack wings; these may resemble insect larvae or leeches.

The most popular wet flies today are specialized types. Large patterns with wings of hair or marabou, often in bright attractor colors, are commonly used for steelhead and salmon. And fat-bodied hackle flies called wooly worms, which have hackle along their entire length, are favorites for trout of all kinds on big western rivers.

Wet flies are often drifted at random, covering lots of potential holding water rather than particular lies. The wet-fly drift technique, with a floating or sink-tip line, works especially well in long runs and riffles that lack large boulders or other obvious cover. In such places, trout take shelter near small obstructions or in depressions in the bottom that may be invisible from the surface.

You can also fish specific targets. Cast across stream and let your fly drift into the calm pockets around logs, rocks and other objects. When it reaches a pocket, feed line into the current; the fly stays where it is, but the belly expands downstream. Otherwise the fly would be swept away immediately.

An old reliable method, all but forgotten by modern anglers, is to fish with two flies at once. The second fly is tied to a dropper 3 or 4 inches long. To make the dropper, leave one of the strands untrimmed when you tie your tippet to the leader with a blood knot. Cast across stream and drift the flies to a likely spot. Then raise your rod tip and jiggle it, so the dropper fly skips on the surface while the tippet fly works underwater.

In fall and winter steelheading, it's usually necessary to fish wet flies very deep. Use the wet-fly drift with a fast-sinking shooting head or a lead-core head. Many wet flies designed for steelhead have weighted bodies or bead heads; they will bounce along bottom without snagging if the rocks are rounded.

**Gold-Ribbed
Hare's Ear**

Fishing with Nymphs

Day in and day out, the odds favor the fly fisherman who uses a nymph. No matter how low or high the stream may be, no matter how cold or warm, the naturals that nymphs imitate are always present and available to the trout.

Nymphs are intended to copy the immature forms of aquatic insects, including mayflies, stoneflies, caddisflies, dragonflies, damselflies and midges. Some nymphs are close imitations of particular species, as

exact as flytiers can make them. Others are impressionistic, meant to suggest a variety of naturals in form, size and coloration. Many nymphs of both these types have bodies that are thick at the front and thinner at the rear, simulating the wing pads and abdomen of the real thing. Usually, there's a soft, sparse hackle to serve as legs.

A nymph pattern may be tied in weighted and unweighted versions. Weighted nymphs have lead or copper wire wound onto the hook shank under the body material. They are used for fishing near bottom, especially in fast currents. Unweighted nymphs work well for fishing shallow; and because they have livelier action, many experts prefer them for fishing deep in slow water as well. To carry them deep, split-shot or lead

wrap is attached to the leader. A few nymphs are designed to float, imitating the immature insect at the moment it arrives on the surface to transform into an adult.

No one becomes a complete nymph fisherman overnight. Techniques for fishing nymphs are far more numerous and varied than those for any other type of fly. Some are simple, but others are the most challenging of all ways of catching trout.

Depending on species and stage of life, the naturals may crawl across the bottom, burrow in it, swim or simply tumble along with the current. Thus the nymph fisherman can work his fly realistically by drifting it freely with the current, or by twitching or stripping it along at various depths.

How to Fish a Nymph

Check for common nymphs by stirring up the bottom, then holding a fine mesh net downstream. Select a fly that resembles the most common insect.

Attach a strike indicator (arrow) to your leader to help detect subtle takes. A strike indicator serves the same function as a bobber.

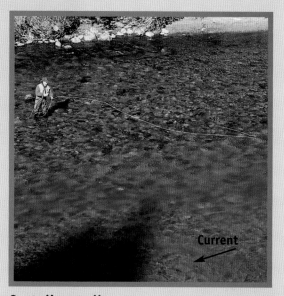

Current

Cast diagonally upstream. Allow the nymph to drift naturally along the bottom. Watch the indicator and set the hook at any twitch or hesitation.

Detecting strikes in nymph fishing can be difficult. When you use a natural drift, it's generally impossible to feel the hit. The best solution is to use a floating line with a bright-colored tip, a leader with a fluorescent butt, or some kind of strike indicator (above) attached to the leader. If you see any twitch or hesitation, set the hook.

For greatest sensitivity, strike indicators should be positioned as close to the fly as possible. To fish shallow, place the indicator just above the tippet knot; to fish deep, move it back toward the leader butt.

Keep your casts short so you can see the twitch more clearly. If you use a sink-tip line, keep an eye on the point where the lighter-colored floating portion disappears below the surface.

One of the easiest nymph techniques, and one of the most effective, is the wet-fly drift (p. 233). It's a good way to fish runs and riffles that lack obvious cover to cast to. By planning a drift carefully, you can also use this technique to swing your fly close to boulders or logs, or to nymphing trout you can actually see.

Sometimes these nymphing fish are visible only as flashes near the streambed as they turn and dart in the current to feed. At other times, their tails make swirls on the surface when they tip nose-down to take nymphs on the bottom, or their backs may break water when they feed on naturals that are only a few inches deep. Anglers often mistake these swirls for rises to adult insects, and make futile attempts to catch the trout

with dry flies.

When drifting a nymph to a feeding fish, try to sink it exactly to the fish's eye level. To increase the depth of a drift, angle your cast farther upstream so the fly will have more time to sink before reaching the trout. Use a weighted nymph if necessary, or add a suitable amount of weight to your leader.

In the still water of pools, try making a long cast, letting the nymph sink near the bottom, then retrieving it in short twitches. In very cold water, especially in the early season, a nymph allowed to lie motionless on the bottom and twitched only occasionally may be more effective than anything else except live bait. Stay alert for strikes; a trout may pick up the loitering nymph and drop it instantly.

Mickey
Finn

Fishing with Streamers

If you're serious about catching big trout, try fishing with streamers. The real heavyweights feed almost exclusively on baitfish; and most streamers are tied to mimic shiners, dace, sculpins, chubs, darters and even young trout.

Not that streamers are invariably the flies to select. When the water conditions are ideal for feeding, trout show more interest in dries, nymphs and wets. Streamers produce most dependably when dries and wets don't: during periods when the water is very cold or discolored.

Pick the right times, and you may come up with a trophy. Not only do streamers attract the attention of big trout better than small flies, they also give you a better chance of hanging on once a fish is hooked. The big, stout hooks hold securely, and the heavy tippets generally used with streamers make break-offs less likely.

The traditional streamer has a wing of long hackle feathers, but other types are more popular today. Patterns with hair wings are often called bucktails, even if the hair is synthetic or comes from animals other than deer. Another type, the zonker, has a strip of soft fur tied along the top of the hook. Muddlers have large heads, usually of clipped deer hair, to simulate the outline of sculpins.

Some brightly colored streamers do not closely imitate any baitfish, but instead work as attractors. Often, these bright flies draw more strikes than realistic ones. Or trout may swirl at an attractor pattern, revealing their whereabouts, but refuse to take it. Then you can switch to a realistic streamer or some other type of fly more likely to draw a strike.

Because of their size and bulk, streamers produce more vibration than other flies when stripped through the water. This extra attraction helps fish locate them in roily water or after dark. Muddler patterns, with their oversize heads, make the most underwater disturbance.

Like nymphs, streamers are tied with or without built-in weight, and may be fished with floating or sink-tip lines, or with sinking shooting heads. Split-shot or other weight may be added to the leader as needed.

The wet-fly drift (p. 233) is a good basic technique for streamers. You can twitch the fly during the drift for a more convincing minnowlike action. Mend the line often, so the fly does not speed unnaturally through the current. Proper mending also keeps the streamer drifting broadside to the current, so it's more visible to fish lying in wait.

In slower current that does not give the fly much action, you can cast across the stream, then strip the fly back toward you as it slowly swings downstream. No mending is needed, since the fly is retrieved before a wide belly can develop. The streamer simulates a baitfish darting across the current. Even when conditions are not ideal for streamers, this technique enables you to cover water very quickly, tempting trout to swirl at the fly as they would at an attractor pattern.

Large trout feed almost exclusively on bait-fish, and most streamers are tied to mimic them.

How to Cover Water with the Deep Streamer Swing

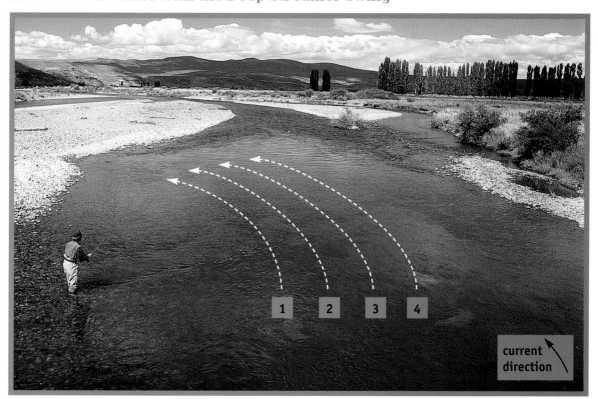

1 2 3 4

current direction

Make a short cast so the fly lands just upstream from the area you want to fish. Allow the fly to swing along arc 1. Lengthen each subsequent cast by 1 to 3 feet, so the fly cover arcs 2, 3 and 4. When you've thoroughly covered the water, take a step or two downstream and repeat the process. Continue moving downstream until the entire area has been covered.

Dave's Crickett

Dave's Hopper

Mouse rat

Fishing with Special-purpose Flies

Historically, almost all flies were tied to imitate insects or baitfish. But anglers have come to realize the fish aren't always interested in such offerings. At times, other foods are more abundant and the trout prefer them to the everyday fare.

Certain of these morsels, such as leeches, crayfish and salmon eggs, seem to defy imitation with fur and feathers. But imaginative flytiers have come up with realistic copies, and inventive anglers have devised techniques to bring them to life.

The most popular of these special-purpose flies are terrestrials. These simulate land insects such as ants, grasshoppers, crickets, beetles and inchworms, any of which may fall onto the water. Terrestrial flies are effective throughout the warm months. They're especially useful in late summer, when aquatic hatches wane. Terrestrials are fished on the surface in slow to moderate current, where the surface is relatively smooth.

Ant imitations often work better than standard dry flies on days when no trout are rising. Floating ants in sizes 18 to 22 are drifted close to the banks, where natural ants are most likely to be. These tiny flies are difficult to see, so keep your casts short and strike gently at any rise near your fly. Sinking ants are usually tied in sizes 8 to 20. Drift ant imitations with a floating line, mending often to avoid drag.

Grasshopper patterns, in sizes 4 to 14, are most productive in meadow streams, particularly on windy days when the naturals are blown onto the water. Dead-drift them along grassy banks, adding an occasional twitch. Beetles and jassids (small flat-bodied insects, also known as leafhoppers) are inconspicuous on the water, but in warm weather the trout may feed on them selectively. Beetle imitations are tied in sizes 10 to 20; jassids, sizes 16 to 22. A dead drift on the surface works best.

Leech flies are among the top lures for big trout. These are big flies, sizes 2 to 10. The dressings, in most cases, consist mainly of marabou or rabbit fur. These soft materials have an undulating action that matches the squirming of the naturals. Work leech flies in slow current with the wet-fly drift, twitching them from time to time. In still water, retrieve with long, slow strips; a jerky action would make the fur or marabou flare out from the hook, spoiling the illusion of a real leech.

Scud patterns imitate tiny crustaceans that are superabundant in many trout streams, especially spring creeks. Trout often gorge themselves on scuds, burrowing into weedbeds and rooting them out. It's not unusual to catch a trout that is so stuffed with scuds that it regurgitates them when you attempt to unhook it. When trout gorge themselves this heavily, they're tough to catch, but you may be able to draw a strike by drifting a scud pattern so it nearly hits the fish on the nose. Scud flies range from size 10 to 20.

Crayfish flies should be worked close to rocky streambeds, either drifting them with the current or stripping them briskly through quiet water. Crayfish are most plentiful in limestone streams, and become most active in low light. A good time to fish the imitations, sizes 1/0 to 8, is at dusk or after dark.

In streams with runs of Pacific salmon, other salmonids like rainbows, Dolly Varden and grayling feed heavily on salmon eggs. Fly anglers take trophy fish by dead-drifting egg flies in fluorescent red, pink or orange. Use just enough weight on your leader to reach bottom; big trout may drop the fly immediately if they feel resistance. Egg patterns also are tied in white and chartreuse to imitate the spawn of suckers and other fishes.

Hair bugs, the same types used for bass, are also effective for trophy rainbows and browns, especially at night. But most bugs are too large for average-sized trout.

When trout are feeding heavily on scuds you may be able to draw a strike by drifting a scud pattern very close to the fish.

Spinning & Baitcasting Techniques

For the average fisherman, spinning and baitcasting are much easier than fly fishing. And in many situations, they catch more and bigger trout. Because trout eat more baitfish and fewer insects as they grow larger, good-sized baits and lures have more appeal than small flies.

The monofilament line used with spinning and baitcasting gear offers several advantages to stream fishermen. The small-diameter line cuts the current much better than fly line, so drag is not as much of a problem, and you can fish deep more easily. Mono is also less wind-resistant, which makes casting in a headwind or crosswind considerably easier. And fly line is highly visible; if you cast over a trout, or allow your line to drift ahead of the fly, the fish may spook. With mono, your presentation need not be as precise.

When heavy rains cloud a stream, fly fishing may be tough, but spinfishermen and baitcasters continue catching trout. The fish can detect the scent of natural bait or the sound and vibration of plugs and spinners.

On a narrow, brushy stream, flycasting is almost impossible because streamside obstacles foul your backcast. But with a short, ultralight spinning outfit, you can flip small lures beneath overhanging branches and fish pockets that otherwise would be difficult to reach. Spinning gear is also an advantage on wide streams because you can make long casts and cover a lot of water in a hurry.

Baitcasting gear is the best choice for exceptionally large trout. The level-wind reel eliminates the line-twist problems that plague spinfishermen when very large trout strip line from their reels.

Jig Fishing

Until recently, jigs were reserved for warmwater species like bass and walleyes. Few anglers even considered using them for trout. But jigs do have a place in trout fishing, and in the hands of an expert they can be deadly.

Jigs resemble favorite trout foods such as minnows, insect larvae, crustaceans, leeches and salmon eggs. Try to match your jig color to the fish's natural food. A black or brown jig, for instance, would be a good match for most insect larvae; an orange jig, for salmon eggs.

When trout are aggressive, a jig with a tail dressing of soft plastic, marabou or hair is all you need. But when they're fussy, try tipping your jig with some type of natural bait, like a piece of worm or a small minnow.

Jigs work well for both small and large trout. They cast easily and sink rapidly in the current. A jig of the proper weight hugs bottom and is not swept by the current as much as most other lures. And jigs are versatile: you can drift them downstream, retrieve them across stream, or jig them vertically.

DOWNSTREAM DRIFTING. To catch trout feeding in riffles, cast a $1/32$- to $1/80$-ounce micro-jig upstream, then let it drift down through the riffle. Keep your rod tip high, reeling up slack as the jig drifts. Strikes may be hard to detect, but you can attach a strike indicator, just as you would in nymph fishing.

For casting these tiny jigs, use a $41/2$- to $51/2$-foot ultra-light spinning rod with a slow to medium action. Spool your reel with limp, 2- to 4-pound mono.

CROSS-STREAM RETRIEVE. In deeper water, use a heavier jig, $1/16$ to $1/4$ ounce. Quarter your cast upstream, aiming for targets like boulders and logs. Let the jig sink to bottom, then retrieve in a series of short twitches, lowering the jig back to bottom with a taut line after each twitch. If the bottom-bouncing technique doesn't pay off, try a twitching retrieve in the mid-depths and just beneath the surface. Sometimes a faster retrieve will trigger a strike.

With these heavier jigs, use a medium-power, fast-action spinning rod, from $51/4$ to 6 feet in length, with limp 4- to 8-pound mono.

VERTICAL JIGGING. This technique works well for large trout in deep pools and runs of good-sized rivers. Simply lower a jig or jigging spoon to bottom, then jig vertically as the boat drifts downstream. Keep your line taut as the lure sinks; set the hook at the slightest tug. Use a lure weighing from $1/8$ ounce to 2 ounces, depending on current speed and water depth.

A medium-heavy baitcasting outfit works best for vertical jigging. Use a $51/2$- to 6-foot, fast-action rod with 12- to 20-pound mono.

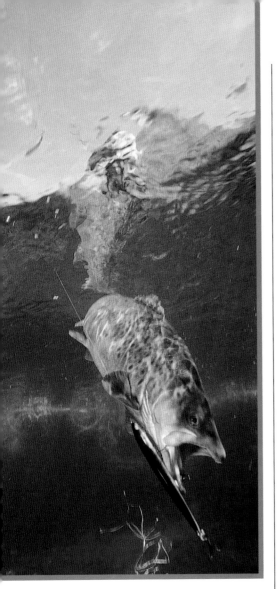

Casting with Hardware

The term "hardware" means all hard-bodied lures like spoons, spinners and plugs. Hardware attracts trout by flash and vibration. By casting with hardware, you can cover a lot of water in a hurry. The technique works best from late spring through early fall, when higher water temperatures make trout more aggressive.

Compared to most other trout-fishing techniques, hardware fishing is easy. Simply cast across stream, then regulate the speed of your retrieve so the lure ticks bottom. When trout are actively feeding, ticking bottom may not be necessary; the fish will swim upward to grab the lure.

Exactly how you angle your cast depends on the lure, the water depth and the current speed. The more you angle it upstream, the deeper the lure will run. If the lure is bouncing bottom too much, angle the cast farther downstream. This way, water resistance from the current will keep the lure off bottom.

Work the cover farthest downstream and closest to you first. Then, a hooked fish will not spook others in unfished water when the current sweeps it downstream, or in unfished water close to you when you reel it in.

Standard spinners and thin spoons are popular in small streams, where distance casting is not important. Sonic spinners, which have a shaft that passes through the blade, are extremely popular in the West. The blade starts turning at a very low retrieve speed.

Weight-forward spinners and medium to thick spoons are a better choice in bigger rivers or in those with deep water or fast current. These heavier lures can be cast much farther, and they run deeper.

Floating minnow plugs work well in small streams, but sinking minnow plugs and diving crankbaits are more effective in deeper current.

With spinners, spoons and sinking minnow plugs, the slower you retrieve, the deeper the lures will run. Floating minnow plugs and crankbaits run deepest with a medium to medium-fast retrieve.

For casting spinners, small spoons and minnow plugs, use a 5- to 6-foot light spinning outfit with 2- to 6-pound mono; for larger spoons and diving plugs, a 5½- to 7-foot, medium-power spinning outfit with 6- to 8-pound mono.

To avoid line twist, attach spinners and spoons with a small ball-bearing snap-swivel. Or, splice in a swivel about 6 inches ahead of the lure. Attach minnow plugs with a small snap or a Duncan loop knot; crankbaits, with a snap or a Trilene knot.

When casting hardware, work the cover farthest downstream and closest to you first. Then, a hooked fish will not spook others in unfished water when the current sweeps it downstream, or in unfished water close to you when you reel it in. Make your casts in the order shown in the photo.

Trolling for Stream Trout

When you troll, your lure is in the water all the time, maximizing your chances of catching fish. Trolling offers several other advantages over casting: it's an easier technique for the novice; it enables you to cover more water; and where multiple lines are legal, you can troll with several lures at once.

Trolling works best in big rivers that have long stretches of deep water with slow to moderate current. It's not well suited to river stretches with lots of riffles or rapids, and not recommended for shallow or very clear water. Because the boat passes over the fish before the lure arrives, spooking may be a big problem. You can reduce spooking by trolling in S-curves. This way the lure does not track continuously in the boat's wake.

Another way to avoid spooking fish is to troll with side planers. These devices attach to your line, pulling it well to the side of the boat's wake. They also let you cover a wider swath of water. Another way to fish side planers is to walk along shore, using the planer to carry your line to midstream waters you couldn't reach by casting.

Diving planes also attach to your line, taking the lure deep. The unweighted type is all you need in most streams; weighted ones generally run too deep.

Baitcasting gear works best for trolling. A good trolling rod is stiff enough to handle the water resistance against the lure, but light enough at the tip to telegraph the lure's action. Use abrasion-resistant mono, from 6- to 12-pound test depending on the size of the trout. A depth finder helps you follow breaks in

Bomber Model A

the bottom contour.

Most anglers troll with deep-diving crankbaits. You can also use minnow plugs, spoons and jigs. It's a good idea to keep your lures near bottom, except when trout are feeding on insects or salmon smolts and will come up for a lure. Normally, no extra weight is needed to get a crankbait to bottom, but you may have to add weight to other lures.

Trolling styles used in stream fishing for trout include: slipping, upstream trolling and downstream trolling.

SLIPPING. The term "slipping" means letting the boat drift slowly downstream, reducing its speed with a motor or oars while allowing the lures to trail in the current. As long as the boat drifts more slowly than the current, the force of the water will give the lures action. Some trout fishermen refer to this technique as "backtrolling."

To cover wide channels, zigzag your boat while slipping. This allows you to cover more water on the drift, a big advantage if you don't have a motor. It also gives your lures more action, causing them to speed up and slow down, rise and fall.

Slipping is effective year-round, but works especially well in cold water; the slow-moving lure appeals to lethargic fish. The technique has one major advantage over other trolling methods: the lure passes over the fish before the boat does, so they're less likely to spook.

UPSTREAM TROLLING. You can troll upstream only in slow current. Otherwise, water resistance is so great that the lure is forced to the surface. Where the current is slow enough, you can troll upstream, then turn around and troll back down, keeping your lures in the water.

DOWNSTREAM TROLLING. This technique is often used to present spinners or other lures that do not require much current for good action. Trolling downstream slightly faster than the current gives these lures enough action, yet they look like drifting food. To troll slowly enough, you may have to shift your motor between forward and neutral every few seconds. When using lures like spoons and crankbaits, you will have to troll somewhat faster.

By trolling downstream, you are in a better position to fight the fish. The current pushes a hooked fish in the direction the boat moves, reducing the possibility of breaking the line or tearing out the hooks.

Spinfishing with Flies

Even if you don't own a fly rod, you can fly-fish with spinning gear. In fact, spinning with flies works better in some situations. In deep water, for instance, you can attach split-shot to mono line and reach bottom more easily than with fly line. And in high winds, mono is easier to control.

In streams with flies-only regulations, spinning gear is usually legal, as long as the lure is a fly. But to cast a fly, you must attach some extra weight.

With a sinking fly, simply add a split-shot or two about a foot up the line. Leader wrap, lead sleeves or a good-sized strike indicator will also add weight. Strike indicators help detect light pickups as well.

Dry flies and sinking flies can be rigged with a weighted float or a plastic bubble, which can be partially filled with water for extra casting weight. If you use a clear float or bubble, trout will pay little attention to it. But a float or bubble splashing down close to a fish, or drifting over it ahead of the fly, may cause it to spook.

A long, soft rod is best for casting flies and manipulating them in the water. A stiff rod doesn't flex enough to cast a light weight, and could snap a light leader when you set the hook. A 6½- to 7½-foot, slow-action spinning rod or an 8½- to 9½-foot, 4- to 6-weight fly rod with a spinning reel is a good choice. Spool your reel with 2- to 8-pound, limp mono.

Many spinfishermen use line that is too heavy, and add too much weight, inhibiting the movement of the fly. Always use the lightest line practical for the conditions, and the lightest weight that will allow you to cast and reach the desired depth. Too much weight causes snagging problems; and even with minimal weight, strikes are more difficult to detect than with fly-fishing gear.

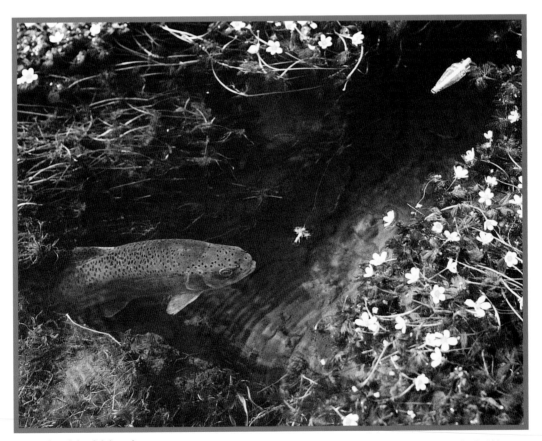

Standard bubble rigs work best for casting across stream or downstream; if fished upstream, the bubble would drift ahead of the fly. Tie the rig by threading a plastic bubble on your line, then attaching a dry fly, wet fly, streamer or nymph. Twist the ends of the bubble so it locks in place a foot up the line. With a dry fly, you can put a little water in the bubble for casting weight; use a drag-free drift. With a sinking fly, you can fill the bubble with water or add split-shot for more depth; dead-drift the fly or twitch it for extra action.

Fishing with Natural Bait

Fly-fishing purists frown on the idea of using spoons, spinners and other hardware to catch trout, and the idea of using natural bait is even farther down their list of tolerable tactics. But there's no denying that natural bait catches lots of trout; in fact, there are times when it badly outfishes flies and hardware.

Trout rely on their sense of smell to a greater extent than most other gamefish. They can detect dissolved substances in minute concentrations, so it's not surprising that they use their remarkable sense of smell to help them find food.

Natural bait appeals to this highly developed sense. Smell is especially important during periods of high, muddy water. Under these conditions, trout cannot see flies or hardware, but they can easily detect the odor of natural bait.

In early spring, when the water is still cold and few insects are hatching, natural bait usually outproduces flies by a wide margin. Natural bait is also a good choice in streams that do not have many insects. And big trout or those in heavily fished streams can be super-wary, closely inspecting any potential food item. They're likely to recognize any imitation as a fake.

Bait fishermen often make the mistake of using heavy line and a big hook, then adding a heavy sinker and a golf-ball-sized bobber. This type of rig is fine for northern pike, but will seldom catch a trout. For most stream trout, bait-fishing specialists use light spinning tackle with 2- to 4-pound mono, size 6 to 12 hooks, and a split-shot for weight. Of course large trout require heavier tackle, but seldom will you need line heavier than 8-pound test or a hook larger than size 2.

The major drawback of natural bait is the problem of deep hooking. Even a small trout often takes the bait so deeply it's impossible to remove the hook without causing serious injury. If you plan on releasing your trout, don't use live bait. If you must release a deeply hooked trout, cut the line rather than trying to remove the hook.

Another disadvantage of many natural baits is the difficulty of keeping them alive and carrying them, especially if you're wading. And in some states, certain natural baits, like minnows, are illegal for trout.

The variety of trout baits is nearly endless. Garden worms and nightcrawlers are the most common baits, along with minnows and fish eggs. Leeches, adult and larval insects, and crayfish are not as popular, but are no less effective. Fishermen have also discovered that certain "grocery baits," like marshmallows and corn, work extremely well, especially for stocked trout.

Although most trout will take any of these baits, some have a distinct preference. Also, a given bait may be more productive at certain times of year or under certain water conditions. Following are details on the most common live baits used for trout:

GARDEN WORMS. Any trout will take a worm. The bait is effective anytime, but works best in early spring when streams are high and discolored. For convenience, carry your worms in a box that attaches to your belt.

Push a size 6 to 10 hook through the middle of the worm, letting the ends dangle; or hook the worm two or three times, letting the tail dangle.

NIGHTCRAWLERS. You can use nightcrawlers and garden worms interchangeably; for small trout, half a crawler is better than a whole one. Crawlers must be kept cooler than garden worms.

Push a size 6 or 8 hook through the broken end of a half crawler, or through the middle of a whole crawler. Or, hook the crawler two or three times, like a garden worm.

MINNOWS. Trout fishermen commonly use fathead minnows and shiners because of their availability, but almost any kind of minnow in the 1½- to 3-inch

Aquatic insects rigged for trout.

range will work. Minnows catch trout year-round, but are most effective in spring and early summer, when young baitfish are most numerous. Live minnows are best in slow-moving water; in current, dead ones work nearly as well.

Trout, particularly browns, eat more fish as they grow older, so minnows are a good choice for the big ones.

Sculpins, often called bullheads by mistake, are the prime bait for trophy browns in numerous western streams. But other baitfish are illegal in most western states, and many other states ban any type of baitfish. These regulations are intended to prevent introduction of non-native fish species, and to reduce the trout harvest. Always check your local fishing regulations before using any kind of baitfish.

To carry minnows when you're wading, put them in a small bucket with a perforated lid, then tie the bucket to your waders. Fatheads are the easiest to keep alive.

Most minnows are hooked through the lips with a size 4 or 6 short-shank hook. You can also hook a sculpin by pushing a size 4 or 6 double-needle hook through the vent and out the mouth, then attaching a special clip to the front of the hook.

AQUATIC INSECTS. Immature aquatic insects work better than adults, mainly because they're easier to keep on the hook. Stonefly nymphs and hellgrammites (dobsonfly larvae) top the list, but mayfly nymphs, caddis larvae, waterworms (cranefly larvae) and other immature forms also catch trout.

Any of these baits will take trout year-round, but stonefly nymphs are best in midsummer; hellgrammites, in spring and early summer. You can find stonefly nymphs clinging to the undersides of rocks and logs in cold streams; hellgrammites are found in warmer water, and can be caught by turning over rocks in a riffle while someone holds a small-mesh seine just downstream. Mayfly nymphs can be found by sifting through mud on the stream bottom; waterworms, by digging through sticks and debris on the bottom or in a beaver dam; caddisworms, by checking the undersides of rocks.

Adult aquatic insects are not as common in a trout's diet as larval forms. But some adults, such as stoneflies, make good trout bait. Watch for them as you walk along the stream, and don't hesitate to give them a try.

Stonefly nymphs should be hooked through the collar with a size 8 or 10 light-wire hook; hellgrammites, under the collar with a size 4 to 8 hook; mayfly nymphs, through the hard plate just behind the head with a size 10 or 12 light-wire hook; caddis pupae (above) or larvae, by pushing a size 12 to 16 light-wire hook through the head or threading it through the body (use several larvae or pupae, or a larva inside its case); waterworms, through the tough skin just ahead of the tail lobes using a size 8 or 10 light-wire hook. Adult mayflies and stoneflies stay on best when hooked through the head with a size 10 or 12 light-wire hook.

TERRESTRIAL INSECTS. In late summer, trout often lie near the bank, waiting for grasshoppers to get blown into the water. Where hoppers are plentiful, you can easily catch them by hand or with a small insect net. They can be fished alive or dead, floating or submerged. Crickets are not used as widely, but are equally effective.

Fishermen have discovered that waxworms (bee moth larvae),

maggots (fly larvae) and other larval baits used for ice fishing are excellent for trout. They work particularly well in winter, when most other baits are hard to find. Their small size is an advantage when the water is cold and trout feeding slows.

Hoppers and crickets are hooked with a size 6 to 10 light-wire hook, either under the collar, or through the body so the point protrudes from the underside of the abdomen. Waxworms and maggots are hooked through the head with a size 10 or 12 light-wire hook; some anglers hook on two or three.

CRUSTACEANS. Crayfish from 1½ to 3 inches long make good summertime bait for big trout, especially browns. For smaller trout, use only the tail. Crayfish work best in streams with high crayfish populations.

You can catch crayfish by quickly grabbing them after turning over rocks in the streambed. You can also use a seine. Try to select crayfish in the softshell stage. Live crayfish can be hooked through the tail, from the bottom up, with a size 2 to 4 hook. Crayfish tails are hooked the same way.

EGGS. All species of trout and salmon feed on each other's eggs. Salmon eggs are most popular for bait because of their large size and commercial availability, but trout eggs also work well.

A single egg will catch trout of all sizes. But for large trout, most anglers prefer egg clusters, either plain or tied in a mesh spawn bag. Eggs are effective year-round, but they work best during and after a spawning run, when the fish are eating eggs.

Fresh salmon eggs deteriorate quickly, but you can preserve them by rolling them in powdered borax or soaking them in a boric-acid solution.

Plunking

Practically every experienced trout fisherman has been badly outfished at some time or other by a kid plunking worms into a pool. While the technique is not glamorous, it accounts for plenty of trout.

The term plunking simply means still-fishing. The usual technique is to attach a sinker to the line, bait up, lob-cast into a pool, then sit back and wait.

Plunking works especially well for big trout. If you sit quietly, they eventually detect the scent and swim over to investigate. If you continually cast and retrieve, you are likely to spook them.

Almost any live bait will work, but nightcrawlers and minnows are most popular. In stocked streams, anglers often plunk with Velveeta® cheese and many junk foods. Browns, rainbows and cutthroat seem most susceptible to plunking.

Use only enough weight to keep your bait from drifting. If you attach a heavy sinker, the fish will feel resistance and spit the bait. In small streams, a split shot is normally adequate, but in bigger streams, you may need a small slip-sinker. Most anglers plunk with light spinning gear and 4- to 8-pound mono, depending on the size of the trout and the snagginess of the bottom.

Freelining

If you stand along a grassy bank on a hot summer's day, you may see trout rising to take grasshoppers and other insects that fall into the stream.

Terrestrial insects rigged for trout.

Crayfish rigged for trout.

When trout are feeding this way, you can catch them by freelining with the insects they are eating. Most fishermen freeline with light spinning gear, but you can also use a fly rod, with either a floating fly line or monofilament. The long rod helps to position the nearly weightless bait over the lie. The technique is simple: attach the bait to a light-wire hook, stand upstream of the lie, then pay out line. With fly-casting gear or light spinning gear, you can also flip the bait upstream and let it float down. Because there is no sinker, the bait will float on the surface or just beneath it.

Freelining works best in late summer, when adult insects are numerous and stream levels low. Any insect-eating trout are susceptible to the technique. The best area for freelining is along a grassy bank or other spot where insects cling to streamside vegetation and commonly fall into the water.

Drift Fishing

Drift fishing accounts for more trout than any other bait-fishing technique. The idea is to present your bait so it drifts naturally with the current, just like real food.

Position yourself to the side and just downstream of a riffle or run likely to hold trout. Most pools do not have enough current to keep your bait drifting. Before casting, look for boulders, logs or other likely cover, then quarter your cast upstream so the bait will skirt the object as it drifts.

Light spinning gear works best for average-sized trout. A 6- to 7-foot, medium-action rod is long enough for good line control, yet flexible enough for lobbing delicate baits. The lighter the line you use, the easier it is to achieve a drag-free drift. Heavy line has more water resistance, so the current creates a larger belly and the bait begins to drift too fast. Limp, clear, 4-pound mono is a good all-around choice, but

you may need heavier line if the bottom is snaggy.

Some drift fishermen use a fly rod with a spinning reel. The longer rod gives them even better line control and makes it easier to dunk the bait into hard-to-reach spots.

In drift fishing, it's important to select a sinker of the proper weight. Too heavy, and it will hang on bottom so the bait cannot drift as fast as the current. Too light, and the current will lift the bait off bottom. You must choose a sinker heavy enough that it just ticks bottom as the bait drifts. Carry a selection of sinkers and split-shot in various sizes, and use different ones to suit the conditions.

Almost any natural bait tough enough to stay on the hook will work for drift fishing. A delicate bait like an adult mayfly would probably tear off. You can add visual appeal by snelling a small piece of fluorescent yarn on your hook just ahead of the bait.

Basic Drift-fishing Technique

Keep your rod tip high and follow the bait as it drifts downstream. Take up slack with your free hand as the angle of your line changes.

Strip off enough line to reach your casting target, hold the slack in your free hand, then bring the rod back over your shoulder. Quarter your cast upstream into a run or deep riffle. Use a gentle lobbing motion. Do not snap the rod or you will tear the bait off the hook.

Set the hook whenever the bait stops moving. When you reach the end of your drift and current begins to lift the bait, strip in line and cast again.

Night Fishing

To many, the notion of fishing a trout stream at night evokes thoughts of tripping over logs and tangling lines in streamside brush. But to others, night fishing means big trout, especially browns.

Big browns stay in heavy cover during daylight hours, but at night they seem to lose their caution. They feed in shallow riffles and tails of pools, often far from cover, and are not nearly as selective as in daylight. Cutthroat and rainbows also feed at night, but to a lesser extent.

Night fishing is most effective during low-water periods in summer, when the clarity increases because of the low flow and the water temperature may rise into the 70s. At night, the water may cool to the mid-60s, a more likely temperature for feeding, and the clarity is actually an advantage. Moonless, starry nights are best; trout are less wary in the dark of the moon, but the stars provide enough light so you can see a little.

Before attempting to fish at night, scout the water during the day. Remember likely trout lies, overhead branches or other obstacles that could foul your cast, deep holes that you could step into while wading, and gradually sloping banks where you could easily land a good-sized trout. Nighttime is not the time to check out new water.

Fly fishermen most commonly use streamers, nymphs or leech imitations, usually in large sizes. During a major hatch, you can often hear trout rising. In this situation, dry flies can be very effective. Many night fishermen prefer big, heavily hackled dry flies because they are easier to see and produce plenty of vibrations so trout can quickly locate them. A light-colored fly is also easier to see, and at night the exact color is not as important as the silhouette.

After dark, spinfishermen catch a lot of big browns by casting minnow plugs, spinners or small spoons into a riffle, then reeling them rapidly downstream. Live bait is usually fished in slower water; a gob of worms, a whole crawler or a chub tail is a good choice.

Because the fish are more aggressive at night, your presentation need not be as delicate as in daylight. In fact, a fly splatting down on the water may actually attract a trout's attention. You can get by with a 6- to 8-pound spinning line or fly tippet, so if you do get snagged in streamside brush you can pull loose. A heavy tippet will also straighten out better on the cast.

You don't need a lot of special equipment for night fishing, but unless you're very familiar with the streambed, it's a good idea to wear waders instead of hip boots. Bug spray, a flashlight and a light that attaches to your vest also come in handy.

Winter Fishing

If you dislike crowds, try fishing your favorite trout stream in winter. Chances are you'll have the whole stream to yourself, and the trout can be surprisingly cooperative.

Of course, you should check the fishing regulations to make sure the stream is open. Many streams close before the fall spawning season and don't re-open until spring, and those that remain open often have special regulations, such as artificials-only or catch-and-release.

Most winter fishing is for browns, rainbows, cutthroat and brook trout, but anglers on Pacific-coast streams catch good numbers of winter-run steelhead. These fish enter the streams in late fall in preparation for spring spawning.

Trout behave much different-ly in near-freezing water than at summertime temperatures. Look for them in slower water and heavier cover. In most cases they're right on the bot-tom, although they will rise to feed on tiny emerging midges, or snowflies. Bright sunlight triggers these midge hatches,

prompting trout to start feed-ing. Fly fishing with midge pupa patterns in sizes 18 to 28 can be very effective, especially on warm, sunny afternoons.

Many anglers think that flies this small must be difficult to use, so they shy away from midge fishing. But you can fish midges much the same way you fish nymphs, only with lighter gear. Most midge fishermen use a 2- to 4-weight fly rod from 8 to 9 feet long. Midges work best when fished just beneath the surface film, so a floating, weight-forward fly line is a good choice. Use a 9- to 12-foot knot-less leader with a 6x to 8x tip-pet. Strikes on midges are often very subtle, so it pays to attach a sensitive strike indicator.

Dry flies are seldom used in winter, but streamers, nymphs and scud patterns account for a fair number of trout. Streamers should be worked deep and slow. Nymphs and scuds should be dead-drifted, just as in summer.

Where live-bait fishing is legal, it works exceptionally well during the winter months. Western anglers catch lots of good-sized brown trout on sculpins. But small baits like waxworms, maggots, mayfly and

stonefly nymphs, salmon eggs and hellgrammites are the best choice for most stream trout fishing. Simply attach a small split-shot, and drift the morsel through a likely spot.

As a general rule, the best winter trout fishing is where the stream is warmest. Trout often congregate around springs because the groundwater is normally warmer than the sur-rounding water. In some tail-water streams, trout stay in the vicinity of the dam because water discharged from the depths of the upstream reservoir is a few degrees warmer than water farther downstream.

Check snowy streambanks to determine if there is a midge hatch. Tiny dark insects resembling mosquitoes are probably midges; select a fly that resembles them. Dead-drift a midge imitation just beneath the surface film, rather than on the sur-face. Your tippet will be less visible and the sunken fly seems to have more appeal.

STREAM TROUT

Fishing for Trophy Trout

An average stream fisherman seldom catches a big trout. It's not that the big ones aren't there; anglers occasionally see them following lures or hear them taking insects on the surface. As proof that big trout exist, fisheries workers regularly take them with shockers during stream surveys, even on streams that are fished heavily.

The trophy fisherman catches considerably fewer trout, but the challenge of outwitting a big one makes up for the lack of quantity. To improve his chances of taking a trophy, he fishes in different places and uses different techniques than other anglers.

Look for big trout in the deepest pools or undercuts, or at least in areas where they can easily reach the deep-water retreat. Just how deep is relative; in a small creek, a 4-foot pool is deep enough to hold a big one. In a large river, an 8-foot pool may not be deep enough.

Big trout prey on smaller ones, so when a likely-looking pool fails to produce even a small trout, this may be a clue that the pool is home to an exceptionally large trout. It pays to try such a pool from time to time rather than giving up on it.

Of course, some streams are more likely to produce big trout than others. Tailwater streams, coastal streams and streams connected to large lakes generally yield the biggest trout.

A trophy trout is more likely to be near bottom than a small one, so sinking flies or deep-running lures are usually more effective than dry flies or shallow-runners.

Because fish make up a greater percentage of a trout's diet as it grows older, fish-imitating lures like minnow plugs, spinners and streamers take larger trout than small, insect-imitating flies. Some trophy hunters use 5-inch minnow plugs, or streamers that measure up to 4 inches.

Trout that have lived in a stream for many years and seen almost every possible lure are difficult to fool with even the most realistic artificial. But these old-timers can often be duped with live bait, preferably a natural food captured in the stream. Western anglers, for instance, know that big browns have a weakness for sculpins, small fish that spend most of their time hiding under rocks. Other good baits for big trout include salmon eggs, chub tails, crayfish, waterworms, hellgrammites and nightcrawlers.

Big dry flies can be deadly during a hatch of large insects. In the northern Rockies, trophy-class trout that normally ignore insects go on a feeding rampage when large stoneflies, known as salmon flies, are hatching. On many eastern streams, big trout gorge themselves during the green drake mayfly hatch.

A hefty trout does not like to exert itself too much. Rather than racing smaller trout to catch fast-moving foods, it lies in wait for the chance to grab unsuspecting prey. Regardless of the type of bait or lure, a slow presentation generally works best.

Any type of trout fishing requires an inconspicuous approach to avoid putting the fish down. But when you're after trophies, stealth is even more important. The reason these trout have grown so large is that they have learned to sense predators, including fishermen. If they detect any unusual movement or vibration, they immediately head for cover and refuse to bite. Some trophy specialists go to extremes to avoid detection; they cast from behind bushes, or stay upstream of the pool and let the current carry their bait to the fish. For trophy browns, serious anglers do almost all their fishing at night.

Steelhead

The fighting ability of steelhead is legend. They have been clocked at more than 26 feet per second, fastest of any freshwater fish. A hooked steelhead may leap repeatedly, sometimes clearing the surface by 2 to 3 feet. When you consider that they're often performing these acrobatics in swift water, it's not surprising that even the best steelhead fishermen land only a small percentage of the fish they hook.

Steelhead are rainbow trout that spend their adult lives at sea or in the open water of huge inland lakes, such as the Great Lakes. Each spring, they migrate up tributary streams to spawn. Great Lakes steelhead may make a "mock spawning run" in fall, but no spawning takes place at that time. Along the Pacific Coast, steelhead may move into a stream in summer or fall and remain until spawning time the following spring. Steelhead can be found somewhere along the Pacific Coast every month of the year.

Pacific Coast steelhead were introduced into the Great Lakes in the late 1800s. Runs have since developed in many streams, especially those with clean, cold water and gravel bottoms. Because nonmigratory rainbows have also been stocked in the Great Lakes, fishermen sometimes mistake these deeper-bodied fish for steelhead.

Steelhead generally grow larger than stream-dwelling

rainbows. The average steelhead weighs 4 to 6 pounds, though some exceed 20 pounds.

Steelhead swim miles up tributary streams to find the right spawning area. They easily navigate raging cascades and most waterfalls. Only a dam or high waterfall blocks their progress.

While in the stream, steelhead bite reluctantly. The best technique is to drift-fish (p. 248) with yarn flies or spawn bags. By drifting a bait past a fish repeatedly, you can sometimes entice a take.

Most drift-fishermen use 8- to 9-foot fly rods, and a high-quality disc-drag fly reel filled with 8- to 12-pound abrasion-resistant monofilament line. About 18 inches in front of the yarn fly, anglers use a barrel swivel, which has a 6-inch dropper of 6- to 8-pound mono tied to it. By adding the appropriate amount of split-shot to the dropper, an angler can fish along the bottom without fear of getting snagged. If the rig does get hung up, the angler simply pulls on the line and the split-shot pulls off the dropper or the dropper line breaks, saving the yarn fly and swivel.

When drift-fishing for steelhead, many fishermen use bright or fluorescent yarn. Fish probably mistake these flies for spawn.

Steelhead Range

Steelhead have a long, sleek, silvery body with a faint pink lateral stripe, or no stripe at all. The gill cover may have a pinkish patch, but unlike a stream rainbow, has few or no black spots. The world-record steelhead weighed 42 pounds, 2 ounces. It was caught at Bell Island, Alaska, in 1970.

How to Tie a Yarn Fly

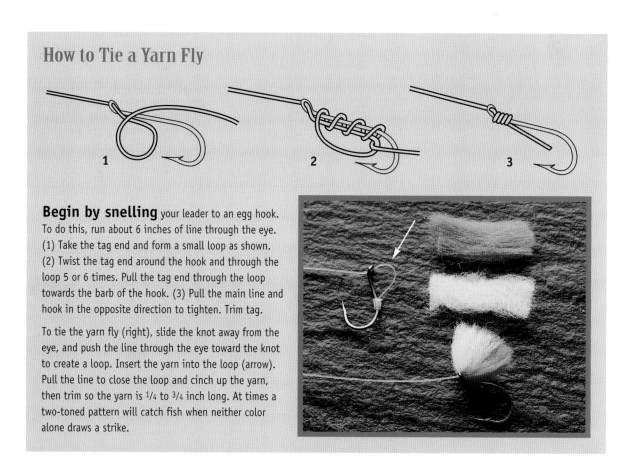

Begin by snelling your leader to an egg hook. To do this, run about 6 inches of line through the eye. (1) Take the tag end and form a small loop as shown. (2) Twist the tag end around the hook and through the loop 5 or 6 times. Pull the tag end through the loop towards the barb of the hook. (3) Pull the main line and hook in the opposite direction to tighten. Trim tag.

To tie the yarn fly (right), slide the knot away from the eye, and push the line through the eye toward the knot to create a loop. Insert the yarn into the loop (arrow). Pull the line to close the loop and cinch up the yarn, then trim so the yarn is 1/4 to 3/4 inch long. At times a two-toned pattern will catch fish when neither color alone draws a strike.

Catching Steelhead in Large Rivers

To locate steelhead, look for areas of moderate current with a bottom of grapefruit- to cantaloupe-sized rocks and water at least 3 feet deep. Usually, the fish lie along a current seam, in the tail of a pool, in troughs on the bottom or in a "soft spot," a slow area surrounded by fast current.

Once steelhead enter fresh water, they stop feeding, but they occasionally strike lures as an instinctive response or in defense of their territory. Anglers are often frustrated when they see fish tailing all around them but fail to get a single bite. While steelhead fishing can be a challenge, there are many ways to improve your odds and tempt even the most uninterested fish.

One of the deadliest techniques is slip-trolling. Anglers run an outboard in forward gear but with very little power to keep the bow pointed into the current while allowing the boat to slip slowly downstream. This technique enables you to hang a lure in the current so it practically brushes the fish's nose, provoking the steelhead to strike.

Slip-trolling gives you excellent boat control. By turning the motor slightly, you can slide sideways in the current without losing ground. Then, by turning the motor back the other way, you can slide back to your original position.

Some refer to the technique as backtrolling or hotshotting. The latter term originated because the lure most commonly used is a trolling plug called the Hot Shot. It dives rapidly, has an erratic darting action and comes in the bright colors that steelhead usually prefer.

When fishing is tough, natural bait often works better than lures. One of the most productive live-bait rigs is a floating spinner tipped with a piece of shrimp or a cluster of salmon eggs. This rig is also fished by slip-trolling.

Other effective methods for big-river steelhead include casting spoons and spinners with light spinning gear, or flycasting with wet and dry steelhead flies.

Steelhead fishing is best

This beautiful steelhead was caught by slip-trolling a Hot Shot on the Snake River near Lewiston, Idaho.

Lures and baits for steelhead include: (1) in-line spinners, such as the Mepps Aglia; (2) heavy spoons, such as the Little Cleo; (3) crankbaits, such as the Storm Wee Steelie Wart; (4) imitation salmon eggs, such as Berkley Power Eggs; (5) flies, such as the Silver Hilton; (6) spawn bags; and (7) single egg imitators, such as the yarn fly.

when the river is low and the fish are confined to deep pools and runs. Otherwise, they're scattered and difficult to find. Of course, your odds are greatest at the peak of the run. Conservation agencies closely monitor the progress of most steelhead runs, and often the number of fish passing through the dams of a river system are published daily in the local newspapers.

Weather and time of day are of little importance in steelhead fishing, but the first person of the day to fish a hole or run generally has the best chance.

Have someone cast to the side and upstream of the boat while others slip-troll. This technique allows you to cover more water and reach fish that have not been spooked by the boat.

How to Slip-troll for Steelhead

Position your boat at the upper end of a likely run with the bow upstream. While holding the boat's position, let out 60 to 70 feet of line.

Allow the boat to slip slowly downstream. It's important to let out the same amount of line on each rod so you present a "wall" of lures.

Continue slipping down the run. Some anglers feel that the wall of lures pushes the steelhead down the run, trapping them at the end and forcing them to strike.

In Wyoming's Flaming Gorge Reservoir, lake trout anglers have great success trolling with downriggers and spoons.

Lake Trout

The prospect of battling a huge lake trout draws anglers to remote lakes as far north as the Arctic Circle. These waters, most of which are in Canada's Northwest Territories, yield many 30- to 40-pound lake trout each year and a few that are considerably larger. The biggest lake trout on record is a 102-pound giant netted in Saskatchewan's Lake Athabasca.

Lake trout prefer water from 48° to 52°F, colder than any other gamefish. They cannot survive in water warmer than 65°F. During summer, lake trout may descend to depths of 100 feet or more to find cold water. Many lakes have water cold enough for lake trout, but if the water is too fertile, the fish cannot make use of the deep, cold water, because it does not have sufficient oxygen. As a result, lake trout are restricted mainly to the cold, sterile lakes of the Canadian Shield, the Great Lakes and deep mountain lakes of the West.

Lake trout grow slowly in these frigid waters. In some lakes of northern Canada, a 10-pound laker might be 20 years of age or even older. The age of a trophy lake trout may exceed 40 years. Because they grow so slowly, they can be easily overharvested. To preserve the quality of their lake-trout fishery, many fishing lodges in the Far North are now requiring that all trophy trout be returned to the water.

Lake trout have excellent vision. But because so little light reaches the depths, they rely heavily on their sense of smell and their lateral line to find food. In some waters, they feed exclusively on aquatic insects, worms and crustaceans. In other lakes, they eat only fish: mainly ciscoes, whitefish, sculpins and smelt. Lake trout feed almost exclusively during the day, although shallow-water fish feed in dim light.

In the western states and parts of Canada, lake trout are known as Mackinaw or gray trout, although the most popular nickname is laker. A lake trout/brook trout hybrid, called the splake, has been stocked in some northern lakes, including lakes Superior and Huron. Splake mature earlier than lake trout and grow faster than either parent, so they are less affected by fishing pressure.

Lake Trout Range

Lake trout have light spots on a background varying from light green or gray to dark green, brown or black. The tail is deeply forked. The world-record lake trout, 72 pounds, was caught in Great Bear Lake, Northwest Territories, in 1995.

Splake have light spots on the sides and light, wormlike markings on the back. The tail is not as deeply forked as that of a lake trout and the tips of the tail are more rounded. World record: 20 pounds, 11 ounces; Georgian Bay, Ontario; 1987.

Where to Find Lake Trout

Following ice-out, lake trout move from deep water into the warmer shallows where they remain for several weeks until the water becomes too warm. Then, they go as deep as necessary to find cold water. In lakes of extreme northern Canada, the shallows are always cold enough for lake trout, so they remain in water of 20 feet or less through the summer.

Lake trout move back to shallow water just before the fall spawning period. They spawn over a bottom of baseball- to football-sized rocks, usually at a depth of 5 to 20 feet. Because spawning lake trout are so easy to catch, most states and provinces close the season in fall.

Following is a list of some of the best spots to find and catch lake trout throughout the season.

Prime Locations for Lake Trout:

• Narrows between two major basins of the lake attract springtime lakers searching for food.

• Extensions from islands and points are ideal lake trout feeding areas in spring and fall.

• Deep slots and deep humps hold summertime lakers when the shallows become too warm.

• Shallow reefs that top off at 10 feet or less attract spawning lake trout in fall.

• Rocky points often attract small lake trout to shallow water on top of the points, while larger fish remain in deeper water off the tips.

• River mouths bring in warm meltwater that attracts lake trout. They are also drawn to schools of baitfish that hang around the plume.

• Islands that slope gently into deep water are excellent springtime laker spots. You'll usually find the fish at depths of 10 to 40 feet.

Lures for lake trout include: (1) trolling spoons, such as the Pro King; (2) dodger and fly combinations, such as the Alderton Action Flasher rigged with the Little Hooker; (3) trolling plugs, such as the Cisco Kid; (4) lead-head jigs, such as the Northland Sting'r Bucktail Jig; (5) vibrating blades, such as the Heddon Sonar Flash; and (6) jigging spoons, such as the Blue Fox Tor-P-Do Spoon.

How to Catch Lake Trout

Lake trout anglers use a wide variety of techniques, depending mainly on the depth of the fish. When lakers move into shallow water in spring and fall, for instance, the best methods are casting with flashy spoons or still-fishing with dead bait. When they go deep in summer, vertical jigging or trolling with downriggers or three-way swivel rigs are the most productive techniques. As a rule, lake trout use the same structure in winter as they do in summer. Jigging is, by far, the most productive method for catching lake trout through the ice.

Because lake trout water is usually free of snags, there is no need for heavy tackle. Most anglers use medium- to medium-heavy power spinning or baitcasting gear. Mono from 8- to 14-pound-test is adequate in shallow water. Spectra line, about 30-pound test, is a good choice for trolling or vertically jigging in deep water. It doesn't stretch and, because of its thin diameter, gets down easily.

Popular Lake Trout Techniques

Troll with downriggers to reach schools of deepwater trout. Note the depth of the trout on your graph and set your downrigger balls slightly shallower. Keep your "leads" no longer than 5 to 10 feet so the lures move up and down with the downrigger balls. If you don't have downriggers, you can troll with a three-way sinker rig (inset) consisting of an 8- to 12-ounce sinker and a 2-foot dropper and a 6-foot leader. The dropper keeps your lure off bottom so it won't snag.

Vertically jig with a heavy spoon (above), vibrating blade or lead-head jig. Use a graph to make sure you are right on top of the fish.

Still-fish with dead bait, such as a cisco or strip of sucker meat. Rig the bait on a size 1 to 2/0 hook and a slip-sinker rig with a 1/2- to 1-ounce egg sinker.

Lead-line and Wire-line Trolling

A popular method for catching lakers in open water without having to deploy downriggers is lead-line trolling. You'll need a medium-power 7- to 8-foot rod and a reel capable of holding 150 yards of lead-core line, 18- to 40-pound test. The line should be color coded at 10 yard intervals.

You can use a variety of baits for lead-lining, but the most popular choices include spoons, squid skirts, minnow plugs and live or dead minnows.

To reach the right depth, "count colors." As a rule one 10 yard section of color gets you down about 5 feet. If you're fishing with two lines it pays to try different color counts (below). Keep experimenting until you find the right depth.

Anglers often use large attractors, such as cowbells, ahead of their lure or bait. The attractor not only draws lake trout but serves as a speed and bottom indicator, transmitting a strong beat up through the line and through the rod. Any change in tempo of the beat indicates a change in trolling speed. If the beat stops, this indicates that the attractor has hit bottom, so you must reel up some line. Try to keep at least one line near the bottom, but don't let it drag.

When lakers are found really deep, it gets difficult to troll with lead-core line. You'll wear yourself out reeling in 15 or more colors, and if you are trolling with two or more lines, they may cross when you make a turn or the wind blows you off course.

Trolling with wire solves these problems. You'll need a different rod for this technique. A stiff rod with a roller tip, and a level-wind reel spooled with at least 100 yards of single-strand stainless steel wire of about 20-pound test works best. Attach the wire to a three-way swivel, then add a 15-pound mono dropper with an 8-ounce weight and a 6-foot leader of 10-pound-test mono. Some anglers do not like trolling with this much weight, but you'll need only about 1/4 the amount of line to reach the bottom as you would when trolling with lead-core.

How to Troll with Lead-core Line

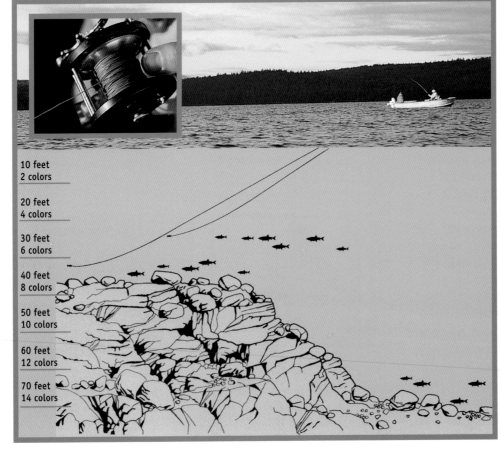

10 feet
2 colors

20 feet
4 colors

30 feet
6 colors

40 feet
8 colors

50 feet
10 colors

60 feet
12 colors

70 feet
14 colors

Let out line
while motoring a little faster than normal trolling speed. Remember to count colors (inset) as the line pays out, then reduce speed. With two anglers, each should fish at different depths until you locate the fish. The scale along the left margin gives you an idea of how deep your lure will run.

Ice Fishing for Lake Trout

As the ice fishing season begins, lakers will move back to the spots they spent the summer in, although they may be shallower in the water column. Prime wintertime spots are humps that top off at 40 to 60 feet in water that is at least 30 feet deeper. Most of the fish will relate to the top of the reef, but some will lie along the drop-off and others will suspend over deep water adjacent to humps and points.

The best way to catch lakers through the ice is to jig with vibrating blades, tube jigs and air-plane or bucktail jigs tipped with minnows. Drill a lot of holes, and keep moving until you find the fish. Using a

Northland Air-plane Jig

medium-power jigging rod about 3½ feet long and a bait-casting or spinning reel spooled with 10-pound mono, start jigging on the bottom and gradually work the lure upward. As in the summer, the "high" fish often bite better than those found near the bottom.

Tip-up fishing with live or dead ciscoes will also produce wintertime lakers, but jigging allows you to move around more easily. Some anglers will jig with one rod while setting a tip-up nearby. Because they inhabit such deep water, lakers show less response to changes in weather than do other game-fish. Open-water anglers prefer fair weather and light winds for easy boat control. Calm weather also makes wintertime jigging easier too.

Lake trout will bite any time of day, but you'll seldom catch them after dark. Often the fastest action is in the middle of the day.

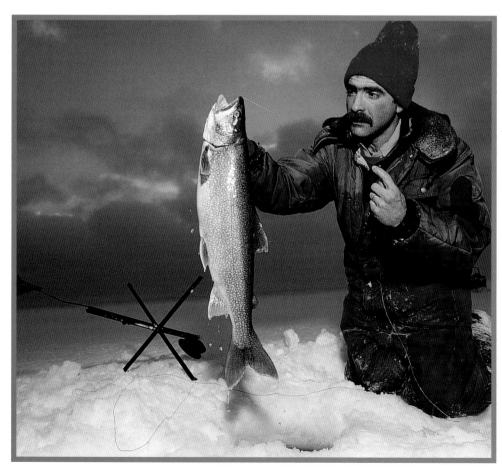

Tip-ups produce good-sized lakers for ice anglers. This fish was taken in Sebec Lake, Maine.

Salmon

Salmon are anadromous fish, meaning that they spend their adult life at sea and then return to freshwater streams to spawn. But scientists do not fully understand how a salmon can cross thousands of miles of open sea and then swim hundreds of miles up a freshwater stream to find the exact spawning site where its own life began. Many believe that they navigate at sea using the stars or the earth's magnetic field and then home in on their spawning stream using scent.

This 11-pound coho was caught in Alaska's Naknek River.

Five species of Pacific salmon – chinook, coho, pink, sockeye and chum – swim into streams from northern California to Alaska. Atlantic salmon enter streams from New York to Labrador.

Pacific salmon differ from Atlantics in that they have a fixed life span; most individuals of the same species return to spawn at the same age, and then die. Atlantics may live to spawn several times.

Salmon are powerful swimmers; on the way to their spawning grounds, they commonly hurdle rapids and falls that would seem impossible to ascend. Because of their tremendous power, speed and stamina, salmon are considered by many anglers to be the ultimate sport fish.

For many years, fisheries agencies tried to stock Pacific salmon in freshwater lakes, with little success. Then, in 1966, cohos were introduced into Lake Michigan in an attempt to control the lake's huge population of alewives and to create a new sport fishery. The salmon thrived on the small baitfish and the project's success led to the introduction of chinooks. Today, all of the Great Lakes support good salmon populations, and salmon have been stocked in many other large lakes. Chinooks are now plentiful in South Dakota's Lake Oahe and North Dakota's Lake Sakakawea, and many deep, cold lakes in the West have been planted with kokanee, the freshwater form of sockeye salmon. Landlocked salmon, the freshwater form of the Atlantic salmon, have been stocked in deep, cold freshwater lakes, mainly in the Northeast, since the late 1800s.

Salmon need cold water to survive, preferring temperatures around 55°F. In large lakes, wind and current move huge masses of water, causing drastic temperature changes over short periods of time. Salmon detect these fluctuations and follow water of their preferred temperature. As a result, salmon may be near the shore one day and miles away the next. Or, they can be schooling on the surface at sunrise and lying in 100-foot depths in the afternoon.

Coho and chinook salmon feed mainly on small fish, while kokanees and Atlantics rely more heavily on crustaceans and insects. The growth rate and ultimate size vary considerably among salmon species, with chinooks growing the fastest. In the Great Lakes, they commonly reach 20 to 35 pounds over a normal 4-year life span. Sea-run chinooks grow even faster, sometimes exceeding 50 pounds in 4 years.

Pacific Salmon Combined Range

Chinook salmon have silvery sides and black spots on the back and both lobes of the tail. The gums are blackish. The anal fin has 15 to 19 rays. The normal life span is 4 years. World record: 97 pounds, 4 ounces; Kenai River, Alaska; 1985.

This spawning male sockeye was photographed in Dumpling Creek, Alaska.

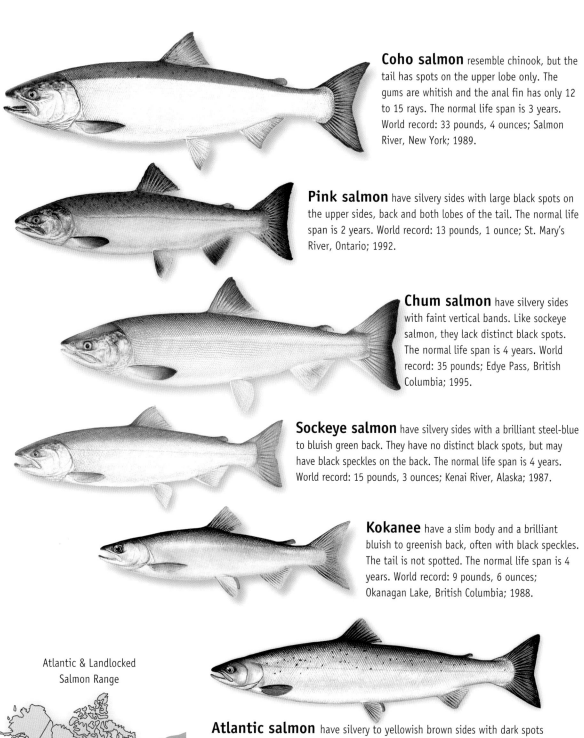

Coho salmon resemble chinook, but the tail has spots on the upper lobe only. The gums are whitish and the anal fin has only 12 to 15 rays. The normal life span is 3 years. World record: 33 pounds, 4 ounces; Salmon River, New York; 1989.

Pink salmon have silvery sides with large black spots on the upper sides, back and both lobes of the tail. The normal life span is 2 years. World record: 13 pounds, 1 ounce; St. Mary's River, Ontario; 1992.

Chum salmon have silvery sides with faint vertical bands. Like sockeye salmon, they lack distinct black spots. The normal life span is 4 years. World record: 35 pounds; Edye Pass, British Columbia; 1995.

Sockeye salmon have silvery sides with a brilliant steel-blue to bluish green back. They have no distinct black spots, but may have black speckles on the back. The normal life span is 4 years. World record: 15 pounds, 3 ounces; Kenai River, Alaska; 1987.

Kokanee have a slim body and a brilliant bluish to greenish back, often with black speckles. The tail is not spotted. The normal life span is 4 years. World record: 9 pounds, 6 ounces; Okanagan Lake, British Columbia; 1988.

Atlantic & Landlocked
Salmon Range

Atlantic salmon have silvery to yellowish brown sides with dark spots that may be X-shaped. Atlantics resemble brown trout, but the tail is slightly forked, rather than square, and the adipose fin is not spotted. World record: 79 pounds, 2 ounces; Tana River, Norway; 1928.

Landlocked salmon have larger spots than sea-run Atlantics, and the spots often have light halos. World record: 22 pounds, 11 ounces; Lobstick Lake, Newfoundland; 1982.

Where to Catch Salmon

Salmon rely on cover and structure less than most other gamefish. They go where they must to find food and a comfortable water temperature.

In the Great Lakes, salmon schools are scattered during spring and early summer. Their search for 53° to 57°F temperatures may take them miles from shore or within casting distance of piers. Although fishing is excellent on some days, catching salmon consistently is difficult. But as spawning time nears, salmon gather near the mouths of spawning streams where finding and catching them becomes easier.

Stream fishing for salmon in Great Lakes tributaries begins in September and continues into October. Along the Pacific Coast, some fish enter rivers and streams as early as April, but the majority of the runs take place from June through September. Atlantic salmon return to fresh water from May through October, with some rivers having both spring and fall runs. Once salmon enter spawning rivers and streams, you'll find them in the same kinds of lies favored by trout.

How Water Temperature Affects Salmon

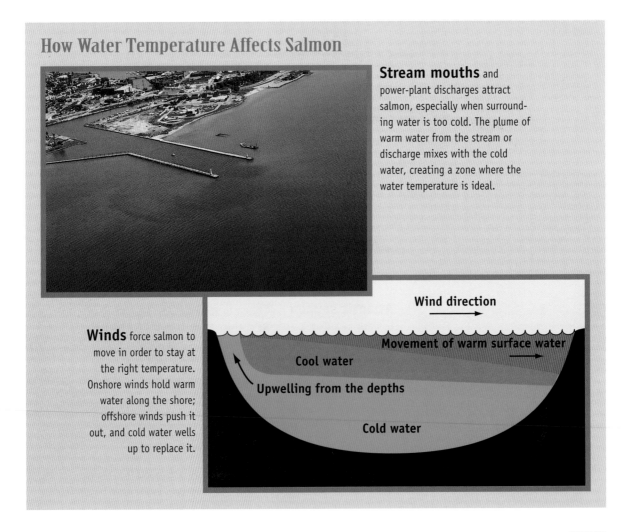

Stream mouths and power-plant discharges attract salmon, especially when surrounding water is too cold. The plume of warm water from the stream or discharge mixes with the cold water, creating a zone where the water temperature is ideal.

Winds force salmon to move in order to stay at the right temperature. Onshore winds hold warm water along the shore; offshore winds push it out, and cold water wells up to replace it.

Wind direction

Movement of warm surface water

Cool water

Upwelling from the depths

Cold water

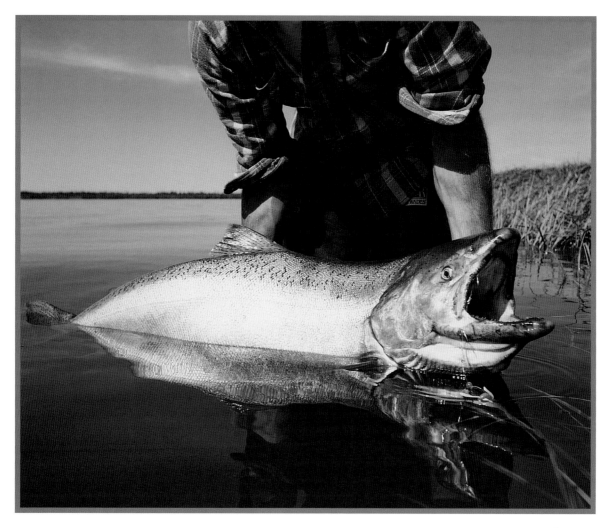

A 38-pound female chinook salmon caught in the Naknek River, Alaska.

How to Catch Salmon

Salmon anglers use a wide variety of natural-bait and artificial-lure techniques. Natural baits are used extensively by West Coast salmon fishermen. Common bait-fishing techniques include still-fishing or drift-fishing with a gob of fresh spawn or a spawn bag, and slow-trolling or mooching with herring. The latter technique involves dropping the bait to the bottom, then slowly raising and lowering it while the boat drifts.

In the Great Lakes, most anglers rely on artificials, particularly trolling spoons, plugs and flies, using side planers and downriggers to spread their lines and work a precise depth range. Silver or white lures with a little blue or green are good choices because they resemble alewives and smelt, important natural foods. But experienced anglers constantly experiment with different colors and actions, often trolling several different lures at the same time to determine the choice of the day.

For extra attraction, salmon fishermen often attach a large metal attractor, called a dodger, just ahead of their spoon or fly.

Downrigger lures for salmon include: (1) flutter spoons, such as the Northport Nailer; (2) dodger and fly combinations, such as the Luhr-Jensen Dodger rigged with the Foil Fly; and (3) plugs, such as the Luhr-Jensen J-Plug.

Downrigger Fishing

Trolling with downriggers and a good graph enables you to keep your lines in the fish zone most of the time. Downriggers also make it possible to fish deep water with relatively light tackle. If you had to add sinkers to get down, you would need a beefy rod to handle the weight.

Most salmon boats are equipped with at least two downriggers and many have four or more. This enables anglers to easily experiment with different depths and different lures until they find the right combination.

To reach the desired depth, simply attach your line (usually 12- to 20-pound mono) to a release device on the cable and then lower the downrigger ball into the fish zone. A strike frees the line from the release, so you can fight the fish without any extra weight. If desired, you can add another release farther up the cable and attach a second line, or stacker.

Fishing with Trolling Boards

Trolling boards keep your lines wide of the boat, a big advantage when fishing in clear, shallow water. Salmon are extremely boat-shy, so drawing the lines to the side of the boat's wake reduces the chance of spooking them.

The boards, which are pulled by cords attached to a pole in the boat, plane 40 to 75 feet to the side. The lines attach to release devices that slide down the cords toward the trolling boards. It is important to twist the line several times before attaching it to the release device (top photo); this way, the line won't slip through the release when a salmon strikes. Two or three lines can be fished off each side of the boat, covering a swath of water more than 100 feet wide.

Some salmon fishermen prefer side planers to trolling boards. Side planers, which are considerably smaller, attach directly to your fishing line, so there is no need for a cumbersome pole and cords. The drawback to side planers is that they stay on your line when you fight the salmon. This takes away from the sport and increases the chance of losing the fish.

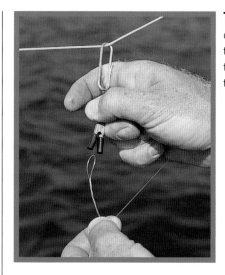

The proper way of attaching the line to the release device is to twist the line several times first.

Trolling Spoon Tip

Bend a spoon to improve its action by putting your thumbs together at its center, then sliding them outward while exerting pressure. The bend should be as smooth as possible. Spoons bent this way catch more water, causing them to veer more sharply to the side and creating a wider wobble. Tie one end of a 2-foot monofilament leader to the ring on the trolling spoon; the other end to a ball-bearing swivel. A snap swivel on the spoon would spoil the action.

Trolling board lures for salmon include: (1) spoons, such as the Blue Fox Trixee; and (2) plugs, such as the Rebel Fastrac.

Shore Fishing

Salmon in the Great Lakes and other large inland waters spend only a small percentage of their time within casting range of shore. But if you carefully pick your times and places, you'll enjoy some fast salmon action.

Pre-spawn salmon begin congregating near stream mouths weeks before the spawning run begins. They generally feed around the stream mouth for a few hours in early morning, move out in midday, and then return again in the evening.

Offshore winds also draw salmon into shore. It pays to carry a water thermometer and periodically check the temperature; as long as it's in the 53° to 57°F range, there's a good chance the fish will be there.

Piers (below) give shore fishermen a big advantage, because they enable anglers to fish water they could not otherwise reach. Anglers also wade out on long points to reach salmon cruising far from shore.

Most shore fishermen use

How to Fish from a Pier

Cast a thick spoon as far as you can. Pay out line as the spoon sinks, counting until the lure hits the bottom. Then, reel in steadily. If the spoon hits bottom on a 10-count on the first cast, count down to 8 on the second cast, 6 on the third, etc. If you catch a salmon, count down to the same depth on the next cast.

spinning rods at least 8 feet in length to power-cast heavy spoons. But when the fish are tightly schooled around stream mouths, still-fishing with a spawn bag or a live alewife on a slip-sinker rig may work better.

Always use a large-capacity reel when shore fishing for salmon. To ensure that a big salmon doesn't spool you, your reel should hold at least 300 yards of 12- to 17-pound-test mono.

River & Stream Fishing

As Pacific salmon move into rivers and streams to spawn, their digestive tract begins to shrink and they stop eating. Their color changes from bright silver to reddish or brownish and finally to black. Males develop a strongly hooked lower jaw, or kype, and large canine teeth to help them defend their spawning territory. But even though the fish aren't feeding, they strike lures out of reflex or territoriality. Male Atlantic salmon also develop a kype but they continue to feed.

During the spawning run, certain pools and runs or the areas below dams and waterfalls literally become jammed with salmon. Once the fish reach their spawning grounds, it pays to concentrate on specific spawning beds, or redds.

When salmon are in slow to moderate current, most anglers cast with spoons, spinners and jigs. In faster current or when salmon are on the redds, try drift-fishing (p. 248) with yarn flies or spawn bags. In the large rivers of Alaska, salmon fishermen slip-troll with deep-diving plugs designed to get down to the bottom, where the majority of the fish are holding.

Although the majority of stream fishing is done by wading, drift boats offer some major advantages. You can cover more water to find the fish, and, because you're drifting at the same speed as the current, drag on your lure is virtually eliminated. This makes it easier to get down to the fish.

River- and stream-fishing lures include: (1) in-line spinners, such as the Worden's Rooster Tail; (2) spoons, such as the Blue Fox Pixee; (3) plugs, such as the Storm Lures King Mag Wart; and (4) flies, such as the Lefty's Deceiver.

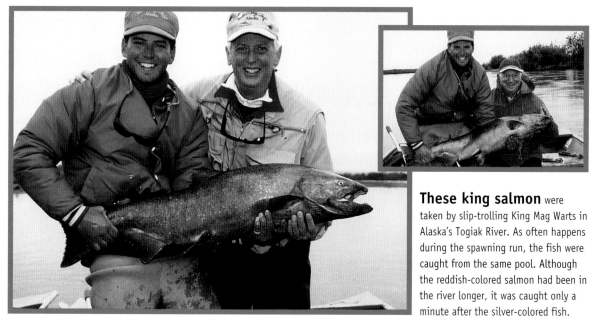

These king salmon were taken by slip-trolling King Mag Warts in Alaska's Togiak River. As often happens during the spawning run, the fish were caught from the same pool. Although the reddish-colored salmon had been in the river longer, it was caught only a minute after the silver-colored fish.

Keeping & Cleaning Fish

Fish are extremely perishable. Fish that do not have red gills, clear eyes and a fresh odor should be discarded. Proper care ensures firm flesh for cooking.

The secret to preserving your catch is to keep it alive or cold. If the surface water is cool, a stringer or wire basket can keep some fish species alive. Bring the fish aboard when moving the boat to a new spot. Return them to the water as soon as possible.

Aerated live wells in many boats keep bass, northern pike and other hardy fish alive. Limit the number of fish; remove dead ones to ice immediately.

Check your catch often, whether the fish are on a stringer or in a wire basket or live well. Transfer dead ones to an ice-filled cooler immediately. Dead fish left in water spoil rapidly.

Burlap bags, newspapers, moss or other materials that "breathe" help preserve fish when ice is not available. Keep the covering moist; evaporation helps cool fish.

Large gamefish should be killed immediately. Use a stout stick and rap the fish across the back of the head. Their flesh can bruise if they flop around in a boat. Field-dress as soon as possible and place the fish on ice.

Keeping fish in good condition on extended trips is difficult. Fish held longer than 2 days should be super-chilled (opposite page), frozen or smoked. You can often take advantage of motel facilities to keep your catch cold or frozen. If shipping fish by plane, place them in a Styrofoam cooler wrapped with a layer of heavy cardboard.

Storing Fish

For top flavor, clean and cook your gamefish within 2 hours after catching it. However, most anglers have to keep their catch for a longer time.

The colder the storage temperature, the longer the fish can be held. If handled and cleaned properly, fish can be refrigerated for 24 hours with little flavor loss. Fish stored on crushed ice in a cooler will remain fresh for 2 or 3 days, but the cooler must be drained often so the catch doesn't soak in the water. Super-chilled fish can be kept up to 7 days.

To keep fillets in the refrigerator, simply rinse them quickly with cold water and pat dry with paper towels. Then, place the fillets on paper towels and cover them tightly with plastic wrap or aluminum foil.

Pan-dressing

Panfish, including bluegills, crappies and yellow perch, are often too small for filleting. They are usually pan-dressed instead. Scales, fins, guts and head are always removed. Scaling fish is quick and easy with a scaler, though a dull knife or a spoon can be used. Wet the fish and scrape off the scales, working from tail to head. This job should be done outdoors, because scales fly in all directions. Or line the kitchen sink with newspapers and scale as carefully as possible. The tail is quite tasty and can be left on. Most of the the tiny fin bones are removed by pan-dressing.

How to Pan-dress Whole Fish

Slice along the dorsal fin of the scaled panfish. Make the same cut on the other side, then pull out the fin.

Cut along both sides of the anal fin. Remove the fin by pulling it toward the tail. Remove the head. Angle the blade over the top of the head to save as much flesh as possible.

Slit the belly and pull out the guts. Cut off tail, if desired. Rinse fish quickly; dry with paper towels.

Super-chilling Fish

It's hard to keep fish fresh on long trips into the backcountry. You'll be lucky to keep them for more than 2 or 3 days on ordinary ice. But you can keep them for a full week by "super-chilling" them with a mixture of ice and salt. Because the ice-salt combination has a lower melting point, about 28°F, the fish stay colder.

You can super-chill fillets, steaks or whole fish that have been gutted and gilled. Wrap the fish in aluminum foil or plastic wrap. Add 1 pound of coarse ice cream salt to 20 pounds of crushed ice and stir thoroughly. If you need less of the salt-ice mixture, reduce the ingredients proportionately.

Place the wrapped fish on a 4-inch bed of the salt-ice. Add alternating layers of fish and salt-ice, finishing with a generous topping of the salt-ice mixture. Later, as the ice melts, drain the cooler and add more of the salt-ice.

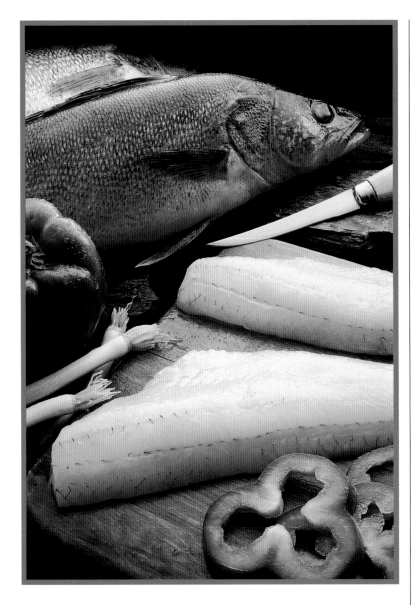

Filleting Techniques

Anglers use a variety of filleting techniques. The Canadian filleting method shown on these pages is the easiest and quickest for most anglers. Fillets can be stripped from the backbone in under a minute with a very sharp knife.

If your fillet board does not have a clip, you can use a fork to pin the head of a small fish. A fork or pliers can also be useful during skinning. Salt on the hands helps hold a slippery fish.

The skin can be removed or left on. Fish such as largemouth bass have strong-tasting skin, so many anglers remove it. However, the skin on small trout and panfish is tasty. Panfish have large scales that must be removed if the skin is retained.

Keep the skin on fillets that will be charcoal grilled. This helps prevent the flesh from falling apart, sticking to the grill and overcooking. Cut long fillets into serving-size pieces before they are cooked or stored. Thick fillets can be divided into two thin fillets for easier cooking.

Remove the thin strip of fatty belly flesh on oily fish such as salmon and large trout. Any contaminants will settle into this fatty tissue. To clean fillets, wipe with paper towels or rinse quickly under cold running water. Dry thoroughly with paper towels.

After filleting, rinse hands with clean water before using soap. Rub hands with vinegar and salt, lemon juice or toothpaste to remove the fishy smell.

Save the bones and head after filleting. These pieces can be used for stock, chowder, fish cakes or other dishes.

Filleting Basics

Filleting is the most common method of cleaning fish. It is easily mastered with a little practice and some knowledge of the bone structure and location of the various fins. The technique is popular because most of the flesh can be quickly removed from the bones without touching the intestines. In addition, the boneless fillets can be cooked in many ways and are easy to eat.

A sharp knife is essential when filleting fish. Use a sharpening stone and steel to touch up knife blades. Fillet knives of hard steel will hold their edge longer than soft steel. However, soft steel requires less effort to sharpen. It is interesting and helpful to watch butchers sharpen and realign knives.

Ideally, the length of the blade should fit the fish. Because good fillet knives last many years, it pays to have two or three sizes. A wooden fillet board with a clip on one end is useful for holding fish. Outdoors, fillet your fish on an oar, a paddle or the lid of a plastic cooler.

Canadian Filleting Technique

1. Cut behind the pectoral fin straight down to the backbone. Angle the cut toward the top of the head.

2. Run the knife along one side of the backbone. The knife should scrape the rib bones without cutting them.

3. Push the knife through the flesh near the vent just behind the rib bones. Cut the fillet free at the tail.

4. Cut the flesh carefully away from the rib cage. To save flesh, the blade should graze the bones.

5. Remove the first boneless fillet by cutting through the skin of the stomach area.

6. Turn the fish over. Remove the second fillet using the same filleting technique.

7. Rinse fillets quickly with cold water or wipe with paper towels. Save head and skeleton for stock.

8. Skin fillets, if desired. Hold the tail with your fingertips and cut between flesh and skin with a sawing motion.

Removing Y-bones

Members of the pike family have delicious, flaky meat. But the Y-bones are bothersome enough that some people refuse to eat these fish.

Although there are a couple of ways to remove these bones, most fishermen don't know how, so they have to pick them out at the table. Shown below is a way to make boneless fillets from pike and pickerel.

Cleaning Catfish & Bullheads

Catfish and bullheads should be skinned (opposite page), regardless of their size. Two basic tools are required: a sharp knife and a set of skinning pliers. A regular set of pliers works, but skinning pliers work better because the jaws are wider, affording a better grip on the catfish's thin, slippery skin.

Some anglers also use a skin-ning board clamp or a board with a nail driven through it to hold the head in place. Large fish may have to be hung from a tree limb or other overhead support to facilitate cleaning. Small fish can be handheld.

Regardless of how you secure the fish, take care to avoid the sharp pectoral and dorsal spines throughout the cleaning process. Kill the fish with a hammer before you start skinning.

Freezing Fish

Many anglers overlook the importance of proper freezing techniques for their catch. They wrap fish fillets loosely in plastic wrap or hurriedly throw it into a used bread bag, then toss the parcel into the freezer. When it comes time to cook, they're surprised that the fish is dried out or freezer burned.

Fish can be preserved by freezing in water. Any dehydration that occurs will first happen to the ice, not the meat; and if the food is frozen in a milk carton or plastic container, dehydration is greatly reduced.

Even foods frozen in water won't last indefinitely, however, especially if stored in a frost-free freezer. In a freezer of this type, a fan unit pulls moisture out of the air to prevent frost buildup. Unfortunately, it also pulls the moisture out of poorly wrapped fish and it will also eventually cause the ice to be eaten away from foods that have been frozen in water. In addition to these problems, fats in fish and game will slowly begin to oxidize even in the freezer. As a result, fatty fish such as salmon, and many types of game, have a shorter freezer life than other foods. In general, fillets from fatty fish have a maximum freezer life of about 1 month; fillets from lean fish, 2 to 3 months.

Fish fillets may be treated to extend their freezer life by 3 months. Mix 2 tablespoons of ascorbic acid (available in drugstores) with 1 quart cold water. Place fish in the mixture for 20 seconds, then wrap and freeze.

Never thaw fish at room temperature, because bacteria can grow as the food is thawing. Place wrapped packages on a plate in the refrigerator for a day; larger pieces may need even longer to thaw.

How to Remove Y-bones from Northern Pike

2. Cut the flesh from the Y-bones by guiding the knife blade along the bones (arrow), scraping lightly. Remove the triangular strip of bones and flesh; save them for stock. Two long boneless fillets remain.

1. Slice through the flesh along the edge of the Y-bones (arrows). The bottom fillet will be boneless.

How to Skin a Catfish or Bullhead

1. Make a cut through the skin behind the head. Start behind the pectoral fin on one side of the fish, and cut up, over and down to the other pectoral fin.

2. Use the point of the knife to split the skin down the middle of the back, from head to tail, running down one side of the dorsal fin.

3. Split the skin on the other side of the dorsal fin, connecting this cut to the one just made. The fish is now ready for skinning.

4. Grasp the skin with pliers and pull toward the tail. It should strip off in one or two pieces. Repeat the process on the other side.

5. Remove the meat along each side of the fish with a fillet knife. Cut around the rib cage for a totally boneless fillet. Cut away all dark red flesh along the lateral line. This meat often harbors contaminants and can have a strong flavor.

How to Freeze Fish in Water

1. Use small pans, freezer containers, or clean milk cartons to freeze meal-sized portions of fish or game. Cover food with cold water, cover container and freeze. If needed, repeat to ensure that food is encased in ice.

2. Pop out block of frozen ice and food by running cold water on the bottom; the ice should release easily from the container.

3. Wrap the solid block of ice and food in plastic wrap or aluminum foil. Overwrap with freezer paper, sealing tight. Label package with species, date, and number of servings, and store in a 0° freezer.

Photographing Your Catch

With catch-and-release fishing growing in popularity among anglers, photography has become an important way to ensure that you will remember a particular fish or memorable trip. However, many anglers find it very difficult to take quality photos that do justice to the fish. Some snapshots are too light, others too dark; some are fuzzy and out of focus, others are too cluttered to clearly show your catch.

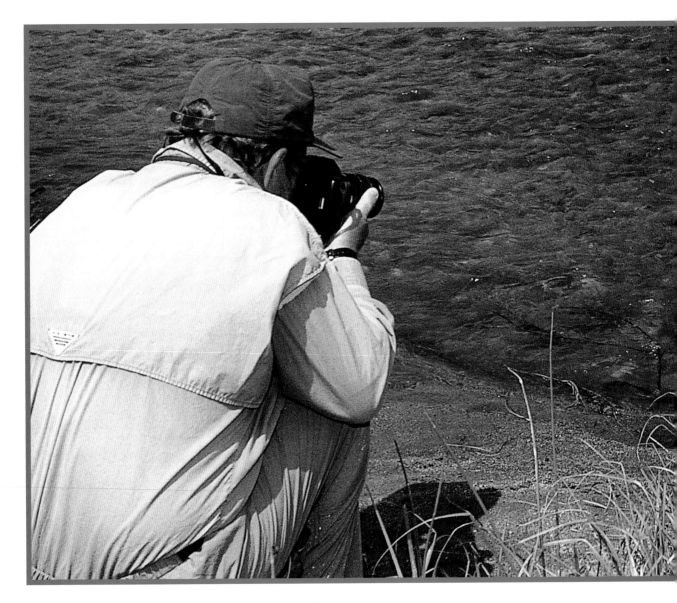

The first step toward taking better photos is to find yourself a good, reliable camera. For the casual photographer, a good choice is a fully automatic 35mm pocket camera with a fixed lens. Some of these models are water-resistant or waterproof. If you frequently fish alone, you'll need a camera with a self-timer – and a small tripod – so you can photograph yourself.

If you are seriously interested in photography, you'll want to get a 35mm camera with optional manual modes, as well as automatic operation. A serious photographer also needs a camera that can accept a range of lenses. Mounting your camera with a zoom lens with a focal length of about 28mm to 80mm is an excellent choice. This type of lens allows you to adjust it from wide-angle to low-power telephoto view in an instant, without the inconvenience of carrying extra lenses and changing them constantly.

If you've never operated a 35mm camera, it pays to enroll in a course to learn the principles of photography and photo operation. Short courses are sometimes available at the store where you purchased your camera, or through community education programs. Perhaps the best way to improve your own photography is to study photos you like and figure out why they appeal to you.

The tips on the following pages will help you take better pictures the next time you go fishing. By paying attention to detail and giving up a few minutes of fishing to concentrate on your photography, you'll be able to bring back photos that capture the live excitement of your catch.

Shooting Posed Photos

An angler posed with a beautiful trophy fish can make for a terrific shot – or a terrible one. The next time you snap a photo of a friend holding a big bass or a child with his or her first sunfish, pay attention to the following details. The result will be a much better photo.

• Take the photo moments after the fish is landed. Don't hurt its chances by keeping the fish out of water for too long. If possible, shoot the picture while holding the fish in the water.

• Choose the background carefully. Sky, water or undeveloped shoreline make good, simple backdrops.

• Have your friend push back his hat and take off his sunglasses to remove shadows hiding his face.

• Don't let your model's hands obscure the fish – especially its head.

• Take photos of normal fish-handling activities to give realism and authenticity to your shots.

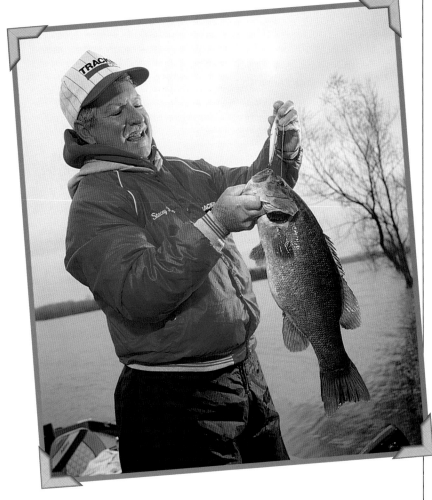

Photography Tips

Shoot Early or Late in the Day

Natural light is most attractive in the early morning or late afternoon, when the angle of sunlight is low. Photos taken at these times will have rich, warm colors and uniform tone, while photos taken at midday have deep shadows and harsh, contrasting tones. Midday light can "burn out" details – such as the natural silvery hue of many fish. If you must shoot in bright light, turn the fish slightly to minimize reflection and get the best coloration and detail.

Use Lots of Film

Film is relatively cheap, compared to other fishing accessories, so take lots of photos to ensure that you get at least one good shot. If you like the look of a shot, take extras to compensate for those that may be ruined by movement or awkward expressions. If you have a camera with manual exposure controls, you can bracket your photos by taking shots on both sides of the setting recommended by your camera's light meter. For example, if the meter indicates an F8 exposure aperture, take one photo at this setting, then take a second at F5.6 and a third at F11. This helps guarantee that you get at least one good exposure.

Too dark

Good exposure

Too light

PHOTOGRAPHING YOUR CATCH

Catch the Action

Keep your camera loaded and set for the prevailing light conditions – and keep it close at hand. Set the shutter speed at 1/500 second to ensure that the action will be frozen. If using an autofocus camera, make sure to keep the subject in the center of the frame.

Look for Angles

In general, you're better off shooting from below or at the same level as your subject. A low camera position allows you to use the sky as a background, which is ideal because the sky is uncluttered. Panfish and bass look the best held vertically using one hand, but long trophy fish often look very impressive when held horizontally using two hands.

Use Fill Flash

When shooting a backlit subject, use "fill flash" to add light to shadowy areas. This technique is possible only if you own a manual camera, or an automatic camera with an override setting that provides fill flash. For a manual camera, fill flash works best if you use a variable-power flash unit. With the camera in manual mode, set your shutter speed to synchronize with the flash – usually 1/60 second. Then, set the F-stop on the lens according to the camera's light meter. Adjust your flash unit according to the F-stop of your camera and the distance to the subject. Turn down the power dial on the flash unit by one F-stop to prevent the flash from "burning out" your subject. Shoot one or two shots; then lower your power setting by one more F-stop and shoot again.

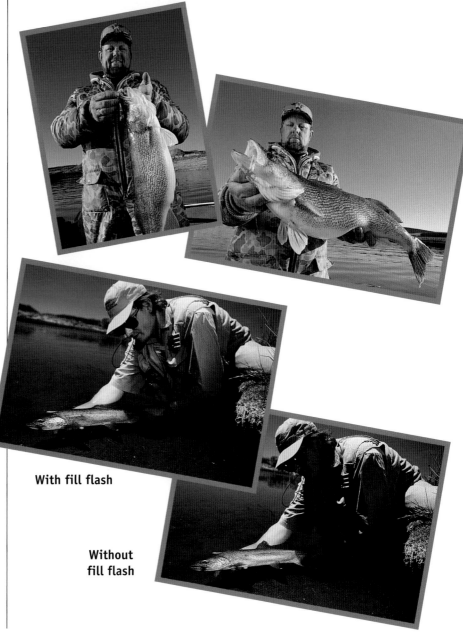

With fill flash

Without fill flash

General-Purpose Tips

No More Messy Worms (p. 284)

General-Purpose Tips

No More Messy Worms

Digging through a pail full of worms and bedding makes a mess of your boat, hands and clothes. Instead, drop several dozen worms in a bucket of ice. Meltwater cleans the worms, and they'll survive all day. When you're done fishing, put the worms back into the bedding. If they crawl down, they're still healthy.

Long Live the Leeches

To ensure you always have leeches on hand, buy several pounds in the spring when they're plentiful and cheap. Leeches can be kept alive for months in a refrigerator. Take out only as many as you will need on your fishing trip. Most of the leeches you don't use will survive a day on the water and can be returned to the fridge. But keep them separate from leeches in long-term storage. Putting dead or dying leeches in with healthy ones may kill them all. Here's how to keep leeches in good shape:

STORE leeches in a Styrofoam bucket in a refrigerator; the water should be barely above freezing — 34 to 38° F. Change water every few days to keep it clean. Store an extra container of water in the refrigerator. When you change water, the fresh water will be at the same temperature and any chlorine will be gone.

ADD a few ice cubes to your bait bucket as you fish to keep the water cool. If the water is allowed to get warm, leeches begin to mature and spawn. The process begins at about 50° F and accelerates as the temperature rises. Once leeches mature, they die within several days, even if you return them to cold water.

Bring the Worms to You

To attract worms and keep them in a spot where they are easily gathered, make a worm bed. Place several inches of matted straw over dirt you have loosened and turned with a garden fork. Keep the straw moist to draw worms.

Fishing a Worm Beneath a Bobber

If you're fishing a nightcrawler with a slip-sinker, hook it once through the head so it trails behind the hook. But don't hook it this way when you bobber-fish because the worm will dangle vertically. You'll miss strikes, and fish will steal your bait. Here's a better way to hook your worm when bobber fishing:

HOOK the worm twice through the middle when suspending it below a bobber. This way, you're more likely to hook a fish that doesn't suck in the entire worm.

Keep Crawlers Lively

Worms kept in something other than a thick Styrofoam container get limp and lifeless on a warm day. If they get too hot, they'll die. Here's a way to keep worms lively, even in the hottest weather.

Put a few ice cubes in a small resealable plastic bag and bury it in the bedding. The worms will stay cool for hours. Without the bag, the melting ice cubes would make the bedding too soggy.

Nightcrawler Substitute

If it's been too dry to collect nightcrawlers or if you can't find them at your local bait shop, it's tough to find a good substitute. Here's a trick that may salvage your fishing trip:

STRING three garden worms on a single hook. Push about ¼ inch of the head of each worm onto the hook and let the tails wiggle freely. The squirming worms work as well as, and sometimes even better than, a crawler.

"Easy Pickin's" for Crawlers

Because crawlers are so expensive, lots of anglers try to collect their own, but most are lucky to get enough for a day's fishing.

Here's how you can catch enough nightcrawlers in just an hour or two to last most of the season. All you need is an underground worm bed or an old refrigerator to keep them in.

- Most worm pickers go out at night, but you can often find more worms in early morning, especially if it has been drizzling all night. By morning, the worms are crawling some distance from their burrows, so catching them is easy. And you don't need a light. The best early-morning spots are golf course greens and the gutters along paved streets.

- Some golf courses produce lots of crawlers; others, very few. The trick is to find the ones that don't apply chemicals to control the worms.

- Check well-established lawns. A newly seeded or sodded lawn may not produce crawlers for several years, and if the soil is too sandy or gravelly, it may never produce.

- Look for crawlers during or after a prolonged light rain or drizzle. Worms don't like being pelted by heavy rain. The air temperature should be at least 50° F. Otherwise, worms stay in the ground.

- Wait until a couple of hours after dark so the night-crawlers are out of their burrows. If their tails are still anchored, the worms will zip back in when they detect a light or feel the vibrations from your footsteps.

- Cover your flashlight lens with red cellophane. This way, the light doesn't seem to bother the worms. Step lightly to keep vibrations to a minimum.

- Pick up crawlers on a paved street using a spatula. It's difficult to get your fingers under the wet, slippery worms.

Follow Birds to Fish

Birds can lead you to good ice-fishing spots. If there are no anglers or fish houses on a lake to give away the location of a hotspot, you can often pinpoint the site of recent fishing activity by watching birds, such as crows or gulls, which often congregate where anglers have discarded bait or small fish.

During the open-water season, look for loons, cormorants or fish-eating ducks diving in off-shore areas. The birds are feeding on small fish, which are probably relating to a reef or some kind of cover. Gamefish are likely to be there along with them.

Acclimate Minnows

Most minnows are sensitive to rapid changes in water temperature. Always keep this in mind when handling your bait.

Many anglers believe they can keep their minnows alive on a hot day by adding ice. But they're often surprised to find all the minnows dead within minutes. Icing your minnows can help, but don't add too much ice at once. If you lower the temperature of the water by more than about 10° F at a time, the minnows will often die from temperature shock.

You can also kill minnows by moving them from cool water to warm. This problem occurs most frequently when anglers transfer minnows in a cool oxygen pack to the warm water of a cooler, bait well or flow-through minnow bucket. Solve the problem this way:

PLACE the unopened oxygen pack into a cooler or bait well to slowly warm the water inside the bag and acclimate the minnows to the change in temperature. After about a half-hour, the water in the pack will be the same temperature, and you can open the bag without harming the minnows.

Finer Fiddle for Worms →

Southeastern anglers collect grunt worms by "fiddling" — rubbing an ax head or piece of steel on a wooden stake driven into the ground. The vibrations draw worms to the surface. Here's a way to make a stake that produces stronger vibrations with less effort and will help you get more worms.

Cut ¼-inch-deep saw kerfs at ½-inch intervals along one side of a 2 × 2 stake about 30 inches long. Make a point on one end and drive the stake about a foot into the ground.

Rub another stick, such as a piece of broom handle, rapidly up and down across the saw cuts.

Save Bug Dope for Bugs

If you get insect repellent containing DEET on your hands, it can soften vinyl fly line coatings, weaken monofilament line, damage lure finishes, eat away at line spools, dissolve non-wormproof tackle boxes and damage the screens of liquid crystal recorders. Here's a way to avoid the problem.

Apply the bug dope first to the *backs* of your hands. Then use the backs of your hands to spread the repellent to your face, neck and arms. This is a good tip for the camp cook as well, so the repellent doesn't get in the food.

Sea Anchor Savvy

Anglers on big water commonly use sea anchors to reduce their drifting or trolling speed. But sea anchors have many other boat-control applications. Here are some important ones:

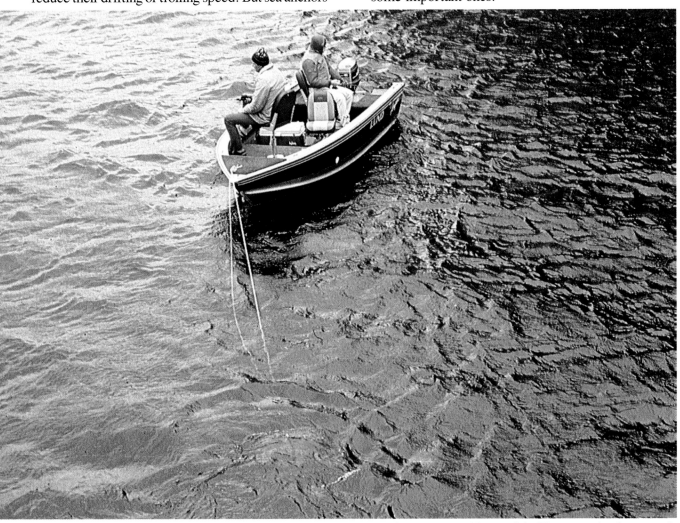

BACKTROLL *with the wind* by extending a sea anchor from your bow and running your motor in reverse. Without a sea anchor, the wind would swing your bow around, making precise boat control impossible. The sea anchor has enough drag to prevent the bow from switching around in the wind, so you can easily follow the bottom contour.

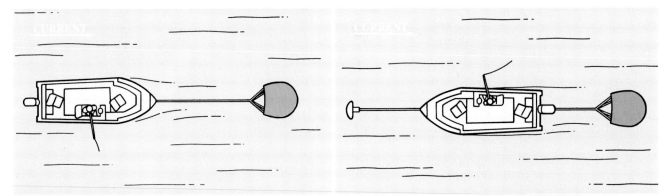

TROLL slowly downstream against a strong upriver wind by running a sea anchor off the bow and pointing the bow into the waves. The force of the current against the sea anchor prevents the wind from swinging the bow around. You could backtroll into the waves, but you might get a bath from water lapping over the stern.

ANCHOR in place on a big, windswept river by dropping a heavy anchor from your bow and running a sea anchor from your stern. The current will pull the sea anchor and stern downstream. The bow will point upriver as the anchor rope pulls tight. Even if the wind blows hard upstream or switches around, the boat will stay in the same place.

Prevent Line Twist ↑

When you're jigging vertically, whether in open water or through the ice, the lure usually spins around and causes severe line twist. The twisted line tends to wrap around your rod tip and tangle in your guides. To prevent the problem, tie a small swivel to your line, a foot or two above the lure.

Avoid Bobber Stop Hang-ups

The advantage of a slip-bobber over a regular bobber is that you can cast it easily, even when you're fishing deep. But the bobber stop (arrow) can interfere with casting. If it happens to wind onto the front edge of your spool, it can catch outgoing line, causing your cast to fall short or to stop suddenly and snap off the bait. Here's how to avoid the problem:

REACH down with your index or middle finger as the bobber stop reaches the bail and guide the line toward the rear of the spool. Then continue reeling as you normally would. With the bobber stop out the way, the line will peel smoothly off the spool on the cast and won't hang up.

Unwrap Line Quickly

It's happened to nearly every angler: when you're fishing, you notice a wrap of line around your rod. You're not sure how the wrap got there, but it seems the only way to get rid of it is to restring your rod. Here's an easier way:

1. GRAB the line where it wraps around the rod between two of the guides.

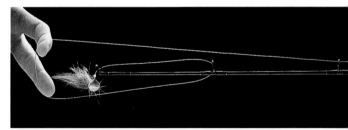

2. PULL the line over the tiptop or butt of the rod, whichever is easier.

3. RELEASE the line, and the line runs from guide to guide without the once-around wrap.

Heading off a Bird's Nest

If you're using a spinning reel and retrieve without much tension on the line, a loop of mono will often form at the front of the spool and interfere with the outgoing line as you cast. If you try to peel off line to get rid of the loop, the loop will also begin to peel off and tangle with the other line, often forming a snarl several feet long. It may be impossible to untangle the line without cutting it.

Here's a good way to head off a tangle before it occurs and save precious fishing time:

OPEN the bail and remove the spool when you notice that a loop has formed. Because these loops form at the front of the spool, it's best to pull line off the *back* of the spool to avoid tangling the outgoing line with the loop. After you pull off the loop, replace the spool, close the bail and reel in the loose line.

Cut a Backlash Short

Even expert baitcasters get backlashes, especially when they're casting into the wind. Here's a trick that minimizes the amount of line involved in a bird's nest and keeps you from ruining all the line on your spool:

LAY a piece of plastic tape across the spool after stripping out a bit more line than you're likely to cast. Reel the line over the tape. Now, even if you get a backlash, the tangle will go no deeper than the tape. If you have to cut the line to clear the spool, you'll still have plenty left.

Trigger Strikes While Trolling

When you're trolling with plugs, spinners or spoons, drop your rod tip back once in a while rather than maintain a steady pull. Dropping back causes the lure to tumble momentarily, triggering strikes from any fish that may be following.

Bobber Helps You Get Unsnagged

River rats know that if you snag your lure downstream, you may be able to pull free by letting out enough line to form a belly several yards below the snag. When you give a sharp tug, water resistance against the line pro-duces a downstream pull that may free the lure. But if the lure is tightly snagged, this technique won't work. Here's a way to produce a stronger downstream pull and free the lure:

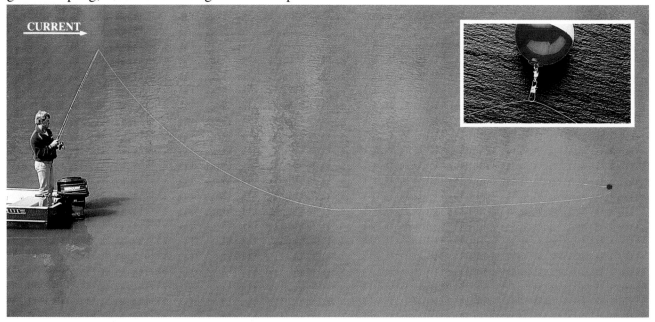

CLIP a big bobber to the eye of a snap-swivel (inset). Close the snap over your line. Open your bail and let the current carry the bobber well past the snag. Close your bail. When the line tightens, give a sharp tug. The added resistance of the bobber results in a stronger downstream pull than that produced by the line alone. Other floats, such as plastic bottles, will also work, and these can be partially filled with water to increase the drag and the power of your pull.

Bonus for Paddlers

Trolling in deep, open water may seem like a waste of time, but some anglers who canoe the wilderness lakes of the northern states and Canada know differently. When paddling across open expanses, they toss out a lure, such as a crankbait or minnow plug.

Pike, walleyes, lake trout and smallmouth bass often suspend in open water, feeding on ciscoes, a common baitfish in many of these lakes. Trolling across the middle of a lake is not a high-percentage method, but it produces a surprising number of fish.

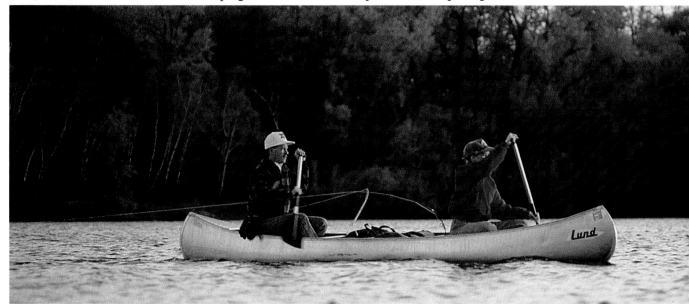

Diagnose Fly-Casting Faults

A good forward cast is easy for most fly-fishermen because they can watch the fly line and correct their casting faults. The problem is the backcast: It's tough to glance backwards over your shoulder to make adjustments to your casting stroke. For that reason, many fishermen have lousy backcasts and cast poorly overall.

If you have trouble with your backcast, such as hitting the water or ground behind you with the line, use this trick to study your problem and correct it:

1. STAND sideways to your target (a Hula Hoop makes a good one) with your feet spread comfortably, like a batter standing at the plate. Lower your rod so it is parallel to the ground and cast sidearm rather than overhand.

2. WATCH the fly line as you make your backcast and forward cast. Adjust your timing and casting stroke until the line unfurls smoothly, forming narrow loops forward and backward.

3. TURN back toward your target and cast with an overhand motion instead of sidearm. The timing and motion remain nearly identical, even though the casting plane changes from horizontal to vertical.

Smooth Fly Casting From a Boat

When fly-fishing from a boat, anglers usually drop extra line in loose coils near their feet. On the cast, the line will lift up and zip through the guides — unless you happen to be standing on it. Cutting a cast short this way is especially frustrating when fishing for shallow-water trophies such as tarpon or bonefish.

Your chances are few, so quick, accurate casts are essential. You can eliminate the problem by fishing without shoes so you can feel any line underfoot. Be sure the area is free of hooks, and if it's sunny, remember to apply sunblock to protect the tops of your feet from a bad burn.

Try Tailwaters After Heavy Rains

Heavy rains cause most streams to rise quickly and turn muddy. The dirty water usually ruins fishing, but you may be able to salvage your trip by moving to the tailwaters of a good-sized reservoir. Silt settles out in the reservoir, so even after a torrential rain, water flowing from the dam will be relatively clear for some distance downstream. It will stay clear until it is muddied by tributaries.

Fly-Fishing in the Wind

Wind gives fly-fishermen fits. You can't drive your forward cast into the wind. And a wind at your back causes the backcast to pile up, which means the forward cast is no good either. But wind doesn't have to ruin your fly-fishing. Here's how to make good casts, either into the wind or with it:

CASTING INTO THE WIND. Cast sidearm, keeping your forward cast as low to the water as possible. This way, the wind, has little effect on it. Loft your backcast a bit (dotted line) so the wind helps straighten it out.

CASTING WITH THE WIND. Cast sidearm, keeping your backcast low and shorter than normal. Aim higher with the forward cast (dotted line) so the wind will catch it, adding to your distance.

Fight Fish Smart

If you hook a large, powerful fish with normal-weight tackle, you may not be able to wear it down by lifting with steady tension. The fish can resist without moving much and doesn't get tired. Here are a couple ways to tire big fish quickly and increase your odds of landing them.

Work a fish in shallow water by pulling it to one side, switching the rod to the other side and pulling from the opposite direction. Pulling from the side with the rod tip low to the water forces the fish to struggle to regain its balance, so it tires quickly. The closer the fish is, the more effectively you can use the rod to wear it down.

If a large fish is sulking underneath the boat, work it with short, quick pumps of the rod, taking in just a few inches of line each time. Those quick tugs get a fish off the bottom and moving in your direction better than either a steady pull or a long, slow pumping motion.

More Accurate Spinning

One problem with open-face spinning: it isn't as accurate at short distances as baitcasting. The baitcaster can lightly thumb the spool to control the cast or press down to stop the plug and make it land in just the right spot.

But once an angler casts a spinning outfit, it's tough to stop the lure on target — unless you use this trick.

Slide your hand back on the handle far enough so you can pinch the line against the spool with your index finger. Flip the bail and cast, releasing line by moving your finger. You can slow the lure down by feathering the line with your index finger, or press the spool to end the cast. This trick works only with small and medium-sized reels; big reels are mounted too far off the rod to reach with your finger.

Extend "Casting" Distance

Success in pier or shore fishing means getting your bait to the fish. If they're too far out, you can't cast to them. Here's a way to use an offshore breeze to get your bait to those hard-to-reach fish:

DOUBLE up your line about a foot above your baited hook and (1) thread the loop through a Lifesaver candy. Pass the loop over the Lifesaver so it (2) cinches up against the candy and keeps it from sliding on the line. Blow up a balloon and tie a knot in the stem. (3) Tie the balloon to the Lifesaver with a few inches of line.

DROP the rig in the water and let the offshore wind carry the balloon out. After about 15 minutes (less if you suck on the candy first), the Lifesaver will dissolve and drop the bait to the bottom.

Avoid a Gummy Mess

Soft-plastic lures will react with many other items in your tackle box, bonding the materials together and bleeding the colors. The warmer the weather, the faster the reaction takes place.

All soft-plastic lures are made of polyvinyl chloride, the same plastic that makes up a rigid PVC pipe. The lures are softer than the pipe because they contain more petroleum-based "plasticizer." The plasticizer oozes to the surface of the lure and dissolves such things as plastic hook boxes, tackle boxes that aren't "worm-proof," paint on many lures, and "living rubber" spinnerbait skirts and jig dressings.

Take plastic grubs off spinnerbaits at the end of the day. Sort all soft plastics by color and store them in separate wormproof compartments or in plastic bags.

No-Tangle Throw Rope

A long rope can save the life of someone who has fallen overboard and is struggling in the water. But it takes too long to untangle a rope that lies in a heap in the bottom of the boat.

Here's a system of rigging a long throw rope so it can be thrown immediately and accurately. It's handy not only in boating accidents, but in ice-fishing mishaps as well.

MAKE a throw rope by punching a ⅜-inch hole in the bottom of a plastic jug. Thread 50 feet of ⅜-inch rope through the bottom hole and out the top. Tie a loop at each end. Pull one knot snug against the outside bottom of the jug. Feed the rest of the rope into the mouth of the bottle.

TOSS the rope to a victim by holding the loop at the mouth of the jug, grabbing the jug by the handle and throwing it underhand. The rope will peel out smoothly from the mouth as the jug sails through the air. The victim can get a firm hold of the loop at the jug end.

Easy-to-See Ice-Fishing Line

The light, clear monofilament used when ice fishing for panfish is difficult to see. You can't tell when your lure is on the bottom, and you can't see the line on the ice. Solve the problem by spooling up with 4-pound-test fluorescent yellow monofilament, which is easy to see. Use a 3-foot leader of clear mono, which is nearly invisible to the fish (see inset).

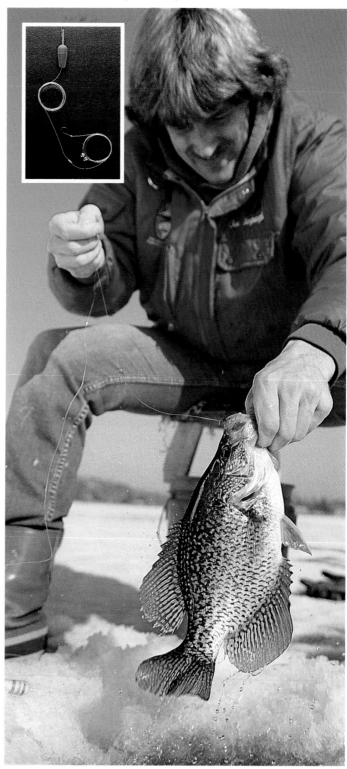

Handy Minnow Storage

Ice fishermen often end the day with a good supply of healthy minnows. Rather than carry them home or throw them away, you can keep them beneath the ice at your fish house. Here's how to store them so they stay healthy for days and are easy to retrieve on your next trip:

1. POUR the minnows into a perforated can attached to a 6-foot rope with a stick tied to the other end. Lower the can down a hole drilled just outside the house, as close as possible to the fishing hole inside the house. Let the rope freeze into the ice.

2. RETRIEVE the minnows by sliding a long hook made from a coat hanger down your ice-fishing hole. Snag the cord, hoist the can into the fish house, and pour the minnows into your bait bucket. When you're done for the day, sink the minnows back down the fishing hole.

De-icing Your Auger

After cutting a hole in the ice, most fishermen set their auger down in the snow. But snow sticks to the wet blades, turns to slush and freezes solid within minutes. Once frozen, the ice is difficult to get off, and if too much builds up on the blades and threads of the auger, the tool won't cut. Here's a simple way to keep your hand or power auger ice free:

KNOCK the ice off the auger with a small hammer you carry in your ice-fishing gear. Be careful not to nick the cutting edge with the hammer.

Ice-Fishing Safety

Unfortunately, some of the year's best ice fishing occurs when the ice is most dangerous: right after freeze-up and just before ice-out. Unless you're sure the ice is safe, stay off it, no matter how well the fish are biting.

River ice can be especially treacherous. The current weakens it and keeps it from freezing uniformly.

Anytime you're ice fishing early or late in the season or on a river, take extra precautions. Test the ice thickness with a sharp ice chisel, and carry an ice pick so you can pull yourself out if you do fall through. Here are a couple of other tips for crossing ice safely.

Carry a long stick or sapling. If you fall in, the stick will bridge the hole and provide support so you can lift yourself onto solid ice. If a friend falls through, you can crawl over the ice, pushing the stick in front of you to reach him and help pull him to safety.

Wear a life vest under your coat. If you break through, the vest will keep you afloat and conserve body heat. A good alternative is a "float coat," which looks like a regular parka but has built-in flotation.

Gamefish Tips

Largemouth & Smallmouth Bass Tips

Better "Pegging" Technique

Plastic-worm anglers peg bullet sinkers with toothpicks to keep the worm and sinker from separating on the cast and retrieve. But the toothpicks jam in the holes, making the sinkers difficult to remove and later reuse without first punching out the toothpick. Here's a method that let's you re-rig quickly:

SLIP a rubber sinker stop onto your line before adding the bullet sinker, hook and worm. To re-rig, simply slide the stop up the line a few inches, snip off the hook, change sinkers, tie on a new hook and slide the stop back into place.

Mono Loop Fends off Weeds

Texas-rigged worms are weedless, but with the hook buried in the worm, you'll miss fish. A worm hooked on a plain jig head has an exposed hook, so you'll hook more fish but snag more weeds. Here's how to rig a worm so it's nearly weedless but still allows a good hook set:

1. TIE a piece of 30-pound stiff mono behind the eye of a 1/0 straight-shank worm hook. Run the line through the eye.

2. SLIDE the worm on the hook, and poke the mono into the worm at the hook bend so the mono forms a loop over the hook point. The loop is stiff enough to fend off weeds and brush but supple enough to give on a strike. Fish the worm with a bullet sinker. Set the hook as soon as a bass hits.

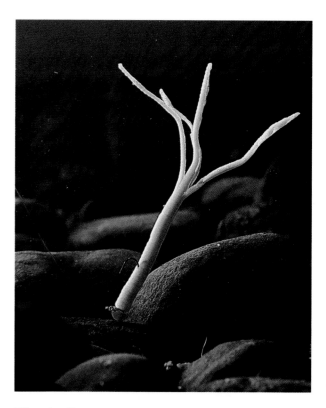

Plastic Surgery Improves Worms

If bass ignore a normal plastic worm, try a high-buoyancy worm made with air bubbles in the plastic, such as a Sportsman's Super Floater, and enhance its action with a razor blade or X-Acto knife.

Slice the worm lengthwise, from the midpoint to the tail. Then slice each half lengthwise again to form four tentacles. Thread the worm on a jig. With the jig head on the bottom, the tentacles wiggle enticingly.

Keep Curly-Tails From Twisting

If you're bothered by severe line twist after casting with a curly-tail plastic worm, you're not alone. Even if the worm is hooked straight, without a kink in the body, it may twist on the retrieve. Here's how to rig a curly-tail worm to keep it from spinning and twisting your line:

HOOK the worm so the curly-tail rides *down* when the hook point rides up. Make sure the body isn't kinked. If the tail is turned up, the worm is much more likely to spin as it moves through the water.

Wind in Rushes Triggers Bass

When a strong wind begins whipping a bed of bulrushes, largemouth bass will move from the cover inside the bed to the windward points (arrows), where they ambush prey and smash lures for two to three hours. Then the bass quit feeding and return to heavy cover or move deep.

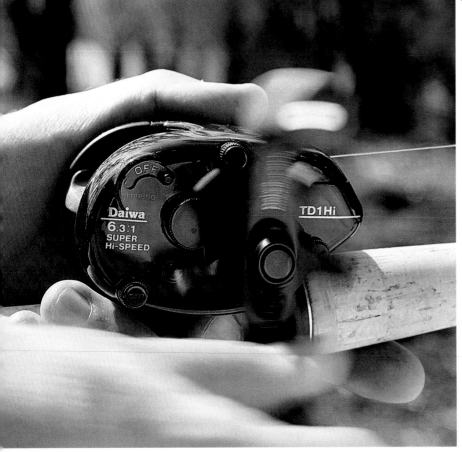

← Fast Reel Helps in Slop

A high-speed reel gives you a big advantage when bass fishing in slop. First, you can get your lure back to the boat in a hurry so you can clean off weeds.

Second, a high-speed reel helps you get a better hook set. You need to hold the rod tip high to keep your lure out of the vegetation, but then you have little hook-setting power. The high gear ratio makes it possible to drop the rod tip, rapidly take up slack, then set the hook.

Third, a high-speed reel enables you to quickly lift a fish and keep it from diving into the slop.

Stiff Rod Rips Weeds

A rod with good backbone works best for ripping a crankbait through weeds. You can't get enough snap with a soft rod to tear the weeds, so they stay on the lure. But with a stiff rod, you can rip the lure free with one sharp tug.

Floating Line Helps Walk the Dog

"Walking the dog" — working a stickbait so it dodges side to side across the surface — is a proven technique for bass. Give the bait a sharp twitch and give it a bit of slack as it veers to one side. When the lure stops, twitch it again and give it slack as it glides in the other direction. Continue the retrieve so the plug dodges side to side (dotted line) as you bring it toward the boat. It's a great way to raise bass out of submerged weeds, brush or timber.

But you'll run into a problem if you let the bait lie motionless for several seconds. The monofilament will sink and the bait will nose-dive rather than dart to the side. Here's how you can solve the problem:

RUB a candle or fly floatant over the first 6 feet of line up from the lure. Either substance will float the line.

Secret Humps

River fishermen know that smallmouth bass and walleyes hold behind bridge pilings to get out of the current, so most of these spots are heavily fished. But there's another kind of cover associated with bridges that is harder to spot and is fished less often. As bridge builders sank bridge footings, they would excavate boulders and rubble from the riverbed and dump the material in a pile nearby. Use your depth finder to sound the river bed in the vicinity of the bridge to find these submerged rock piles. Most anglers overlook such spots, yet they make ideal cover for smallmouth, walleyes and other gamefish.

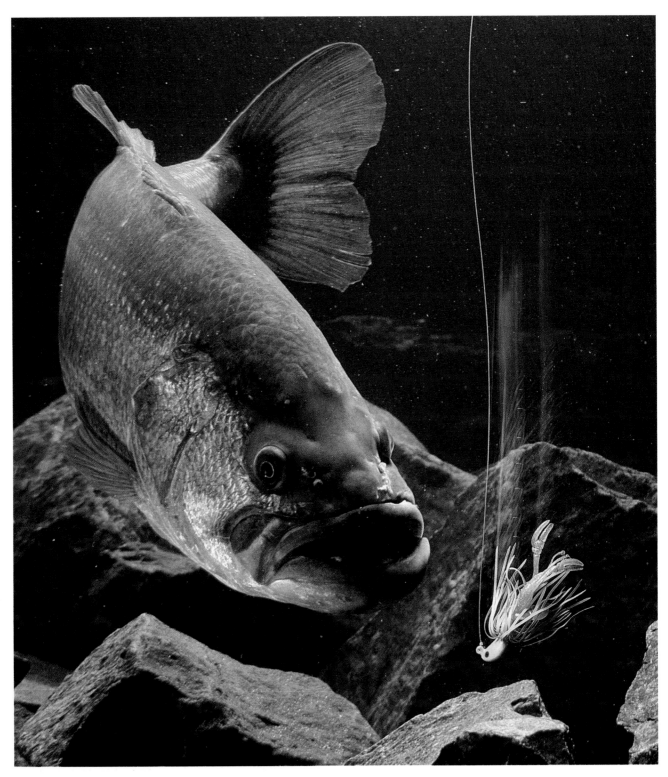

Bang Jigs for Bass ↑

If you're over a school of bass on a rock pile, but ordinary jigging fails to trigger them to strike, get their attention by "banging" a jig.

Drop a heavy jig to the bottom, raise it up a few inches and let it fall. Continue to bounce it on the rocks with short vertical movements of the rod. It's hard for bass to ignore the repeated clunking.

Keep Pork Rind Fresh

Left in the open air and hot sun, pork rind quickly dries and looses its suppleness and action. When you set down a pork rind lure for a while but don't want to return the pork to the jar, wrap the pork in a damp rag. When you unwrap the pork later in the day, it will still be soft and full of action.

Write off Weeds

Spinnerbaits are a favorite for bass in heavy cover. They're nearly weedless, but the swivel often catches bits of fine weed, stopping the blade. Here's a way to use a ballpoint pen to keep the swivel weed free:

CUT the (1) last ¾ inch to 1 inch off the pointed top of a ballpoint pen. Poke or drill a small hole through the tip. Using a needlenose pliers, open up the loop at the end of the spinner arm and remove the swivel and spinner blade. (2) Slide the plastic cone onto the spinner arm. Then reattach the blade and push the cone back along the arm so it covers the swivel.

Pack Pork in Plastic Bags

Jars of pork rind are bulky. To carry pork in a vest or small tackle box, pack a few pieces and some of the brine in a small resealable plastic bag.

Add Spice to Spinnerbaits

Many anglers fish shiners for bass, but when the bait dies, they simply throw it away. Instead, you can use the shiner to tip a skirtless spinnerbait. It makes the lure more attractive and also slows the sink rate so you can work near the surface without speeding up the retrieve. Here's how to rig the minnow:

SLIP a (1) worm hook with an offset shank onto the spinnerbait hook as a trailer. (2) Hook the shiner through the lips with the spinnerbait hook, and bind it to the trailer with a rubber band. The offset shank lets the hook lie flat against the minnow.

Easy-to-Open Pork Rind

As you use pork rind, the brine corrodes the cover of the jar and forms a salty deposit on the threads. As a result, the jar can be impossible to open by hand. Try this trick to keep the cover from sticking.

Spread a thin coat of petroleum jelly on the threads of the cover and jar when you first use the pork rind; repeat occasionally during the season. The petroleum jelly will prevent corrosion and lubricate the cover, so it comes off easily.

Weedguards for Light Cover

In sparse weeds or brush, nylon bristle weedguards may protect the hook more than is necessary, causing missed strikes. Here's a simple way to modify the weedguard:

CLIP several bristles at the base with a scissors or nail clipper. A dozen or so fibers remaining (lower) will protect the hook in thin cover and yet be supple enough to hook most of the fish that hit.

Weedguards for Heavy Cover

In slop, thick lily pads, bulrushes or timber, ordinary weedless jigs still hang up because the nylon bristles don't shield the hook point from the sides. A quick adjustment makes the weedguards work better.

Flare the bristles across the point and heat them with a lighter or match. Be careful not to melt them. The nylon will take a set and stay in position.

Vertical Jigging From a Distance

Jigging directly below the boat catches bass in cold weather or at other times when fish are inactive. It's hard for a bass to resist the temptation of a jig repeatedly bouncing right in front of its nose. But if the water is clear, you can't park your boat directly over fish without spooking them. Try this instead:

VERTICAL-JIG a ¹⁄₁₆-ounce squid-tail jig below a large slip bobber, setting the bobber stop to put the jig at the same level as the fish. The large bobber has enough flotation and water resistance so a sharp pull will lift the jig rather than sink the bobber or pull it back toward you.

Save Light Tippets

Fly-fishermen who stalk small, clear streams for smallmouth bass often find that light tippets used with tiny jigs and poppers are a winning combination. But the continual shock of false-casting even these small lures will eventually weaken a clinch knot tied with a 4-pound-test tippet. If you don't retie often, you may lose a big fish.

Solve the problem by using a Duncan loop instead of a clinch knot or other knot that snubs down on the hook. The Duncan loop better withstands the shock of false casting a weighted fly. As a bonus, the loop allows small poppers and jigs freer play for better action. Here's how to tie the Duncan loop:

THREAD the tippet through the hook eye and then (1) form a loop next to the standing line. (2) Make five turns around one side of the loop and the standing line. Wet the knot and (3) tighten it by pulling on the fly and the free end. (4) Slide the knot to within ¼ inch of the hook eye. Trim.

Prevent Line Twist With Bass Bugs

Large bass bugs, especially frog imitations with big splayed legs, may spin in the air as you cast, twisting your leader and line. Attaching the lure to a snap-swivel will eliminate line twist but will also cause a bug to ride low in the water or sink, ruining the action. Here's a way to keep twist out of your line without sinking the bug:

ATTACH a short piece of 30-pound mono to the fly line (p. 117). Tie the mono to a small swivel; attach the leader to the other end of the swivel. The swivel may sink the tip of the fly line, but it won't affect the bug.

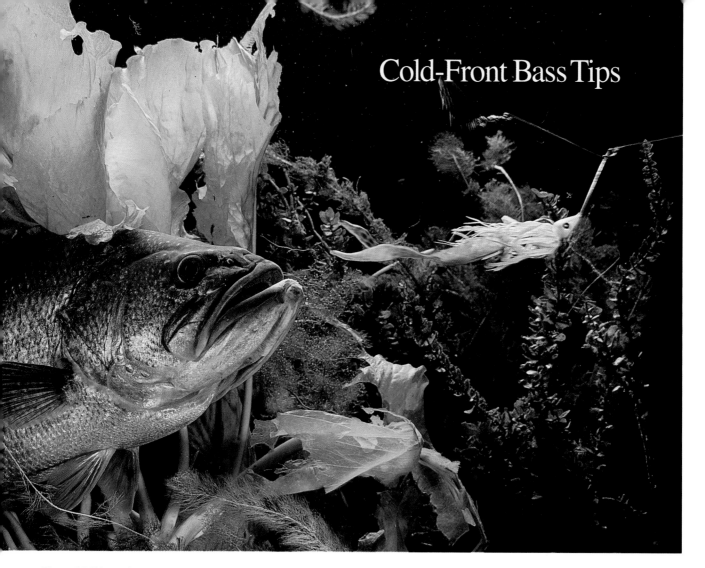

Cold-Front Bass Tips

Good Vibrations

Fishing gets tough with a sudden change in weather — the dreaded cold front. Still, cold-front bass aren't impossible to catch. Bass are sure to notice big baits that make strong vibrations in the water. Here are a couple of examples.

A big, single-bladed spinnerbait with a size 6 or 8 Colorado blade (above) produces a strong, slow vibration that can tempt lethargic bass. Put a jumbo pork frog on the hook to slow the sink rate. Cast the lure into heavy cover and retrieve slowly.

Crankbaits run deep enough to reach bass that have been pushed into deeper water by a cold front, and the strong vibrations can trigger strikes, even from inactive bass. Cast out a big, sinking, deep-diving crankbait. Reel fast to get it deep, then slow down so it swims along the bottom.

Looking for Active Fish

Under cold-front conditions, most anglers slow down their presentation to entice fish that aren't interested in feeding. Some fishermen, however, do just the opposite: they work fast, hoping to find and catch the few fish that are relatively active.

Fish water you know well and move quickly from one proven spot to another, fishing each no more than 10 minutes. Pepper the areas with lures you can work fast, such as spinnerbaits and crankbaits. By covering a lot of water, you should be able to find a few active, catchable bass.

Stick to Bread-and-Butter Spots

Fish the spots that normally produce bass; exploring new water is a bad bet when fish aren't feeding. Usually bass will be in the areas you found them before the front passed. But they may hold tighter to cover or in slightly deeper water.

Finding Weedline Bass

As a cold front passes, bass holding at various depths along a weedline move to the base of the weeds. Inside turns in the weedline are usually best.

Slow and Subtle

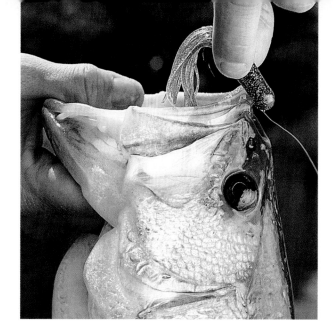

Although big, noisy lures can catch cold-front bass, a slow presentation with a small lure usually works better. Here's one proven method for cold-front bass: Rig up with clear, light mono and a 1/16-ounce to 1/8-ounce tube jig. If the water is deep or cloudy enough that you can put the boat over fish without spooking them, try vertical jigging, which lets you work a lure right in front of fish until one decides to strike.

If the water is clear or shallow, and scaring fish is a possibility, cast and jig instead. Either way, work the jig as slowly as you can.

"Doodlin' " Brass and Glass

Doodlin' — twitching a Texas-rigged plastic worm along the bottom — catches bass in a lot of situations, but it can be one of the best approaches to try after a cold front has passed. Doodlin' can be even more effective if you add a brass bullet weight and a glass bead to the worm. As you're trolling, drifting or retrieving, twitch the rod tip rapidly, keeping the worm on the bottom. The brass and glass will click together, making far more noise than an ordinary lead sinker. Here's how to rig the brass and glass:

SLIDE a brass bullet weight and a good-sized glass bead onto 6-pound-test monofilament. Tie on a worm hook and rig a plastic worm Texas style. Brass is not as dense as lead, so you'll need a larger-than-normal sinker to get down. (Get brass weights and glass beads from Cemco, Box 1015, Starkville, MS 39759.)

Jigging a Worm in Place

Working a Texas-rigged plastic worm slowly through heavy cover is an effective cold-front technique. But even the slowest retrieve may be too fast when bass are off the bite. Here's a way to entice them.

When the worm hangs up on submerged branches or weeds, resist your first reaction to rip it free. Instead, after you feel the sinker hit the obstruction, drop the rod tip a bit so the worm sinks a few inches. Then pull the line tight again to raise the worm. If a bass is around, the action of a worm jigged repeatedly in front of its nose may be too much to resist.

Target Shallow Weeds

With the change in weather, many bass will head to the thickest weeds available. Some of this cover may be deep, some as shallow as 3 or 4 feet. Make best use of your time by trying the shallow weeds first.

In the shallows you can easily see where the cover is thickest and provides the most security, so you can flip or pitch a jig-and-pig or plastic worm practically on a fish's nose. Getting close in deeper water is far more difficult, because you can't see the nooks and crannies of the cover and aren't so sure where fish are likely to be holding.

Walleye & Sauger Tips

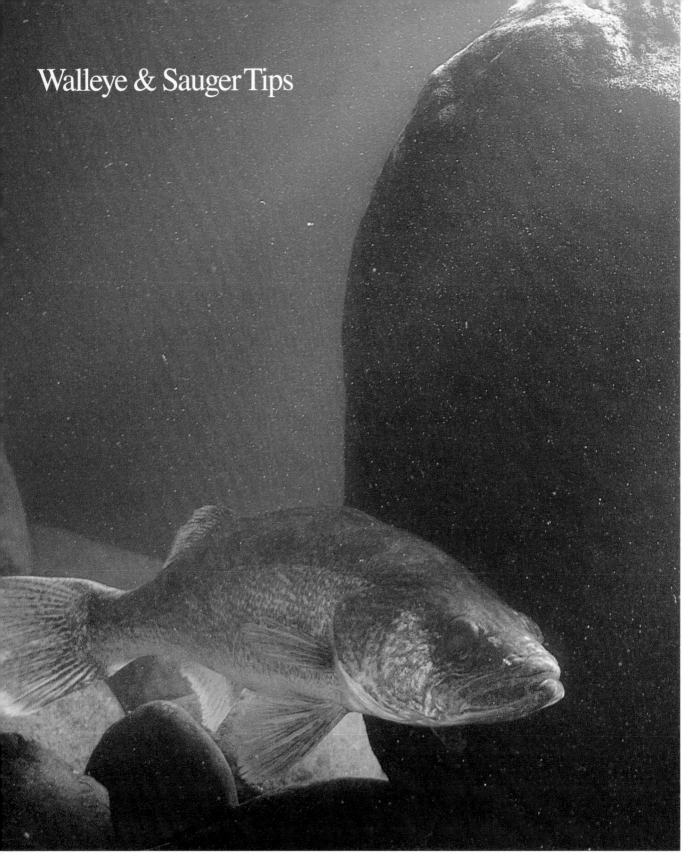

A Rocky Start for Walleyes

Look for early-season walleyes on rock piles in water less than 10 feet deep. The rocks absorb sunlight and warm the surrounding water. Most of the lake is still cold, so walleyes are attracted to these zones of warmer water. These areas appeal to walleyes for an-

other reason: The warmth activates invertebrates, which attract baitfish on which the walleyes feed. Walleyes frequent big boulders later in the year as well. The large rocks cast shadows where the walleyes can hide and avoid bright sunlight.

Go Light After a Cold Front

Walleyes and saugers don't feed much following a cold front. But they may nip at a small, slow-moving bait. Here's a trick that can put a few walleyes in your boat when fishing really gets tough.

Spool a light spinning outfit with 2- to 4-pound mono, tie on a 1/16- or 1/32-ounce jig and tip it with a small minnow or leech. Use a trolling motor to keep your boat over a spot where you suspect fish are holding, then drop the jig to bottom. Lift and lower it slowly, move it in very short hops or just hold it steady; set the hook if you feel a tap or the line tightens. One problem: light jigs are tough to fish in windy weather.

Double Bait for Big Fish

If you're catching only little walleyes and saugers, you may be using minnows that are too small. Bigger fish often want bigger bait. If you run out of big minnows, here's a way to save the day:

HOOK two small minnows on a jig or split-shot rig. Don't bury the hook too deeply or the minnows will jam up in the bend of the hook and won't trail naturally.

Jigs for Weed Walleyes

Stocked walleyes spend a lot of time in the thick vegetation usually associated with largemouth bass. You can catch these walleyes by casting jigs into this heavy cover. But ordinary walleye jigs don't work well; the exposed hook point and attachment eye on top of the jig head snag weeds. And most weedless bass jigs are too big.

Try a 1/8-ounce weedless jig with the attachment eye at the front of the head, which lets the lure slip through weeds easily. Some of these jigs also have a flattened head to slow the sink rate, so you can swim them over very dense weeds. (These special weedless jigs are available from J. M. Tackle, Route 4, Hayward, WI 54843.)

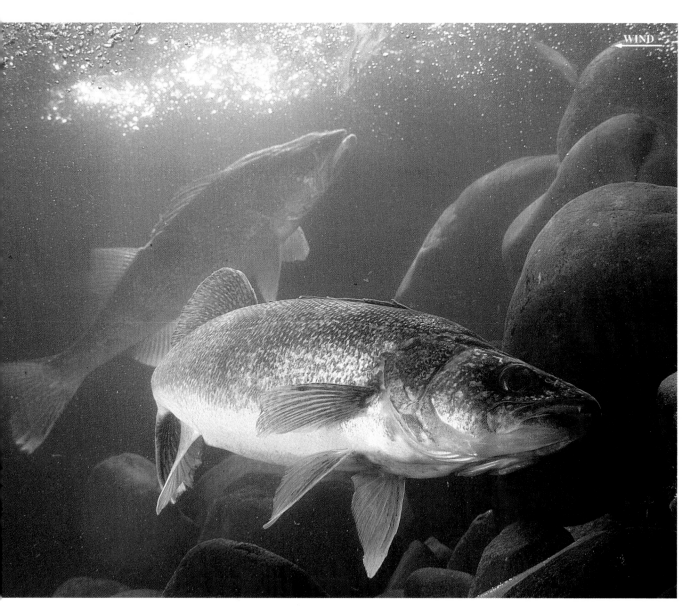

WIND

Check the Downwind Side ↑

On a windy day, walleye anglers normally fish the windward side of an underwater hump or point. But there are also times when fish feed on the downwind side. On a shallow hump or point, strong wind whips up a great deal of turbulence, causing various kinds of invertebrates to drift off the downwind side of the rocks. Baitfish gather to feed on the small organisms. Then gamefish, including walleyes, largemouth bass and muskies, move in to feed on the baitfish.

A Long Reach Means Fewer Snags

Submerged boulder piles and rocky reefs are top spots for walleyes. But it's nearly impossible to fish a jig or slip-sinker rig in the rocks without getting hung up. You can minimize snags by keeping your line straight up and down, but even then, you'll hang up once in a while. Here's how to improve your chances of freeing

Slip in on Walleyes

The sound of an outboard, the whir of an electric trolling motor, or the clunk of an anchor can spook walleyes off a shallow reef. To approach such a spot silently, anchor at least 50 feet upwind, and pay out rope until you're within casting range. If you need to check the reef with your depth finder, let your boat blow right over the spot, take your readings, and then move slightly upwind by taking in anchor rope.

a lure if you do get snagged. Use a longer rod so you can reach out farther to change your angle of pull, making it possible to dislodge the hook without repositioning the boat. Some anglers use specially designed spinning rods up to 8 feet long or they rig a fly rod with a spinning reel (p. 117).

Springtime Walleye Magnet

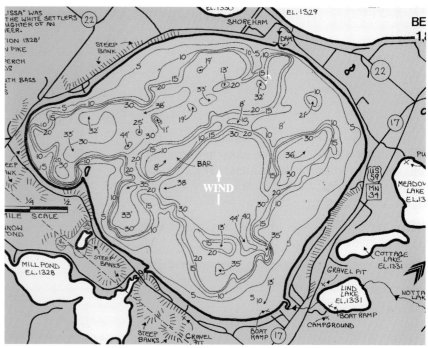

Walleye fishermen know that the fish feed in the shallows in spring because the water there is warmer than in the main body of the lake. The difference may be only a degree or two, but it's enough to attract baitfish, and the walleyes soon follow.

But some areas along shore are warmer than others, so they draw more walleyes. Water in a sheltered bay, for instance, warms faster than water along a straight shoreline because the wind can't mix it with deeper, cooler water.

Bays are obvious spots to check, but here's another type of spot that's not so obvious:

INDENTATIONS in the breakline (arrow) function much like bays, but are not obvious from looking at the shoreline. Sunlight heats the surface layer of the lake, and if the wind pushes the warm water toward shore, it will collect in the depression. An indentation on the downwind side of the lake may have water 10 degrees warmer than nearby shallows.

Slow Down Slip-Bobbers

Slip-bobbers are tough to beat when fishing live bait for walleyes. A breeze can make the rig even more effective by slowly moving the bobber and bait through water that might hold fish. Yet a strong wind will move the bobber and bait too fast to interest any but the most active fish. Here are some ways to slow down the drift and catch walleyes that aren't willing to chase a fast-moving bait:

SELECT (1) a smaller slip bobber, which will catch less wind and move the bait more slowly than a large float. (2) Use enough weight on your line that the bobber barely floats; this way it is little affected by wind. (3) Choose a wooden float; it's denser than foam so it rides lower, drifts slower and casts better. (4) Use a bobber weighted with a lead sleeve. It will ride low and drift slowly, and the extra weight will increase casting distance.

There's More Than One Way to Hook a Leech

Most fishermen hook their leeches in or around the sucker, the large disc on the wide end (tail). This method of hooking works well for most types of fishing, but there are times when other ways are more effective.

Here are the best ways to hook leeches for various fishing situations:

THROUGH THE SUCKER. Hooking in or near the sucker is recommended for most casting and trolling. Because you pull the leech backwards, it always tries to swim away.

THROUGH THE NECK. This method is best when nipping panfish are a problem. The flesh in the neck region is very tough, making it harder for them to steal your bait.

THROUGH THE MIDDLE. This method is ideal for bobber fishing. The leech is balanced on the hook, so it undulates more than it would if hooked in the end.

Cure for Balled-up Leeches

When the water is cold (below 50° F), leeches tend to ball up on the hook (inset). Even in warm water, a leech occasionally decides to roll itself up tight. Regardless of what you do, you can't get them to unwind and swim. The problem occurs most often when the leech is hooked through the neck, though some leeches ball up no matter where you hook them. Unfortunately, a balled-up leech is worthless for walleyes.

Prevent the problem by sliding a short piece of surgical tubing over the collar of the jig. Hook the leech far enough ahead of the sucker so the sucker can attach to the tubing. A leech with its sucker attached to something is not as likely to ball up.

Free-Standing Stinger ↑

Walleyes often nip at a jig and minnow without getting hooked. Many anglers tie a small treble to the bend of the jig hook and imbed this "stinger" in the minnow's tail. But even light mono between the jig and treble inhibits the action of the bait. And the line often wraps around the minnow, cinching it into a half-circle and ruining its action. Here's a better way.

Tie a size 14 or 16 treble hook to the bend of the jig hook with a short length of stiff line, such as Mason hard mono, 15-pound test or heavier. The stiff line holds the treble straight out behind the jig, so you don't need to hook it in the minnow. The bait moves freely, as if the stinger weren't there at all. Yet when a fish nips the tail, it gets hooked.

Cut Through Stringy Weeds

Walleyes are sometimes found in stringy weeds, such as coontail. The weeds catch on your line, slide down and foul your lure. Sometimes you can shake them off during the retrieve, but more often you have to reel in the lure and remove the weeds by hand. Here's an easier way.

Add a short leader of thin multistrand wire, such as 12-pound-test Sevenstrand, between your line and lure (p. 114). When you feel resistance from a weed, jerk the rod. The thin wire will cut through the stem, and the weed will fall off the line. The wire leader also ensures that sharp-toothed fish such as northern pike won't bite off your lure.

Durable Natural Jig Dressing

If you run out of bait and walleyes refuse artificials, try tipping a jig with throat tissue cut from a walleye you've already caught. The thin flesh wiggles enticingly on the hook, emits natural scent and is remarkably durable.

When you clean a batch of walleyes, cut out these throat pieces and freeze them for later use. Here's how:

CUT out the throat tissue by slicing along the dotted lines as shown. Then cut the tissue loose at the point of the chin. Drive the jig hook through the front of the piece of throat tissue (inset). The meat there is thicker and tougher, so the hook won't tear out.

Early-Bird Walleyes

Walleyes in heavily used lakes often feed earlier in the day than those in less popular lakes. Speedboaters, jet-skiers, water-skiers and other commotion drive them into deep water or heavy cover. Often, the traffic stays heavy until dark, and walleyes don't feed much before the lake settles down.

To catch these early feeders, start fishing at the crack of dawn. The bite may end by breakfast time.

Clean Jig Eyes

Most jigs you buy are painted by dipping the entire head. Usually the attachment eye is clogged with paint, so you have to poke a hole to attach your line. But if you use another hook to open the eye, as many anglers do, some paint will remain on the eye. When you tie on your jig, the knot won't snug up properly, and the rough edge can fray your line. To avoid these problems, clean out the eye like this:

PUSH the point of a knife blade into the eye and give it a half twist. Usually, all of the paint will chip away from the eye. If not, scrape away any that is left to make a smooth surface for your knot.

Chart Depth While Ice Fishing

Often walleyes will school on a small point or in a tiny indentation along the breakline. It takes a lot of depth readings to find these spots, and even then, you may not get a clear picture of the bottom unless you keep track of the depth at each location.

After you sound through the ice (below) or through an ice hole, use the handle of your ice scoop to scratch the depth in the ice or snow. You can even stomp contour lines in the snow, joining holes of equal depths.

Once you have marked the depths and contours, you will have a much better understanding of the structure and where fish might be.

Improved Willow Rig

Veteran walleye and sauger anglers often use a willow twig to detect subtle bites while ice fishing. They anchor a 2- to 3-foot twig in the slush removed from the hole, then center the tip over the hole, about a foot above the water. Then they make a loop in the line and hang it over the tip of the twig. A light bite pulls the willow down slightly; a hard bite bends the willow far enough down so the loop slips off. Normally, line is spread on the ice so the fish can run with no resistance.

But the loop often catches on the end of the willow, and the loose line sometimes catches on ice chips. The fish feel the resistance and drop the bait. Here's how to overcome these problems:

THREAD a light float on the line and drape the float over the tip of the twig (inset). The minnow will not be strong enough to dislodge the float, but a firm strike will pull it free. Set a small spool of mono in a shallow circular depression you've formed in the snow or chipped in the ice. As a fish takes line, the spool will spin in the cavity until you grab the line and set the hook.

Don't Drill at Dusk

Many ice fishermen make the mistake of showing up at dusk, just when the walleyes are moving in to feed. When they drill their holes, they spook the fish. You can avoid the problem by drilling your holes an hour earlier.

Northern Pike & Muskie Tips

Spokes for Spinners

A lot of muskie and pike fishermen make their own spinnerbaits and in-line spinners. Most of the components are readily available from specialty fishing tackle stores and mail-order firms. But you may have trouble finding the stiff, heavy stainless steel wire (at least .060 inch) you need to make really large spinners and spinnerbaits. If the wire is too light, fish will bend it and the spinners won't spin properly. A ready source of heavy wire: bicycle wheel spokes. The rustproof spokes are available in any bicycle shop.

← Add Flash to Muskie Lures

Muskies are notorious for following lures to the boat and turning away at the last minute without striking. If you are getting follows but no strikes, try dressing up the lure with a small spinner. The added flash and vibration is often all it takes to trigger a strike. Here's how to add spinners to three different kinds of lures:

JERKBAITS with metal tail blades, such as Suicks, can be modified by drilling a small hole at the center of the rear edge of the tail blade. Add a split ring, a snap-swivel and a size 0, 1 or 2 spinner. The greater drag of sizes larger than this inhibits the lure's action. The snap allows you to easily remove or change the spinner blade.

GLIDEBAITS and other jerkbaits without metal tail blades, such as Reef Hawgs and Eddie Baits, can also be fitted with a spinner blade. Remove the rear treble hook. Then replace it with a split ring, a snap-swivel and a size 0, 1 or 2 spinner blade.

CREATURES, such as big soft-plastic waterdog imitations, can be modified by threading a long needle with 10-pound mono (1) into the "chest" of the creature and out the tail. If you can't find a needle long enough to do the job, use a piece of stiff piano wire with a loop in one end. (2) Pull the needle and line out the tip of the tail. (3) Tie line to a snap-swivel and number 1, 2 or 3 spinner. (4) Pull the swivel snug to the end of the tail. Insert a large jig with a stout hook into the head of the lure; tie off the line on the bend of the hook.

Weed-Resistant Pike Plugs

Pike are suckers for big, metal-lipped plugs such as Pikie Minnows, but when the fish are lurking in shallow weeds, these plugs are impossible to use. They run too deep, and the lip collects weeds.

Here's a way to modify these plugs so they run shallower and don't pick up as many weeds:

DRILL a hole near the end of the lip and insert a split ring; attach your leader. The plug will run just under the surface. And weeds will slip down the line and pass under the plug, rather than hang up on the lip.

Muskies After Dark

Boat traffic and fishing pressure can force muskies to feed at night. Successful fisherman change their habits, too. Fish the same areas you would during the day, and try shallower areas as well. Use bucktails or jointed plugs, working them with a steady retrieve so the fish can easily home in on them.

Go Deep for Big Summertime Pike

Fishermen catch plenty of good-sized pike in shallow weedy bays in spring, but when the water warms up, they get nothing but "hammer handles" in these areas. The lack of big pike in summer had led to the mistaken belief that big pike lose their teeth or have sore mouths in summer and don't feed. But in reality, they're feeding more than ever.

The main reason for the scarcity of big pike in summer is that anglers aren't fishing deep enough. As pike get larger, they prefer cooler water. In some cases, they'll stay in shallow water and congregate around spring holes, artesian wells, the mouths of trout streams, or other specific point sources of cold water. But if there are no point sources, pike have no choice but to go deep.

If there is adequate oxygen in the lake depths, they'll go as deep as 50 feet and occasionally down to 100. Lake trout anglers sometimes catch big pike. At these depths, they're generally feeding on good-sized baitfish, such as ciscoes and whitefish, and you'll have to use similar-sized baits to catch them.

Improve Glidebait Action

A wire leader deadens the action of a glidebait, such as an Eddie Bait or Reef Hawg. But you can increase the glide and the side-to-side motion by inserting a split ring (arrow) between the leader and the bait. The ring allows freer play between the steel leader loop and the eye of the plug.

If you're using heavy line and are concerned about the strength of the connection, solder the ring, making sure to file all rough edges that would inhibit movement of the lure. Or you can fit a small split ring inside a larger one (p. 88).

Weight Bucktails Quickly

Fishermen often weight bucktails to make them run deeper or to cast farther into a stiff wind. But sinkers added to the line makes casting awkward; the sinker and lure twirl like a bolo. You can eliminate tangles by adding weight directly to the lure. Here's how:

ATTACH a Snap-Loc bell sinker of the appropriate weight to the split ring or wire loop that holds the treble hook. These sinkers make changing or removing weight easy.

Protect Hands From Sharp Teeth

The needle-sharp teeth of pike and muskies, and the large hooks you use to catch these fish, are a constant danger and can inflict serious wounds in an instant. Protect your hands with heavy buckskin gloves while landing and unhooking these fish. The hooks aren't likely to penetrate the thick leather.

Split Rings Improve Hooking

Muskies and big pike often manage to throw the hook by twisting and thrashing against the weight of a plug. Improve your chances of landing the fish by inserting split rings between the lure and trebles. The rings allow the hooks freer play so big fish can't twist free or bend hooks as easily. Here's how to add them:

CUT off the old treble hooks or remove them by opening the eye of the hook hanger.

ADD split rings or double split rings (p. 88) and new trebles; close the eye of the hook hanger.

Bucktails With Spice

More muskies are caught on bucktails than on any other lure. But here's a way to make bucktails work even better:

ADD a split ring and snap to the wire loop holding the rear treble. Clip a 2-inch white split-tail pork rind onto the snap. If necessary, trim the rind at the leading end and punch a new hole. The rind should stick only ½ inch beyond the bucktail. If you attach the rind directly to the treble and it trails back too far, muskies may strike short.

A Stinger for Pike Plugs

When a big pike or muskie grabs a large wooden plug, it's difficult to get a good hook set because their teeth penetrate the wood, preventing you from moving the

More Hookups on Jerkbaits

Jerkbaits account for plenty of good-sized pike and muskies, especially in fall. But many fishermen work jerkbaits too erratically. They sweep the rod 3 to 4 feet at a time, causing the lure to dodge rapidly from side to side. As a result, fish often miss the lure. Here's a better way.

Work the lure with smooth, slow and regular 2-foot sweeps of the rod tip. The lure will still have enough swimming action to attract pike and muskies, but they'll have an easier time catching it, and you'll get more hookups.

Continuous Figure Eight

This unique two-person procedure has produced dozens of 30-pound-plus fish for northern Wisconsin muskie experts. It would work for muskies anywhere.

While one person casts, another figure-eights alongside the boat (opposite page). When the first person completes his retrieve, he starts figure-eighting, and the other person makes a cast. This way, someone is figure-eighting at all times.

The continuous motion evidently arouses the curiosity of big muskies. Even fish that haven't been seen following the lure being retrieved will suddenly appear and strike the figure-eighted lure.

plug enough to sink the hooks. Here's a way to rig a large plug that will improve your chances of hooking pike and muskies:

RIG a 4-inch wire leader with a snap at one end and a treble hook at the other. Clip the snap to the eye at the nose of the lure. Lay the treble along the plug's back and secure the hook with a rubber band. The treble should be big enough to hold a large fish, but not heavy enough to throw the plug out of balance.

Finer Points of Figure-Eighting

Muskies are notorious for following a lure to the boat. Good muskie anglers know how to figure-eight a lure (dotted line) to get the fish to strike. But the technique involves more than just sweeping the rod back and forth through the water. Done poorly, figure eights result in little more than good arm exercise. Done right, they can more than double your muskie catch. Here are some tricks the experts recommend:

- Use a heavy-duty baitcasting reel with the drag set tight. When a muskie follows your lure to the boat, thumb the spool and push in the free-spool button. Then, should a big fish strike next to the boat, you can set the hook and give line when the fish runs.

- When you see a muskie behind your lure, it's important to read its mood to determine how to proceed. If the fish is "hot," you stand a good chance of enticing it to strike. But if it's only mildly interested, you may be better off leaving it alone.

- Watch the fish's head; if it stays within a few inches of the lure and the mouth is opening and closing, the fish is hot. Begin tracing a big figure eight with the rod tip. The lure should be about 2 feet underwater. If the fish continues to follow but doesn't strike, bring the lure back over its snout. This maneuver often triggers a strike.

- If you see a fish following a few feet behind the lure and swimming lazily, chances are it's not ready to strike. You may want to try one or two figure eights, but if the fish doesn't respond, don't continue. You may end up spooking the fish. Instead, note the precise location. Then come back and try again later. By that time, the fish may be in a more aggressive mood.

- To make a muskie take the lure, do everything you can to keep it away. Many fishermen make the mistake of slowing the lure when they see a fish following, but this is a sure way to make the fish lose interest. Slow down only when the fish quits following, then speed up again. Sometimes the change in speeds will bring the fish back.

- If a muskie follows a surface lure to the boat, don't figure-eight the lure on top. It's nearly always a waste of time. Even if you're using a surface crawler with no underwater action at all, plunge the rod tip into the water and figure-eight the lure a couple feet beneath the surface.

Better Hook Sets With Big Bait

Anglers sometimes use suckers more than a foot long to catch trophy pike and muskies. These baitfish are usually hooked through the nose, but the thick snout of a really large sucker fills up the hook gap and makes a good hook set difficult. Here are two ways to rig these big baitfish so the hook point remains exposed and the bait stays alive. With either of these methods, you'll have to pause long enough for the fish to swallow the bait before attempting to set the hook.

METHOD 1: Open the gap of the hook slightly; this way the point is more likely to hook a fish and less likely to get buried in the bait. Thread on a "keeper" made of a strip of surgical tubing or a heavy rubber band to keep the sucker from sliding up and down the hook shank. Hook the sucker upward through the snout only, not both lips, to keep more of the hook point exposed. Finally, slide the other end of the rubber keeper onto the hook.

METHOD 2: Thread a large needle with a foot of heavy braided Dacron fishing line. (1) Push the needle through the eye sockets of the sucker. Draw the line through the head of the bait, and (2) tie the ends together to form a loose loop. Trim the ends. (3) Insert a large hook in the loop and twist it several times so the line tightens across the head of the bait. (4) Slip the hook under the taut line and adjust it so the point rides up.

Prevent Bait Tangles

Monofilament line absorbs water and sinks, sometimes causing problems for bobber fishermen. When you fish a big minnow below a bobber, the bait may swim near the surface, crossing the submerged line between the rod tip and bobber and causing a tangled mess. Even if the sucker doesn't cause a tangle, the sag in the line may prevent a good hook set. You can solve the problem by applying candle wax or fly floatant to the line. The mono will float and stay out of the way of the swimming baitfish.

Jerking Live Bait for Pike

This unusual but effective method for big pike and muskies combines the action of a jerkbait with the appeal of live bait.

Hook a 6- to 10-inch sucker minnow upward through only the snout with a 2/0 to 5/0 short-shanked bait hook attached to a foot-long wire leader. Cast the minnow with a heavy baitcasting or spinning outfit.

Retrieve the sucker with 2-foot jerks, occasionally pausing to let the bait glide and roll. When you see or feel a strike, wait until you think the fish has swallowed the bait before setting the hook.

Where it is legal, you can rig a small treble hook as a stinger, joining it to the eye of the other hook with a 6-inch section of wire. Hook one prong of the treble in the tail. With this rig, set the hook immediately.

When it is necessary to sink the bait several feet, pinch a large split-shot to the wire leader, several inches above the nose of the sucker.

Keeping the Kinks Out

Many anglers use twisted multistrand steel leaders to keep pike and muskies from biting through the line. But these leaders easily get kinks that are impossible to remove. Then, as you work a lure, the leader flexes at the kink, eventually weakening and perhaps breaking as you play a fish. Get around the problem this way. Buy single-strand leaders or make them yourself from stainless steel wire. It kinks less than twisted wire, and kinks that do form are easier to remove. As a result, a leader that is no heavier remains stronger.

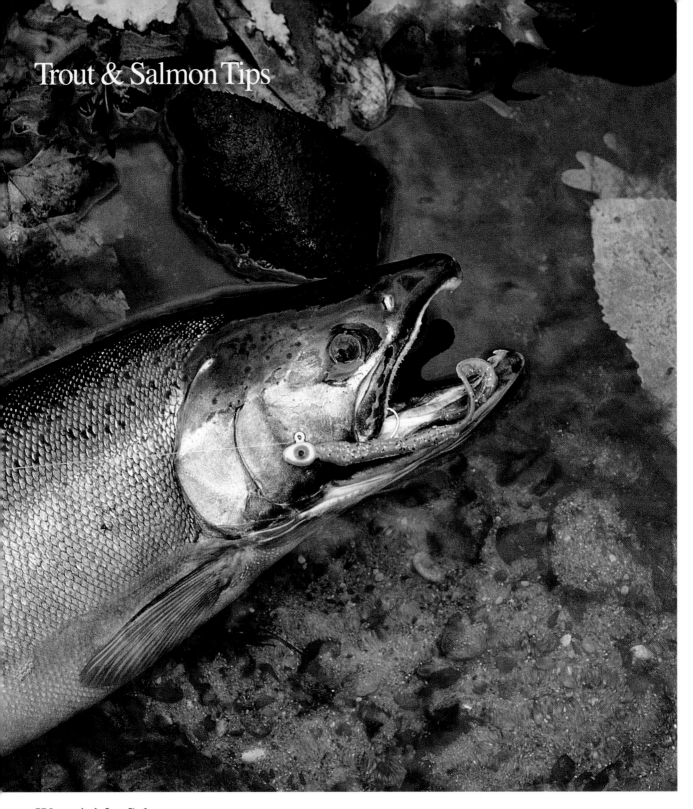

Wormin' for Salmon

During their life at sea, chinooks, cohos and other Pacific salmon eat small eels of various kinds. Once the salmon enter rivers to spawn, they no longer feed, but they still strike lures resembling eels. As a result, they can be caught on the curly-tailed worms normally used for bass.

Hook a 3- to 5-inch worm on a stout-hooked jig heavy enough to run just off the bottom. Bright or fluorescent colors are usually best, but black and purple work well on bright days.

Anchor your boat above a holding area, then angle your cast down and across the river. Let the current swing the worm in front of the salmon. Or troll the worm through deep water on bends or by creek mouths. Salmon usually hit these lures hard; set the hook as soon as you feel the strike.

Peanuts Give Bait a Lift

Lake trout will take dead smelt or ciscoes lying on the bottom, but these baits are more effective when floated up a foot or two. Because lakers are usually found in very deep water, using a slip bobber to suspend the bait is not practical.

Here's a way to float dead bait just off the bottom, where it's visible and appears to be barely alive. It works not only for lakers, but also for big pike.

STUFF a (1) Styrofoam packing peanut inside the mouth of the bait and (2) run the hook through both lips to keep the mouth shut. If more flotation is needed to make the bait float, (3) cut a small slit in the belly and stuff another peanut or two into the abdomen. If the bait is small, use pieces of a peanut. (4) Slip a rubber band over the fish or tie mono around the bait to keep the peanut in the body. Fish the bait 2 feet behind a ½- to 1-ounce sinker.

Easy-to-See Strike Indicators

Even fluorescent strike indicators can be tough to see in cloudy or hazy weather when you're squinting into the brightest part of the sky. Here's a solution:

COLOR one end of a strike indicator with a black water-proof marker to provide a dark silhouette. Now, in any light, at least half of the indicator will be visible.

Double-Duty Steelhead Plug

West Coast steelheaders often use a crankbait, such as a magnum Hot 'N Tot, to carry bait to the bottom of a steelhead run and also to act as an attractor. Normally, the hooks are removed so they don't foul the trailing bait rig. But then you miss the occasional steelhead that strikes the plug.

Here's a way of rigging the crankbait so you can catch fish on the plug as well as the bait:

REMOVE the (1) front treble and split ring; then remove the rear treble, leaving the split ring on the plug. (2) Slide a short piece of surgical tubing over the rear hook shank and then reattach the hook. (3) Slide the tubing forward so it covers the rear eye, split ring and hook eye, and fasten the desired bait rig to the front eye. The tubing will cause the treble hook to stick straight off the rear of the plug so it won't foul the trailing bait rig.

Keep Reels Dry When Wading

Wading anglers who fish with a fly rod or long spinning rod are familiar with the problem: to unwrap line from the rod tip or restring the tip section of the rod, you must dunk the reel in the water to reach the last few guides. But then sand gets in your reel. Immersion also causes the drags of some reels to slip.

You can avoid these problems by pulling the rod apart at the ferrule. Now you can untangle the line from the end of the rod or string up the tip section without putting the reel in the water.

Better Fly Floatant

Silicon gel fly pastes are handy but are difficult to apply to flies evenly and thoroughly. If you don't apply enough, the fly won't float long. If you dab on too much, the hackles, wings and tail mat down. What you need is a dressing that cleans and treats every part of the fly, evaporates quickly, and floats a fly a long time. Here's how to make a dressing that does just that:

MIX one part silicon gel fly floatant with three parts lighter fluid. Store the mixture in a small jar or squeeze bottle, after first adding a little to the bottle to make sure the plastic doesn't dissolve. Squeeze a drop or two directly onto the fly or apply it with your fingers or a toothpick. The lighter fluid will evaporate in seconds, leaving a thin coat of the gel on the hackles and body of the fly.

Ice Jigs Score in Streams

If you're fishing worms for stream trout, you'll generally need a bit of weight to aid casting and get the worm down to the fish. Pinching a split-shot or two several inches above the bait does the trick, but the shot and hook will revolve around one another on the cast, making accurate placement difficult. Here's a way to make your bait easier to cast and also more appealing to the fish:

HOOK the worm on a gold, silver or fluorescent panfish ice fly. For best casting, use 2- or 4-pound mono on an ultra-light spinning rig. The ice fly and worm will cast as a unit, improving your accuracy.

Ski Wax Tames Dubbing

Spinning short animal hair onto a thread, a process called "dubbing," is the first step in forming the bodies of many dry flies, wet flies and nymphs. However, the process can be tricky and messy, especially for a beginning flytier, because short hair doesn't adhere very well to the thread. Instead, it sticks to the tier's fingers or falls into his lap.

Here's a way to make the hair stick so it's easier to spin onto the thread:

1. APPLY a light coating of soft (warm-weather) cross-country ski wax to several inches of thread.

2. DAB on the hair. Pinch the thread below the hair; roll the thread between your thumb and forefinger to form yarn.

Watching Hard-to-See Flies

It's important to watch the drift of a dry fly so you can detect strikes and set the hook. But there are times glare or darkness makes it hard to see dry flies, especially those that imitate small naturals, such as midges. The next time poor lighting makes dry-fly fishing difficult, try this trick:

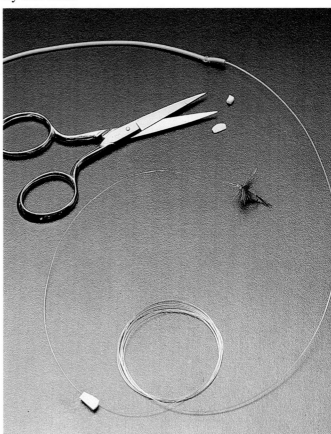

WRAP half of an adhesive foam strike indicator (the kind used by nymph fishermen) around the tippet, about 10 inches above the fly. Trim it to the size of a BB so it doesn't hinder casting or spook fish. This small piece of white foam will be much easier to follow in poor light than a tiny, dark fly. When a fish takes the fly, the foam disappears.

Stopping a Strong Run

When hooked, a big salmon or steelhead makes a swift, powerful run, sometimes stripping off a hundred yards of line or more. If you're fishing in a boat, you may have no choice but to turn around and chase the fish. When wading in a stream, you may have to follow the fish downstream. If you can't, it will break off in seconds. Here's a trick that will stop a streaking fish nine times out of ten.

Give the fish complete slack. They run because they feel resistance; when there is no resistance, they usually stop. In a stream, they often swim back upriver. Once you gain back some line, you can put the pressure on again.

A Shoulder to Lean On ↑

Slippery rocks and swift water can make wading treacherous. If you're fishing a stream with a friend, wade across fast riffles or runs while gripping each other's vest or jacket. Your footing and balance will be much surer than if you had tried to wade alone.

Find Trout Lies Quickly

Fly-fishermen can improve their success by learning where the trout are before they start fishing. Catch a few terrestrial insects, such as grasshoppers, crickets or beetles. Toss them into the stream and watch them carefully. When a trout grabs one, note the location so you'll know where to cast your fly.

"Unmatch" the Hatch to Take Trout

Sometimes, even dedicated match-the-hatch fly-fishermen have to admit defeat. If trout refuse a fly intended to match the insects on the water, here's a trick that may provoke a strike.

Instead of dead-drifting a dry fly, give it a twitch or two, or let the line belly out so the fly skates across the surface. Another option: try a fly that differs from the naturals in size, shape and color.

Trout will closely inspect and often reject a fly that is almost, but not quite, identical to the insect that is hatching. But they will hit something that is completely different.

Dacron Backing Saves Fly Reels

Steelheaders often drift flies or bait along the bottom in swift current using a long fly rod rigged with monofilament. The line is stripped off by hand rather than cast off the reel. Many anglers prefer a fly reel to a spinning reel, because the loose loops that form when lobbing and drifting a bait are less likely to tangle on its smaller handle and more compact form. But don't fill a fly reel only with monofilament. Mono stretches under the tension of loading the line or reeling in a fish. Then it constricts on the spool, exerting force not only against the arbor but the sides of the spool as well. This sideways force may cause the spool to spread and bind against the frame.

To avoid ruining your fly reel, fill it to within ½ inch of the pillars with braided Dacron line, which stretches very little. Top off the spool with about 100 yards of 8- to 12-pound mono, joining the mono to the Dacron as shown below:

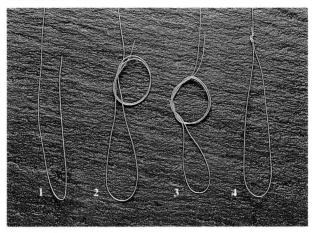

TIE a double surgeon's loop in the end of each line by (1) doubling over the line, (2) tying an overhand knot with the loop, and (3) pushing the loop through the knot a second time. (4) Pull tight and clip the end.

INTERLOCK the two loops by threading the mono loop through the Dacron loop and then passing the mono spool through the mono loop. Pull the loops tight. Then fill your reel with mono to within ⅛ inch of the pillars.

Pretied Tippets Save Time

Some predictable mayfly hatches occur late in the evening. The hatch — and the fishing — can turn on suddenly and proceed at a furious pace. When it's dark and the fish are feeding aggressively, it's easy to break off a fly on a fish or snag it in the brush. Because these hatches may peak and end within minutes, the time-consuming task of trying to tie on a small fly in the dark is especially frustrating. And even a small flashlight can ruin what night vision you do have.

Here's how a little preparation at home can save time and prevent frustration once you're on the stream:

ATTACH 2-foot tippets to several flies of the pattern you think you'll need. Tie a double surgeon's loop (photo at left) in the other end of each tippet. Coil the tippets and tuck them in your hat band, sandwich them in a Velcro fastener on your vest, or hook the flies in a fleece patch and let the tippets dangle. Tie a double surgeon's loop in the end of your leader, and loop on one of the pretied tippets and flies. This way, if you break off a fly, you can simply replace the tippet. Changing tippets is much faster and easier than tying on small flies — especially if it's dark and you're surrounded by hungry trout.

Add Yarn to an Egg Loop

Fresh spawn with a bit of bright yarn is a top steelhead and salmon bait. Most anglers snell the eggs and yarn on the hook. But a snell (opposite page), may pinch off the eggs. An egg loop won't pinch off spawn, but it doesn't draw tight enough to hold the yarn. Here's how you can add yarn to an egg loop:

TIE an egg loop by threading (1) the end of a 24-inch piece of mono through a hook with an upturned eye. (2) Wrap the long end around the shank and tag end six to eight times. (3) Make a loop, then push the long end back through the eye. (4) Hold the wrapped portion while making six or eight more wraps over the tag end and the other line. (5) Insert a small bunch of yarn in the rear loop, and then pull on the long end of the line to tighten the knot and secure the yarn. Trim the tag end of the line. (6) Grasp the yarn in a single bunch and clip it with a scissors to form an egglike ball. (7) Cut a marble-sized ball of spawn from a skein of fresh salmon eggs, leaving as much of the membrane as possible to hold the eggs together. Open the front loop of the knot, slip the eggs inside, and pull the loop tight, securing the eggs to the hook. The knot won't pinch off the eggs, yet the rear loop will hold the yarn firmly in place.

No-Cling Guides for Drift Fishing

When you drift yarn or spawn for steelhead or salmon, it pays to use as long a rod as possible. A long rod holds the line off the water better than a short one, making it easier to control line during the drift. But if you use a fly rod and mono, as many anglers do, the snake guides let the line slap against the rod shaft. In rainy weather, the mono clings to the wet rod, cutting the cast short. You can avoid the problem by modifying your existing fly rod or building a new one especially for drift-fishing. Here's how:

USE single-foot guides instead of the snake guides usually found on fly rods. The single-foots do a better job of holding the wet line away from the rod shaft. The result: your line zips through the guides with less drag.

"Popping" a Lure Can Bring a Strike

A sudden change in the action, speed and direction of a trolled lure can cause a salmon or trout to strike, but when fishing with downriggers, it's tough to vary the action of the lures. If you have no luck trolling through a school of fish that shows on your graph, try this: Jerk on the rod to pop the lure from the downrigger release. Then do nothing. Let the lure rise and trail near the surface for a moment. The sudden change in the action often draws a strike. After popping the release, you must raise the ball to re-rig, so it's a technique to use mainly when you will be lifting the ball to change or inspect the lures.

Offbeat Colors for Steelhead

When drift-fishing for steelhead or salmon, many fishermen use bright or fluorescent yarn. Fish probably mistake these flies for spawn. But don't limit yourself to old standards, such as orange, pink and chartreuse. Here are some other colors and color combinations that often work when the usual colors don't:

INSERT (1) two pieces of contrasting yarn into the loop (arrow) of a snelled egg hook. (2) Pull the line to cinch up the yarn, then trim so the yarn is ¼ to ¾ inch long. The two-toned pattern will sometimes catch fish when neither color alone draws a strike.

MAKE a fly from black, tan or brown yarn. These flies don't resemble spawn at all, but rather natural foods, such as stonefly and mayfly nymphs. Also effective at times is blue yarn, though it resembles nothing steelhead or salmon would normally eat.

An Ant for All Seasons

If rising trout won't take an exact imitation of the insects that are emerging, try this trick.

Tie on a black ant pattern that is smaller than the insects the trout are eating. Cast upstream and fish the ant on a dead drift. Trout that reject exact imitations will often take small ant patterns, even during winter and early spring, when no real ants can be found. In

fact, the trick of using a fly that's smaller than the natural works with other patterns, too.

When matching a hatch with a dry fly, it's usually better to use a size smaller than you think you should. Why? First, we overestimate the size of insects in the air. Second, the hackle of a dry fly makes it look larger than a natural with the same length body and wing.

Snagproof Salmon Flies

Standard salmon streamers and wet flies are tied to ride with the wing up and the hook point down. But a fly tied this way hangs up easily and is likely to snag a salmon if the leader drifts over the fish's back during the retrieve. Fighting foul-hooked salmon takes time better spent fishing, and if you break off, you lose leaders and flies. Even if you don't foul-hook the fish, it may feel the hook across its back and dart away. Here's a trick some fly-fishermen have borrowed from saltwater anglers to avoid snagging bottom or the fish:

TIE your favorite streamer patterns upside down, like bonefish flies. The hook rides point up and is protected by the wing.

Cheap No-Slip Soles

The algae-covered boulders in some trout streams are as slick as grease. With ordinary rubber-soled boots you can fall flat on your face. Many anglers buy expensive boots or waders with felt soles to get traction on slippery rocks, but here's a cheap way to improve your footing with waders you already own:

1. GRIND the lugs off the soles of your boots with a coarse-grained belt or disk sander to provide a roughed-up but flat surface for gluing.

2. TRACE the outline of the boots onto a scrap of indoor-outdoor carpet. Scrape any foam backing off the carpet soles with a wire brush.

3. COAT the sole and carpet with a strong adhesive. Follow the directions that come with the glue. Tape on the soles until the adhesive sets.

Interchangeable Sinking Tips

Many fly-fishermen use sink-tip lines to get streamers or nymphs down to trout feeding near the bottom in a fast run. The sink rate and length of the sinking portion varies from line to line. The best combination for one situation won't necessarily be the best choice in another. You could solve the problem by carrying several different sink-tip lines. But here's a cheaper and more convenient way:

1. CUT lead-core line in several lengths from 18 inches to 6 feet long. Form small loops on the end of each piece, just as you would on the end of a fly line (p. 117).

2. LOOP a section of lead core between your fly line and a 3-foot mono leader. Use a short piece to sink a fly in shallow water, a longer one in deeper water.

Panfish Tips

Finesse Picky Perch

The motion and flash of a small jigging spoon will get a perch's attention. If the fish is aggressive, it will hit the spoon right away. A less active fish, however, will watch the spoon but won't bite.

When finicky fish are giving you fits, try this rig. It catches these inactive perch and the aggressive ones at the same time, whether you're fishing open water or through the ice.

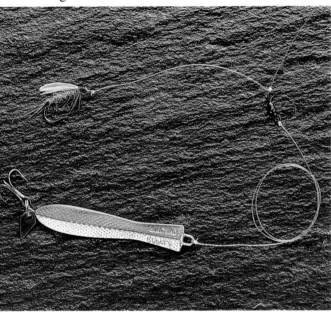

MAKE a tandem rig by tying a barrel swivel to the line. Add 8 inches of 6-pound mono and tie a small jigging spoon on the end. Attach 6 inches of 4-pound mono to the swivel; add a small wet fly or nymph. Even perch with a full belly are curious; they'll move in to inspect the flashy spoon and may take a nip at the fly.

Outwit Fussy Crappies

In spring, you'll find crappies preparing to spawn in shallow water near cover such as brush or bulrushes. But often they don't feed much and shy away from most lures and baits.

Coax them into hitting by casting a lively minnow without a sinker. With no weight to hold it back, the minnow moves naturally and appeals even to the fussiest crappies.

Detect Light-Biters

At times, crappies swim upward as they suck in a small jig, so you can't feel the strike. If you're using a regular bobber, it moves too little to notice. Here's a way to catch these fish, no matter how delicately they take your lure:

USE a European-style slip bobber (inset) on 2-pound-test mono to detect subtle takes. Tie on a 1/64- or 1/32-ounce jig. Add enough split-shot above the jig that only about 1/4 inch of the bobber sticks out of the water. Tiny European shot is best for the fine adjustment necessary. If a crappie swims upward as it sucks in the jig, taking some of the weight off the line, the super-sensitive bobber rises enough to clearly indicate a strike.

No-Tangle Tandem Rig

Popper-and-nymph combos are great for bluegills in shallow water. The popper attracts the fish, but most of them, particularly the big ones, hit the nymph.

One common way of rigging flies in tandem is to cut your leader and join the pieces with a blood or barrel knot, leaving a tag end long enough for the dropper. But tying a dropper this way is time consuming, and the flies often tangle. Also, you need to tie up a new leader or cut the dropper off to go back to fishing one fly.

Here's a rig that's quick and easy to assemble, doesn't tangle, and is easy to take apart when you want to use a single fly:

ATTACH a small cork- or foam-bodied popper to a 6-foot leader. Tie 2 feet of 4-pound mono to the bend of the popper hook with a clinch knot, then attach a size 12 weighted nymph. The popper makes a good strike indicator, disappearing when a fish takes the nymph.

A Little Leech Lasts Longer

Sunfish will gobble up a small jig tipped with a piece of garden worm or nightcrawler. Trouble is, after one or two bites, the worm is gone. Here's a bait that's just as appealing but lasts much longer. Tip a $\frac{1}{32}$-ounce jig with a $\frac{1}{2}$-inch piece of a leech, preferably from the narrow head end, where the flesh is toughest. The bait is small enough to catch nibblers, yet it will stay on the hook indefinitely.

Modify Jigs for Papermouths

If you hook a crappie in the thin membrane around its mouth, the hook can tear out easily. Here's a way to increase your chances of hooking a crappie in the tough tissue in the roof of the mouth:

BEND the hook of a crappie jig about 10 degrees past its original position (dotted line). Now the hook is more likely to stick in the roof of the mouth than in the membrane.

Brush Beater Crappie Jigs

Crappies often hang out in heavy brush and timber. No matter how carefully you work a jig through the branches, you snag up. Even if you don't lose the jig, you'll shake the branches as you try to rip free, usually spooking the fish.

One solution would be to put a mono-loop weedguard on your jig (p. 31). Here's another way of rigging a snag-free crappie jig.

BEND the hook of a bare jig (1) downward about 20 degrees from the normal position (dotted line). (2) Thread on a plastic grub so the hook point is barely exposed.

Pennants for Panfish

Catching spawning bluegills or yellow perch is easy because you can see them in the shallows. But once the fish move to deeper water, they can be hard to locate. Here's a way to bring the fish to you:

DROP a rope of colorful pennants (the kind car dealers use) in an area likely to hold bluegills or perch. A weight on one end of the pennants will keep them from drifting and a float on the other end will mark the spot. Leave the area for an hour or more. The bright flags attract these panfish and keep them in the area until you return. Fish around the flags with small jigs or live bait, either anchoring over the flags or casting from a short distance away.

Scout Ice-Fishing Spots in Summer

Finding crappies under the ice is tough. You may have to drill dozens of holes before you get onto fish. And using a fish finder through the ice is far more time consuming than in open water.

When fishing in the spring and summer, find landmarks that will help you pinpoint your crappie spots once the ice forms. In early winter, the fish are found in the same shallow areas they occupy in the spring. By midwinter they move into the same deepwater spots they occupy in midsummer.

Read Depth Through Bad Ice

In early winter, you can easily sound through the ice with a depth finder. But later in winter, snow, slush and air bubbles interfere with the signal, so you have to drill a new hole each time you want to take a reading. Here's how you can sound through the ice, even if the lake is covered by slush and snow:

SOUND through recently drilled holes, where the ice is smooth and clear. Pour a little water on the ice, set the transducer in the puddle and take a reading.

See Light Bites in the Dark

In midwinter, panfish sometimes mouth the bait so lightly you don't feel a thing. Or they grab the bait and swim up with it. Here's a way to detect these soft bites and set the hook.

Fish from a darkhouse or cover the windows of your fish house so you can see down the hole. In clear water, you'll be able to watch the fish take the bait. In deeper or murkier water, you probably won't be able to see the fish, but if you're using a light-colored bait, it will disappear when a fish grabs it.

Super-Tough Perch Bait ↑

The way yellow perch steal bait, you can spend more time baiting your hook than fishing. When you're jigging through the ice and fishing is hot, try this trick to make a bait that attracts perch with smell, taste and action and won't tear off the hook:

SCALE the belly of a small perch and cut out an inch-long strip (dotted lines). Split one end of the meat to form two tails. Hook the other end of the strip on the jig.

Preserve Perch Eyes

Perch eyes make great bait for walleyes, saugers and even perch. So, when you clean a mess of perch, poke out the eyes with your thumb and save them. But don't put the eyes in a freezer or they'll get mushy. Instead, put them in a small jar and fill it with salt water. Keep the jar in the refrigerator until your next ice-fishing trip. Use an eye to tip a lure, or thread one on a plain hook and fish it on a 4-inch dropper beneath a small jigging spoon.

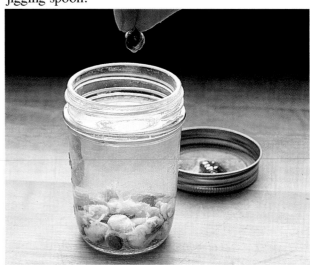

Light up Ice-Fishing Holes

When ice fishing at night, it's tough to see a bobber. Most anglers set a lantern on the ice, but the bobber may be hard to see because of the shadow cast by the rim of the hole. And when a fish pulls the bobber under, you can't see it at all. Try this trick to help you see better. It works with a light source as small as a candle or as large as a lantern.

BORE a hole in the ice between the holes you're fishing in, stopping just before the auger breaks through. Set a candle or lantern in the hole. Light will travel through the ice to nearby holes, illuminating the bobbers from the side and below so they're plainly visible (photo at right). Cover the hole on windy nights to keep the flame from blowing out, but be sure enough air gets in so the flame doesn't smother.

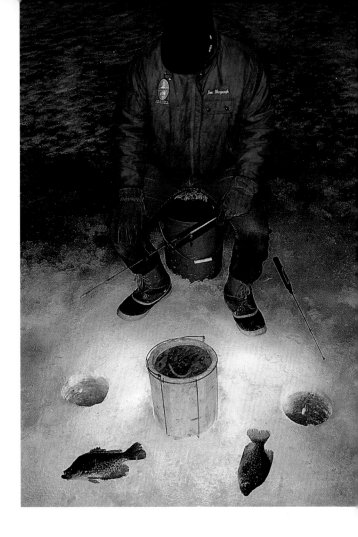

Chum for Panfish

It's easier to bring panfish to you than for you to find them, especially when you're fishing through the ice. Borrow a tip from the saltwater angler's bag of tricks and try chumming. It works best for sunfish and perch, stirring up their competitive instincts so they feed more aggressively and keeping their interest so they stay around longer. Because fish must be able to see the chum from some distance away, chumming works best in clear water over a clean bottom, rather than in heavy cover. Here's how to do it:

DROP a few BB-sized chunks of frozen shrimp down the hole. Once the fish move in, chum sparingly but often to keep them around. As you change bait, use your old bait for chum. It's important to drop the chum in the same spot each time. When fishing in open water, drop the chum next to a marker or other stationary object.

Catfish Tips

Keep Baitfish on a Short Leash

Flathead catfish anglers often weight a big, frisky sun-fish, sucker or bullhead with a slip-sinker and put a sinker stop about 18 inches above the hook so the bait can move freely. But in the tangled timber big flatheads love, a baitfish on an 18-inch tether will hide in the wood or wrap your line around a snag.

Keep the baitfish close to the sinker by eliminating the sinker stop entirely or by placing a stop only a few inches up the line. Reel in the slack. If you want the baitfish to swim a little more, feed a few inches of line through the sinker. With the baitfish on such a short leash, a catfish can catch it easily.

Line Release for Bank Fishing

When bottom fishing from shore with live bait, you should keep the line under a little tension so the wind or current doesn't carry it out. Yet line must pay out when a fish bites or it will drop the bait. To get just the right amount of tension, try this trick:

SLIP a loop of line under a matchstick held to the foregrip with a rubber band. The match will keep the line from drifting away, but will release the line when a fish hits. If the current or wind is strong, increase the friction on the loop by pulling the line in tighter to the rubber band. If there is little current, or if you feel that light-biting catfish are dropping the bait because they feel resistance, move the line farther from the rubber band. This way, the slightest tug will pull it free.

Wild Baitfish Tame Cats

Veteran catfishermen know that baitfish caught from the river they're fishing are far superior to pond-reared baitfish purchased from the local bait shop.

Almost any kind of wild baitfish, including chubs, suckers and sunfish, will work.

The reason is simple: to baitfish that inhabit the river, catfish are natural enemies. When a hooked baitfish spots a cat, it struggles frantically to escape. The commotion arouses the cat's interest. A pond-reared baitfish, on the other hand, has never seen a catfish and has no reason to fear it.

Keep Chicken Liver on the Hook

Chicken liver is a top channel cat bait, but liver won't stay on a hook if it gets warm and mushy. If you fish from the bank or a boat, keep the bait in a cooler. If you wade, pack the liver in a plastic bag and drop it in a canvas creel with an ice pack. Here are three other tricks that help keep the bait on the hook:

IMPALE the chicken liver on a number 8 or 10 treble hook, making sure each hook point pierces the bait. Whether the liver is firm or mushy, a treble hook holds it more securely than a single hook.

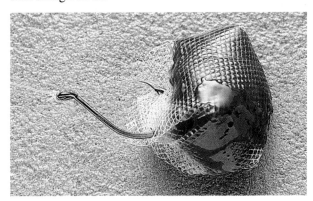

WRAP mushy liver in a patch of nylon mesh or stocking. The mesh lets odors escape yet keeps the bait from falling apart. Form a bag by gathering the edges of the fabric with the hook, twisting the hook to close the top and hooking the mesh again to keep the bag from opening up. Or tie the bag shut with thread before pushing a hook through it.

MIX chicken liver with Wheaties in a blender to form a thick paste. Mold the bait around a bait-holder treble hook to form a doughball.

Longer-Lasting Scent

Catfish are drawn to some commercial and homemade scents, but many of these concoctions wash off after a few minutes in the water. Here's a way to make the scent last longer.

Cut a piece of sponge about 1-inch square and bury a bait hook in it. Soak the sponge in scent. Fish the sponge in one spot or drift it slowly along the bottom. Reapply scent every half hour or so.

The sponge stays on the hook well and releases the scent slowly. Because it has a soft texture like real food, a catfish will pick it up and swim off, giving you time to set the hook.

Enhance Natural Odor

Flatheads, blues and big channel cats are lazy; they'll eat a good-sized baitfish but usually won't go much out of their way to do it. Here's how you can make any baitfish more appealing to big cats by slowing it down so they can catch it more easily, and at the same time increasing the amount of scent it gives off:

TRIM part of the tail and pectoral fins before rigging the bait with a slip-sinker. The smell of fluids that seep from the cuts will attract catfish. The bait will move frantically, but without normal fins won't be able to dodge a big cat.

Jigs for Cats

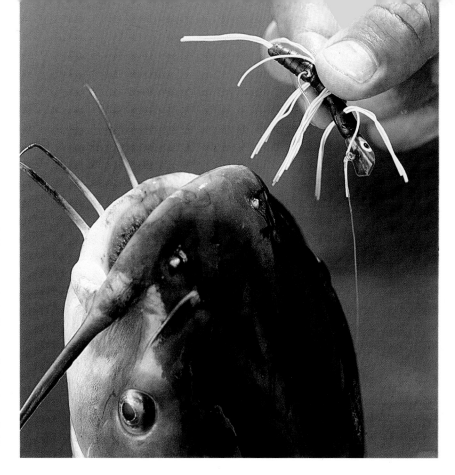

Few anglers think of jigs as catfish lures, but jig fishermen who target walleyes or bass in catfish waters catch plenty of cats by accident. It's not hard to understand why jigs catch so many catfish: They can easily be fished on the bottom, right where the catfish are.

Jigs tipped with live bait such as minnows, nightcrawlers or leeches work best, although it's not unusual to catch catfish on plain bucktail, twister-tail or rubber-legged jigs. Work the lure along the bottom in slow hops, just as you would for walleyes or bass.

Keep Clam Meat on the Hook

Clams make good bait for catfish and many bottom-feeding saltwater fish, such as flounder and surfperch. The meat of a clam consists of the firm muscle mass, called the "foot," and some other tissue, which is softer. The foot is easy to keep on the hook; the other tissue is not. Most anglers use only the foot, but here's a way to make use of the soft meat as well:

WRAP the soft meat with about 8 inches of thread, leaving the hook point exposed. The thread will cut into the meat, making a knot unnecessary.

Junkyard Slip-Sinkers

The debris-strewn bottoms of good catfish holes can gobble up a lot of sinkers. Here's how to cut your losses by making your own slip-sinkers out of otherwise worthless scrap:

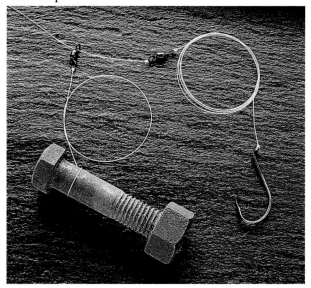

TIE a heavy washer, bolt, nut or other scrap to a 12-inch piece of mono. Attach a barrel swivel to the other end. Slip the line from your rod through the free end of the swivel, and tie it to a second swivel. Run a short leader and bait hook off the second swivel. The "junkyard dropper" should be lighter than the main line. That way, if the scrap hangs up, the dropper will break, sparing the rest of the rig.

← Toughen up Bait

Almost any kind of dead minnows will catch channel cats, but dead bait softens up with use and tears off the hook. Here's a way to keep it on the hook much longer.

Spread the minnows on a screen and let them dry in the sun for several hours. The screen lets both sides dry out and toughen up. Use the minnows as soon as they're dry, or freeze them in a plastic bag to use later.

Cats Want Leeches — Dead or Alive

Most anglers think of leeches as good bait for walleyes, but leeches also work well for a lot of other species, including channel cats.

Walleyes seldom bite on dead leeches, but channels don't seem to care whether they're dead or alive. In fact, when cats are off the bite, the rank smell of the dead leeches often stirs their interest.

Save your dead leeches; you may want to use them in combination with live ones or with some other type of live bait. Dead leeches will keep for several days in cold water.

Remove Bullheads Fast

Bullheads often swallow the hook. Digging it out, even with a needlenose, is messy and time consuming. Here's a quick way to get a bullhead off your line and get back to fishing.

Tie up several bait hooks on 1-foot leaders, each with a loop at the other end. Tie a snap to your fishing line and clip it to a leader loop. Bullheads aren't leader shy and won't notice the snap. If one swallows the hook, unsnap the leader, clip on another, bait up and return to fishing. Recover the hooks when you clean the fish.

Lift Baits Above Snags

Years after a reservoir fills, a tangle of roots, limbs and logs remains on the lake bed, making it difficult to reach bottom-hugging fish without snagging the debris on the bottom. Here's how some southern catfish anglers solve the problem. The technique will work in any snag-filled lake or slow-moving stream.

RAISE the bait off the bottom by pegging a 2- to 3-inch Styrofoam float about a foot up the leader (inset). The float lifts the hook and bait. The closer the float is to the hook, the higher the bait will ride.

Feel Your Way Around Snags

Big flatheads lie in deep holes filled with sunken timber. It's tough to know where to cast. Get too close to the wood, and the sinker or hook will hang up. Stay too far away, and the big cats won't find the bait. To place the bait properly, you need to figure out the precise location of the logs and limbs. Here's how:

FAN-CAST with a 1-ounce bell sinker tied to the end of your line. Retrieve it along the bottom. The sinker seldom hangs up, and you can feel it crawl over logs, limbs, brush and rocks. Once you get a clear picture of the bottom, you can cast near snags but not into them.

Steelheading for Catfish

Most catfishermen add a good-sized sinker to their line and let their bait rest motionless on the bottom of the river. In time, a catfish will usually find it. But enterprising anglers have discovered a quicker way to get a cat's attention.

Remove the front treble from a crankbait and substitute a leader and hook baited with a minnow, a gob of worms, chicken liver or cut bait. Except that the baits are different, this is the same rig steelheaders use to fish along the bottom of a swift run (p. 57).

Anchor below a riffle, or wade out into it, and let the rig trail in the deeper run downstream. You can move the bait from side to side simply by repositioning your rod. Reel in or let out line to move the bait farther upstream or downstream.

Even if the catfish are not in position to smell the bait, they can home in on the vibrations of the crankbait using their lateral line sense. Once they get close, they smell the bait and grab it, though occasionally a cat will hit the plug.

Making & Modifying Lures

An Improved Texas Rig (p. 350)

Making & Modifying Lures

An Improved Texas Rig

With a regular Texas-rigged worm, you miss strikes because fish grab the worm behind the hook. But if you rig the plastic worm as shown below, the hook is far enough back to catch short-strikers. The sinkers are inside the worm, offering several other advantages:

They keep the worm from sliding down the shank when you set the hook; they won't separate from the worm, so pegging is unnecessary; and they're covered by soft plastic, so bass hang onto the worm longer. Here's how to make an improved Texas rig:

Thread (1) the line through a plastic worm so it comes out about one-fourth of the way back. Simply use the hook as a needle. (2) Thread several 1/64- or 1/32-ounce bullet sinkers onto the line nose first and tie on the hook. (3) Draw the sinkers and the eye of the hook into the worm by pulling on the line; push the hook into the worm so the point barely protrudes. The worm should hang straight so it doesn't twist your line.

Spinning Worms for Bass

Most plastic worm fishermen bump the lure slowly along the bottom. It's a deadly but very slow method. But when bass are scattered in the shallows, you can often catch more fish by using a faster retrieve to cover more water. Here are two ways to rig a worm so it can be worked rapidly across the surface. Because the worms are rigged crooked, they spin on the retrieve, drawing explosive strikes.

THREAD a (1) 6-inch worm on a barbed-shank worm hook so half the bend is covered. Add a swivel above the hook to prevent line twist. Slide the end of the worm over the hook eye; poke a piece of toothpick or mono (see below) through the eye to keep the worm in place. The worm has a kink in it so it spins when reeled in. Make a (2) weedless version by threading the worm on a worm hook and twisting it a quarter turn before reinserting the hook Texas style.

Pliable Pegs

Some anglers peg their worms by pushing a toothpick through the hook eye to keep the worm from sliding down the hook. But when you pull through weeds or set the hook on a short-striking fish, you may tear the worm off the toothpick. Here's how to keep the worm from ripping off as easily:

PEG the worm with a short piece of 80-pound mono; trim the ends flush with the worm. The mono has more give than a toothpick, so when you jerk, the mono bends instead of ripping through the worm.

Depth Control for Spinnerbaits

How deep a spinnerbait runs depends on how fast you retrieve it. The slower you reel, the deeper it tracks. But changing speeds to run at the right depth may reduce the number of strikes you get. Here's a way to change the running depth of a spinnerbait without altering the speed:

BEND the arm from its normal position (dotted line) to widen the angle and make the lure run shallower. To fish deeper, bend the arm the other way.

Hard-to-Throw Buzzbaits

Buzzbaits stir up plenty of action in heavy cover, but a leaping bass can easily throw the heavy, long-bodied lure. As the bass shakes it's head, the lure flops back and forth, twisting the hook, enlarging the hole in the fish's mouth and allowing the hook to back out. But here's a way to doctor a buzzbait so it's considerably harder for a bass to throw:

MODIFY the buzzbait by snipping the shaft, forming eyes in the wire and joining them with a split ring. It's important to form the eyes by bending the wire *up* (arrows) so the ends are behind the prop arm, where they won't catch weeds. The hook of this jointed buzzbait moves independently of the heavy blade, so bass have a hard time shaking it loose.

Mow Weeds With a Spinnerbait

Thick submerged weeds, such as hydrilla and coontail, cling to a spinnerbait and ruin its action. Here's a clever way to modify a spinnerbait so you can work it through the weeds with fewer hang-ups. Select a spinnerbait with a heavy brass willowleaf blade and an attachment eye that is not twisted to form a loop in the wire. If the lure has a twisted eye, a clevis or beads, it will catch more weeds on the retrieve.

FILE the leading edges of the blade and hone them until they're razor sharp. Now, the blade will cut through the weeds so they can't foul the lure.

Tuning Spinner Blades

Commercial spinnerbaits and in-line spinners have cupped blades that start turning easily and spin rapidly. But sometimes fish don't respond to the vibrations of a standard blade. Here's a way to modify your spinner blades so they make a different sound, which may be more appealing:

FLATTEN the blade on a rock or anvil. The flat blade creates more resistance and a slower, more throbbing beat than the original.

Two-Way Trailer →

When spinnerbait anglers add a trailer hook to catch short-striking fish, they push it over the main hook point up (top).

This system works fine in heavy cover. The trailer doesn't snag many weeds because the hook point is protected.

But when you're working open water, try rigging the trailer point down (bottom). With one hook pointing up and the other pointing down, your hooking percentage will increase.

Homemade Trailer Hooks

Many commercially made trailer hooks have vinyl-coated eyes to hold them firmly on the bend of the main hook. Otherwise, the trailer would flop around or fall off entirely.

If you can't find trailer hooks with vinyl-coated eyes, or if they're not available in the style or size you want, you can easily make your own using almost any long-shanked hook with a large straight eye. Here's how to do it:

COAT the eye of the hook with a waterproof, flexible adhesive (the kind you would use to patch waders). Or, dip the eye in the liquid vinyl sold in hardware stores to coat and insulate tool handles. When the coating dries, push the trailer hook onto the main hook.

Double-Skirted Spinnerbaits

Most spinnerbaits and buzzbaits have rubber skirts to add action, color and a full silhouette to the lure. Sometimes anglers want to add yet another skirt to make the lure appear larger, or to add another color or to slow the sink rate to keep the lure near the surface on the retrieve. But with a second skirt, bass may strike short. Here's how to add a skirt without reducing your hooking percentage:

MAKE a double-skirted spinnerbait by sliding a skirt over a trailer hook. Then push the main hook through the skirt's rubber sleeve and the eye of the trailer. Push the trailer into place on the bend of the main hook.

Snag-Resistant Snake Plugs

Fish can't resist the wild action of a jointed minnow plug. But it's almost impossible to use these lures in weedy or brushy cover because they foul immediately.

Here's a way to make a jointed minnow plug more weedless while adding the enticing swimming action of a plastic worm:

1. REMOVE the back end of a medium-sized jointed minnow plug by cutting or opening the rear eye (arrow); take off the front treble and split ring.

2. TWIST the eye on the front section so it is horizontal (arrow). Slide a split ring onto a 3/0 worm hook; then join the split ring to the plug so the hook rides point up.

3. RIG a 4-inch plastic worm on the hook Texas style. Fish the lure in pads, stumps and trees, retrieving it steadily so it

swims at or near the surface like a snake. When a fish hits, pause a second before setting the hook.

Modify Spoons for Different Speeds

Lightweight trolling spoons have good action within a narrow range of speed. Troll too fast, and they spin, twisting your line; too slow, and they drag through the water without much wobble at all. You can find the best speed by trolling your spoon next to the boat and

varying your speed until it wobbles just right. But a problem arises when you want to run that spoon with other lures that troll best at different speeds. Here's a way to make the spoon work at higher or lower speeds so you can use it with these other lures:

TUNE the spoon for higher speeds by straightening it (red line). Make it wobble more at lower speeds by increasing

the bend (blue line). Bend the spoon by hand, being careful not to kink the metal.

Fizzing for Fish ↑

When fish are fussy, even the slow movement of a plastic worm or soft-plastic tube jig may not get them to strike. Here's an unusual presentation that can really pay off:

CRUMBLE an Alka-Seltzer tablet and slide the chunks in the rear of a soft-plastic tube jig. Stuff cotton in the tube to hold the Alka-Seltzer in place. Fish the lure slowly. As water soaks through the cotton, the Alka-Seltzer begins to fizz. The bubbles that stream from the rear of the jig attract fish and often trigger a strike. This is a proven tactic for largemouth bass, but don't hesitate to try it on other species, as well.

Hook Big Fish Better

Most plugs, spoons and spinners come with treble hooks. But if you're after trophy-class fish, ordinary trebles may not be strong enough. Big-fish specialists know that a good-sized single hook will sink deeper and hold better than a treble, and no fish is likely to bend or break it.

If you're fishing in waters where there's a good chance of hooking something big, replace your trebles with single Siwash hooks. A Siwash has a sturdy shank and an extra-long slow-tapering point that penetrates like a needle. Once a fish is on, there's little chance it will get away.

Lures with a single Siwash hook offer another advantage: they can be used in waters where treble hooks are banned.

If the trebles are attached with split rings, you can simply open the ring, take off the treble and substitute the Siwash. If the ring is welded, you'll have to cut it off and add a new one. If a lure has two or three trebles, you may want to remove all of them and add just one Siwash where the rear treble was. Changing hooks may disrupt the lure's balance and ruin its action, so be sure to test it before fishing.

Fixing the Weak Link

You hook a big fish, it thrashes wildly, but then it's gone.

After you reel in, you find a hook is missing from your lure. A split ring broke, and the fish swam off with the hook.

This all-too-common problem can be prevented by soldering your split rings to keep them from pulling apart. Even if you have a soldering gun handy, however, you may have trouble getting the solder to stick.

Here's an easy way to beef up your split rings so they won't break at a critical moment:

1. REMOVE the original split ring and treble hook. Find two split rings that will nestle together, so one fits snugly inside the other.

2. JOIN the hook and plug with the small ring first. Start the large ring on the plug (shown); then put it on the hook. A split-ring pliers makes the job easier.

3. FIT the small ring inside the larger one. Often, it will snap into place. Even if it doesn't fit snugly, the connection has been strengthened.

Easy Jig Eyes

Many anglers are convinced that eyes make lures more effective. But the eyes are tough to paint on neatly if you don't know how. Here's a way to do it right every time:

DIP the head of a large nail in light-colored paint and dab it on the lure to form the eye. Let it dry. Dip a finishing nail in dark paint to make the pupil.

Quick Paint Stirrer

Many of the paints you use on jigs, poppers and other lures are hard to mix by hard shaking when the bottles are full. And as the paint gets older and thicker, it gets even tougher to mix thoroughly. You could use a stick to stir the paint, but here's a method that's quicker and not as messy:

DROP a buckshot, small bullet (not the whole cartridge) or large split-shot into the bottle. As you shake the bottle, the pellet stirs up the paint.

Finding the Leak

A leak in a hollow plastic plug will reduce the lure's buoyancy and may ruin its action. If a plug isn't running right, shake it while holding the hooks and split rings against the body so they don't rattle. If you hear water inside, you've found the problem. Here's how to find the leak and plug it:

LOWER the lure, which has been frozen, into hot water. The rapid warming will cause the cold air in the lure to expand and bubble out of the leak, pinpointing its location.

Shake out water if you can. If not, suck the water out through the leak or enlarge the hole with a hot pin. Patch the leak with epoxy.

Remembering the Right Crankbait

Different crankbaits run at different depths. If you're fishing in 8 feet of water, you'll probably want a lure that runs 6 or 7 feet deep. If you can't recall how deep your crankbaits run, try this trick:

WRITE the running depth of each lure on the body or lip with an indelible marker so you know at a glance which crankbait to use. Running depths are often listed in catalogs or the instructions that come with the lures, but it's best to test them yourself. Different line weights and retrieve speeds will cause the lures to run at different depths.

High-Vis Dry Flies

Dry flies can be tough to see as it gets dark. And if you can't see a dry fly, it's tough to fish it. Here's a trick flytiers can use to make dry flies that are visible, even in low light:

TIE in a tuft of fluorescent yellow or chartreuse steelhead yarn where the wing would be. Then wind the hackle "parachute" style around the base of the yarn rather than the hook. This method keeps the hackle from hiding the yarn, which will be easy to see, even at dusk. But trout will see the fly in silhouette and won't be spooked by the color.

Better Sinking Flies

Most flytiers wrap lead wire around the hook shank of streamers and nymphs to make them run deeper. But the lead wire causes the fly to sink horizontally. The water resistance against the entire length of the fly minimizes the sink rate. Also, the fly doesn't have much action. Here's a better way to weight flies.

Instead of wrapping lead on the hook, tie the fly on a bare jig. Flies tied on jig hooks have an appealing jigging action and sink head first, so they get down to

the fish faster. Because they ride point up, they don't snag as often.

For best casting, use a jig no larger than 1/32 ounce. But jigs this size usually have hooks too small for good-sized fish. To get the hook you want, you can mold your own jigs. Or use bigger jigs and shave off some lead with a file or old knife. Another solution is to buy plain jig hooks (without the lead) and squeeze on a split-shot of the desired weight.

Tooth-Proof Streamers

Toothy gamefish cut ordinary tinsel-bodied streamers to shreds. Streamer bodies made by slipping woven mylar tubing over the shank aren't very durable, either. If a few individual strands are cut, the body unravels.

You can use that same mylar tubing (with the string core removed) to make a much tougher streamer. Because the mylar is wrapped on, the strands bind one another to the shank, so the fly won't fall apart, even if several are cut. Here's how to tie one of these durable streamer bodies:

MAKE a body by first putting a few wraps of thread around the shank. Lay the mylar along the hook, wrap thread over it, then wrap the mylar around the shank (shown). Tie off the mylar with thread. Continue tying the fly.

Snag-Resistant Wooly Buggers

The Wooly Bugger is one of the best flies for big trout and smallmouth bass. Most anglers fish it deep, with a split-shot next to the hook eye, so it moves up and down like a jig. Using a split-shot rather than tying the fly on a jig head allows you to change weight for varying circumstances. But the hook point rides down as often as up and frequently snags on rocks. Here's a way to correct the problem:

TIE the fly to the tippet with a Duncan loop (p. 37). Hold the fly with the hook point up, and clamp a split-shot (BB or larger) to the *lower* strand of the loop. The weight keeps the point riding up so you'll snag less.

Weedless Poppers

Most fly rod poppers aren't weedless, so they hang up in the heavy cover where bass hide. Here's how you can make two types of weedguards that will allow your popper to slip through weeds and brush.

MONO WEEDGUARD. Poke (1) a pair of holes (arrow) on each side of the hook shank using a needle. Angle the holes out and back. Dip the ends of a piece of 30-pound-test mono in 5-minute epoxy, and (2) insert them into the holes to form a loop just large enough to protect the hook.

WIRE WEEDGUARD. Punch a needle (1) through the lip of the popper on either side of the hook eye to make a pair of holes (arrow). Bend a short length of stainless steel wire (about .010-inch diameter) so it has a tight loop in the middle. (2) Push the legs of the wire down the holes. (3) Fit the loop over the hook eye, then pull the wire legs to tighten the loop. Trim the legs so they are just long enough to protect the hook point.

Enlightened Fishing

As the sun sinks below the horizon, a red-hot evening bite suddenly turns ice-cold. What happened? Is it possible the fish simply couldn't find your lure in the dark?

That may indeed be the case. When the sun goes down, light penetration may be reduced to the point where fish cannot see your bait. Lack of sufficient light is obviously a problem early or late in the day, but it may also be a problem in midday if it is overcast or windy;

if the lake is covered by ice and snow; or if the water is deep or murky.

A study on an algae-clouded Michigan lake shows just how much murky water can reduce light penetration in both summer and winter (see chart on p. 93). In summer, for instance, 95 percent of the light was filtered out at depths of 8.53 feet. In winter, under snow and ice, 95 percent of the light was filtered out at a depth of 2.79 feet. With so little light available, even fish such as walleyes, with eyes adapted to darkness, stop biting because they can't see the lure.

But fishermen can beat the low-light problem by using lures that produce their own light. Some lures come with a glow-in-the-dark finish, but experts prefer to

Use flexible luminescent tape for easy application

doctor their own lures with luminescent tape or paint. The tape can be applied when you're fishing and is much easier to work with than paint. Be sure to use tape that is thin and flexible so it will mold to the shape of your lure.

If the lure glows too brightly, as many commercially made luminescent lures do, it will spook more fish than it will attract. Don't cover the whole lure with tape. A small spot or strip is enough to attract a fish's attention.

Don't flash luminescent lures with a camera strobe or Q-beam; it will make them glow too much. Instead, simply lift the lure from the water every 5 to 10 minutes to recharge it. At night, illuminate it occasionally with an flashlight.

Recharge luminescent lures with an ordinary flashlight

Here are some ideas for doctoring your lures:

• Place one small luminescent spot or strip on each side of your lure to make it more visible in deep or murky water.

• If fish are right on the bottom, put a small piece of tape on the lure's belly so fish can easily spot the lure from below.

Dip sinkers in luminescent paint after applying white base coat

• Use a sinker with luminescent tape or paint ahead of a leech, worm or minnow. The glowing sinker leads fish to the bait.

• When trolling for salmon or trout, put a little tape on your dodger as well as your plugs and spoons.

• Add small dots or ovals of tape to spinner blades to make them more visible in dark water.

Depths at Which Light Is Filtered out in an Algae-Clouded Lake*

PERCENTAGE OF LIGHT FILTERED OUT	DEPTH (FEET)	
	SUMMER	WINTER
20	1.97	0.66
40	3.94	0.82
60	4.92	0.98
80	6.23	1.64
90	7.87	1.90
95	8.53	2.79
100	16.07	no data

*Based on July and February data from Wintergreen Lake in southwestern Michigan

Tackle Tips

Budget Line Stripper (p. 364)

Tackle Tips

Budget Line Stripper

Removing old line by hand is tedious. You can buy a line stripper to make the job easier. But either way, you end up with a tangled pile of line you can't reuse.

If you're stripping off expensive line, such as braided Dacron or lead-core, you'll probably want to save it. This makes the job even more time-consuming because you have to wind the line onto another spool.

To remove line quickly and save it to use another time, put a 6- to 8-inch dowel in the chuck of an electric drill. Tie the line to the dowel, and run the drill at low to medium speed until all the line is removed (pages 94–95). With a baitcasting reel, use the clicker or your thumb to keep the spool from overrunning and causing a backlash.

When the line is on the dowel, secure it this way:

TIE the line to a rubber band, then put the rubber band around the dowel so the line doesn't unravel.

Quick and Easy Line Holder

It's a good idea to carry extra spools of line. But spools lying loose in a tackle box take up a lot of space and are almost sure to tangle with your tackle. Here's an easy-to-build rack that will keep line in order and fit in a storage compartment in your boat.

Nail or screw together a three-sided rack from scrap lumber. Drill a ⅜-inch hole completely through one end piece and partly through the other. Slide a ⅜-inch dowel through the first hole and seat it in the opposite hole. Trim the dowel flush with the outside of the end piece.

Nail or screw a small metal flap to the end piece to cover the end of the dowel and keep it from sliding out. The flap pivots so you can remove the dowel.

Put a rubber band around each spool to keep line from unwinding. Slide the dowel through the spools, seat it and drop the flap. Keep a nail clipper handy by tying it to the rack with a short piece of fishing line.

Drill Hole Partially Through This Side

Metal Flap

Drill Hole Completely Through

Tame Springy Mono

When first put on a spinning reel, heavy mono may spring from the spool as you open the bail, making casting difficult. You have the opposite problem with old line: it's so coiled it doesn't peel off the reel and pass through the guides smoothly. Here's a solution to both problems:

COILED mono (left) or line that springs off the reel can be softened by soaking your spool in warm tap water for about 10 minutes. When you put the spool back on the reel (right), the line will be much more manageable.

Easy Pull-off Sinker Rigs

If you're fishing a bait rig over a rocky bottom, it's a good idea to use a sinker that will pull off if the weight hangs up in rocks. That way, you just add a new sinker rather than make a whole new rig. But tying most pull-off sinker rigs takes time. The line, leader and dropper are usually attached to a three-way swivel, requiring three knots. Here are two simpler rigs that take less time to make:

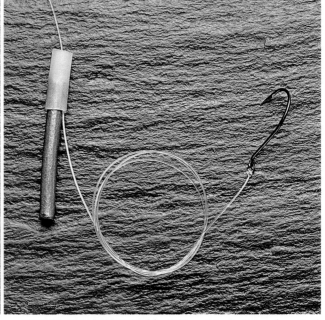

SPLIT-SHOT DROPPER. Tie the leader to a barrel swivel. Tie the line to the other eye, leaving a tag end several inches long for a couple of split-shot. This rig uses one less knot than a three-way swivel rig, yet it works the same way: if the sinkers hang up, a hard tug will pull them off the dropper, and you get the rest of your rig back.

PENCIL-LEAD DROPPER. Slide a 1-inch piece of surgical tubing over your line. Jam the lead about ¼ inch into the tubing. Slide the tubing to the desired distance above your hook. If the lead snags bottom, a hard tug will pull it out of the sleeve. If it pulls out too easily, increase the friction by pushing it farther into the tubing.

The Cat's-Paw Connection

Double-strand leaders save lots of fish, but the way most anglers tie them, the hook will pull off if one strand breaks. Solve the problem with a "cat's-paw," a knot used by many saltwater anglers to attach a hook to a double-strand leader. The knot will hold the hook securely, even if a fish bites through one strand. Here's how to tie the cat's-paw:

TIE a 1-foot loop in your line with a strong knot, such as a double surgeon's loop (p. 61), and (1) thread the loop through the hook eye. (2) Spread the loop and the two leader strands, and (3) pass the hook through the loop and between the two leader strands (arrow) about five times. (4) Start to tighten the knot by holding the hook while pulling with the standing line. (5) Moisten the knot, then pull it snug. The finished knot resembles the pads of a cat's paw.

Conserve Rubber Stops

The small rubber stops you buy already threaded on a wire loop make handy sinker or bobber stops. Simply slip them from the wire loop onto the line and slide them into position. The rubber won't scuff your line the way other stops sometimes do.

But the stops are fairly expensive, and once you take them off the line, they're difficult to put back on because the hole is too small to push the line through. You could rethread them with a sewing needle, but here's an easier way:

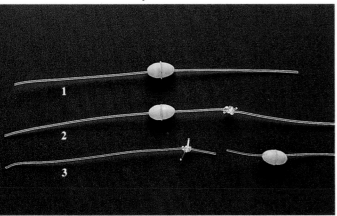

SAVE a rubber stop by (1) cutting it off along with a section of your old mono. To reuse the stop, (2) tie the piece of old mono to your new line. (3) Push the stop over the knot onto the new line, then cut off the knot. Slide the stop into the desired position.

Save Your Slip Bobber

When slip-bobber fishing, your sinker may snag and you'll have to break the line. Without the sinker to stop it, the bobber will slide off, and you'll have to chase it. Try this to keep your bobber on the line:

TIE a slip-bobber rig as you normally would, with a bobber stop above the float. Then, add a second bobber stop *below* the float; it should ride just above the sinker. Now if you break off the sinker, the extra stop will keep the bobber from sliding off.

Better Spring-Lock Bobber

Many anglers like spring-lock bobbers because the long upper tip telegraphs light bites and is easy to see. But these floats have a couple of drawbacks: They are held on the line by a metal spring that may kink and weaken the monofilament. Also, pulling hard on a fish or snag can lift the spring, causing the bobber to pop off the line.

Here's an easy way to modify the float to solve these problems:

REPLACE the spring with a half-inch piece of surgical rubber tubing that fits snugly over the lower stem. Thread the line through the tubing, then push it into the notch in the stem. Slide the tubing up over the notch (inset). Roll back the tubing to move the bobber. The soft rubber does not kink the line, and even the strongest pull won't cause the bobber to pop off.

Bobber Getter

Large cylindrical slip-bobbers are popular with shore-bound catfish anglers. The floats are quite expensive, so it's painful to break your line on a snag and watch your float drift slowly from sight. Here's how some ingenious anglers recover their floats:

1. MAKE a "bobber getter" from a large cylinder float. Straighten a dozen large hooks, clip off the eyes, and shove the shanks into the float so the points angle toward one end. Wrap electrical tape around the float and the base of the spines to reinforce them. Run heavy mono through the float. Tie a barrel swivel to the end the hooks point toward and a ⅜-ounce sinker to the other end. The sinker provides casting weight and tips the float but won't sink it.

2. CAST the bobber getter beyond the free-floating bobber. Retrieve it to within a few inches of the drifting float. Then jerk the rod to sink the spines.

A Clip-Slip Bobber

If you need a slip-bobber but have only a common round clip bobber (everybody has at least one), try this simple trick:

DEPRESS the button, pushing out the bottom clip (arrow). Turn the button to rotate the clip 180 degrees so it rests on the bobber rather than seating in the hole. Thread a bobber stop onto your line, add the hook and sinker, then clip on the bobber.

Keep Skirts Pliable

The rubbery skirts on spinnerbaits, jigs and Hula Poppers tangle and get stiff as they age, losing their appealing action. Here's a way to keep them pliable:

SPRAY the skirts with Armor All Protectant, sold in auto stores to keep vinyl upholstery in good condition. Wipe off the excess with a cloth.

Getting Pigs off Jigs

New pork chunks can be hard to get off hooks because the hole is too small to pass over the barb. Try this method to get the pig off your jig. Twist the pork chunk hard one way and then the other to enlarge the hole. Then stretch the hole over the barb and slide the pork off the hook.

No-Slip Crimps

To attach a swivel or other terminal tackle to braided wire line or downrigger cable, you can make a loop in the wire and crimp a metal sleeve over the wire and tag end. But if the crimp loosens, you lose tackle. Here's how to crimp wire so it won't pull out:

THREAD the wire (1) through the sleeve, through the swivel eye and back through the sleeve. (2) Push the tag end of the wire back through the sleeve. Pull the end to snug up the loop, but don't pull the loop into the sleeve. (3) Crimp the sleeve with a crimping tool; clip the tag end.

Vest-Pocket Tackle Box

Anglers who wade or hike in to fishing spots have to keep their gear compact as well as orderly. Here's one way to organize small items such as leaders, hooks and spinner blades when space is limited:

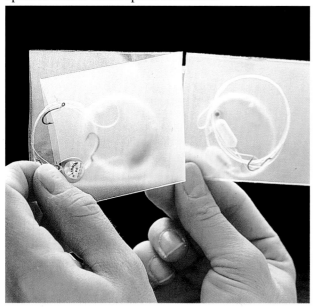

SLIP coiled leaders and other small, flat items into the sleeves of a credit card wallet.

Organize Your Worm Hooks

Rummaging through loose worm hooks is a hassle. And if your hooks aren't sorted by size and type, you can run short of the ones you need without knowing it. Here's how to keep your hooks in order:

BIND the hooks of each type and size together with a rubber band. You'll be able to find the proper bundle and slip a hook out in a moment.

Leader Tamer

Tossed loose in your tackle box, pretied rigs such as leaders, worm harnesses and snelled hooks end up a hopeless mess. Here's one way to keep them from tangling while removing any kinks:

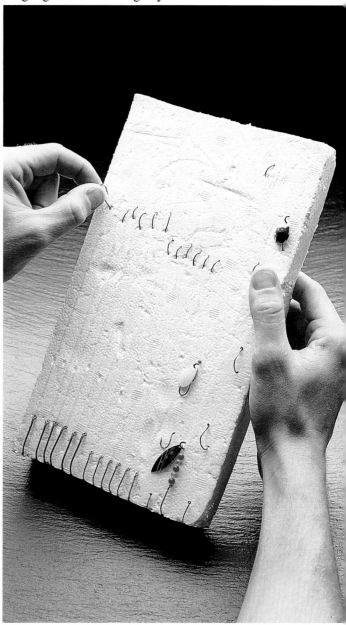

STRETCH out your pretied leaders after sinking the hooks in the edge of a piece of durable packing foam. Pin the loop of each leader to the foam (shown), using an ordinary hook as a staple.

Straighten Up Snaps and Swivels

The right snap, swivel or hook is hard to find if you dump all your terminal tackle into one or two compartments of your tackle box. You can find these small items more easily if you sort them by size and string them on safety pins or paper clips.

Do You Get the Point?

Everyone knows that sharp hooks are important, yet few anglers take time to sharpen their hooks. To make matters worse, they often buy the cheapest hooks, rather than spend a little extra to get good sharp ones.

The photos below depict just how dull some hooks really are and show the best ways to ensure that your hooks are sharp:

ORDINARY HOOKS (1) are surprisingly dull. You can (2) sharpen them to a triangular point with a file or hook hone. (3) Chemically sharpened hooks are even sharper than filed hooks, but they cost up to 10 times more. (4) A good motorized sharpener makes the keenest point of all, though they're a bit too bulky to carry if you fish on foot. One of the best is the Pointmatic Hook-Hone-R, which is easy to use and has long-lasting rechargeable batteries.

Handy J-Plug Box

J-Plugs and similar conical trolling plugs with removable hook harnesses are popular for salmon, and many anglers carry dozens of them. To prevent tangling, some fishermen store the hooks and plug bodies separately. But the bodies take up a lot of space in a tackle box, and if you pile them together in the same tray, you risk damaging the finish. Here's a neat way to protect the plugs' finish and keep them in order, making it easy to find the one you want:

MODIFY a tackle box by cutting a sheet of plastic, plywood or durable packing foam so it fits snugly in the box as shown. Drill rows of holes large enough to accommodate the plug bodies. Put the holder in place and set the plugs in the holes, head up. Store the hook harnesses in a separate container.

Controlling Leader Coils

Long wire and mono leaders are a nuisance to store. If you coil them and then wrap an end several times around the coils, it can be tough unwrapping the leader when you want to use it. Taping the coil is time-consuming and difficult to undo. Here's an easier and faster way:

LOOP a thick rubber band around one side of the coil and cinch it up tight. No knot is necessary, so you can unwrap the leader in a hurry.

Easy-Spinning Spinners

Most spinner-and-bait rigs have a series of beads between the hook and clevis. Sometimes, friction between the clevis and the last bead prevents the blade from turning freely, especially on a slow retrieve. Here's a simple modification that lets the blade spin more easily:

ADD a very small bead (arrow) between the clevis and the larger beads. The small bead has less surface area, reducing friction against the clevis.

Waterproofing Maps

Lake and river maps are always near water. If the maps you use while fishing aren't water resistant, protect them this way. Apply a waterproof sealant such as Thompson's Water Seal, designed for treating concrete block and wood. Spread the sealant on both sides of the map with a foam varnish brush. Cover the surface, but don't drench it. Use clothespins to hang the map from a line until it dries.

Better Hook Sets With Diving Planes

Diving planes work well for deep trolling, but setting the hook may be a problem. Because of the water resistance of the planer, the full force of your hook set doesn't reach the fish. You can set the hook with considerably more force by rigging the diving plane the following way:

TIE about a foot of heavy monofilament and a barrel swivel to the front clip of a diving plane such as a Luhr Jensen Jet Planer. Run your line through the other end of the swivel and tie it to a second swivel, fastened to a leader and your lure. The diving plane will now slide along your line, much as a slip-sinker does. When a fish strikes, it pulls enough line through the swivel so you pull directly against the fish when you set the hook.

Long-Distance Baitcasting

Modern baitcasting reels are precision instruments, capable of casting long distances. But there are times when even longer casts are needed.

Shorefishermen, for instance, may have to make super-long casts to reach fish in midriver or to reach a drop-off in a lake.

If distance is important, you can modify an ordinary baitcasting reel to reduce friction against the spool, allowing you to cast a heavy lure or sinker 100 yards or even farther. Because the spool will spin much more freely, you'll have to thumb the reel more skillfully to avoid backlashes. Here's how to get extra distance from your reel:

1. CLEAN out the heavy grease in bearings, gears, the levelwind mechanism and other moving parts by spraying them with a light lubricant, which dissolves the grease and washes it away.

2. REMOVE the sleeves that rub against the spool and act as centrifugal brakes. If backlashes are a problem after removing the sleeves, replace one of them. On magnetic reels, remove the small magnets.

3. FILL the spool to increase its circumference. That way, the same number of revolutions of the spool will produce a longer cast. Small-diameter line also increases distance; use the lightest line practical for the water you're fishing.

Budget Marker Buoys

If you're moving from spot to spot or following a long breakline, it pays to carry a lot of marker buoys. Here's a way to make cheap buoys that are as good as the ones you can buy:

CUT an H-shaped piece from a thick sheet of tough packing foam. Tie one end of a 50-foot cord to the center of the H, then wind it on. Attach a 4- to 8-ounce sinker to the end of the cord. When you toss out the marker, the cord will unwind as the weight sinks. The marker's flattened shape will keep it from unwinding once the weight hits bottom. If the marker doesn't unwind, use a heavier sinker or cut down the height of the H.

Easy Hook Keeper

A hook keeper near the rod butt comes in handy, yet many rods don't have one. Here's an easy way to make a hook keeper from materials you're likely to have on hand:

1. TAPE down the ends of a loop made from 5 inches of heavy mono. The loop should point toward the rod butt.

2. LAY the loop back over the tape. The loop should now point toward the rod tip.

3. WRAP tape over the mono two or three more times. Slip the hook into the loop.

Keep Cold Metal Under Wraps

One of the coldest things about fishing in chilly weather is the metal reel seat of a spinning rod. Here's how to keep the cold metal off your hands:

WRAP the reel seat with the tape sold in bike stores to cover handlebars. Another option is the cloth self-adhesive tape that is sold in drug stores and resembles an Ace bandage. Either material insulates your hand from the cold and provides a comfortable grip on the reel seat.

Bundle Rods Quickly

When storing or transporting two-piece rods without a case, it's a good idea to bundle the easily damaged tip with the stiffer butt section. But putting rubber bands where you want them and getting them off again can be difficult. Here's a simple way to put a rubber band wherever there's a guide:

LOOP a rubber band over a guide, wrap it around the rod sections once or twice, and loop it over the guide again.

No-Tangle Rods

When you carry a bundle of strung-up rods in your boat or car, you invariably end up with a tangle of lines and rod tips. Then, as you go to use a rod, you have to spend time unwrapping it from the other lines before you can fish.

Next time you carry a bunch of rods, try this method of rigging them before tossing them in your rod box or vehicle:

SECURE the hook on the reel, grab the line halfway up the rod, wrap it once or twice around the rod, and loop it over a guide. This way the line can't tangle.

Cane Pole Line Holder

Two-piece cane poles and telescoping poles are usually rigged with a line about as long as the pole. When you collapse or unjoint the pole, you have extra line and nowhere to put it. Here's a solution.

Tape two paper clips to the rod near the butt. Space them about 3 feet apart with their opposite ends exposed. After you break down the rod, wrap the extra line between the clips.

Case Your Rod and Reel

A long fishing rod is a nuisance when you drive from one fishing spot to another. You can take off the reel and case the rod, which is time consuming. Or you can break the rod down and, leaving it strung up, toss it in the back-seat or trunk, where it's likely to get broken. Here's a way you can safely stow a spinning, baitcasting or fly rod in a vehicle without having to unstring it and take off the reel:

MAKE a case for a rod *and* reel by first cutting an inch-wide slot in a PVC or ABS pipe. The slot should be a bit longer than the distance from the rod butt to the reel seat. Drill a hole in each side of the pipe, about a foot from the end, and two more holes in a cap that fits the pipe. Thread elastic shock cord through the holes and knot the ends. The cord will keep the cap on snugly, but you can pull it off to put a rod in the tube. Glue a permanent cap on the other end.

Freeing Jammed Ferrules

Graphite ferrules sometimes jam so tight that all the standard ways of freeing them, such as holding the rod behind your knees and pushing out with your legs to separate the joint, don't work. Trying to muscle the sections apart may break the rod. Here's how to get them apart without forcing them:

1. COOL the ferrule by placing ice cubes on it or simply leaving the rod outside in cool weather. Both sections of the ferrule will contract.

2. GRASP the female ferrule at the end. Hold it for 20 seconds; it will warm and expand before the male section does, so you can easily separate the two.

Cork Caulk

If your dog chews up the cork handle of your best fishing rod or a toothy fish takes a chunk out of a popper, don't worry. Here's an easy way to repair gouges in cork:

FILL the gouges with a paste made by mixing five-minute epoxy and cork sawdust. Sand the filler flush with the cork after it hardens. Rod builders create a lifetime supply of cork sawdust when they turn down rod handles. Otherwise, get the sawdust you need by filing on a large cork.

Ice-Resistant Tiptop

Frozen tiptops plague ice fishermen. The ice clings to the guide struts, sharp metal edges and ceramic inserts and is hard to remove. Here's how to get rid of the ice easily:

REPLACE the standard tiptop (top) with a fly rod tiptop (bottom). It has a much smoother shape, no struts, and the thin wire has less surface area to collect ice. Any ice that forms is easily removed with your fingers.

No-Slip Tiptop

Anglers commonly replace the broken or damaged tiptops on their rods by bonding them on with ferrule cement. They melt the cement, smear some on the rod, and put on the tiptop. But the tiptop strips off most of the cement as you push it on, so it soon comes loose. Here's how to install a tiptop that won't slip off or twist around on the rod.

Heat the old tiptop to melt the ferrule cement and pull it off with a pliers. Apply cement to the last ¼ inch of the rod and install the new tiptop like this:

PUSH the new tiptop partway on and then heat it to draw the cement inside. Push the tiptop on the rest of the way and turn it so it aligns with the other guides.

Ultralong Ultralights

Short ultralight spinning rods are ideal for fishing in tight, brushy cover. But longer ultralights are a better choice for most other circumstances. They have extra flex for casting light lures, cushion light line against the thrashing of a fish and give you better line control and stronger hook sets. Unfortunately, long ultralight rods are hard to find.

Build your own from a 3- to 5-weight graphite fly rod blank. Outfit the rod with the handle, reel seat and guides you would put on a standard spinning rod.

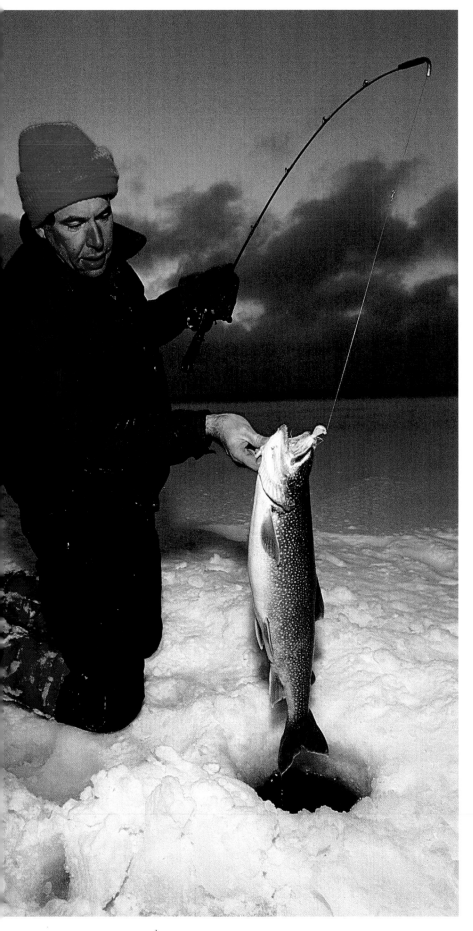

Wear-Resistant Tiptop

Winter lake-trout anglers often use braided wire line for vertical jigging in very deep water. Wire line stretches less than mono or Dacron, making it much easier to detect strikes. But wire cuts through tiptops like a hacksaw. You could use a tiptop with a line roller, but it will ice up in cold weather. Here's how to make a tiptop that will stand up to wire line and won't freeze up:

1. FILL a brass tube 6 inches long and 3/16 inch in diameter with sand. Tape the ends closed to keep the sand from spilling out of the tube.

2. BEND the tube in a right angle around a 1-inch dowel or pipe. The sand will keep the tube from collapsing. Pour out the sand; smooth any rough edges.

3. TAPE the tube to the end of a stiff 3- to 4-foot rod after removing the old tiptop. The tube lasts because it distributes wear over a large area.

Bank Fisherman's Strike Indicator

When you're bank fishing with your rod propped on a stick, a strong wind can buffet the tip. Other times, poor light can make it tough to see the rod tip move. Either way, a bite is hard to detect. You can tell when a fish is biting under these conditions by making a strike indicator.

One way is to clip the eye of a snap-swivel to a small clip bobber, and hang the snap on your line between the first and second guides. The bobber will rise as a fish takes the bait.

Trouble is, to reel in a fish, you must pull the bobber off the line, and that takes time. Then, if you're not careful, the bobber may fall in the water and you'll lose it. Here's a rig that solves those problems:

1. BEND 12 inches of stainless steel wire in half and twist a small loop in one end. Push the wire legs through a large cork as shown. Bend the legs outward and then back inward, so they cross and touch. The cork should be painted or wrapped with reflective or luminescent tape so it's more visible. Tie the cork to a ½-ounce sinker.

2. HANG the wire legs of the strike indicator on the line between the first and second guides. As a fish takes the bait, the strike indicator will rise. When a fish runs, line will slide through the wire legs. Jerk the cork off the line when you pick up the rod. The tether and sinker will keep it from blowing or drifting away.

Swivel Gaff

When you hook a big fish on your gaff and it starts thrashing wildly, it can twist the handle out of your hand. Here's how to keep a grip on the gaff:

MAKE a swivel gaff (inset) by forming a hook from a sharpened metal rod about 20 inches long and ¼ inch in diameter. Thread the last 2 inches of the straight end. A machine shop can do the job. Cut a 1-inch hardwood dowel about 8 inches long for the handle, and drill a hole through the middle large enough for the rod to turn easily inside. Thread a nut on the rod, followed by a washer, the handle, another washer and two nuts. Now, when a big fish thrashes, the gaff swivels inside the handle, so the fish can't twist the gaff from your hand.

Replacing Rod Guides

Rod guides wear out, they break, they loosen. Or, you may just want to replace your guides with better ones. A rod shop could do the job, but so can you.

First, you'll need something to hold the rod while you wrap the guides and apply the finish. You can make a good rod holder from a cardboard box by cutting the front and sides as shown above. Cut a straight notch in one side of the box and an L-shaped notch in the other. This way, you can let go of the rod and the weight of the handle won't tip it. When you're done wrapping the rod, the box comes in handy for storing your tools and materials.

Remove the old guides by cutting off the rod windings with a razor blade or X-Acto knife. Be careful not to nick the rod blank. Remove any hardened epoxy by dampening a cloth with nail polish remover, acetone, or epoxy thinner, and holding the rag on the rod for a few moments. Then scrape away the old epoxy with your thumbnail. Now you're ready to put on the new guides. Here's how:

1. TAPER the top of the guide feet with a grinder so the thread wraps on smoothly. If the feet have blunt edges, there will be a gap in the thread at the end of each foot.

2. RUN the thread between the pages of a phone book or other heavy book to provide tension as you wrap the guide. The more pages on top of the thread, the greater the tension.

3. TAPE down one foot of the guide. Using D-weight nylon winding thread, start wrapping about ¼ inch beyond the tip of the other foot. Turn the rod to wrap the thread over itself.

4. CONTINUE to turn the rod, making sure the thread wraps evenly without gaps or overlap. The thread will climb the guide foot smoothly. Trim the tag end of the thread.

5. LAY down a separate loop of thread when the wraps are about 1/16 inch from the guide support. Continue wrapping to the support. Clip the thread several inches from the rod.

6. PUT the tag end of the thread through the loop. As you do this, make sure you hold the last few wraps with your thumb and forefinger so they don't loosen.

7. PULL the loop to draw the tag end underneath the wraps and out the side. Trim the excess thread. Wrap the other guide foot. Sight down the rod and align the guide.

8. REMOVE any gaps or overlap by gently rubbing across the thread with a smooth, blunt object, such as the barrel of a ballpoint pen.

9. APPLY rod-winding finish (see below) with a brush while turning the rod. Wait a day, trim rough spots with a razor, then add another coat.

No-Drip Rod Finish

The thin epoxy used on rod wraps is more durable than other finishes but has this fault: it forms drips before it hardens, unless the rod is held in a horizontal position and rotated. Rod builders often use small, low-speed motors to do this job. Otherwise, you'll have to rotate the rod a quarter turn every 30 seconds for the first half-hour and less often during the next hour as the epoxy thickens. It's a good job to do while watching television. If you don't have the patience to rotate the rod by hand, try this: Brush on two very thin coats of the glossy polyurethane finish used on wood. Or use a quick-setting rod finish, such as Speed Coat. If applied sparingly, neither of these finishes will drip, and no turning is necessary.

Tying Multistrand Leaders

If you're tired of getting bit off by pike or pickerel, tie up a leader from small-diameter wire, such as 12- or 18-pound Sevenstrand. This twisted multistrand material doesn't kink as easily as solid wire, and it's thinner than nylon-coated wire. The problem comes in trying to fasten the leader to your lure, snap or swivel, because multistrand wire, unlike solid wire, is too springy to twist with your fingers.

Here's an easy way to rig up one of these leaders:

1. RUN the wire through the eye of the lure or snap, leaving a 6-inch tag end, and clamp on a forceps.

2. SPIN the forceps around the main strand of the leader (arrow) 10 to 15 times, keeping the wraps close together. The centrifugal force wraps the leader tightly.

3. CLIP the tag end of the twisted wire close to the wraps. Attach a small barrel swivel to the other end of the leader in the same way.

Airline Emergency Kit

You've shelled out a lot of money for an exotic fishing trip, but when you step off the airplane, your tackle is nowhere to be found. The stores available in many remote locations can't outfit you properly, so your vacation dreams are put on hold until the airline tracks down your fishing gear. In some cases, your tackle never arrives, and your fishing trip is ruined. Granted, the chances of losing your tackle in transit are small, but the result is often disastrous. Here's a way to guard against it.

Pack an emergency fishing kit and carry it on the airplane. Pack light because your baggage must fit under the seat or in the overhead luggage compartment. The kit should consist of a rod or two that can be broken down, reels, a spool of line and a selection of lures and terminal tackle. You may not be able to pack everything you want, but make sure you have enough to get by.

Fixing Sticky Ferrules

The graphite ferrules on some fishing rods often stick together. Pulling them apart is a hassle, and if you're not careful you may damage or break the rod. If you have a ferrule that sticks, try rubbing the male section with ordinary pencil lead. The thin film of graphite will lubricate the connection. After your next fishing trip, the rod should pull apart easily.

If the ferrule sticks and won't come apart at all, try freeing it as shown on page 108.

A Better Needle Knot

A needle knot is a popular way to connect a fly line and leader. But it's difficult to tie because you must slide heavy mono up the thin core of the fly line. The method shown below offers two advantages over an ordinary needle knot. First, it lets you slide heavy mono up the fly line core more easily. Second, you don't need a knot to join the line and leader, so the connection passes through the rod guides without a hitch. Here's how it's done:

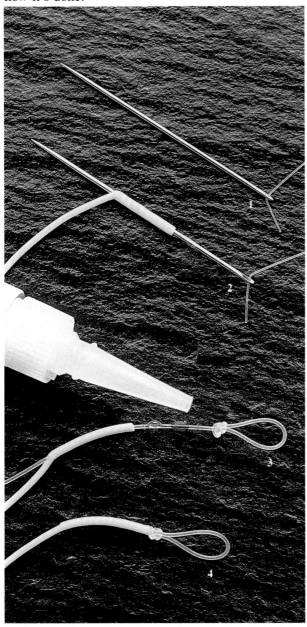

THREAD (1) the *thin* end of a tapered leader through the eye of a needle. (2) Slide the needle up into the fly line core and out the side, about ½ to 1 inch from the end. Pull the leader through until the pretied loop is within 1 inch of the fly line. (3) Coat the leader between the fly line and loop with super glue. (4) Pull the loop snug against the fly line. Trim. Within seconds, the glue will bond the leader securely inside the line, forming a strong splice.

Stringing up a Fly Rod — the Right Way

You rush to get on a trout stream during a big hatch. You're anxious. Time is slipping away. While stringing up your rod, you drop the fly line, which slips backwards through all the guides and lies in a coil near the reel. Now you have to do the job over again. Here's how to do it right:

DOUBLE over the fly line or butt section of the leader and push the loop through each guide. Now, if you drop the line, the loop springs open and catches in the guide, so you won't have to start over.

Stripping off Fly Line Coating

Some fly line knots and splices require you to strip several inches of vinyl coating off the line. You could use a wire stripper for the job, but it can nick and weaken the braided core. Or you could use nail polish remover to soften the coating, then strip it off with your thumbnail, but that's messy and inconvenient. Here's how to avoid these problems:

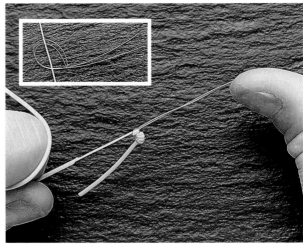

CINCH a loop (inset) of 20-pound monofilament onto the fly line, 2 to 3 inches from the end. With the doubled-up mono in one hand and the fly line in the other, pull hard and steady. The mono will cut into the coating and strip it off the core without damaging the core itself. If you have to remove a lot of the coating, strip it off 2 to 3 inches at a time.

Repair Damaged Fly Line

The vinyl coating on a fly line is surprisingly tough, but fly lines still get damaged. If a little of the coating gets scraped off, an otherwise perfect line is ruined. The damaged area isn't as stiff as the rest of the line is, so it "hinges" and causes troublesome tangles. The edges of the damaged vinyl hang up in the guides, cutting your casts short. The exposed braided core is subject to abrasion that will weaken the line.

The coating is often damaged when it gets pinched between two metal surfaces, such as the seat and hull of an aluminum boat. If you do damage the line, here's a good way to repair it, saving an expensive line that still has plenty of life:

1. WRAP the damaged area with nylon thread or floss by twirling the spool around the line (arrow) while holding the end of the thread under your thumb. A rubber band around the spool (inset) keeps the thread from unwinding.

2. GUIDE the thread with your fingertips to cover the damaged area and about ⅛ inch on either side. Perfect wraps aren't needed. Finish the wraps using a loop of thread, just as in wrapping a rod guide (p. 113).

3. COAT the thread with a pliable waterproof adhesive, such as Pliobond or Goop. When the adhesive dries, the repaired area won't hinge and will shoot through the rod guides smoothly.

Strong Line-to-Leader Loops

The same wrapping technique used to repair a fly line (opposite page) lets you make a strong loop in the end of the line for attaching your leader. This kind of connection is more durable than the common needle knot and you won't need a mono connector on your line. Here's how to make the loop:

STRIP (1) the coating off the last inch of fly line with a loop of heavy mono (p. 115). Fray the last ⅛ inch of the core to make a smoother wrap. (2) Double over the last 1½ inches of line. (3) Wrap thread tightly over the exposed core and last ⅛ inch of the vinyl coating. (4) Coat well with a pliable, waterproof adhesive.

Manageable Marabou

Fluffy marabou streamers and jigs look great in the water. But in the tackle box, the marabou mats down and picks up rust stains from other hooks. Here's a way to keep the flies in good shape:

CUT sections of plastic drinking straws a bit longer than the flies or jigs. Cut a slot for the hook in each and slip the tubes over the flies.

Prevent Fly Rod Hangups

When a big salmon, trout or saltwater fish grabs your fly and makes a run, any knot or tangle in the fly line can hang up in the guides, popping one off or snapping the tippet. If you build your own rods, you can reduce the chances of this happening.

Use stripper guides, snake guides and a tiptop that are all a bit larger than you'd find on a commercially made rod built on the same blank. A knot in the line stands a better chance of clearing these larger guides without damage to the rod or tippet.

Double-Duty Fly Rods

Many anglers who wade streams are faced with a difficult choice as they begin to assemble their tackle: fly-fishing or spinning? It's tough to carry and fish two rods, so you have to choose. Or do you?

Resolve the dilemma by using your fly rod for both fly-fishing and spinning. A fly rod can easily double as a spinning rod. Its length is useful for drifting bait or small jigs, and it flexes enough to cast light lures. You'll be ready for anything, no matter what the fish are biting on. Here's how to rig it:

TAPE on the spinning reel when you want to spin fish, mounting the reel in the middle of the grip so it feels like a spinning outfit. If you build rods, you can make a straight cork handle without a reel seat and tape either reel wherever you want. Or you can install sliding rings to hold the reels in place. Outfit these combination rods with larger-than-normal guides so coils of mono can pass through with less resistance as you cast.

Equipment Tips

No-Hands Flashlight (p. 388)

Equipment Tips

No-Hands Flashlight

Night fishing can be frustrating. You can't see well enough to tie knots, untangle backlashes or unhook fish. Many of these jobs require two hands, so it's tough to hold a flashlight. But here's a way to see at night while keeping both hands free.

Strap a compact, battery-operated headlamp to your forehead. These lights, available in many sporting goods stores, are lightweight, and you can aim them simply by turning your head.

Some headlamps come with two lights: a small one aimed downward for close-up work and a larger, brighter one for distance.

Headlamps also come in handy when gathering nightcrawlers. You can carry your worm container in one hand while grabbing the crawlers with the other.

Pinpoint Pinholes

Pinholes and leaky seams in rain gear are an all-too-common problem. You can patch most of these leaks with a waterproof sealer, but first you have to find them. Here's how:

TURN on a bright overhead light and hold the raingear up to it. Spots of light reveal the location of leaks.

Personal Bug Deflectors

As you motor back toward the landing at dusk, you get pelted by insects. Unless you wear glasses, it's nearly impossible to keep the bugs out of your eyes. Here's an easy solution to your problem, if you have a cap with a mesh crown support:

PULL the mesh down so it covers your eyes. The mesh is porous enough to see through, yet fine enough to stop bugs.

Reusable Hand Warmers →

Chemical warmers keep hands and feet toasty in cold weather. They start heating as soon as you expose the contents to air. Though they produce heat for up to 12 hours, many outdoorsmen use them for only a couple hours and then throw them away, never realizing it's possible to stop the reaction and save the warmers for later. Here's how.

Seal the warmer in a small resealable plastic bag. The reaction requires oxygen, so it stops. As soon as you open the bag, the reaction starts up again.

Bag Cold Feet

Cold feet are a big problem for ice fishermen. Perspiration condenses in your boots, dampening socks and wool liners and reducing their insulating value. Here's a way to keep your socks and boot liners dry and your feet warm:

TRAP moisture by slipping a bread bag over a light wool sock before putting on a heavy sock. Then put on your boot. Your inner sock will get damp, but the bag will keep your heavy sock and boot liner dry, so your foot doesn't get cold.

Wader Wick

Once waders and hip boots get wet inside, they may take weeks to dry out. In the meantime, the cloth lining mildews or rots. And, of course, they're uncomfortable to use. Here's a way to dry them out quickly, and you don't even have to hang them up.

Fold down the tops as far as you can to expose the lining to the air. Then stuff loosely crumpled sheets of newspaper inside the boots. The paper wicks out moisture, which then evaporates. If the boots are very wet, replace the paper after a day.

Dead Zone

← Understand Your Blind Spot

It's a mistake to fish only where you "see" fish with your graph, LCR or video. These devices detect bottom-hugging fish only if they're directly beneath the transducer. Elsewhere in the sound cone is a "blind spot" or "dead zone" just above the bottom. If fish are in this zone (photo at left), you won't see them.

Transducer

Zone Where
Fish Are Visible

Dead Zone   Dead Zone

As the illustration shows, the dead zone is thickest at the edge of the cone and thinnest beneath the boat. The deeper the water and the wider the cone angle of your transducer, the thicker the blind spot will be.

You can't eliminate the blind spot, but you can gain a better understanding of what's happening beneath the boat by determining how thick the zone really is. Drop a jig to the bottom. Lower the rod tip to the water and reel in any slack. Lift the rod tip until the jig appears on your depth finder, and note the distance between the water and rod tip. That distance is the thickness of your blind spot in that particular part of the sound cone and depth of water.

Substitute Transducer Bracket

You may have trouble getting a suction cup bracket to stick on the transom of a rented or borrowed boat. Or you may break a permanently mounted transducer bracket while launching. Either way, you can't use the depth finder. But here's a solution.

Put the transducer in a small heavy-duty plastic bag filled with water. Seal the bag around the cord, then set the bag directly on the bottom of the boat (not on a false floor). You can also set the transducer in the bilge without the bag, making sure there's enough water in the bottom of the boat to keep the face of the transducer wet. As long as there is no air space between the transducer and the water, the unit will read through the hull, though signal strength and reception will be reduced.

Get Better Readings Through the Ice

When using a depth finder for ice fishing, you won't be able to see your lure and the fish below your hole unless the transducer points straight down. But it's hard to aim the transducer simply by eyeballing it. Here's a trick to get it lined up right every time:

MOUNT a surface, or "bull's-eye," level on the top of the transducer with silicone caulk. Before the caulk dries, make sure that the transducer is pointing straight down by placing the depth finder on the edge of a table (top), aiming the transducer at a hard floor, and adjusting it until you get the most intense signal. Then, with the transducer in the proper position, seat the level in the caulk (bottom) until the bubble is centered. When fishing, simply center the bubble to make sure the transducer is in the right position.

Big "Hooks" Can Be Misleading

Many fishermen think a big hook on their paper graph, LCR or video means a big fish. It could be, but it could also mean a small fish. Here's why.

Suppose two fish of equal size swim underneath your stationary boat. The first fish (number 1 in diagram below), is only a few feet down, where the cone is narrow. As a result, it passes through the cone quickly and makes only a short mark. The second fish (2), swims near the bottom, where the cone is wide. It spends more time in the cone, and consequently makes a much longer mark.

Here's another example: You're drifting or slow-trolling and pass over a bluegill (3) that is motionless or swimming slowly with the boat. It makes a long mark because it stays in the cone until the boat moves away. Then a good-sized bass (4) swims rapidly through the cone. It makes a shorter mark because it passes through the cone more quickly.

Yet another possibility: You pass over two fish of identical size resting just off the bottom. The cone's edge passes over one (5), the center over the other (6). The fish in the center, where the cone is widest, stays in the cone longer and makes a bigger mark.

A more reliable indicator of fish size than arc length is arc *thickness*. The thickness depends on the strength of the reflected signal. And big fish reflect a much stronger signal than little fish.

Avoid Depth Finder Interference

Some anglers run two or more depth finders simultaneously. But two units with transducers operating at similar frequencies will interfere with each other.

If you plan to use two depth finders at the same time, make sure they have transducers with operating frequencies separated by at least 50 kilohertz. A flasher with a 192-kHz transducer, for instance, will work fine with a 107-kHz LCR but a 192-kHz and 200-kHz unit are not compatible.

Here's how to recognize interference:

LOOK for scattered red bands that spin around the dial on a flasher (top). Interference on a graph, LCR or video appears as clutter (bottom).

Make Your Anchor Bite

When a strong wind blows, even a heavy anchor may drag across a sand or gravel bottom without digging in. A much heavier anchor might do the trick but would be a chore to use. Here's a way to make an ordinary anchor bite when you need it to:

1. LOOP a small second anchor onto the rope, about 6 feet above the main anchor.

2. TIGHTEN the rope. The small anchor won't slide on the rope, and you can easily take it off later.

3. DROP both anchors. The small one will hold the rope down so the big one digs in. If you don't have a small anchor, use any heavy weight.

Stay Dry in Big Waves

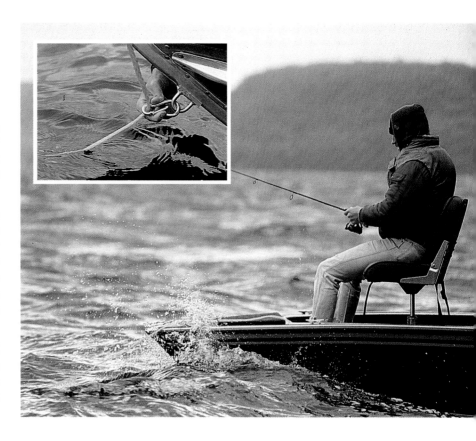

An anchored boat can be a wet place on a windy day, especially if your anchor rope is tethered to the highest point of your bow. The bow can't rise in big waves, so water splashes in.

The solution: Tie the anchor rope to the bow eye, which is closer to the waterline. If you have an anchor winch on the bow, clip the rope to the bow eye (inset). Any spring-loaded clip will work. Even with the clip in place, you can let out and take in rope with your anchor winch.

Now, with the anchor rope attached near the waterline, the boat will be able to rise and fall with the waves rather than to plunge bow first into each one.

Portable Anchor

Most anchors are too heavy to lug into hard-to-reach lakes. And it's often difficult to find a rock with the right shape to tie a rope around. Here's how to rig and use an anchor you can take anywhere:

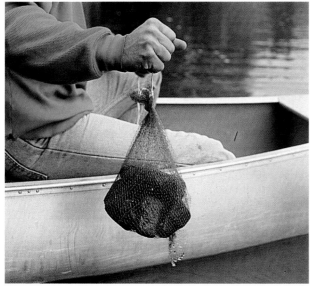

LOWER a mesh onion bag filled with rounded rocks and tied to your anchor rope. If you're fishing over a rocky bottom, put one bag inside another for extra strength. You can make an even more durable anchor bag from a basketball net. Cinch the bottom shut by running a short length of rope through the netting, place rocks inside, and cinch the top with the anchor rope.

Snagproof Anchor

If you fish over a bottom strewn with big rocks or man-made obstructions such as concrete slabs, you may hook your anchor so solidly you can't raise it. In fact, there may be nothing you can do but cut the rope. Here's how you can fish over rocky bottoms without losing your anchor:

USE an anchor with soft lead flukes. If the anchor hangs up, cinch off the rope and run the motor. The snagged fluke will straighten, and the anchor will pull free. Pound the fluke back into place with a hammer.

Bargain Wading Staff

A wading staff is a handy but pricey tool for stream fishermen.

Here's a way to make your own wading staff from a bamboo or fiberglass cross-country ski pole, which you can buy at closeout prices at the end of the ski season. Ski poles are strong and have a point that digs in for a good grip. A loop on the other end keeps the pole fastened to your wrist in case you stumble and makes a good place to tie a lanyard for clipping to your vest or belt.

But the circular basket on most ski poles hangs up in brush. Here's a way to fix that problem:

TRIM back the plastic basket at the bottom of the pole so only 1-inch stubs remain. They will keep the pole from sinking in a soft bottom but won't catch on brush as easily as the full basket does.

Cheaper Propane

Stoves and lanterns fueled by small propane cylinders are convenient for camping and fishing, but the cylinders are expensive and last only a few hours. Here's a way you can substantially reduce the cost of the propane and avoid frequent trips to the store to buy replacement cylinders:

REFILL a small cylinder from a large propane tank, using a brass coupler (left) designed for that purpose (contact K-M Products, 110 Tamara, Kalkaska, MI 49646). Pressure from the large tank (right) forces the propane into the small tank with a hiss that sounds like air filling a tire. When the sound stops, the tank is full. Instructions come with the coupler; follow them for safety. By refilling cylinders, you pay only a tenth as much for the propane.

Cheap "Power-Trim"

If your motor doesn't have power-trim or a shallow-water tilt mechanism, you've got a problem when running in shallow water. Here's a way to prevent grinding your prop into the bottom:

RAISE the outboard by hand, then lay a 2 × 2, an ax handle or a piece of closet pole between the motor and the bracket that attaches it to the transom. Be sure the wood doesn't rest against and damage the reverse lock mechanism, a latch that prevents the motor from tilting up when you run it in reverse or neutral.

Cushion Gas Cans

A gas can will vibrate as the motor runs, and its metal edges will scuff the boat floor. As you fish and move around in the boat, the can rocks against the floor and makes noise. Here's a way to protect the floor and keep the can quiet:

SLICE a piece of garden hose lengthwise and slide it over the metal rim on the bottom of the can.

Long-Lasting Trailer Lights

Leakage into trailer lights causes bulbs to burn out, and corrosion in the sockets ruins the fixtures. If you have to replace your factory trailer lights, try this:

INSTALL sealed, waterproof lights. If you can't find those made for boat trailers, you can use taillights designed for tractor-trailer rigs. Sealed lights are a little more expensive than non-waterproof lights, but they last much longer.

Don't Tire While Tubing

In a float tube, you can maintain your position in a breeze by kicking your feet, leaving your hands free to fish. But a stiff breeze can wear you out. And if you let yourself drift, it may be a long way back to your put-in point. Here's a simple way of holding your position when you get tired of kicking:

LOWER an anchor tied to a stout cord. Any weight will do, but a couple pounds is all that's needed to hold a tube in a light wind. Tie the other end of the cord to the tube. Wrap the extra cord on a marker buoy or chunk of packing foam to keep it from tangling. When you drop anchor, simply half-hitch the line around the buoy and put it in a pocket of the tube. The anchor also lets you maintain your position over fish. Otherwise, it's easy to lose your bearings and drift away, even on a calm day.

Cold-Climate Boat Storage

If you store your boat in a cold climate, don't keep it in a level position. Water can puddle between the ribs and hull, inside gunwales, and in other small spaces, loosening or breaking parts of the boat as it freezes and expands. Even aluminum and fiberglass, materials normally considered weatherproof, can be damaged this way.

You can solve the problem by storing the boat with the bow raised slightly so water drains away. If you keep the boat right side up, remove the drain plug. Even if the boat is kept outside and exposed to rain and freezing temperatures, most water will run out before it can turn to ice.

The Lowdown on Motor Height

To get the best performance from your outboard, it must be set to the right height. If the shaft extends too far into the water, the extra drag reduces your speed, increases fuel consumption and sprays water.

If the motor is too high, the hull interferes with the flow of water to the prop, causing it to over-rev and lose thrust. Here's how to determine if your motor is set to the proper height and what to do if it isn't:

1. CHECK the height of the outboard's cavitation plate (arrow); it should be at about the same height as the bottom of the hull.

2. ELEVATE the motor if it's too low. Set a board on the transom as shown before putting on the motor and tightening the bracket. To elevate a motor that is bolted on, remove the bolts and reinsert them through holes lower in the bracket. If the motor is too high, lower it by reinserting the bolts in holes higher in the bracket; you may have to notch the transom to lower the motor.

Launching Without a Ramp

Occasionally you may want to launch your boat where there's no concrete ramp or where low water has left several feet of soft sand between the ramp and the lake or river. If you try to back the boat in with your vehicle, you may get stuck. Here's a way to launch your boat under these difficult circumstances:

1. TIE a strong rope from your trailer tongue to your hitch while the vehicle is parked on solid ground. Lower the tongue jack, if there is one. Then unhook the trailer, making sure it doesn't get away from you.

2. ROLL the trailer and boat down to the water. In soft sand, you may have to push a bit. The rope should be short enough to keep the trailer from rolling all the way into the water. As you launch, stand on the trailer tongue for counterweight.

3. HAUL the trailer slowly to solid ground while lifting the tongue enough to keep it from digging in. Don't attempt to roll the trailer out on the tongue jack, because the jack may catch on the ground and bend or break.

4. LOAD the boat after rolling the trailer back into the water with the rope attached. As you crank, you must stand on the trailer tongue to keep it from lifting. Hold the tongue up as the vehicle pulls the boat out.

Easy Tie-Down for Cartop Loads

When carrying a canoe or small boat on a car, it's important to use a knot that can be tied and untied easily but holds the load securely. Many people throw the rope over the boat, tie a loop in the rope, run it under the rack and back through the loop, then pull the rope

tight and tie it off. But when you want to use the rope again, you have a loop in it that's too tight to untie. Here's how to tie a knot, called the trucker's hitch, that gets the job done but won't leave a permanent loop in your rope:

1. FORM a loop with two twists about a foot above the roof rack by slipping your fingers under the rope and rotating your wrist twice.

2. DRAW the lower strand of the rope through the original loop (arrow), forming a second loop as shown. Pull the second loop tight.

3. RUN the free end of the rope around the rack and then through the loop. Pull on the free end to tighten the rope over the load.

4. WRAP the free end around both strands of rope and tie a half-hitch (shown), pulling it snug against the loop. Finish with a second half-hitch.

Canoe Rod Holders

Most canoes have no good place to lay a fishing rod. If you set them in the bottom, they slide to the center, where they can get broken. Here's a good way to keep rods where they're handy but out of the way:

SLIP the tip and handle of each rod into 2-inch-diameter PVC pipe couplings attached to the cross members and seats of the canoe with 6-inch-long nylon wire ties, available in hardware stores.

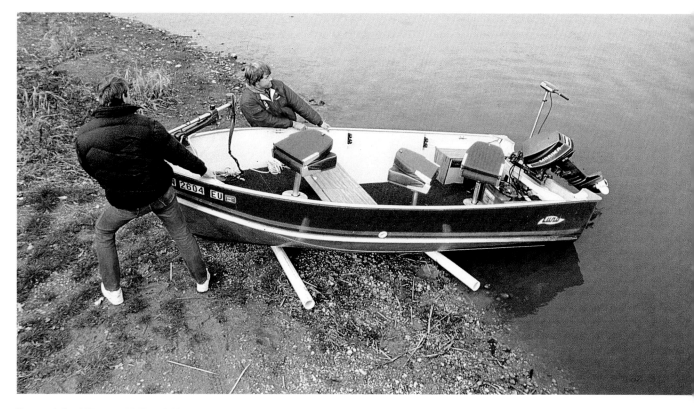

Portable "Boat Winch"

If you want to pull your boat up on shore and leave it for awhile, you'll have to get it far enough out of the water that waves or wakes from passing boats can't pile over the transom. Pulling up a 12-footer is no problem, but a 16-footer is another story. Here's how to save your back. Lay two sections of 3-inch-diameter PVC pipe under your boat; roll the boat over them until it's high and dry.

Walk the Plank

When launching a boat from a trailer with bunks, you may have to walk partway down the trailer frame to push the boat off. And to get it back on the trailer, you may have to walk on the frame once again, often in the dark. Trying to keep your balance is nearly impossible. Eventually you'll slip off and fall in the water and perhaps get seriously hurt. Here's something you can do to keep your footing:

STAND on a 1-by-8-inch plank that you've bolted to the trailer frame, while launching and loading your boat. Apply non-skid tape to the plank, or paint it and sprinkle on sand before the paint dries to create a rough surface.

Charge Two Batteries at a Time ↑

You come in after a day's fishing with two drained batteries and want to head out again first thing in the morning. How can you charge both with only one battery charger? You could charge one battery at a time, but you'd have to get up in the middle of the night to switch the cables. Instead, try this trick.

Connect the batteries in parallel (positive-to-positive, negative-to-negative) with 10-gauge or heavier cable. Hook the charger to one of the batteries. Use a trickle charger (also known as a taper-type), which includes most marine and automotive chargers. These gradually reduce the amount of current as the batteries approach full charge.

Multiple batteries take longer to charge than a single one. Two fully discharged batteries, for example, take about twice as long as a single fully discharged battery of equal size. For that reason, you'll need at least a 20-amp charger to do the job overnight. To make sure both batteries are fully charged, check each with a battery gauge or voltmeter (opposite page).

Charging in parallel works even if batteries have been discharged to different levels. But if the difference is great, one battery reaches full charge long before the other and may overcharge while the other is still charging. In this situation, it's best to charge the batteries separately.

Battery Safety

Batteries are filled with corrosive chemicals and produce explosive gases when charging. For these reasons, they are hazardous if used or charged improperly. Take these precautions to avoid trouble:

• Don't check the battery's charge, as some people do, by laying a wrench or other heavy piece of metal between the posts to make a spark. That test tells you little about the charge level. But the surge of current through the wrench from a fully charged battery can melt lead posts in a fraction of a second, and the sparks can ignite accumulated hydrogen and oxygen, causing an explosion.

• To avoid sparks, connect the charger to the battery posts before plugging it in. When finished, unplug the charger before unhooking the leads. If the posts are dirty, they'll spark when you try to make the connection. Clean them with a wire brush first.

• Keep the vent caps on a standard battery when charging it. The caps are designed so that flames from igniting gas can't follow back into the battery.

• If you spill battery acid, sprinkle on an equal volume of baking soda to neutralize it. Then add water to form a slurry, which you can clean up. Wear glasses and rubber gloves to protect eyes and hands.

Avoid Alligators

Some electric trolling motors come equipped with alligator clips that connect to the battery terminals. The clips are quick and convenient. But with little surface area touching the terminals, alligator clips make a poor connection, causing a drop in voltage. To compensate, the trolling motor draws more current, draining the battery more quickly.

Here's how to improve the connection and get more running time out of your battery:

REPLACE the alligator clips with connectors, such as those shown, that can be attached snugly to the battery terminal with wing nuts. Connectors of this type provide plenty of surface area for the current to flow across. Crimp and then solder the connectors for the best conductivity. When installing any connector, be careful not to cut individual strands in the cable as you strip insulation. Losing even a few reduces conductivity and drains the battery faster.

Storing a Battery

If you store a boat battery improperly during the off-season, you may shorten its life or reduce its capacity. These tips will keep a battery in good shape.

Disconnect the battery. Charge it fully and store it in a cool, dry place. Outside is fine, but be sure to keep it fully charged. Don't store a battery in a warm place; higher temperatures speed up the self-discharge reaction that causes lead sulfate crystals to form on the plates, ruining the battery.

Contrary to popular belief, modern batteries can be stored on a cement floor without discharging.

Check the charge level every two months; never let it fall below 75 percent charge (12.4 volts). Subzero temperatures can freeze a discharged battery, almost always ruining it.

Extend Battery Life

Many anglers charge their marine batteries with automatic battery chargers designed for automobiles. To provide a margin of safety against overcharging, many units shut off before they deliver a full charge. As a result, the battery discharges before it should. More important, repeated undercharging allows lead sulfate crystals to build up on the plates, reducing the battery's capacity and shortening its life. Here's how to tell if you're getting a full charge on your battery.

Charge the battery as usual. Wait 24 hours or turn on the boat's running lights for five minutes to get rid of "gas voltage" that causes a deceptively high reading right after charging. Then use a battery gauge (shown) to measure charge level. If you don't have a battery gauge, use a voltmeter and the table below.

If your automatic charger isn't fully charging your battery, use one with a timer or manual shut-off. By knowing the charge level, battery capacity and charger output, you can use the information that came with your battery to calculate how long to leave the battery on your manual charger. Charging too long corrodes the plates, shortening battery life.

How to Determine Charge Level From Voltage*

12.6 volts	100% charged
12.4	75%
12.2	50%
12.0	25%
11.9	Discharged

* Some batteries may reach full charge at a slightly higher voltage. Consult battery label, instructions or manufacturer for details.

Photographing Your Fish

Good photos prolong the memory of a trip, but many folks have trouble taking interesting pictures. Their photos are out of focus or poorly lit, the background is cluttered, the fish looks stiff and lifeless. The problems are endless.

The first step toward taking better photos is to start with a reliable camera. Casual photographers can take good photos with one of the many fully automatic 35mm pocket cameras, some of which are water-resistant or waterproof.

If you're really interested in photography, you'll want to get a 35mm camera with manual, as well automatic, modes of operation. Serious photographers also want interchangeable lenses. A zoom lens, about 28mm to 80mm, is an excellent choice because you can adjust it from wide-angle to low-power telephoto in an instant without the inconvenience of carrying extra lenses and changing them.

If you've never owned a good 35mm camera, it pays to enroll in a course to learn the principles of photography and camera operation. Short courses are sometimes available at the store where you bought your camera or through community education programs. Perhaps the best way to improve your own photography is to study photographs you like and try to figure out why they appeal to you.

The tips that follow can help you take better pictures next time you go fishing. By paying attention to detail and giving up a few minutes of fishing to concentrate on your photography, you'll bring back photographs that are exciting and alive, even if the subject is a half-pound sunfish.

Making Posed Photos Look Good

An angler posing with a big fish can make a terrific or terrible shot. The next time you take a picture of a friend with a fish, pay attention to the following details. The result will be a better photo.

- Take a picture when the fish is still alive — best of all, moments after it's landed. That's when the colors are brightest, the fins flare the most and the fish looks most vigorous. Dip the fish in the water before the shot to wash off dirt, blood or weeds.

- Choose the background carefully. Sky, water or undeveloped shoreline looks better than a backyard, the inside of a tackle shop, or a cluttered boat.

- Push back your subject's hat and take off sunglasses to keep shadows from hiding the face.

- Don't let your subject's hands obscure the fish, especially its head.

- Get a shot with the lure in the corner of the fish's mouth, but don't let the lure cover the eyes.

- Cover up a torn or stained shirt with another shirt or jacket, especially one in a bright color.

- Photograph a single good-looking fish rather than a big stringer. Don't throw a pile of fish on the ground and have your subject stand behind it.

Dead fish, shaded face, cigarette and a dirty T-shirt are hallmarks of a lousy photo

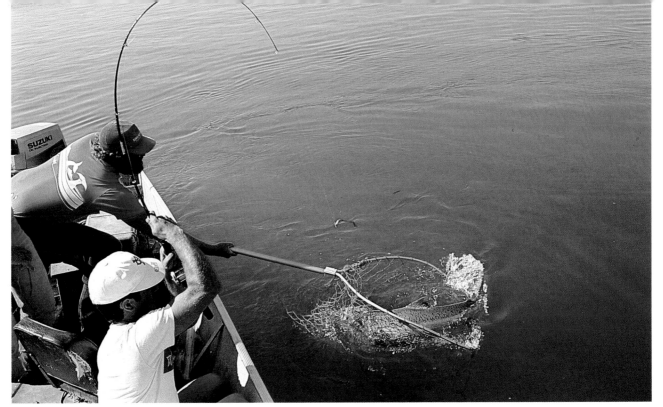

Action shots capture the excitement of fishing

Catch the Action

Try shooting action photos. Keep the camera loaded, set for the prevailing light, and close at hand. Use a wide-angle lens to get the angler and the fish in the frame and in focus. Set the shutter speed at 1⁄500 second to stop the action. With an auto-focus camera, remember to keep whatever you want in focus in the center of the frame.

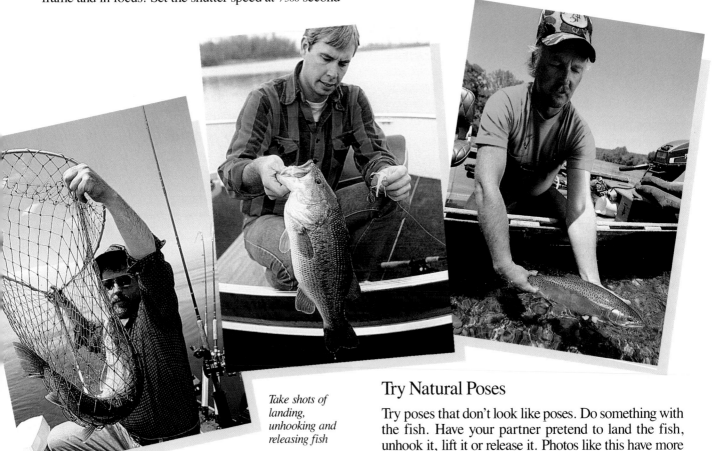

Take shots of landing, unhooking and releasing fish

Try Natural Poses

Try poses that don't look like poses. Do something with the fish. Have your partner pretend to land the fish, unhook it, lift it or release it. Photos like this have more life than the usual "meat" shot.

Try shots from below (left) or above (right) your subject

Play the Angles

Move higher or lower than your subject to make shots more interesting. Get below the level of the fish and shoot upward to emphasize the fish's size and eliminate boat clutter from a shot. On a stream, shoot down from a bank or bridge to get a good view of your friend as well as the surroundings.

Low-Light Advantage

Shoot in the morning or evening, when the sun is low, for the warmest, richest light. Good light makes a photo look vivid. The same shot at midday would have deep shadows and contrasting bright spots.

Midday glare presents another problem: the bright light can overpower all detail in a fish. Silvery fish such as trout and salmon are most likely to "burn out" by reflecting too much light. If you must shoot in bright light, turn the fish slightly until you get the best coloration and detail.

Harsh midday light casts dark shadows (left); low light makes a subject come alive (right)

Too bright

Just right

Too dark

Take Lots of Photos

Don't spare the film. Compared to gas, tackle and other expenses, film is cheap. If you like the looks of a shot, take extras to compensate for those that are inevitably ruined by movement or awkward expressions. To make sure the exposure is correct, "bracket" your photos the way professional photographers do. For example, if you set your shutter speed at $1/250$ second and your light meter says f8, try a second shot at f5.6, and a third at f11. That way you're sure one will have the proper exposure.

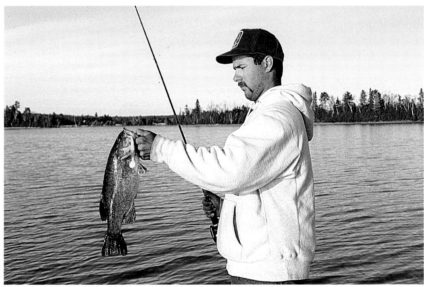

A vertical fish fills the frame of a vertical shot (left) better than a horizontal (right)

Fill the Frame

Turn your camera and take some "verticals" as well as the usual "horizontals." By matching your format to the shape of the subject, you can fill the frame with the fish and angler and eliminate dead space. The result: more interesting photos with greater impact.

Fill flash (right) gets rid of shadows for a vivid image

Fill Flash Fixes Flat Fotos

If your subject is backlit, use "fill flash" to eliminate shadows and make your photo "pop."

Fill flash works best with a variable-power flash unit. With the camera in manual mode, set your shutter speed to synchronize with the flash, usually ¹⁄₆₀ second. Then set the aperture (f-stop) according to the cameras's light meter.

Adjust your flash unit according to the aperture setting of your camera and the distance to the subject. Then turn down the power dial by one f-stop. Otherwise the

flash will "burn out" your subject. Shoot one or two shots. For insurance, lower your power setting by one more f-stop and shoot again.

You can't use fill flash with some fully automatic cameras because the flash won't fire in bright light. Other automatics have fill-flash buttons, so you can use the flash anytime.

Wide-Angles Add Interest

A short, wide-angle lens (a 24mm or 28mm) makes objects in the foreground of your photo look bigger while shrinking objects in the background. As a result, a wide-angle image is often more interesting than a similar picture taken with a "normal" 50mm lens. Wide-angle lenses also let you keep both foreground and background objects in focus in the same photograph.

The same fish looks much bigger with a wide-angle lens (left) than with a normal lens (right)

Glare from the water (left) is reduced with a polarizing filter (right), which also protects the lens

Cheap Lens Protection

A polarizing filter, like polarized sunglasses, cuts glare from the water and other objects. You can adjust the filter for greater or less polarization. A filter also serves to protect the more expensive camera lens. A "skylight" or UV-haze filter gives protection without noticeably affecting the photo.

Adjust for Bright Snow

Dazzling white backgrounds, such as new-fallen snow or a big rapids, often fool photographers. For example, a picture of an ice fisherman on a sunny day is likely to be badly underexposed. The ice and snow will appear light gray, and the angler's face will be a dark shadow.

That happens because the camera's light meter reads and adjusts for the intense light of the background rather than the light coming off the subject's face. Here are two ways to remedy the problem.

If you're using a camera that can be operated in a manual mode, move close to your subject and set the exposure by metering off the person's face. Step back and take the photo. The angler's face will be properly exposed. The snow will be bright white and lack detail, but no one will care about that.

Some automatic cameras without a fully manual mode can be set to overexpose by up to two full stops, which will correct for snow or white water in the background. Some fully automatic cameras can be "fooled" by setting them to meter for a slower film. But many cameras read the film speed electronically off the film canister and can't be adjusted to compensate for these conditions.

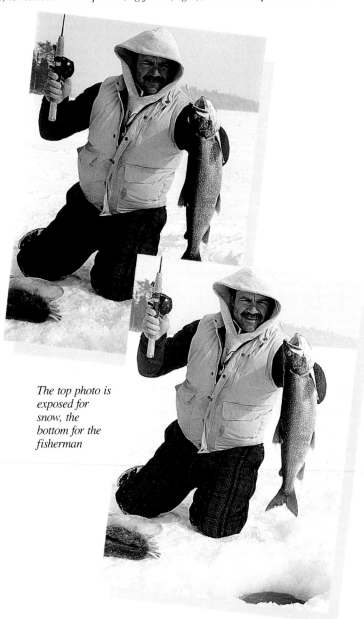

The top photo is exposed for snow, the bottom for the fisherman

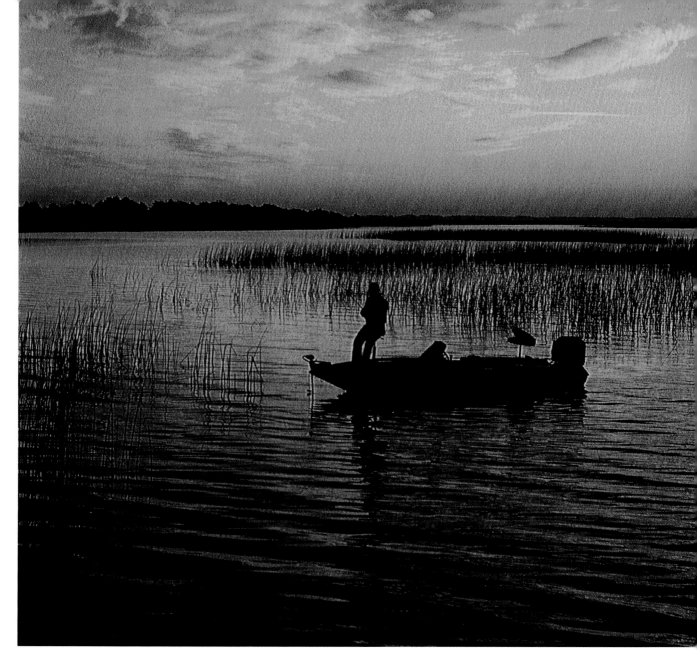

There's More to Photos than Fish

There's more to fishing than fish, and there's more to fishing photography than pictures of fish. Try photographing your surroundings and the entire fishing experience. Little things like running the boat, changing lures and casting can make shots that are every bit as interesting as a picture of a trophy.

Keep Film Safe

Beginning photographers don't realize film can be easily damaged. Here are a couple tips to keep your film in good shape.

Water, heat and light all damage film. Keep unexposed and exposed film in the plastic canisters it comes in to help protect it. On a hot day, keep the containers in your cooler.

Radiation, such as the X-rays used in airport luggage-scanning equipment, can damage film. The machines are billed as "film safe" and may not damage ordinary film the first time through. But X-ray damage is cumulative, building up with each additional exposure. If your film is checked several times before it is developed, the pictures are likely to have streaks or lines on them, or they may be slightly fogged. "Fast," light-sensitive film (ASA above 400) is more easily damaged than other film. If you're traveling with light-sensitive film or expect to pass through security checks at several airports, ask the agents to inspect the film by hand rather than pass it through the X-ray machine. Most of them are willing to do so.

How to Build and Use a Cradle

MATERIALS needed to build a cradle include (1) two 4-foot 2 × 2s, (2) heavy string and (3) a 4-foot-by-5-foot piece of ¼-inch nylon mesh. You'll also need a staple gun.

BUILD the cradle by centering a 2 × 2 along each 5-foot edge of the mesh. Staple on the 2 × 2s. Weave string through the mesh and tie the ends closed (shown).

Taking Care of Your Trophy

You've just brought the fish of a lifetime to boatside. This is the one you want for the wall. Be sure the things you do from here on out keep the fish in good condition so it will look as realistic on the wall as it does in the water.

If possible, land trophy muskies, pike, lake trout and other big fish with a cradle (photo at left), by hand, by carefully gaffing them in the mouth or by beaching them. A landing net will knock off scales and split the tail and fins. Repairing the damage is difficult.

Fish begin to decompose shortly after death, so freeze them as soon as you can. On trips where no freezer is available, keep the fish alive until you are ready to leave. Tether it on a 30-foot nylon cord tied to its lower jaw. Attach the cord along a steep shoreline where the bottom is free of snags; this way, the fish can rest in deep, cool water (photo below).

Take a color photograph of the fish while it is still alive. A photo will help your taxidermist restore the fish to its original color. Kill the fish by whacking it on the

In remote country, tether your fish in deep water to keep it alive

LEAD the fish into the cradle headfirst, then scoop it up. The mesh closes around the fish so it can't thrash. The fins and tail stay in good shape.

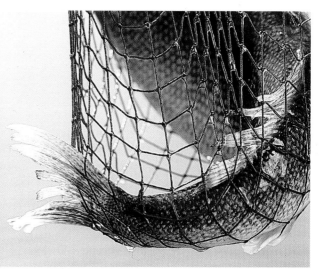

AVOID landing the fish with a net if you want to mount it. As the fish thrashes in the net, the tail and fins poke through the mesh and split.

head with a blunt object. Don't use anything that would cut the skin or remove scales. Don't remove the entrails or gills.

Sprinkle powdered borax or a commercial color preservative on the fish's skin.

Wrap the fish in a wet towel, binding the fins tightly against the body to protect them. Don't fan the tail; doing so makes it easier to damage. Don't wrap the fish in newspaper; the ink discolors the skin.

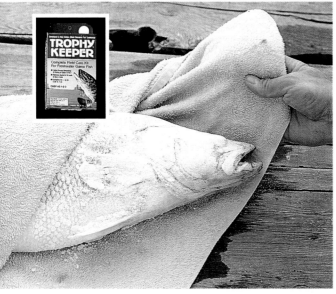

Sprinkle color preservative (inset) on the fish before wrapping it in a wet towel to protect the skin, fins and tail

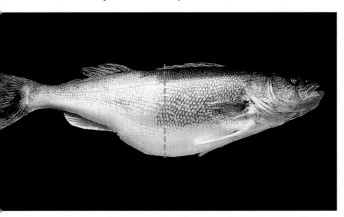

Color preservative was used to the right of the dotted line for demonstration purposes; the area to the left wasn't treated

Put the fish, still wrapped in the towel, in a large plastic bag. Squeeze out the air, wrap the bag with tape, then freeze. Label the bag with your name, address, fishing license number, and date the fish was caught. This information will aid any conservation officer that checks your catch. It will also help your taxidermist identify the fish as yours.

If possible, store the fish in a chest freezer, which keeps items colder than freezer-refrigerator combinations. Avoid frost-free freezers, which rely on a small

fan to circulate air to prevent frost build-up. The circulation can dry out the fish and contribute to freezer burn.

If a mount you admire was done by a taxidermy company, get the name of the person who did the work. Some companies employ many taxidermists, and all are not equally skilled.

When finding a place on your wall for your trophy, avoid heat and humidity. A fish may look great over the fireplace, but the heat will dry it out. Also, direct sunlight will cause the fish to fade.

Dust your mount occasionally with a featherduster or a soft cloth dampened with water. Gently stroke the fish from the head toward the tail to avoid damaging any of the scales.

More and more anglers release their trophies and buy "museum mounts" — fiberglass or carbon-fiber

Measure length and girth to order a proper-sized reproduction

replicas of their catches. To get the best likeness of your fish, carefully measure its length and girth. Weigh it if you have a scale. Finally, take a color photo to help match the model to the original.

Certifying a Record

If you catch a fish you think may qualify as a record, you'll have to follow several procedures to get it certified. The following tips are based on the requirements of the IGFA (International Game Fish Association), the major international record-keeping organization. These procedures will also satisfy the state-record requirements of most conservation agencies.

Should you hook a potential record, don't let anyone touch your line or rod or help you land the fish. Any assistance will disqualify the catch, with this exception: someone else may net or gaff the fish.

Weigh the fish as soon as possible on a scale checked and certified for accuracy by a government agency or accredited commercial organization. These scales may be found in sporting goods stores, grocery stores and butcher shops. The scale should bear a stamp with a number, date of inspection, and name of inspector. Record this information. If the scale available is not certified, weigh the fish anyway. The scale can be verified for accuracy later, and the weight of the fish adjusted, if necessary.

Weigh the fish *only once* in the presence of two witnesses. Record their names and addresses. You cannot be a witness to your own application.

Measure (1) the fish's girth; (2) total length; and (3) fork length (photo below).

Photograph everything. Take photos of the fish lying on a flat surface to aid in determining what species it

is. If you have a ruler, lay it next to the fish. Photograph the fish hanging vertically. Take photos of the angler with the fish. Photograph the tackle used to land it. Also take a picture of the fish on the scale with the weight clearly visible. These photos must accompany your application.

A professional taxonomist or fisheries biologist must examine the fish if it's a potential all-tackle record, if you think it's a hybrid, or if for any reason the identification of the species will be in doubt from a photo alone. In these instances, the biologist must attest to the identification in writing.

Don't cut the fish open; this raises suspicions that weight may have been added to the fish and later removed. The record-keeping agency may ask that the fish be opened to verify no weight was added.

If you are applying for a line-class record, clip a line sample to send in with your application. Save the first 50 feet of line from a spinning or baitcasting outfit. For a fly-fishing record, the IGFA requires the fly, entire leader, and 1 inch of fly line, all knots intact. Wrap the line on notched cardboard. The sample will be laboratory tested for strength.

This is only a partial list of requirements. If you think you have a world or line-class record, consult the IGFA or their annual publication, *World Record Game Fishes*, for more details.

If you wish to submit a claim to the IGFA, you can obtain an application form by writing to the International Game Fish Association, 3000 E. Las Olas Blvd., Fort Lauderdale, FL 33316-1616.

The IGFA requires that your application be filled out and returned within 60 days of catching the fish.

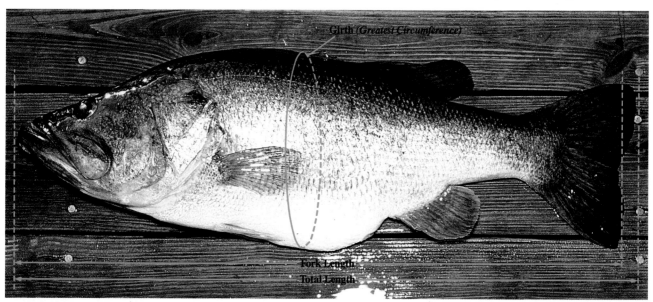

MEASURE fork length from the tip of the lower jaw (or the upper jaw if that sticks out farther) to the fork of the tail.

Measure total length from the tip of the jaw to the end of the tail. Measure girth around the largest circumference.

Print a Trophy

Fish prints, or *gyotakus,* are popular in Japan and are gaining popularity in this country. Many people consider them more interesting and attractive than mounted fish; they certainly are cheaper. You can make fish prints at home with a minimum of equipment and a bit of experimentation.

Flat fish, such as sunfish and crappies, print well. So do largemouth bass and other fish with big scales. It's harder to print long, cylindrical fish or those with small scales, such as trout.

Before you start, you'll need water-based printer's ink (black is traditional, but other colors will work), a 1-inch paint brush, a fine brush for detail, cotton balls, two paper cups (one for ink and one for water), toothpicks, old newspapers, several boards about half the thickness of the fish, a little water, and blank newsprint or Japanese rice paper.

Follow these steps to make a fish print:

1. Wash the fish with salt water, which cuts slime better than fresh water.

2. Place the fish on open newspapers and pat it dry with paper towels. If necessary, raise the dorsal fin and prop it up with a toothpick (below), stuck in the fish on the side you will not print.

3. Using a toothpick, push a small wad of cotton into the fish's vent and place another in the gill on the side you will print. The cotton will absorb fluids that would otherwise discolor the paper.

4. Place boards or stacked magazines under the fins to provide support. Let the fish set about five minutes so it stiffens slightly.

5. Use the 1-inch brush to spread ink on the side, fins and head of the fish (above). Don't paint the eye.

6. Press the paper against the fish, moving from the head to the tail. Be careful not to double print or slide the paper. Peel the paper away (above).

7. If the image prints too dark, thin the ink on the fish by brushing on a bit of water. Make several more prints, adding water or ink as necessary.

8. Paint an eye on the best print with the fine brush.

Care & Preparation of Fish

Blackened Fish

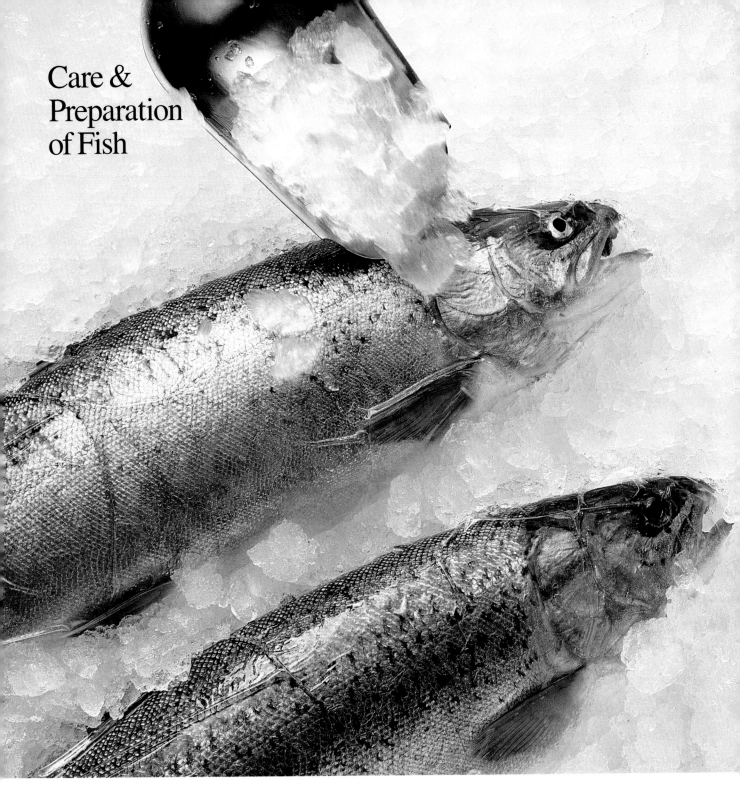

Care & Preparation of Fish

Super-Chilling Fish

It's hard to keep fish fresh on long trips into the back-country. You'll be lucky to keep them more than two or three days on ordinary ice. But you can keep them for a full week by "super-chilling" them with a mixture of ice and salt. Because the ice-salt combination has a lower melting point, about 28 degrees, the fish stay colder.

You can super-chill fillets, steaks or whole fish that have been gutted and gilled. Wrap the fish in aluminum foil or plastic cling wrap. Add 1 pound of coarse ice-cream salt to 20 pounds of crushed ice and stir thoroughly. If you need less of the salt-ice mixture, reduce the ingredients proportionately.

Place the wrapped fish on a 4-inch bed of the salt-ice. Add alternating layers of fish and salt-ice (photo above), finishing with a generous topping of the salt-ice mixture. Later, as the ice melts, drain the cooler and add more of the salt-ice.

Freshwater "Scallops"

Many anglers cut fillets off walleyes and discard the rest. They don't realize they're throwing away some of the best meat — the cheeks. They have a taste and texture very much like scallops. But cheeks of even a good-sized walleye are tough to skin because they don't give you much to hold onto. Here's a trick that makes the job quicker and easier:

1. CUT under the cheek, leaving the cheek connected to the fish by a small flap of skin just behind the eye.

2. SKIN the cheek meat by peeling it off with your thumb and forefinger.

Freeze Fish Longer

Most anglers freeze much of the fish they catch. But fish loses its fresh taste after a while in the freezer. Lean fish, such as walleyes, will keep well for three to four months. Oily fish, such as salmon or trout, will begin to develop a strong, fishy taste in only about half that time.

Here's a trick to extend freezer life by several months. Soak the fish for 20 seconds in lemon juice or a solution of 2 tablespoons of ascorbic acid (available in drugstores) in 1 quart of water. The ascorbic acid, which is also present in lemon juice, retards spoilage by counteracting oxidation and slowing the growth of microorganisms. After soaking, double-wrap the fish and freeze it immediately.

Reduce Contaminants

It's a sad fact of life that many waters contain pollutants such as pesticides, heavy metals and industrial chemicals, all of which concentrate in fish flesh.

You can reduce your consumption of harmful chemicals by eating small fish of a given species, rather than large ones. The small fish have had less time to accumulate pollutants.

Predator fish usually have the most contaminants. They're highest on the food chain, so they concentrate the chemicals found in the smaller fish they eat.

Many contaminants, including PCBs, dioxin and DDT, are soluble in oil, so fatty fish, such as trout and salmon, have a higher contaminant level than lean fish, such as walleyes and pike.

Here's how to minimize the amount of oil-soluble contaminants by trimming away the fatty tissue as you clean fish:

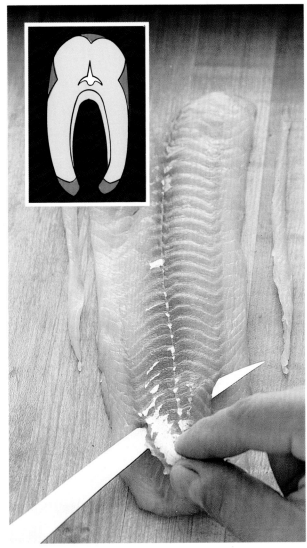

CUT away the fatty tissue found along the lateral line, back and belly (shaded areas on inset).

Breakable Fish Bricks

Resealable plastic bags come in handy for freezing fish. Simply drop the fish in the bag, fill the bag with water, seal it and freeze it. The fish will stay fresh for months. But the bags freeze in irregular shapes that don't stack well in the freezer. And you have to thaw out the entire bag to use a small portion.

Here's a way to freeze fish in plastic bags so the packages stack neatly, and the contents are easy to identify. Best of all, individual pieces of fish can be removed so you don't have to thaw the whole package.

1. COVER whole fish or fillets with water as they lie side-by-side in a resealable bag in a cake pan. Leave a little space between them. Squeeze out the air, and seal the bag. Prepare several bags of fish, laying them in the pan in layers. Put the pan in the freezer. When the fish is frozen, remove the bags from the pan and stack them in the freezer.

2. BREAK off as many pieces of fish as you need for a meal by pushing the bag against the edge of a countertop (shown). Don't rip the plastic. Remove the broken-off portion, reseal the bag and return it to the freezer.

No Bones About It

The fillets of many kinds of fish contain a row of small bones, called epipleural ribs, that lie right above the rib cage. Here's an easy way to get rid of these bones:

REMOVE the row of bones after first locating it with your finger. Slice through the fillet along one side of the bones (shown) for the length of the body cavity. Then slice along the other side, forming a thin strip (dotted lines) that you can lift out to leave a completely boneless fillet.

No More Awful Offal

If you clean fish on Sunday, but your garbage collector doesn't come till Wednesday, the carcasses will have a long time to ripen and smell. Prevent the problem by sealing the fish remains in a plastic bag and freezing them solid. Set them out, still frozen, on the day of garbage pickup.

Five-Piece Y-Bone Method

Members of the pike family have delicious, flaky meat. But the Y-bones (photo at right) are bothersome enough that some people refuse to eat these fish.

Although there are a couple of ways to remove these bones, most fishermen don't know how, so they have to pick them out at the table.

Here's one easy way to make boneless fillets from pike and pickerel. Then you can forget about Y-bones and enjoy your meal.

1. CUT down behind the head. Turn the blade toward the tail and run it along the backbone (dotted line). Slice upward just ahead of the dorsal fin, cutting away the back fillet.

2. LOOSEN the skin along each edge of the back fillet so it will lie flat on the cutting surface. Now you can skin the fillet as you would any other.

3. REMOVE the side fillets by first cutting down to the backbone, once behind the head, and a second time ahead of the dorsal fin (arrows). Feel along the back to find the Y-bones (row of dots). With the fish on its side, insert your knife just above the Y-bones and cut away a fillet (shown) so the Y-bones remain attached to the fish. Remove the fillet from the other side in the same way. Skin the fillets.

4. CUT off the fillets from each side of the tail section by slicing along the backbone. There are no Y-bones in this part of the fish. Skin the tail fillets. You now have five boneless fillets.

"Butterfly" Your Fish

Butterflying is a fast way to prepare an appetizing cut from a large smooth-skinned fish, such as salmon, large trout and catfish. It also works well with some saltwater fish, such as wahoo and tuna.

You can butterfly fillets quickly. You don't cut through the heavy backbone, so you don't dull your knife, as you would by steaking a fish. The finished cut is easier to eat than a steak because it has no bones. Finally, butterflied fillets are more appealing because the flesh is on the outside; the inedible skin and fat are tucked away on the inside (photo at left). Here's how to butterfly a fillet:

CUT a (1) fillet from the fish. Remove the rib bones, but don't skin the fillet. (2) Slice across the fillet, about an inch from the end, cutting through the meat but not the skin. (3) Make a second cut, parallel to the first and about an inch farther from the end; slice completely through both the meat and the skin. (4) Fold the piece of fish backwards along the first cut so the meat is on the outside and the skin is on the inside. Butterfly the rest of the fillet, except the tail section.

Get Rid of Muddy Taste

Some fish, such as bass and catfish, pick up a weedy or muddy taste from the water they live in. But you can get rid of most of this strong flavor by using either of the following methods:

Method 1. Soak the pieces of fish for approximately 30 minutes in a mixture of a quart of water and ½ tea-spoon of baking soda. After soaking, rinse the fish with water.

Method 2. Soak the fish for an hour in fresh, cold whole milk. Then rinse the fish with water. Many of the molecules that cause the disagreeable flavor bind to the proteins in the milk and wash away.

Smoke-Flavored Fish

Grilling over charcoal or hardwood coals is a great way to cook your catch. It works best with fish such as salmon or trout, because they're oily enough to remain moist. You can give grilled fish an even richer, smokier flavor by adding wood chips to the coals. Hardwoods, such as mesquite, hickory or fruitwood, are best. But if you put wood chips directly on the coals, they're likely to start on fire. Here's a way to use wood chips in your cooking without having your meal go up in flames:

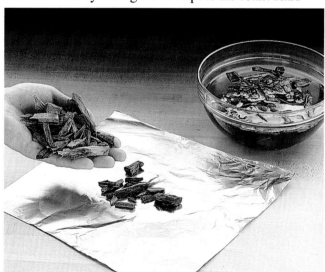

1. PUT 2 cups of wood chips on heavy-duty aluminum foil after soaking them in water for an hour and draining them. Though different kinds of woods smell different on the grill, all produce about the same taste.

2. ROLL the foil into a tube, leaving the ends open. Put the tube on the coals (top photo). Brush the fish with oil or butter and lay it on the grill when smoke begins pouring from the ends of the foil. Cover the grill for a smokier flavor.

Recipes

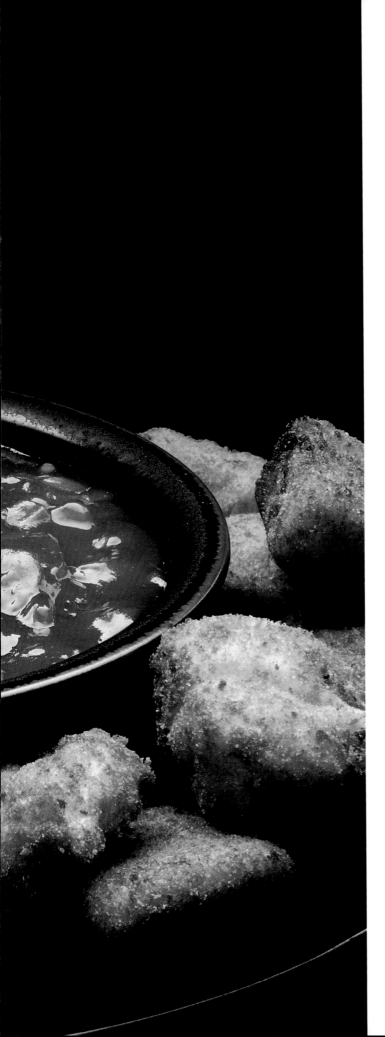

Appetizers

Serve small helpings of appetizers to stimulate the appetite but not satisfy it. Make appetizers from fresh fish or from cooked leftovers. Store leftover fish in the refrigerator no longer than 2 days before using it in appetizers.

Cook appetizers shortly before serving and keep warm in 175° oven. Keep cold appetizers in the refrigerator until serving time.

Sweet and Sour Fish Nuggets

Vegetable oil
1/2 pound bass or other lean fish fillets (page 34),
    1/4- to 1/2-inch thick
1 egg
2 teaspoons water
1/3 cup dry bread crumbs
    Sweet and Sour Sauce (page 141)

20 to 25 appetizers

In deep-fat fryer or saucepan, heat oil (2 to 3 inches) to 375°. Cut fish into 1 1/2-inch pieces. In small bowl, blend egg and water. Dip fish into egg mixture, then coat with bread crumbs.

Fry a few at a time, turning occasionally, until deep golden brown, 1 1/2 to 2 1/2 minutes. Drain on paper towels. Keep warm in 175° oven. Prepare sauce as directed. Serve fish nuggets with sauce.

Beer-Poached Chunks ◇ LOW-FAT ⬤ FAST

Cocktail Sauce (page 139)
½ pound perch or other panfish fillets (page 34),
    ¼- to ½-inch thick
1 can (12 ounces) beer

20 to 25 appetizers

Prepare Cocktail Sauce as directed. Cut fish into 1½-inch pieces. In 1½-quart saucepan, heat beer to boiling. Stir in half of the fish. Reduce heat to medium. Cook, stirring gently, until fish flakes easily, about 2 minutes. Remove with slotted spoon. Repeat. Serve with Cocktail Sauce.

Lemony Fried Fish Balls →

Basic Tartar Sauce (page 137) or Cocktail
    Sauce (page 139)
2 tablespoons finely chopped onion
1 tablespoon margarine or butter
2 tablespoons all-purpose flour
¼ cup half-and-half
½ teaspoon salt
    Dash pepper
1 egg, slightly beaten
1 cup flaked cooked trout or other oily fish
    (page 34)
1 to 1½ teaspoons grated lemon peel
2 tablespoons all-purpose flour
1 teaspoon water
¼ cup fine dry bread crumbs
    Vegetable oil

18 to 20 appetizers

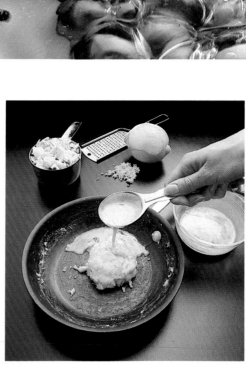

How to Prepare Lemony Fried Fish Balls

PREPARE one or both sauces as directed. Set aside. In small skillet, cook and stir onion in margarine over medium heat until tender, about 1 minute. Stir in 2 tablespoons flour.

BLEND in half-and-half, salt and pepper. Cook and stir over low heat until mixture is very thick and forms a ball. Remove from heat.

STIR in half (about 2 tablespoons) of the beaten egg. Mix in fish and grated lemon peel. Cover and refrigerate about 30 minutes, until chilled.

SPRINKLE 2 tablespoons flour on plate or waxed paper. Drop the chilled fish mixture by scant table-spoonfuls onto flour; roll to coat and shape into balls.

MIX water with remaining half of egg. Pour bread crumbs into small dish. Dip balls in egg mixture; roll in bread crumbs. In deep-fat fryer or saucepan, heat oil (2 to 3 inches) to 375°.

FRY five or six balls at a time, turning occasionally, until deep golden brown, 2½ to 3½ minutes. Drain on paper towels. Keep warm in 175° oven. Serve with sauces.

← Fish Toast 🍅 VERY FAST

¼ cup all-purpose flour
¼ cup finely chopped almonds
¼ cup water
1 egg
2 tablespoons snipped fresh parsley
1 tablespoon cornstarch
1 teaspoon soy sauce
½ teaspoon salt
½ teaspoon sugar
¼ teaspoon sesame oil
¼ pound walleye or other lean fish fillets
   (page 34), about ½-inch thick
   Vegetable oil
5 slices white bread

20 appetizers

In medium bowl, mix flour, almonds, water, egg, parsley, cornstarch, soy sauce, salt, sugar and oil. Cut fillets into 20 pieces. Stir into flour mixture.

In deep-fat fryer or saucepan, heat vegetable oil (2 to 3 inches) to 375°. Remove crusts from bread; cut each slice into four squares. Top with fish-flour mixture. Fry five squares at a time, turning several times, until golden brown, 2 to 3 minutes. Drain on paper towels. Keep warm in 175° oven.

Salmon Quiche

CRUST:
3 cups all-purpose flour
1 teaspoon salt
⅔ cup vegetable oil
¼ cup plus 2 tablespoons milk

FILLING:
1 cup shredded Monterey Jack cheese
1 to 1½ cups flaked cooked salmon
5 eggs
2 cups half-and-half
¾ teaspoon salt
⅛ teaspoon pepper
   Dash ground nutmeg
2 tablespoons snipped fresh parsley

36 appetizers

Heat oven to 350°. In medium bowl, mix flour, salt, oil and milk lightly with fork until blended. Pat into 13 × 9-inch baking pan, patting dough 1 inch up side of pan. Bake for 8 minutes.

Sprinkle cheese over hot crust, then sprinkle with fish. In small mixing bowl, blend eggs, half-and-half, salt, pepper and nutmeg. Pour over fish. Sprinkle with parsley. Bake until knife inserted in center comes out clean, 30 to 35 minutes. Cool for 10 minutes. Cut into 2 × 1½-inch pieces.

Broiled Bass Canapés ◇ LOW-FAT ● VERY FAST ↑

1 cup flaked cooked bass or other lean fish
   (page 34)
½ cup finely chopped cucumber
2 tablespoons mayonnaise or salad dressing
1 tablespoon dairy sour cream
¼ teaspoon steak sauce
⅛ teaspoon salt
⅛ teaspoon dried dillweed
   Dash pepper
2 drops red pepper sauce
24 to 30 Melba toast rounds or rich round
   crackers
   Sliced pimiento

24 to 30 appetizers

In small bowl, mix fish, cucumber, mayonnaise, sour cream, steak sauce, salt, dillweed, pepper and red pepper sauce. Spread about 1 heaping teaspoonful of mixture on each cracker. Place crackers on baking sheet.

Set oven to broil and/or 550°. Broil 4 inches from heat until light brown, 3 to 5 minutes. Top each with pimiento slice before serving.

Broiled Trout Canapés ◇ LOW-FAT ● VERY FAST ↑

1 cup flaked cooked trout or other oily fish
   (page 34)
1 cup shredded Monterey Jack cheese
⅓ cup finely chopped celery
¼ cup dairy sour cream
2 tablespoons finely chopped onion
⅛ teaspoon pepper
30 Melba toast rounds or rich round crackers

30 appetizers

In small bowl, mix fish, cheese, celery, sour cream, onion and pepper. Mound about 1½ teaspoonfuls of mixture on each cracker. Place crackers on baking sheet. Sprinkle with paprika, if desired.

Set oven to broil and/or 550°. Broil 6 inches from heat until cheese melts, 2½ to 3½ minutes.

← Trout Cheese Ball

1 package (3 ounces) cream cheese, softened
¼ cup margarine or butter, softened
1 tablespoon grated onion
1 teaspoon grated lemon peel
½ teaspoon prepared horseradish
¼ teaspoon prepared mustard
⅛ teaspoon salt
⅛ teaspoon pepper
1 cup finely flaked cooked trout or other oily fish
   (page 34)
½ cup finely chopped pecans
3 tablespoons snipped fresh parsley

3½-inch cheese ball

In medium bowl, blend cream cheese, margarine, onion, lemon peel, horseradish, mustard, salt and pepper. Stir in fish. Cover and refrigerate 1 to 2 hours, until chilled.

Mix pecans and parsley; sprinkle on plate or waxed paper. Shape fish mixture into ball. Roll in pecans and parsley to coat. Place on serving plate. Cover and refrigerate 3 to 4 hours. Serve with crackers.

← Salmon Spread ◇ LOW-FAT

1 package (3 ounces) cream cheese, softened
⅓ cup dairy sour cream
2 tablespoons finely chopped celery
1 tablespoon finely chopped green onion
1 tablespoon fresh lime juice
1½ teaspoons Worcestershire sauce
⅛ teaspoon salt
   Dash pepper
1 cup flaked cooked salmon or other oily fish
   (page 34)

About 1⅓ cups

In small bowl, mix all ingredients except fish. Stir in fish. Cover and refrigerate at least 2 hours. Serve with crackers or bread sticks.

Creamy Dill Dip

1 cup cottage cheese
2 tablespoons mayonnaise or salad dressing
2 tablespoons fresh lemon or lime juice
¼ teaspoon dried dillweed
1 cup finely flaked cooked bass or other lean fish
   (page 34)
2 tablespoons finely chopped almonds

About 2 cups

In food processor or blender, blend cottage cheese, mayonnaise, lemon juice and dillweed until smooth. Stir in remaining ingredients. Cover and refrigerate at least 1 hour. Serve with vegetable dippers.

Smoked Fish Dip ↑

1 cup dairy sour cream
½ cup mayonnaise or salad dressing
1 cup flaked smoked fish
3 tablespoons chopped green onion
½ teaspoon Worcestershire sauce
   Dash garlic powder

About 1½ cups

In small bowl, blend sour cream and mayonnaise. Stir in remaining ingredients. Cover and refrigerate at least 1 hour. Serve with vegetable dippers or potato chips.

Fish Salads

Salads are a good way to use leftover cooked fish. They can also be made from fresh fish. Chill leftover fish in the refrigerator and use for salad within 48 hours. If leftovers are not available, poach, steam or microwave (pages 48 and 56) fresh fish for salad recipes that call for cooked fish. Chill immediately after cooking.

Salmon Potato Salad ◆LOW-FAT

⅔ cup dairy sour cream
2 tablespoons plus 1 teaspoon cider vinegar
2 tablespoons chopped green onion
1 tablespoon plus 1 teaspoon sugar
1¼ teaspoons prepared mustard
½ teaspoon salt
    Dash pepper
1 quart water
1 teaspoon salt
2 medium red potatoes (about ¾ pound)
2 cups flaked cooked salmon
1 small onion, finely chopped
¼ cup finely chopped celery
1 tablespoon snipped fresh parsley
4 to 6 tomatoes, optional

4 to 6 servings

In small bowl, blend sour cream, vinegar, green onion, sugar, mustard, ½ teaspoon salt and the pepper. Cover and refrigerate.

In 2-quart saucepan, heat water and 1 teaspoon salt to boiling. Add potatoes. Return to boiling. Reduce heat. Cover and simmer until fork tender, 25 to 35 minutes. Drain. Cool.

Peel potatoes; cut into ½-inch cubes. In medium bowl, combine potatoes, salmon, onion, celery and parsley. Add sour cream dressing, tossing to coat. To serve salad in tomato shells, remove stem ends of tomatoes and scoop out center pulp and seeds.

Confetti Salad

SALAD:
1 medium green pepper
2 cups flaked cooked panfish or other lean fish (page 34)
2 cups shredded carrot
½ cup sliced fresh mushrooms
¼ cup thinly sliced celery
¼ cup sliced black olives
¼ cup snipped fresh parsley
2 radishes, thinly sliced
2 tablespoons chopped onion

DRESSING:
⅓ cup vegetable oil
3 tablespoons cider vinegar
2 teaspoons lemon juice
¼ teaspoon sugar
¼ teaspoon salt
⅛ teaspoon dry mustard
⅛ teaspoon pepper
    Dash garlic powder

4 to 6 servings

Cut green pepper into 2½ × ¼-inch strips. In medium bowl, combine green pepper with remaining salad ingredients.

In small bowl, blend dressing ingredients. Pour over salad, tossing to coat. Refrigerate at least 1 hour. Garnish with lemon slices, if desired.

← Garden Salad 🔴 **VERY FAST**

SALAD:

3 cups torn iceberg lettuce
1 cup flaked cooked panfish or other lean fish
    (page 34)
1 large tomato, cut into 8 wedges
2 hard-cooked eggs, sliced
½ small onion, thinly sliced and separated into
    rings, optional
¼ cup sliced green olives
4 radishes, thinly sliced

DRESSING:

¼ cup vegetable oil
3 tablespoons white vinegar
2 tablespoons catsup
⅛ teaspoon pepper

4 to 6 servings

In medium bowl, combine salad ingredients. In
small bowl, blend dressing ingredients. Pour dressing over salad, tossing gently to coat.

Trout Salad With Mustard Dressing

DRESSING:

2 packages (3 ounces each) cream cheese,
    softened
⅓ cup mayonnaise or salad dressing
¼ cup half-and-half
1 tablespoon plus 1 teaspoon prepared mustard
⅛ teaspoon celery salt
⅛ teaspoon curry powder
3 to 4 drops red pepper sauce

SALAD:

2 tablespoons margarine or butter, melted
    Dash garlic salt
½ pound raw shrimp, peeled and deveined
1 bunch romaine
3 cups flaked cooked trout
10 cherry tomatoes, quartered
2 hard-cooked eggs, sliced
1 avocado, peeled and sliced
½ cup sliced black olives

4 to 6 servings

In small bowl, blend cream cheese and mayonnaise.
Stir in remaining dressing ingredients. Cover and
refrigerate dressing at least 1 hour. In small bowl,
mix margarine and garlic salt. Set oven to broil
and/or 550°. Place shrimp on broiler pan. Brush
with margarine. Broil 4 inches from heat until
opaque, 4 to 7 minutes, brushing with remaining
margarine once. Turn large shrimp over once.

Arrange romaine on large serving plate. Mound fish
in center and arrange shrimp and remaining ingredients around fish. Serve with dressing.

Salmon Salad →

1 cup uncooked small shell macaroni
2 cups flaked cooked salmon
⅓ cup sliced black olives
¼ cup finely chopped green pepper
1 tablespoon grated onion
¼ cup vegetable oil
2 tablespoons red wine vinegar
¼ teaspoon dried oregano leaves
¼ teaspoon salt
⅛ teaspoon pepper

4 to 6 servings

Prepare macaroni as directed on package. Rinse under cold water; drain. In medium bowl, combine macaroni, salmon, olives, green pepper and onion. In small bowl, blend oil, vinegar, oregano, salt and pepper. Pour dressing over salad, tossing to coat. Refrigerate at least 1 hour before serving.

Northern Pike Salad ● VERY FAST

2 cups flaked cooked northern pike or other
    lean fish (page 34)
⅓ cup mayonnaise or salad dressing
¼ cup finely chopped celery
2 tablespoons finely chopped onion
1½ teaspoons prepared mustard
¼ teaspoon salt
⅛ teaspoon pepper

4 to 6 servings

In small bowl, blend all ingredients. Refrigerate at least 30 minutes. Serve on lettuce leaves. Sprinkle with paprika, if desired.

Fish Slaw ◇ LOW-FAT

3 cups coarsely chopped cabbage
1 cup flaked cooked bass or other lean fish
    (page 34)
¼ cup finely chopped carrot
1 tablespoon finely chopped onion
3 tablespoons mayonnaise or salad dressing
2 teaspoons lemon juice
2 teaspoons sugar
½ teaspoon salt
⅛ teaspoon pepper

4 to 6 servings

In medium bowl, combine cabbage, fish, carrot and onion. In small bowl or 1-cup measure, mix mayonnaise, lemon juice, sugar, salt and pepper. Pour dressing over salad, tossing gently to coat. Refrigerate at least 1 hour before serving.

Tossed Spinach Salad

½ pound walleye fillet, about ½-inch thick

MARINADE:
½ cup water
2 green onions, cut into 2-inch pieces
1 teaspoon soy sauce
½ teaspoon salt
¼ teaspoon sesame oil
⅛ teaspoon ground ginger
   Dash garlic powder

SALAD:
½ medium green pepper
2 cups torn fresh spinach
1 cup fresh bean sprouts
½ cup diagonally sliced celery
½ cup sliced fresh mushrooms
4 cherry tomatoes, cut in half

DRESSING:
⅓ cup vegetable oil
¼ cup white wine vinegar
½ teaspoon sugar
½ teaspoon soy sauce
¼ teaspoon salt
⅛ teaspoon sesame oil
   Dash ground ginger
   Dash pepper
1 tablespoon toasted sesame seed, optional

4 to 6 servings

Cut fillet into 1-inch chunks. Place in small bowl. In small saucepan, blend marinade ingredients. Heat to boiling. Pour over fish, stirring to coat. Cover by placing plastic wrap directly on surface of fish. Refrigerate at least 1 hour.

In small skillet, cook fish and marinade over medium heat, stirring gently, until fish flakes easily, 4 to 7 minutes. Remove fish with slotted spoon to paper towel-lined plate. Refrigerate about 30 minutes, until cool. Discard marinade and onions.

Cut green pepper into 2½ × ¼-inch strips. In medium bowl, combine green pepper strips, spinach, bean sprouts, celery, mushrooms and tomatoes. Add fish chunks. In small bowl, blend dressing ingredients. Pour dressing over salad, tossing gently to coat. Serve immediately.

NOTE: To toast sesame seed, cook in small skillet over medium-high heat, stirring constantly, until light brown, 2 to 3 minutes.

Fish Creole Salad   ↑

½ cup thinly sliced celery
¼ cup chopped onion
¼ cup chopped green pepper
2 tablespoons margarine or butter
1 can (16 ounces) whole tomatoes
¼ cup white wine
1 teaspoon Worcestershire sauce
1 bay leaf
¼ teaspoon salt
⅛ teaspoon cayenne
   Dash garlic powder
½ pound walleye fillet, about ½-inch thick
5 to 6 cups torn iceberg lettuce

4 to 6 servings

In 10-inch skillet, cook and stir celery, onion and green pepper in margarine over medium heat until tender. Add tomatoes, wine, Worcestershire sauce, bay leaf, salt, cayenne and garlic powder. Heat to boiling. Reduce heat. Simmer, stirring occasionally and breaking up tomatoes, for 10 minutes.

Cut fillet into 1-inch pieces. Stir into tomato mixture. Cook over medium heat, stirring gently, until fish flakes easily, 5 to 7 minutes. Remove bay leaf. Serve over lettuce.

Salmon Louis FAST ↑

DRESSING:

½ cup mayonnaise or salad dressing
3 tablespoons catsup
2 tablespoons dairy sour cream
2 tablespoons half-and-half
1 tablespoon chopped green onion
2 teaspoons chopped sweet pickle
1 teaspoon fresh lemon juice
½ teaspoon Worcestershire sauce

SALAD:

4 cups torn iceberg lettuce
2 cups flaked cooked salmon
1 tomato, cut into wedges
1 hard-cooked egg, sliced, optional
¼ cup sliced black olives, optional

4 to 6 servings

In small bowl, blend dressing ingredients. Refrigerate at least 30 minutes. Arrange lettuce in medium bowl or on serving plate. Mound fish in center. Arrange tomato wedges, egg slices and olives around fish. Pour half of dressing over salad. Reserve remaining dressing for serving.

Molded Waldorf Salad

1 to 1½ cups flaked cooked bass or other lean fish (page 34)
1 can (8 ounces) crushed pineapple, drained and ¼ cup juice reserved
⅔ cup chopped celery
1 medium red apple, cored and chopped
1 envelope unflavored gelatin
1 tablespoon cold water
¾ cup boiling water
1 tablespoon sugar
1 tablespoon lemon juice
1 cup mayonnaise or salad dressing

6 to 8 servings

Lightly oil 4- to 6-cup mold. In medium bowl, combine fish, crushed pineapple, celery and apple. In small bowl, mix gelatin with cold water. Stir in boiling water, mixing until gelatin dissolves. Stir in reserved pineapple juice, sugar and lemon juice, mixing until sugar dissolves. Blend in mayonnaise until smooth. Stir into fish, pineapple, celery and apple. Pour into prepared mold. Refrigerate about 4 hours, until firm.

Unmold onto serving plate lined with lettuce leaves. Garnish with apple slices, if desired.

Fish Soups
& Chowders

Fish soups can be light and delicate, or rich and hearty. Serve them as a first course or as a complete one-dish meal.

Make soup from fresh or frozen fish, or from cooked leftovers. Watch the soup carefully after adding the fish, because it can easily overcook. Refrigerate leftover soup for use within 2 days, or freeze in plastic containers and use within a month.

← Hearty Vegetable and Panfish Soup

    4 slices bacon, cut up
    1 medium onion, chopped
    1 small green pepper, chopped
    ¼ cup chopped celery
    1 clove garlic, minced
    4 tomatoes, peeled and chopped
    2 cups sliced fresh mushrooms
    2 cups water
    1 can (6 ounces) tomato paste
    ½ cup white wine
    1 tablespoon plus 1 teaspoon instant chicken
        bouillon granules
    1 bay leaf
    ½ teaspoon dried oregano leaves
    ½ teaspoon sugar
    ¼ teaspoon ground sage
    1 pound panfish fillets

4 to 6 servings

In Dutch oven, cook bacon over medium-high heat, stirring occasionally, until crisp. Remove with slotted spoon; set aside. Add onion, green pepper, celery and garlic. Cook and stir over medium heat until vegetables are tender, 6 to 7 minutes. Add bacon and remaining ingredients except fish. Simmer, stirring occasionally, for 30 minutes. Cut fillets into 1-inch pieces. Add to soup. Simmer, stirring gently, until fish flakes easily, about 8 minutes.

Trout Gumbo

    3 slices bacon, cut up
    2 medium onions, chopped
    ½ cup chopped celery
    1 clove garlic, minced
    1 quart hot water
    1 can (28 ounces) whole tomatoes
    1 package (10 ounces) frozen whole okra
    ⅓ cup uncooked long-grain rice
    1 tablespoon fresh lemon juice
    1½ teaspoons instant chicken bouillon granules
    1 teaspoon salt
    ½ teaspoon dried basil leaves
    ⅛ to ¼ teaspoon cayenne
    ⅛ teaspoon pepper
    1 small bay leaf
    1 pound trout fillets

6 to 8 servings

In Dutch oven, cook bacon over medium-high heat, stirring occasionally, until crisp. Remove with slotted spoon; set aside. Add onion, celery and garlic. Cook and stir over medium heat until vegetables are tender-crisp, about 4 minutes.

Add bacon and remaining ingredients except fish. Heat to boiling. Reduce heat. Cover and simmer until rice is tender, 20 minutes. Cut fillets into 1-inch pieces. Add to soup. Cook over medium heat, stirring gently, until fish flakes easily, about 6 minutes.

Walleye Noodle Soup

    2 medium carrots
    1 stalk celery
    1 quart water
    1 small onion, cut into thin wedges
    ¼ cup snipped fresh parsley
    2 teaspoons instant chicken bouillon granules
    ½ teaspoon salt
    ¼ teaspoon dried thyme leaves
    ⅛ teaspoon pepper
    ½ cup uncooked narrow egg noodles
    1 cup flaked cooked walleye or other lean fish
        (page 34)

4 to 6 servings

Cut carrots into thin diagonal slices. Cut celery into thin slices. In 2-quart saucepan, combine water, carrots, celery, onion, parsley, bouillon granules, salt, thyme and pepper. Heat to boiling. Reduce heat. Cover and simmer 10 minutes. Add noodles; return to boiling. Cook until noodles are tender, 8 to 10 minutes. Stir in fish. Simmer for 1 minute.

Hot and Sour Bass Soup ◈ LOW-FAT

5 cups water
2 tablespoons instant chicken bouillon granules
¼ cup white vinegar
1 medium onion, cut into thin wedges
8 whole peppercorns
¾ pound bass fillets, about ½-inch thick
1 can (4 ounces) sliced mushrooms, drained
1 tablespoon soy sauce
1 clove garlic, minced
¼ to ½ teaspoon dried crushed red pepper
2 tablespoons cornstarch
2 tablespoons cold water
1 egg, beaten
1 green onion, chopped

4 to 6 servings

In Dutch oven, combine 5 cups water, the bouillon granules, vinegar, onion and peppercorns. Heat to boiling. Add fillets. Reduce heat. Cover and simmer until fish flakes easily, about 5 minutes. Remove fish. Cut into 1-inch pieces; set aside. Remove peppercorns. Stir mushrooms, soy sauce, garlic and red pepper into soup. Heat to boiling. Reduce heat. Cover and simmer for 15 minutes.

In small bowl, blend cornstarch into 2 tablespoons water. Stir into soup. Heat to boiling. Cook, stirring constantly, until soup is thickened, about 1 minute. Add fish. Reduce heat and simmer for 1 minute. Remove from heat. Pour beaten egg slowly in thin stream over soup; do not stir. Top with green onion.

Herbed Walleye Soup ◈ LOW-FAT

1 medium onion, cut into thin wedges
1 clove garlic, minced
2 tablespoons margarine or butter
2 cups hot water
1 tablespoon instant chicken bouillon granules
1 cup white wine
¼ teaspoon dried thyme leaves
¼ teaspoon dried basil leaves
¼ teaspoon pepper
⅛ teaspoon dried rosemary leaves
¾ pound walleye fillets, skin on

6 to 8 servings

In 3-quart saucepan, cook and stir onion and garlic in margarine over medium heat until onion is tender, about 7 minutes.

Blend the hot water and bouillon granules into onions. Add remaining ingredients except fish. Heat to boiling. Reduce heat. Cover and simmer, stirring occasionally, for 30 minutes.

Cut fillets into 1-inch pieces; add to soup. Simmer, stirring occasionally, until fish flakes easily, about 10 minutes. Skim fat, if desired.

Fish and Citrus Soup ◈ LOW-FAT

¾ pound panfish fillets
2 tablespoons soy sauce
1 medium onion, chopped
2 cloves garlic, minced
2 tablespoons olive or vegetable oil
2¼ cups water
¼ cup fresh orange juice
¼ cup fresh lemon juice
1½ teaspoons instant chicken bouillon granules
1 teaspoon grated orange rind
1 teaspoon grated lemon rind
1 teaspoon sugar
⅛ teaspoon pepper

4 to 6 servings

Cut fillets into 1-inch pieces. In small bowl, mix fish and soy sauce. Cover and refrigerate at least 1 hour, stirring once to keep fish pieces coated.

In 2-quart saucepan, cook and stir onion and garlic in olive oil over medium heat until tender, about 3 minutes. Add remaining ingredients except fish. Heat to boiling. Reduce heat and simmer for 5 minutes. Add fish and soy sauce. Simmer, stirring gently, until fish flakes easily, about 8 minutes.

Bouillabaisse ◇ LOW-FAT ● FAST →

1 medium green pepper, chopped
1 medium onion, chopped
2 cloves garlic, minced
2 tablespoons olive or vegetable oil
3 cups fish stock (page 26)*
1 cup clam-tomato juice cocktail
1 can (16 ounces) whole tomatoes
½ teaspoon sugar
½ teaspoon salt
¼ teaspoon dried thyme leaves
¼ teaspoon ground turmeric
⅛ teaspoon pepper
1 bay leaf
½ pound trout fillets, skin on
½ pound walleye or other lean fish fillets
   (page 34), skin on
½ pound raw shrimp, peeled and deveined
1 can (6½ ounces) minced clams, drained

6 to 8 servings

In Dutch oven, cook and stir green pepper, onion and garlic in olive oil over medium heat until onion is tender, about 4 minutes. Add fish stock, clam-tomato juice, tomatoes, sugar, salt, thyme, turmeric, pepper and bay leaf. Heat to boiling. Reduce heat. Cover and simmer, stirring occasionally to break up tomatoes, for 15 minutes.

Cut trout and walleye fillets into 1-inch pieces. Add fish, shrimp and clams to stew. Cook over medium heat, stirring gently, until fish flakes easily and shrimp turns opaque, about 5 minutes.

*Or, substitute 1 can (14½ ounces) ready-to-serve chicken broth and 1¼ cups water; omit the salt.

Cream of Salmon Soup ● VERY FAST

1 cup sliced fresh mushrooms
¼ cup finely chopped onion
¼ cup margarine or butter
3 tablespoons all-purpose flour
2 tablespoons snipped fresh parsley
½ teaspoon salt
⅛ teaspoon white pepper
⅛ teaspoon dried rosemary leaves
1½ cups milk
1½ cups half-and-half
1½ to 2 cups flaked cooked salmon

4 to 6 servings

In 2-quart saucepan, cook and stir mushrooms and onion in margarine over medium heat until just tender, about 5 minutes. Stir in flour, parsley, salt, pepper and rosemary. Remove from heat. Blend in milk and half-and-half. Cook over medium heat, stirring constantly, until thickened and bubbly, 7 to 10 minutes. Add fish. Cook and stir 1 minute.

Creamy Tomato and Panfish Soup 🔻LOW-FAT

2 large red potatoes (about 1 pound)
1 medium onion, chopped
¼ cup chopped celery
3 tablespoons margarine or butter
2 cups water
1 can (16 ounces) whole tomatoes, drained
½ cup white wine
1 teaspoon salt
    Dash pepper
3 tablespoons all-purpose flour
¼ cup cold water
½ cup half-and-half
1 pound panfish fillets

4 to 6 servings

Peel potatoes; cut into ¼-inch cubes. Set aside. In 3-quart saucepan, cook and stir onion and celery in margarine over medium heat until tender-crisp, about 5 minutes. Add potato cubes, 2 cups water, the tomatoes, wine, salt and pepper. Blend flour into ¼ cup cold water; stir into vegetable mixture. Heat to boiling. Reduce heat. Cover and simmer, stirring occasionally, until potatoes are tender, 20 minutes. Stir in half-and-half. Cut fillets into 1-inch pieces. Add to soup. Cover and simmer, stirring gently one or two times, until fish flakes easily, about 8 minutes.

← Panfish Chowder

  6 slices bacon, cut up
  3 medium red potatoes (about 1 pound)
⅔ cup chopped onion
½ cup chopped celery
  2 cups fish stock (page 26)*
  1 cup sliced fresh mushrooms
½ cup chopped carrot
¼ cup snipped fresh parsley
  1 tablespoon fresh lemon or lime juice
  1 teaspoon salt
½ teaspoon dried dillweed
⅛ teaspoon dried fennel seed
⅛ teaspoon garlic salt
⅛ teaspoon pepper
  1 cup half-and-half
1½ cups cut-up cooked panfish
    (about 1½-inch pieces)

4 to 6 servings

In 3-quart saucepan, cook bacon over medium-high heat, stirring occasionally, until crisp. Remove with slotted spoon; set aside. Peel potatoes and cut into ¾-inch cubes; set aside.

Cook and stir onion and celery in bacon fat over medium-high heat until tender, about 5 minutes. Add bacon, potato cubes, fish stock, mushrooms, carrot, parsley, lemon juice, salt, dillweed, fennel seed, garlic salt and pepper. Heat to boiling. Reduce heat. Cover and simmer until vegetables are tender, 15 to 20 minutes. Blend in half-and-half. Gently stir in fish pieces. Skim fat, if desired.

*Or, substitute 2 cups water and 2 teaspoons instant chicken bouillon granules; omit the 1 teaspoon salt.

Tomato-Dill Fish Soup 🔻LOW-FAT VERY FAST

3 cups water
1 teaspoon dried dillweed
½ teaspoon salt
    Dash pepper
1 pound muskie or other lean fish fillets
    (page 34), about ½-inch thick
1 can (10¾ ounces) condensed tomato soup
2 tablespoons margarine or butter

4 to 6 servings

In Dutch oven, combine water, dillweed, salt and pepper. Heat to boiling. Add fillets. Reduce heat. Cover and simmer until fish flakes easily, about 5 minutes. Remove fish with slotted spatula.

Add tomato soup and margarine to cooking liquid. Cook over medium heat until bubbly, about 4 minutes. Cut fish into bite-size pieces. Reduce heat. Gently stir fish into soup. Simmer for 2 minutes.

Country Trout Chowder LOW-FAT FAST ↑

1 small onion
½ cup chopped celery
2 tablespoons margarine or butter
2 small zucchini (about ½ pound)
3 cups fish stock (page 26)*
2 cups coarsely chopped cabbage
1 can (15 ounces) Northern beans, drained
2 tablespoons snipped fresh parsley
1 tablespoon fresh lemon juice
½ teaspoon salt
4 whole peppercorns
1¼ pounds trout steaks, about 1-inch thick
    Thin lemon wedges

4 to 6 servings

Cut onion into thin slices and separate into rings. In Dutch oven, cook and stir onion and celery in margarine over medium heat until onion is tender, about 5 minutes.

Cut zucchini into ½-inch slices. Add zucchini, fish stock and remaining ingredients except fish and lemon wedges to onion and celery. Heat to boiling. Reduce heat. Cover and simmer, stirring occasionally, until zucchini is tender, 6 to 8 minutes.

Add fish to soup. Simmer, stirring gently one or two times, until fish flakes easily, about 10 minutes. Garnish with lemon wedges; squeeze juice over chowder before eating.

*Or, substitute 1 can (14½ ounces) ready-to-serve chicken broth and 1¼ cups water; omit the ½ teaspoon salt.

New England Chowder

1 quart water
1 teaspoon salt
4 large red potatoes (about 2 pounds)
1 pound bass or other lean fish fillets (page 34)
6 slices bacon, cut up
1 small onion, chopped
¼ cup all-purpose flour
½ teaspoon salt
⅛ teaspoon pepper
⅛ teaspoon dried thyme leaves
3 cups milk
1 small bay leaf
2 cups half-and-half

6 to 8 servings

In 2-quart saucepan, heat water and 1 teaspoon salt to boiling. Add potatoes. Return to boiling. Reduce heat. Cover and simmer until tender, 25 to 35 minutes. Drain; cool. Peel and cut into ½-inch cubes. Set aside. Cut fillets into 1-inch pieces; set aside.

In Dutch oven, cook bacon over medium-high heat, stirring occasionally, until crisp. Remove with slotted spoon; set aside. Add onion. Cook and stir until tender, about 2 minutes. Reduce to medium heat. Stir in flour, ½ teaspoon salt, the pepper and thyme. Add bacon. Blend in milk. Add bay leaf. Cook over medium heat, stirring constantly, until thickened and bubbly. Reduce heat to low. Blend in half-and-half. Stir in potato cubes and fish. Cook over low heat, stirring gently, until fish flakes easily, about 12 minutes. Garnish each serving with chopped chives, if desired.

447

Main Dishes

Fish is easy to prepare but the cooking time should be carefully watched. Test for doneness before the time given in the recipe. A perfectly cooked fish is moist and flaky.

The whole fish used in these recipes are drawn (see Field Dressing, page 8). This means they are gutted and gilled, but the head, fins and tail are retained.

← Rye-Stuffed Trout

    4 slices rye bread
1/3 cup chopped celery
    2 tablespoons chopped onion
    1 teaspoon grated orange peel
1/4 cup margarine or butter
    2 tablespoons fresh orange juice
1/4 cup snipped fresh parsley
1/4 cup coarsely chopped cashews or peanuts
    4 small drawn trout, about 1/2 pound each

4 servings

Set oven to broil and/or 550°. Cut bread into 1/2-inch cubes. Spread bread cubes on baking sheet. Broil 5 to 6 inches from heat, stirring one or two times, until toasted, about 4 minutes. Set aside. Set oven to bake and/or 375°. Grease 13 × 9-inch baking pan.

In 1 1/2-quart saucepan, cook and stir celery, onion and orange peel in margarine over medium heat until tender, about 5 minutes. Stir in orange juice. Heat until bubbly. Stir in parsley and nuts. Add bread cubes; toss to coat. Remove from heat.

Place fish in prepared pan. Stuff with bread mixture. If desired, brush fish with 2 tablespoons melted margarine or butter before baking. Bake until fish flakes easily at backbone, about 20 minutes.

Deep-Fried Catfish 🍳FAST

    Vegetable oil
1/2 cup buttermilk
3/4 cup yellow cornmeal
1 1/2 to 2 pounds small whole catfish or bullhead,
        head and skin removed

4 servings

In deep-fat fryer or saucepan, heat oil (2 to 3 inches) to 375°. Pour buttermilk into shallow dish or pie plate. Sprinkle cornmeal on plate or waxed paper. Dip fish into buttermilk. Coat with cornmeal. Fry a few pieces at a time, turning over one or two times, until deep golden brown, about 4 minutes. Drain on paper towels. Keep warm in 175° oven. Repeat with remaining fish.

← Vegetable Stuffed Walleye

1 medium zucchini
1 small onion, thinly sliced
1 cup sliced fresh mushrooms
3 thin lemon slices
2 tablespoons olive or vegetable oil
2 tablespoons margarine or butter
2 tablespoons grated Parmesan cheese
¼ teaspoon pepper
⅛ teaspoon garlic powder
2 to 3-pound drawn walleye
2 tablespoons margarine or butter, melted

4 to 6 servings

Heat oven to 375°. Grease 13 × 9-inch baking pan. Cut zucchini in half lengthwise, then into thin slices. In 9-inch skillet, cook and stir zucchini, onion, mushrooms and lemon slices in olive oil and 2 tablespoons margarine over medium heat until tender, about 3 minutes. Remove lemon slices; set aside. Stir Parmesan cheese, pepper and garlic powder into vegetables.

Place fish in prepared pan. Stuff with vegetable mixture, placing any extra stuffing around fish. Brush fish with melted margarine. Place lemon slices on top of fish. Bake until fish flakes easily at backbone, 30 to 35 minutes.

Walleye With Rice Stuffing ◆ LOW-FAT

1 package (6 ounces) wild and long grain rice mix
1 teaspoon instant chicken bouillon granules
1½ cups sliced fresh mushrooms
½ cup chopped celery
2 tablespoons margarine or butter
1 jar (2 ounces) sliced pimiento, drained
⅛ teaspoon ground sage
2 to 2½-pound drawn walleye

4 to 6 servings

Prepare rice as directed on package, adding bouillon granules to water. Set aside. Heat oven to 375°. Grease broiler pan or 13 × 9-inch baking pan.

In small skillet, cook and stir mushrooms and celery in margarine over medium heat until mushrooms are tender, about 5 minutes. Stir in pimiento and sage. Stir vegetables into rice.

Place walleye on broiler pan. Stuff with rice mixture, placing any extra stuffing around fish. Cover rice only with foil. Bake until fish flakes easily at backbone, 20 to 25 minutes. If desired, serve with Citrus Butter, page 138.

Lemon-Cucumber Stuffed Trout →

½ cup chopped, seeded, peeled cucumber
½ cup shredded carrot
 2 tablespoons chopped onion
½ teaspoon lemon pepper
¼ cup margarine or butter
½ cup hot water
 1 teaspoon instant chicken bouillon granules
 2 tablespoons snipped fresh parsley
 3 cups dry bread cubes
 4 small drawn trout, about ½ pound each

4 servings

Heat oven to 375°. Grease 13 × 9-inch baking pan. In small skillet, cook and stir cucumber, carrot, onion and lemon pepper in margarine over medium heat until tender, about 6 minutes. Blend in water and bouillon granules. Heat to boiling. Add parsley. Remove from heat.

In medium bowl, stir bread cubes into vegetables until coated. Place fish in prepared pan. Stuff each trout with one-fourth of bread mixture. If desired, brush fish with 2 tablespoons melted margarine or butter before baking. Bake until fish flakes easily at backbone, about 20 minutes.

Wild Rice Stuffed Trout

 1 cup uncooked wild rice
2½ cups hot water
 1 teaspoon salt
⅓ cup chopped water chestnuts
¼ cup chopped green onions
 1 tablespoon chopped stuffed green olives
 3 tablespoons margarine or butter
 4 small drawn trout, about ½ pound each

4 servings

Rinse and drain rice. In 3-quart saucepan, combine rice, water and salt. Heat to boiling, stirring one or two times. Reduce heat. Cover and simmer until rice is tender, 40 to 50 minutes, checking one or two times to be sure rice is not sticking. Add a few tablespoons water, if necessary. Set aside.

Heat oven to 375°. Grease 13 × 9-inch baking pan. In small skillet, cook and stir water chestnuts, green onions and olives in margarine over medium heat for 2 minutes. Stir into rice.

Place trout in prepared pan. Stuff with wild rice. If desired, brush fish with 2 tablespoons melted margarine or butter before baking. Bake until fish flakes easily at backbone, about 20 minutes.

Baked Walleye and Ratatouille ↑

1 medium onion
2 cloves garlic, minced
¼ cup olive or vegetable oil
1 eggplant (about 1 pound)
3 medium zucchini (about 1 pound)
1 medium green pepper
2 cups sliced fresh mushrooms
1 can (16 ounces) whole tomatoes, drained, cut up
1 teaspoon salt
¾ teaspoon dried basil leaves
½ teaspoon dried oregano leaves
¼ teaspoon pepper
2 to 3-pound drawn walleye

2 to 4 servings

Heat oven to 350°. Cut onion into thin slices and separate into rings. In Dutch oven, cook and stir onion and garlic in olive oil over medium heat until onion is tender, about 5 minutes. Peel eggplant and cut into ¾-inch cubes. Cut zucchini into ¼-inch slices. Core and seed green pepper; cut into ½-inch strips. Stir eggplant, zucchini, green pepper, mushrooms, tomatoes, salt, basil, oregano and pepper into onions. Cook over medium heat, stirring occasionally, for 10 minutes. Set aside.

Place fish on large sheet of heavy-duty aluminum foil. Spoon vegetables over and around fish. Wrap tightly. Place on baking sheet. Bake until fish flakes easily at backbone, about 35 minutes.

Bullheads Marinated in Barbecue Sauce ▷ LOW-FAT

3 tablespoons chopped onion
1 tablespoon olive or vegetable oil
¼ cup packed dark brown sugar
¼ cup catsup
¼ cup cider vinegar
2 tablespoons Worcestershire sauce
½ teaspoon dry mustard
¼ teaspoon salt
¼ teaspoon pepper
⅛ teaspoon dried oregano leaves
1½ to 2 pounds small whole bullheads, heads and skin removed

4 to 6 servings

In small skillet, cook and stir onion in olive oil over medium heat until tender, about 3 minutes. Stir in brown sugar, catsup, vinegar, Worcestershire sauce, dry mustard, salt, pepper and oregano. Cook, stirring occasionally, until bubbly. Reduce heat. Simmer, stirring occasionally, for 10 minutes.

Place fish in medium bowl. Pour marinade over fish; cover. Refrigerate at least 30 minutes, turning fish over once. Set oven to broil and/or 550°. Grease broiler pan. With slotted spoon, remove fish from bowl and place on pan. Baste with marinade. Broil 4 to 5 inches from heat for 8 minutes; turn. Baste with marinade. Broil until fish flakes easily at backbone, about 7 minutes.

Sesame-Dill Broiled Salmon VERY FAST ↑

1 tablespoon sesame seed
1 teaspoon dried dillweed
3 tablespoons margarine or butter
¼ teaspoon salt
⅛ teaspoon pepper
4 salmon steaks, about 1-inch thick

4 servings

Set oven to broil and/or 550°. Grease broiler pan. In small skillet, cook and stir sesame seed and dillweed in margarine over medium heat until sesame seed is light brown, about 4 minutes. Stir in salt and pepper. Remove from heat.

Place fish on broiler pan. Brush with half of sesame seed mixture. Broil 5 to 6 inches from heat for 5 minutes; turn. Brush with remaining sesame seed mixture. Broil until fish flakes easily in center, about 5 minutes.

Sherry Poached Salmon LOW-FAT FAST

2½ quarts hot water
1 cup sherry
1 stalk celery, cut into 1-inch pieces
½ teaspoon dried bouquet garni seasoning
½ teaspoon garlic salt
⅛ teaspoon whole peppercorns
4 salmon steaks, about 1-inch thick
Sherried White Sauce Variation (page 139)

4 servings

In fish poacher or Dutch oven, combine water, sherry, celery, bouquet garni, garlic salt and peppercorns. Heat to boiling. Reduce heat. Cover and simmer for 15 minutes.

Lower fish into simmering liquid. Fish should be covered; add boiling water as needed. Cover poacher. Simmer until fish flakes easily in center, about 10 minutes. Remove from liquid. Prepare Sherried White Sauce as directed. Spoon over fish.

← Marinated Salmon Steaks

½ cup vegetable oil
½ cup white wine vinegar
1 teaspoon sugar
1 teaspoon dried parsley flakes
½ teaspoon dried Italian seasoning
¼ teaspoon garlic salt
¼ teaspoon onion powder
⅛ teaspoon paprika
⅛ teaspoon pepper
4 salmon steaks, about 1-inch thick

4 servings

In shallow bowl, blend oil, vinegar, sugar, parsley flakes, Italian seasoning, garlic salt, onion powder, paprika and pepper. Place fish in plastic bag. Pour marinade over fish. Seal bag. Refrigerate 1½ hours, turning bag over two or three times.

Set oven to broil and/or 550°. Grease broiler pan. Remove fish from marinade. Reserve marinade. Arrange fish on broiler pan; baste with marinade. Broil 4 to 5 inches from heat for 5 minutes; turn. Baste with remaining marinade. Broil until fish flakes easily in center, about 5 minutes.

Crunchy Oriental Fillets

½ cup water
⅓ cup teriyaki sauce
½ teaspoon ground ginger
   Dash dry mustard
1 pound panfish or other lean fish fillets
   (page 34), ¼- to ½-inch thick
3 cups chow mein noodles, crushed
¼ cup margarine or butter, melted
½ cup dairy sour cream
2½ teaspoons soy sauce
⅛ teaspoon ground ginger
1 tablespoon finely chopped green onion

2 to 4 servings

In small dish, combine water, teriyaki sauce, ½ teaspoon ginger and the dry mustard. Cut fish into serving-size pieces. Place in plastic bag. Pour marinade over fish. Seal bag. Refrigerate at least 30 minutes, turning bag over one or two times. Drain and discard marinade.

Heat oven to 375°. Grease 13 × 9-inch baking pan. Sprinkle chow mein noodles on plate or waxed paper. Dip fillets in melted margarine. Coat with crushed chow mein noodles, pressing lightly. Place in prepared pan. Bake until fish flakes easily at thickest part, 15 to 20 minutes.

In small dish, blend sour cream, soy sauce and ⅛ teaspoon ginger. Spoon over baked fish. Top with green onion.

Almond Fried Trout ↑

¼ cup all-purpose flour
⅛ teaspoon pepper
1 egg
3 tablespoons milk
1 cup cracker crumbs
½ cup sliced almonds, coarsely chopped
1½ pounds trout fillets, about ½-inch thick
2 tablespoons margarine or butter
¼ cup plus 1 tablespoon vegetable oil

4 servings

Heat oven to 450°. On plate or waxed paper, mix flour and pepper. In shallow dish or pie plate, blend egg and milk. On another plate or waxed paper, mix cracker crumbs and almonds. Cut fish into serving-size pieces. Coat fish with flour, dip in egg, then coat with almond mixture, pressing lightly.

In 13 × 9-inch baking pan, combine margarine and oil. Place pan in oven for 5 minutes to heat oil. Add fish, turning to coat with oil. Bake 5 minutes. Turn fish. Bake until fish is golden brown and flakes easily at thickest part, about 5 minutes. Drain on paper towels. Serve with lemon wedges, if desired.

Tempura Fried Walleye

1 egg, separated
1 cup very cold water
1 cup all-purpose flour
¼ teaspoon salt
¾ teaspoon sesame oil, optional
  Vegetable oil
1½ pounds walleye or other lean fish fillets
  (page 34), about ½-inch thick
1 cup fresh parsley sprigs, optional

4 to 6 servings

In medium bowl, blend egg yolk and water. Blend in flour, salt and sesame oil until smooth; cover. Refrigerate at least 30 minutes. (Do not refrigerate egg white.) In small bowl, beat egg white until stiff peaks form. Gently fold into chilled batter.

In deep-fat fryer or deep skillet, heat oil (1½ to 3 inches) to 375°. Cut fish into serving-size pieces. Dip fish into chilled batter. Fry a few pieces at a time, turning over one or two times, until light golden brown, about 3 minutes. Drain on paper towels. Keep warm in 175° oven.

With slotted spoon, dip one-fourth of the parsley in the remaining batter. Fry, turning over once, until light golden brown, about 45 seconds. Repeat with remaining parsley. Serve with fish.

455

Potato Chip Coated Fillets ▷ LOW-FAT ● VERY FAST

⅓ cup buttermilk
⅛ teaspoon pepper
 1 bag (4 ounces) potato chips, crushed
¾ cup cornflake crumbs
¼ teaspoon paprika
1½ pounds northern pike or other lean fish
    fillets (page 34), about ½-inch thick

4 to 6 servings

In shallow dish or pie plate, mix buttermilk and pepper. On plate or waxed paper, mix crushed potato chips, cornflake crumbs and paprika. Set oven to broil and/or 550°. Grease broiler pan.

Cut fish into serving-size pieces. Dip in buttermilk. Coat with potato chip mixture, pressing lightly. Place on broiler pan. Broil 6 inches from heat for 3 minutes; turn. Broil until fish flakes easily at thickest part, 2 to 3 minutes.

Crunchy Fried Walleye ● VERY FAST

 1 egg
 1 cup evaporated milk
 2 cups cracker crumbs
⅛ teaspoon salt
⅛ teaspoon pepper
1½ pounds walleye or other lean fish fillets
    (page 34), about ½-inch thick
 2 to 4 tablespoons vegetable oil

4 to 6 servings

In shallow dish or pie plate, blend egg and milk. On plate or waxed paper, combine cracker crumbs, salt and pepper. Cut fish into serving-size pieces. Dip in milk. Coat with cracker crumbs.

In 9-inch skillet, heat oil. Fry a few pieces at a time until golden brown, about 3 minutes; turn. Fry until golden brown, 1½ to 3 minutes. Drain on paper towels. Keep warm in 175° oven. Repeat with remaining fish.

Parmesan Bass Fillets

1½ pounds bass or other lean fish fillets
    (page 34), about ¾-inch thick
¼ cup margarine or butter
½ teaspoon salt
⅛ teaspoon pepper
1 tablespoon fresh lemon juice
1 tablespoon white wine
3 tablespoons grated Parmesan cheese
  Paprika

4 to 6 servings

Heat oven to 450°. Cut fish into serving-size pieces. Place margarine in 13×9-inch baking pan. Place pan in oven for 5 minutes to melt margarine. Place fish in pan, skin side up. Sprinkle with salt and pepper. Bake for 5 minutes; turn. Sprinkle with lemon juice and white wine. Top with Parmesan cheese. Sprinkle with paprika. Bake until fish flakes easily at thickest part, about 5 minutes.

Lemon Fried Panfish

1 cup all-purpose flour
2 teaspoons grated lemon peel
½ teaspoon salt
¼ teaspoon pepper
1 cup water
  Vegetable oil
1½ pounds panfish or other lean fish fillets
    (page 34)
  All-purpose flour

4 to 6 servings

In medium bowl, combine 1 cup flour, the lemon peel, salt and pepper. Blend in water; cover. Refrigerate at least 30 minutes.

In deep-fat fryer or deep skillet, heat oil (1½ to 3 inches) to 375°. Coat fish with flour, then dip in chilled batter. Fry a few pieces at a time, turning occasionally, until light golden brown, about 3 minutes. Drain on paper towels. Keep warm in 175° oven. Repeat with remaining fish.

Tomato Baked Walleye Fillets ⟩LOW-FAT ↑

1 medium onion
2 tablespoons olive or vegetable oil
1½ pounds walleye or other lean fish fillets
    (page 34), about ½-inch thick
1½ cups sliced fresh mushrooms
1 can (7½ ounces) whole tomatoes,
    drained, cut up
⅓ cup white wine
½ teaspoon salt
⅛ teaspoon pepper
⅛ teaspoon garlic powder
1 medium tomato, thinly sliced
½ teaspoon dried oregano leaves
2 tablespoons snipped fresh parsley

4 to 6 servings

Cut onion into thin slices and separate into rings. In 9-inch skillet, cook and stir onion in olive oil over medium heat until tender-crisp, about 5 minutes. Set aside.

Heat oven to 350°. Place fish in 13 × 9-inch baking pan. Top with onion rings. Sprinkle mushrooms over onions. Set aside.

In small bowl, combine canned tomatoes, wine, salt, pepper and garlic powder. Spoon evenly over fish and vegetables. Top with tomato slices. Sprinkle oregano and parsley over tomato. Bake until fish flakes easily at thickest part, 25 to 30 minutes.

Herbed Northern Pike and Vegetables ⟩LOW-FAT ●FAST

2 medium zucchini (about ½ pound)
¼ pound fresh broccoli
1 small onion, cut into thin wedges
½ cup thinly sliced celery
¼ cup thinly sliced carrot
2 tablespoons olive or vegetable oil
1½ pounds northern pike or other lean
    fish fillets (page 34), about ½-inch thick
2 tablespoons margarine or butter
¼ teaspoon dried basil leaves
¼ teaspoon salt
⅛ teaspoon dried rosemary leaves
⅛ teaspoon garlic salt
⅛ teaspoon pepper
Paprika

4 to 6 servings

Cut zucchini into 2 × ½-inch strips. Chop broccoli. In 9-inch skillet, cook and stir zucchini, broccoli, onion, celery and carrot in olive oil over medium heat until tender-crisp, about 10 minutes. Spread evenly on broiler pan. Cut fish into serving-size pieces. Arrange on top of vegetables.

Set oven to broil and/or 550°. In ½-quart saucepan, melt margarine. Stir in basil, salt, rosemary, garlic salt and pepper. Brush on fish.

Broil 5 to 6 inches from heat until fish flakes easily at thickest part, 5 to 8 minutes. Sprinkle with paprika before serving.

Cheesy Northern Pike Bake

1 pound fresh broccoli
1 pound fresh cauliflower
    (about ½ medium head)
1 quart water
½ teaspoon salt
½ cup thinly sliced carrot
2 tablespoons margarine or butter
2 tablespoons all-purpose flour
½ teaspoon salt
⅛ teaspoon dry mustard
⅛ teaspoon white pepper
    Dash cayenne
1 cup milk
¾ cup shredded Cheddar cheese
1½ pounds northern pike or other lean fish fillets
    (page 34), about ½-inch thick, skin removed
2 tablespoons margarine or butter, melted
½ cup fine dry bread crumbs
⅛ teaspoon paprika

4 to 6 servings

Cut broccoli stems into ¾-inch thick slices; separate tops into flowerets. Separate cauliflower into flowerets. In 3-quart saucepan, heat water and ½ teaspoon salt to boiling. Add broccoli, cauliflower and carrot; cover. Cook over high heat for 5 minutes. Drain. Rinse under cold running water; drain well. Set aside.

In 1-quart saucepan, melt 2 tablespoons margarine over medium heat. Stir in flour, ½ teaspoon salt, the dry mustard, white pepper and cayenne. Blend in milk. Cook over medium heat, stirring constantly, until thickened and bubbly, about 4 minutes. Stir in cheese until melted. Remove from heat. Set aside.

Heat oven to 325°. Grease 13 × 9-inch baking pan. Place vegetables in pan. Evenly spread half of the cheese sauce over the vegetables. Cut fish into serving-size pieces. Place on vegetables. Evenly spread remaining cheese sauce over fish. Set aside.

In small dish, mix 2 tablespoons melted margarine, the bread crumbs and paprika. Sprinkle over cheese sauce. Bake until fish flakes easily at thickest part, 25 to 30 minutes.

← Sour Cream Fish Bake

    1 quart water
    1 teaspoon salt
    4 large red potatoes (about 2 pounds)
    6 slices bacon, cut up
1½ pounds northern pike or other lean fish fillets
       (page 34), about ½-inch thick
    1 medium onion
    1 medium green pepper
1½ cups dairy sour cream
    ½ cup half-and-half
    2 teaspoons dried chopped chives
    ½ teaspoon salt
    ⅛ teaspoon pepper
    ¼ cup snipped fresh parsley

6 to 8 servings

In 2-quart saucepan, heat water and 1 teaspoon salt to boiling. Add potatoes. Return to boiling. Reduce heat. Cover and simmer until potatoes are fork tender, about 30 minutes. Drain. Cool and slice.

In small skillet, cook and stir bacon over medium-high heat until brown, but not crisp, about 7 minutes. Drain, reserving 2 tablespoons fat. Set bacon aside. Cut fish into serving-size pieces. Slice onion and separate into rings. Core and seed green pepper; cut into rings. Set aside.

Heat oven to 325°. Grease 13 × 9-inch baking pan. Layer potato slices in pan. Pour reserved bacon fat over potatoes.

In small bowl, blend sour cream, half-and-half, chives, ½ teaspoon salt and the pepper. Spoon one-third of mixture over potatoes. Layer fish and onion rings over sour cream and potatoes. Spoon on remaining sour cream. Top with green pepper rings, parsley and bacon. Bake until fish in center of pan flakes easily, about 1 hour.

Bass With Blue Cheese Sauce

    1 tablespoon all-purpose flour
    1 cup dairy sour cream
  ¾ cup white wine
    2 ounces blue cheese, crumbled
    1 tablespoon dried chopped chives
      Dash white pepper
1½ pounds bass or other lean fish fillets (page 34),
      ¼- to ½-inch thick

4 to 6 servings

Heat oven to 300°. Grease 13 × 9-inch baking pan. In small bowl, mix flour and sour cream. Blend in wine, cheese, chives and white pepper. Cut fish into serving-size pieces. Place in prepared pan. Spread with sauce. Bake until fish flakes easily at thickest part, 30 to 40 minutes. Place fish on warm serving plate. Stir sauce before serving.

Walleye in Creamy Orange Sauce FAST ↑

2 tablespoons margarine or butter
2 tablespoons finely chopped onion
1 tablespoon all-purpose flour
1 teaspoon grated orange peel
¼ teaspoon salt
⅛ teaspoon pepper
1 cup half-and-half or milk
1½ pounds walleye or other lean fish fillets
   (page 34), about ½-inch thick

4 to 6 servings

Heat oven to 300°. Grease 13 × 9-inch baking pan. In small saucepan, melt margarine over medium heat. Stir in onion, flour, orange peel, salt and pepper. Blend in half-and-half. Cook over medium heat, stirring constantly, until thickened and bubbly, about 4 minutes. Set aside.

Cut fish into serving-size pieces. Place in prepared pan. Pour sauce over fish. Cover with foil. Bake until fish flakes easily at thickest part, about 25 minutes. Garnish with orange slices, if desired.

Marinated Bass Fillets

½ cup bottled creamy French dressing
2 tablespoons fresh lime juice
¼ teaspoon salt
⅛ teaspoon pepper
1½ pounds bass or other lean fish fillets
   (page 34), about ½-inch thick
1 can (3½ ounces) French-fried onion rings,
   coarsely crushed
⅓ cup grated Parmesan cheese
½ teaspoon dried parsley flakes

4 to 6 servings

In small bowl, blend French dressing, lime juice, salt and pepper. Cut fish into serving-size pieces. Place in a plastic bag. Add dressing mixture; seal. Refrigerate at least 30 minutes, turning over once.

Heat oven to 375°. Grease 13 × 9-inch baking pan. With slotted spoon, remove fish from marinade; place in pan. Mix onion rings, cheese and parsley. Sprinkle over fish. Bake until fish flakes easily at thickest part, about 20 minutes.

Florentine-Stuffed Northern Pike →

2 packages (10 ounces each) frozen chopped
   spinach, thawed
2 cups sliced fresh mushrooms
3 tablespoons olive or vegetable oil
1 cup ricotta cheese
1 egg, slightly beaten
1/3 cup herb-seasoned stuffing mix
1/4 cup grated Parmesan cheese
1 jar (2 ounces) sliced pimiento, drained
1/2 teaspoon salt
1/4 teaspoon pepper
1/4 teaspoon dried basil leaves
1/8 teaspoon onion powder
2 northern pike or other lean fish fillets (page 34),
   1 pound each, about 3/4-inch thick,
   skin removed
   Almondine Butter (page 138)
   Paprika

6 to 8 servings

How to Prepare Florentine-Stuffed Northern Pike

DRAIN thawed spinach in colander, pressing out excess moisture. Set aside. In 9-inch skillet, cook and stir mushrooms in olive oil over medium heat until tender, about 4 minutes.

COMBINE mushrooms, spinach, ricotta cheese, beaten egg, stuffing mix, Parmesan cheese, pimiento, salt, pepper, basil and onion powder in medium bowl. Mix well. Set aside.

HEAT oven to 325°. Grease broiler pan. Place one fillet on pan. Spread about half of the spinach stuffing on the fillet.

CUT a slit lengthwise through middle of other fillet, leaving 3 inches uncut on each end. Place on top of spinach and other fillet. Spoon remaining spinach stuffing in center of split fillet.

PREPARE Almondine Butter. Spoon half of butter over fish. Sprinkle with paprika. Bake until both fillets flake easily at thickest part, 35 to 40 minutes. Serve with remaining butter.

Vegetable-Dressed Fillets FAST

½ cup chopped celery
⅓ cup chopped green pepper
¼ cup chopped onion
¼ cup thinly sliced carrot
¼ cup margarine or butter
1 medium tomato
1 cup dry bread cubes
1 tablespoon snipped fresh parsley
¼ teaspoon dried dillweed
¼ teaspoon salt
　Dash pepper
1½ pounds bass or other lean fish fillets (page 34),
　　about ½-inch thick
2 tablespoons white wine

4 to 6 servings

Heat oven to 350°. Grease 13×9-inch baking pan. In small skillet, cook and stir celery, green pepper, onion and carrot in margarine over medium heat until tender, about 5 minutes. Set aside.

Peel and seed tomato; chop. In small bowl, combine tomato, bread cubes, parsley, dillweed, salt and pepper. Add vegetables. Set aside.

Cut fish into serving-size pieces. Arrange in prepared pan. Cover fillets evenly with vegetable mixture. Sprinkle with wine. Bake until fish flakes easily at thickest part, about 25 minutes.

Spicy Poached Fish LOW-FAT FAST

1½ quarts hot water
1 medium onion, chopped
2 lemon slices
1 clove garlic, minced
2 teaspoons salt
½ teaspoon whole allspice
½ teaspoon whole cloves
¼ teaspoon dried crushed red pepper
1 bay leaf
1½ pounds walleye or other lean fish fillets
　　(page 34), ¼- to ¾-inch thick, skin on
　Zesty Tomato Sauce (page 139) or
　Lemony White Sauce (page 137)

4 to 6 servings

In fish poacher or large skillet, combine hot water, onion, lemon slices, garlic, salt, allspice, cloves, red pepper and bay leaf. Heat to boiling. Reduce heat. Cover and simmer for 15 minutes.

Lower fish into simmering liquid. Fish should be covered; add additional boiling water as needed. Cover poacher. Simmer until fish flakes easily at thickest part, 5 to 8 minutes. Remove from liquid. Prepare Zesty Tomato Sauce or Lemony White Sauce as directed. Spoon over fish.

Italian Fish ◈ LOW-FAT · ● FAST ↑

1½ pounds northern pike or other lean fish
 fillets (page 34), about ½-inch thick, skin
 removed
1 jar (16 ounces) spaghetti sauce
2 tablespoons snipped fresh parsley
½ teaspoon dried basil leaves
¼ teaspoon dried oregano leaves
⅛ teaspoon pepper
1 cup shredded mozzarella cheese

4 to 6 servings

Heat oven to 350°. Cut fish into serving-size pieces.
Arrange in 13 × 9-inch baking pan. Pour spaghetti
sauce over fish. Sprinkle with parsley, basil, oregano and pepper. Top with cheese. Bake until fish
flakes easily at thickest part, 20 to 25 minutes.

Broiled Tarragon Fillets ● VERY FAST

1½ pounds walleye or other lean fish fillets
 (page 34), about ½-inch thick, skin removed
½ cup margarine or butter
2 tablespoons snipped fresh parsley
2 teaspoons fresh lemon juice
1½ teaspoons dried tarragon leaves
¼ teaspoon salt

4 to 6 servings

Set oven to broil and/or 550°. Grease broiler pan.
Cut fish into serving-size pieces. Set aside. In
1-quart saucepan, melt margarine over medium
heat. Stir in parsley, lemon juice, tarragon and salt.

Place fish on broiler pan. Baste with margarine.
Broil 3 to 4 inches from heat for 3 minutes; turn.
Baste with remaining margarine. Broil until fish
flakes easily at thickest part, 2 to 3 minutes. Drizzle
with remaining margarine before serving.

Northern Pike With
Swiss Cheese Sauce ● FAST

2 tablespoons margarine or butter
2 tablespoons all-purpose flour
½ teaspoon salt
 Dash ground nutmeg
1 cup milk
1 tablespoon sherry, optional
1 cup shredded Swiss cheese
1½ pounds northern pike or other lean
 fish fillets (page 34), about ½-inch thick
½ teaspoon celery salt
⅛ teaspoon pepper
3 tablespoons margarine or butter
½ cup fine dry bread crumbs
1 green pepper

4 to 6 servings

Heat oven to 325°. Grease 13 × 9-inch baking pan.
In 1-quart saucepan, melt 2 tablespoons margarine
over medium heat. Stir in flour, salt and nutmeg.
Blend in milk and sherry. Cook over medium heat,
stirring constantly, until thickened and bubbly,
about 4 minutes. Stir in cheese until melted. Remove from heat; set aside.

Cut fish into serving-size pieces. Place in prepared
pan. Combine celery salt and pepper; sprinkle on
fish. Pour cheese sauce over fish.

In small saucepan or skillet, melt 3 tablespoons
margarine. Stir in bread crumbs until coated. Sprinkle over fish. Core and seed green pepper; slice into
thin rings and place on fish. Bake until fish flakes
easily at thickest part, 20 to 25 minutes.

Fish Pinwheels

¹/₂ cup chopped fresh mushrooms
2 tablespoons finely chopped celery
2 tablespoons finely chopped onion
2 tablespoons margarine or butter
¹/₂ cup herb-seasoned stuffing mix
2 tablespoons hot water
¹/₂ teaspoon salt
¹/₈ teaspoon pepper
¹/₈ teaspoon ground sage
4 northern pike or other lean fish fillets
    (page 34), about ¹/₄-inch thick,
    12 to 15 inches long, skin removed
1 tablespoon margarine or butter, melted
  Mushroom Sauce (page 140)

4 servings

How to Prepare Fish Pinwheels

HEAT oven to 375°. Grease 8 × 4-inch loaf pan. In small skillet, cook and stir mushrooms, celery and onion in 2 tablespoons margarine over medium heat until tender, about 4 minutes.

REMOVE skillet from heat. Add herb-seasoned stuffing mix, hot water, salt, pepper and sage to vegetables. Stir until mixture is moistened.

SPREAD one-fourth of the stuffing mixture evenly on each fillet, pressing lightly. Roll up fillets, starting with narrow ends.

PLACE rolls upright in prepared pan, arranging in staggered pattern. Brush with 1 tablespoon melted margarine. Cover pan with foil.

BAKE until fish in center of roll flakes easily, 30 to 35 minutes. Prepare Mushroom Sauce as directed and serve with fish.

Trout Kabobs 🥩 FAST

1 large green pepper
1 quart water
4 small onions (about ½ pound)
2 pounds trout or other oily fish fillets or
    steaks (page 34), about ¾-inch
    thick, skin removed
16 French bread cubes, 1½ × 1½-inch
1 cup margarine or butter
¾ teaspoon garlic salt
4 metal skewers, 16 inches long
4 lemon wedges

4 servings

How to Prepare Trout Kabobs

CORE and seed green pepper; cut in half. In 3-quart saucepan, heat water to boiling. Add green peppers and onions; cover. Cook over high heat for 4 minutes. Drain. Rinse under cold running water; drain.

CUT onions in half. Cut green pepper into 1-inch pieces. Cut fish into 1-inch chunks. Alternately thread two onion halves, one-fourth of the green pepper pieces, one-fourth of the fish and four bread cubes on each skewer.

PLACE kabobs on lightly greased broiler pan. Set oven to broil and/or 550°. In 1-quart saucepan, heat margarine and garlic salt over medium heat until margarine is melted. Brush on fish, bread and vegetables.

BROIL kabobs 8 to 9 inches from heat, turning and brushing with margarine four times, until fish flakes easily at thickest part, about 8 minutes. Serve kabobs with lemon wedges.

Panfish Stir-Fry

1 pound panfish or other lean fish fillets
    (page 34), ¼- to ½-inch thick, skin on
1 teaspoon cornstarch
2 tablespoons vegetable oil
¼ cup teriyaki sauce
1 tablespoon fresh lemon juice
¼ teaspoon salt
¼ teaspoon garlic powder
⅛ teaspoon pepper
1 pound fresh broccoli
¼ cup vegetable oil
½ cup thinly sliced green onion
1 cup thinly sliced carrot
1 cup sliced fresh mushrooms

                        4 to 6 servings

Cut fillets into 1-inch diagonal strips. In medium bowl, toss fish strips with cornstarch until coated. Add 2 tablespoons vegetable oil, the teriyaki sauce, lemon juice, salt, garlic powder and pepper. Cover and refrigerate at least 30 minutes.

Cut broccoli into flowerets; cut stems into thin slices. In 10-inch skillet, heat ¼ cup vegetable oil. Add broccoli, green onion and carrot, stirring to coat with oil. Cook and stir over medium heat until vegetables are tender-crisp, about 3 minutes.

Stir in fish and marinade; add mushrooms. Cook and stir over medium-high heat until fish flakes easily at thickest part, 4 to 6 minutes.

Variation: Substitute 1 cup thinly sliced celery for the carrot.

Poor Man's Lobster   LOW-FAT   FAST

2½ cups hot water
½ cup white wine
1 small onion, sliced
4 lemon slices
1 teaspoon salt
⅛ teaspoon whole peppercorns
1 small bay leaf
1½ pounds northern pike fillets, about ¾-inch
    thick, skin removed

                        4 to 6 servings

In 10-inch skillet, combine water, white wine, onion, lemon slices, salt, peppercorns and bay leaf. Heat to boiling. Reduce heat. Cover and simmer for 15 minutes.

Cut fish into 1½-inch chunks; add to liquid. Cover and cook over medium heat, occasionally stirring gently until fish flakes easily at thickest part, about 7 minutes. Serve with melted butter and fresh lemon wedges, if desired.

Trout Newburg ↑

1 quart water
1 small onion, sliced
1 lemon slice
1 small bay leaf
⅛ teaspoon whole peppercorns
1 pound trout or other oily fish fillets
    (page 34), ½- to 1-inch thick
1 cup sliced fresh mushrooms
¼ cup margarine or butter
2 tablespoons all-purpose flour
¾ teaspoon salt
1½ cups half-and-half
¾ cup milk
¼ cup sherry
¼ teaspoon paprika
⅛ teaspoon cayenne
3 egg yolks, beaten
8 baked patty shells or 8 pieces toast,
    cut into triangles

                        4 servings

In fish poacher or 10-inch skillet, combine water, onion, lemon slice, bay leaf and peppercorns. Heat to boiling. Reduce heat. Cover and simmer for 15 minutes. Add fish. Simmer until fish flakes easily at thickest part, 5 to 10 minutes. Remove fish with slotted spatula. Cut into bite-size pieces. Set aside. (Liquid can be strained and refrigerated or frozen for use in soups or chowders.)

In 2-quart saucepan, cook and stir mushrooms in margarine over medium heat until tender, about 4 minutes. Stir in flour and salt. Blend in half-and-half, milk, sherry, paprika and cayenne. Cook over medium heat, stirring constantly, until thickened, about 5 minutes.

Stir about ½ cup of hot mixture into beaten egg yolks. Return to hot mixture. Cook over medium heat until thickened, 1 to 2 minutes. Stir in fish. Serve over patty shells or toast points.

Variation: Substitute ⅓ cup white wine for sherry.

Fish and Vegetable Pie

PASTRY:

  2 cups all-purpose flour
  1 teaspoon salt
⅔ cup shortening
  3 tablespoons margarine or butter,
    room temperature
  5 to 7 tablespoons cold water

FILLING:

  1 tablespoon margarine or butter
  2 tablespoons all-purpose flour
  1 tablespoon snipped fresh parsley
½ teaspoon instant chicken bouillon granules
½ teaspoon salt
⅛ teaspoon pepper
⅛ teaspoon garlic powder
¾ cup milk
  2 medium white potatoes (about 1 pound)
  2 cups flaked cooked trout or other oily fish
    (page 34)
  1 cup sliced fresh mushrooms
½ cup thinly sliced carrot
½ cup frozen peas
  3 tablespoons finely chopped onion
  1 egg
  1 tablespoon water

4 to 6 servings

In medium bowl, combine 2 cups flour and 1 teaspoon salt. Cut shortening and 3 tablespoons margarine into flour until particles resemble coarse crumbs or small peas. Sprinkle with cold water while tossing with fork, until particles are just moist enough to cling together.

Divide pastry in half and shape into two balls. Wrap and refrigerate one ball. On lightly floured board, roll other ball into thin circle at least 2 inches larger than inverted 9-inch pie plate. Fit crust into pie plate, pressing gently against bottom and side. Trim overhang ½ inch from rim. Cover and set aside.

In 1-quart saucepan, melt 1 tablespoon margarine over medium heat. Stir in flour, parsley, bouillon granules, salt, pepper and garlic powder. Blend in milk. Cook, stirring constantly, until thickened and bubbly, about 5 minutes. Set aside.

Heat oven to 375°. Cut potatoes in half lengthwise, then into thin slices. In large bowl, combine potatoes and fish. Add mushrooms, carrot, peas and onion. Stir in sauce.

Fill pastry-lined pie plate with fish mixture. Roll out remaining pastry. Place on filling. Seal and flute edges. Cut several slits in pastry top. Blend egg and 1 tablespoon water. Brush over top before baking. Bake until crust is golden brown, about 1 hour.

Salmon Pie →

CRUST:
2 cups cooked rice
3 tablespoons grated Parmesan cheese
1 egg white

FILLING:
1 cup flaked cooked salmon or other oily fish
   (page 34)
½ cup half-and-half or milk
3 eggs, slightly beaten
1 cup ricotta cheese
¼ cup chopped onion
2 tablespoons all-purpose flour
2 tablespoons snipped fresh parsley
⅛ teaspoon salt
⅛ teaspoon pepper
⅛ teaspoon ground oregano
   Paprika, optional

4 to 6 servings

Heat oven to 375°. Grease 9-inch pie plate. In medium bowl, mix rice, Parmesan cheese and egg white. Press into prepared pie plate to form crust. Set aside.

In medium bowl, blend filling ingredients. Pour into rice crust. Sprinkle with paprika. Bake until knife inserted in center comes out clean, 30 to 40 minutes. Let stand 10 minutes before cutting.

Variation: Substitute flaked smoked salmon; omit the salt.

Salmon Loaf With Horseradish Sauce ◈ LOW-FAT

2 cups flaked cooked salmon or other oily fish
   (page 34)
2 eggs, slightly beaten
1 cup milk
½ cup fine dry bread crumbs
1 tablespoon snipped fresh parsley
1 tablespoon sliced green onion
½ teaspoon grated lime peel
½ teaspoon salt
⅛ teaspoon pepper
3 tablespoons prepared horseradish
1 tablespoon plus 1 teaspoon soy sauce

4 to 6 servings

Heat oven to 350°. Generously grease 8×4-inch loaf pan. In medium bowl, combine all ingredients except horseradish and soy sauce. Spread in prepared pan. Bake until center is firm and loaf is golden brown, 55 to 60 minutes. Loosen edges with spatula and turn out of loaf pan; cut into slices.

In small dish, blend horseradish and soy sauce. Serve with salmon loaf.

← Layered Salmon Loaf

2 tablespoons margarine or butter
2 tablespoons all-purpose flour
⅛ teaspoon salt
⅛ teaspoon pepper
1 cup half-and-half
2 cups flaked cooked salmon or other oily fish
  (page 34)
1 egg
2 slices soft bread, crusts removed, and bread
  crumbled (about 1¼ cups)
2 hard-cooked eggs
2 tablespoons chopped green onion
1 teaspoon prepared mustard

4 to 6 servings

Heat oven to 350°. Generously grease 8 × 4-inch loaf pan. In 1-quart saucepan, melt margarine over medium heat. Stir in flour, salt and pepper. Blend in half-and-half. Cook over medium heat, stirring constantly, until thickened and bubbly, about 4 minutes. Remove from heat.

In medium bowl, combine fish, one egg, the crumbled bread and ¾ cup hot white sauce; set aside. Finely chop hard-cooked eggs. In small bowl, combine chopped eggs, onion, remaining sauce and mustard. In prepared pan, layer half the fish mixture, then the egg mixture. Top with remaining fish mixture. Sprinkle top of loaf with paprika, if desired. Bake until center is firm, 45 to 50 minutes.

Easy Northern Pike Loaf ◆ LOW-FAT

1½ cups cracker crumbs
⅓ cup milk
2 cups flaked cooked northern pike or other lean
  fish (page 34)
1 can (10¾ ounces) condensed cream of
  shrimp soup
2 eggs, slightly beaten
2 tablespoons finely chopped green onion
¼ teaspoon lemon pepper
⅛ teaspoon garlic powder

4 to 6 servings

Heat oven to 350°. Generously grease 8 × 4-inch loaf pan. In medium bowl, combine cracker crumbs and milk. Let stand to moisten crumbs, about 5 minutes. Stir in fish, cream of shrimp soup, eggs, green onion, lemon pepper and garlic powder. Spread mixture in prepared pan.

Bake until knife inserted in center comes out clean and loaf is golden brown, 55 to 60 minutes. If desired, serve with Mushroom Sauce, page 140.

Variation: Substitute 1 can (10¾ ounces) condensed clam chowder for the cream of shrimp soup.

Oven-Fried Trout Cakes FAST ↑

1 1/2 cups cold mashed potatoes*
1 1/2 cups flaked cooked trout or other oily fish
   (page 34)
1 egg, slightly beaten
2 tablespoons snipped fresh parsley
2 tablespoons grated onion
1 teaspoon fresh lemon juice
1/2 teaspoon celery salt
1/8 teaspoon pepper
1/4 cup all-purpose flour
1 egg
1 tablespoon milk
1 cup fine dry bread crumbs
1 tablespoon snipped fresh parsley
1/2 teaspoon paprika
6 tablespoons vegetable oil
   Lemon-Parsley Sauce (page 137)

4 servings

In medium bowl, combine mashed potatoes, fish, one beaten egg, 2 tablespoons parsley, the onion, lemon juice, celery salt and pepper. Set aside.

Heat oven to 450°. Sprinkle flour on plate or waxed paper. In shallow dish or pie plate, blend one egg and milk. On another plate or waxed paper, combine crumbs, 1 tablespoon parsley and the paprika.

Drop 1/3 cup of fish mixture into flour. Roll gently to coat. Place in egg mixture. Flatten slightly to form 1/2-inch thick patty. Turn to coat with egg. Carefully coat with bread crumbs. Repeat with remaining fish mixture. Set aside.

Coat bottom of 13 × 9-inch baking pan with oil. Place pan in oven for 5 minutes to heat oil. Add fish cakes. Bake for 8 minutes; turn. Bake until golden brown, about 7 minutes.

Prepare Lemon-Parsley Sauce as directed. Serve over fish cakes.

*Use leftover mashed potatoes or substitute cooked instant mashed potatoes.

Northern Pike Patties

2 cups water
1/2 teaspoon salt
1 medium red potato (about 6 ounces)
1 pound skinless northern pike or other lean fish
   fillets (page 34)
1 egg
1 cup milk
1/2 cup cracker crumbs
2 tablespoons finely chopped onion
1 teaspoon Worcestershire sauce
1/2 teaspoon salt
1/4 teaspoon pepper
1 cup dry bread crumbs or cornflake crumbs
2 tablespoons vegetable oil
1 tablespoon margarine or butter
   Mustard Sauce (page 140)

4 to 6 servings

In 1-quart saucepan, heat water and 1/2 teaspoon salt to boiling; add potato. Return to boiling. Reduce heat. Cover and simmer until potato is tender, about 20 minutes. Drain. Cool.

Cut fish into 3-inch pieces. Place fish and egg in food processor.* Process, slowly adding milk, until smooth, 1 to 2 minutes. In medium bowl, mix fish, cracker crumbs, onion, Worcestershire sauce, 1/2 teaspoon salt and the pepper. Peel potato and shred; stir into fish mixture. Refrigerate 30 minutes.

Sprinkle bread crumbs on plate or waxed paper. Form fish mixture into eight 1/2-inch thick patties. Coat with bread crumbs, pressing lightly. Place on baking sheet or tray.

In 9-inch skillet, heat oil and margarine over medium-high heat. Place four patties in skillet. Fry for 2 minutes; turn. Fry until golden brown, about 2 minutes. Drain on paper towels. Keep warm in 175° oven. Repeat with remaining fish mixture. Prepare Mustard Sauce as directed. Serve with fish patties. If desired, serve patties in hamburger buns with lettuce and tomato slices.

*If using blender, purée half the fish and milk at a time. Proceed as directed.

Stuffed Cabbage Rolls

    2 quarts water
    8 large cabbage leaves*
 ⅓ cup finely chopped celery
 ¼ cup finely chopped onion
    1 tablespoon margarine or butter
    2 cups flaked cooked northern pike or other
        lean fish (page 34)
    1 cup uncooked instant rice
    1 egg, slightly beaten
    2 tablespoons snipped fresh parsley
    1 tablespoon fresh lemon juice
 ½ teaspoon salt
 ¼ teaspoon garlic salt
 ⅛ teaspoon pepper
    4 drops red pepper sauce
SAUCE:
    1 can (15 ounces) tomato sauce
1½ teaspoons sugar
 ⅛ teaspoon garlic salt
    4 thin lemon slices

                                    4 servings

*To loosen leaves from cabbage head, cut out core. Place cabbage in bowl; cover with cold water. Let stand about 10 minutes; remove leaves.

How to Prepare Stuffed Cabbage Rolls

HEAT water to boiling in Dutch oven. Add four cabbage leaves; cover. Cook over high heat until pliable, about 2 minutes. Remove with slotted spoon to colander. Rinse under cold running water; drain. Repeat with remaining four leaves. Set aside.

COOK and stir celery and onion in margarine in small skillet over medium heat until tender-crisp, about 2 minutes. In medium bowl, mix celery and onion with remaining ingredients except sauce ingredients. Set aside. Heat oven to 350°.

CUT out hard center rib from each cabbage leaf. Overlap cut edges of leaves; place about ⅓ cup of fish mixture on base of each. Fold in sides; roll up to enclose filling. Place rolls, seam side down, in 9×9-inch baking pan.

COMBINE tomato sauce, sugar and ⅛ teaspoon garlic salt in small bowl or 2-cup measure. Pour over cabbage rolls. Top with lemon slices. Cover with foil. Bake until heated, about 35 to 40 minutes.

Smoked Fish and Potato Casserole

4 medium white potatoes (about 2 pounds)
1 medium onion, chopped
1½ cups flaked smoked fish
3 tablespoons margarine or butter
2 tablespoons snipped fresh parsley
¼ teaspoon pepper
⅓ cup water

4 to 6 servings

Heat oven to 350°. Grease 2-quart casserole. Cut potatoes into thin slices. Layer half each of the potato slices, onion, fish, margarine, parsley and pepper in casserole. Repeat layers. Pour water over layers in casserole; cover. Bake until potatoes are tender, about 1¼ hours. Serve with margarine and snipped fresh parsley, if desired.

Trout and Corn Bake

1 medium green pepper
1 tablespoon margarine or butter
4 slices bacon, cut up
1½ cups flaked cooked trout or other oily fish
  (page 34)
1 package (10 ounces) frozen whole kernel corn
1 cup coarse cracker crumbs
1 can (13 ounces) evaporated milk
3 tablespoons margarine or butter, melted
2 tablespoons grated onion
2 tablespoons snipped fresh parsley
½ teaspoon celery salt
⅛ teaspoon pepper
⅓ cup grated Parmesan cheese
⅛ teaspoon paprika

4 to 6 servings

Heat oven to 350°. Grease 9×9-inch baking pan. Core and seed green pepper. Cut two thin rings and set aside. Chop remaining green pepper. In 9-inch skillet, cook and stir chopped green pepper in 1 tablespoon margarine over medium heat until tender-crisp, about 4 minutes. Remove to medium bowl. Set aside.

In 9-inch skillet, cook and stir bacon over medium-high heat until crisp. Remove bacon with slotted spoon. Add bacon and 1 tablespoon bacon fat to green pepper. Discard remaining bacon fat. Stir in fish, corn, cracker crumbs, evaporated milk, melted margarine, onion, parsley, celery salt and pepper. Spread fish mixture in prepared pan.

In small dish, mix Parmesan cheese and paprika. Sprinkle over fish. Top with reserved green pepper rings. Bake until knife inserted in center comes out clean, 40 to 45 minutes. Let stand 5 minutes. Cut into squares to serve.

Creamy Northern Pike Casserole

1 cup thinly sliced celery
1 tablespoon margarine or butter
2 cups flaked cooked northern pike or other lean
    fish (page 34)
1 can (10¾ ounces) condensed cream of shrimp
    soup
1 cup frozen green beans
1 can (5.3 ounces) evaporated milk
1 can (4 ounces) sliced mushrooms, drained
1 can (3 ounces) French-fried onion rings, crushed
⅛ teaspoon pepper

4 to 6 servings

Heat oven to 350°. In small skillet, cook and stir celery in margarine over medium heat until tender, about 6 minutes. Set aside.

In 2-quart casserole, mix fish, cream of shrimp soup, green beans, milk, mushrooms, ½ cup of the crushed onion rings and the pepper. Stir in celery.

Bake for 30 minutes. Top with remaining onion rings. Bake until hot and bubbly, 15 to 20 minutes.

Cheesy Bass and Rice Casserole ◆ LOW-FAT

2 cups flaked cooked bass or other lean fish
    (page 34)
⅔ cup uncooked long-grain rice
⅔ cup shredded Cheddar cheese
⅓ cup sliced celery
⅓ cup chopped green pepper
¼ cup chopped onion
1 can (10¾ ounces) condensed chicken broth
1 can (4 ounces) mushroom pieces, drained
1 jar (2 ounces) sliced pimiento, drained
1 tablespoon Worcestershire sauce
¼ teaspoon salt
⅛ teaspoon pepper
½ cup herb-seasoned croutons
⅓ cup shredded Cheddar cheese

6 servings

Heat oven to 350°. In 1½-quart casserole, mix all ingredients except croutons and ⅓ cup cheese. Cover. Bake until rice is tender, 50 to 55 minutes. Stir. Sprinkle with croutons and ⅓ cup cheese. Bake, uncovered, until cheese melts, about 5 minutes.

Panfish Asparagus Biscuit Bake ↑

1 cup diced carrot
1 small onion, chopped
2 tablespoons margarine or butter
2 cups flaked cooked panfish or other lean fish
  (page 34)
1 can (10¾ ounces) condensed cream of
  mushroom soup
1 package (10 ounces) frozen asparagus
  cuts, thawed
¼ cup milk
2 teaspoons fresh lemon juice
¼ teaspoon salt
⅛ teaspoon pepper
1 cup buttermilk baking mix
⅓ cup milk
1 teaspoon dried parsley flakes
  Dash paprika

4 to 6 servings

Heat oven to 375°. In 9-inch skillet, cook and stir carrot and onion in margarine over medium heat until tender, about 11 minutes. Remove to 1½-quart casserole. Stir in fish, cream of mushroom soup, asparagus cuts, ¼ cup milk, the lemon juice, salt and pepper. Set aside.

In small bowl, combine baking mix, ⅓ cup milk, the parsley flakes and paprika. Mix with fork. Drop eight mounds of dough on fish mixture in casserole.

Bake until biscuits are golden brown and casserole is bubbly, about 35 minutes. Brush biscuits with melted margarine before serving, if desired.

Spicy Trout and Rice Casserole

1 medium zucchini (about ¼ pound)
½ cup chopped celery
⅓ cup chopped onion
1 clove garlic, minced
2 tablespoons vegetable oil
1 can (8 ounces) tomato sauce
½ cup water
1 tablespoon fresh lemon juice
1 teaspoon sugar
½ teaspoon chili powder
¼ teaspoon salt
⅛ teaspoon cayenne
2 cups flaked cooked trout or other oily fish
  (page 34)
½ cup uncooked instant rice
⅓ cup shredded Cheddar cheese
⅓ cup shredded Monterey Jack cheese
  Paprika

4 to 6 servings

Heat oven to 350°. Cut zucchini lengthwise into fourths, then into ¼-inch thick slices. In 9-inch skillet, cook and stir zucchini, celery, onion and garlic in oil over medium heat until tender, about 7 minutes. Stir in tomato sauce, water, lemon juice, sugar, chili powder, salt and cayenne. Heat to boiling. Reduce heat. Cover and simmer for 10 minutes.

Pour into 1-quart casserole. Stir in fish and rice. Sprinkle Cheddar and Monterey Jack cheese on top. Sprinkle with paprika. Bake until casserole is heated and rice is tender, about 30 minutes.

Fish Melt VERY FAST ↑

1½ cups flaked cooked northern pike or other
   lean fish (page 34)
  ¼ cup finely chopped cucumber
  2 tablespoons chopped radish
  1 tablespoon mayonnaise or salad dressing
  1 tablespoon dairy sour cream
  ½ teaspoon salt
  ⅛ teaspoon pepper
  4 large thin tomato slices
  4 to 8 slices whole wheat bread, toasted
  4 slices American cheese

2 to 4 servings

Set oven to broil and/or 550°. In small bowl, mix
fish, cucumber, radish, mayonnaise, sour cream,
salt and pepper. Place one tomato slice on each of
four toasted bread slices. Spread fish mixture over
tomatoes; spread to edges of bread. Top each piece
with one piece of cheese. Place sandwiches on baking sheet. Broil 2 to 3 inches from heat until cheese
melts, about 2 minutes. Top each sandwich with
another piece of toast, if desired.

Baked Salmon Sandwiches FAST

1½ cups flaked cooked salmon or other oily fish
   (page 34)
  ¼ cup mayonnaise or salad dressing
  2 tablespoons finely chopped onion
  2 tablespoons sliced stuffed green olives
  1 tablespoon sweet pickle relish
  2 teaspoons lime juice, optional
  ½ teaspoon salt
  ⅛ teaspoon pepper
  4 hamburger buns
  ½ cup shredded Monterey Jack cheese

2 to 4 servings

Heat oven to 400°. In small bowl, mix fish, mayonnaise, onion, green olives, pickle relish, lime juice,
salt and pepper. Spread fish mixture on buns. Top
with cheese. Replace tops. Wrap sandwiches in foil.
Bake until fish mixture is hot and cheese is melted,
about 15 minutes.

Smoked Fish Omelet VERY FAST

 3 eggs
 2 tablespoons milk
 ⅛ teaspoon pepper
 1 tablespoon margarine or butter
 ½ cup flaked smoked fish
 ¼ cup shredded Cheddar or Swiss cheese

2 servings

In small bowl, blend eggs, milk and pepper. In 10-inch skillet, melt margarine over medium heat. Pour eggs into skillet. Cook until eggs are set, about 5 minutes. Sprinkle fish and cheese over one half of the omelet. With spatula, carefully fold other half over filling. Cook until cheese melts, 1 to 2 minutes.

Egg Foo Yung LOW-FAT FAST

 ¾ cup water
 1 teaspoon instant chicken bouillon granules
 1 tablespoon plus 1 teaspoon soy sauce
 2 teaspoons sugar
 1 tablespoon cornstarch
 2 tablespoons cold water
 6 eggs
 1½ cups flaked cooked northern pike or other
     lean fish (page 34)
 1 can (16 ounces) bean sprouts, drained
 1 can (4½ ounces) small shrimp,
     rinsed and drained
 1 can (4 ounces) sliced mushrooms, drained
 2 tablespoons thinly sliced green onion
 1 teaspoon soy sauce
 ⅛ teaspoon pepper
 1 tablespoon margarine or butter

4 to 6 servings

In 1-quart saucepan, combine ¾ cup water, bouillon granules, 1 tablespoon plus 1 teaspoon soy sauce and the sugar. Heat to boiling. In small dish, blend cornstarch into 2 tablespoons cold water. Stir into boiling mixture. Return to boiling. Cook, stirring constantly, until thickened and translucent, about 2 minutes. Keep warm over very low heat.

In medium bowl, beat eggs well. Stir in fish, bean sprouts, shrimp, mushrooms, green onion, 1 teaspoon soy sauce and the pepper. In 9-inch skillet, melt margarine over medium heat. Form four patties by dropping ⅓ cup of egg mixture for each patty into skillet. Cook over medium heat for 3 minutes; turn. Cook until set, 2 to 3 minutes. Repeat with remaining egg mixture. Keep warm in 175° oven. Serve warm sauce over patties.

Mushroom Fish Omelet FAST ↑

 1 cup sliced fresh mushrooms
 2 tablespoons chopped green pepper
 2 tablespoons chopped onion
 2 tablespoons margarine or butter
 3 eggs
 2 tablespoons milk
 ⅛ teaspoon pepper
 1 tablespoon margarine or butter
 ½ cup flaked smoked fish

2 servings

In 10-inch skillet, cook and stir mushrooms, green pepper and onion in 2 tablespoons margarine over medium heat until tender, about 5 minutes. Remove to small dish; set aside.

In small bowl, blend eggs, milk and pepper. In 10-inch skillet, melt 1 tablespoon margarine over medium heat. Pour eggs into skillet. Cook until eggs are set, about 5 minutes.

Spoon vegetables and fish over one half of the omelet. With spatula, carefully fold other half of omelet over filling. Cook until hot, about 1 minute.

Fish Complements

Some dishes such as coleslaw, French fries and hush puppies just naturally go with fish. Other dishes, especially vegetables and salads, taste good and add color and appeal to the fish. Both types of dishes are included in this section.

← Beer Batter Onion Rings

1 cup all-purpose flour
1 cup beer
½ teaspoon salt
1 large onion (about 1 pound)
2 cups milk
  Vegetable oil
½ cup all-purpose flour

35 to 40 onion rings

In medium bowl, beat 1 cup flour, the beer and salt with fork. Cover and refrigerate batter 3 hours. Cut onion into ½-inch slices and separate into rings. Place onion rings in shallow dish. Pour milk over onions. Cover with plastic wrap. Refrigerate 3 hours, turning rings over one or two times.

In deep-fat fryer or saucepan, heat oil (2 to 3 inches) to 375°. Place ½ cup flour in paper or plastic bag. Shake onions in flour until coated, then dip in batter. Fry a few rings at a time, turning over one or two times, until golden brown, 1½ to 2 minutes. Drain on paper towels. Keep warm in 175° oven.

Corn Muffins ◆ LOW-FAT ● FAST

1 cup yellow cornmeal
1 cup all-purpose flour
2 tablespoons sugar
1 tablespoon baking powder
½ teaspoon salt
1 cup milk
1 egg
3 tablespoons vegetable oil
2 tablespoons chopped green pepper, optional
2 tablespoons chopped onion, optional

8 × 8-inch pan or 12 muffins

Heat oven to 425°. Grease 8 × 8-inch baking pan or line 12 muffin cups with paper liners. In medium bowl, combine cornmeal, flour, sugar, baking powder and salt. Beat in remaining ingredients until smooth. Pour batter into prepared pan or fill muffin cups one-half full. Bake until light golden brown, about 25 minutes.

Buttermilk Batter Onion Rings

1 large onion (about 1 pound)
1 cup buttermilk pancake mix
1 cup buttermilk
1 egg
  Vegetable oil

35 to 40 onion rings

Cut onion into ½-inch slices and separate into rings. Spread pancake mix on waxed paper or place in paper bag. In medium bowl, beat buttermilk and egg with fork until smooth. Dip a few onion rings at a time into buttermilk mixture, then coat thoroughly with pancake mix. Let stand on wire rack until dry, 1½ to 2 hours.

In deep-fat fryer or saucepan, heat oil (2 to 3 inches) to 375°. Fry a few rings at a time, turning over one or two times, until golden brown, 1½ to 2 minutes. Drain on paper towels. Keep warm in 175° oven.

Potato Salad

1 quart water
1 teaspoon salt
4 medium red potatoes (about 2 pounds)
3 hard-cooked eggs
½ cup chopped onion
¼ cup shredded carrot
1 stalk celery with leaves, chopped
½ teaspoon salt
⅛ teaspoon pepper
1 cup mayonnaise or salad dressing
1 teaspoon prepared mustard
  Paprika

4 to 6 servings

In 3-quart saucepan, heat water and 1 teaspoon salt to boiling. Add potatoes. Return to boiling. Reduce heat. Cover and simmer until tender, 25 to 35 minutes. Cool. Peel and cut into ¾-inch cubes.

Chop two eggs. Cut remaining egg into slices. In medium bowl, combine potato cubes, chopped eggs, onion, carrot, celery, ½ teaspoon salt and the pepper. Stir in mayonnaise and mustard until just combined. Garnish with sliced egg; sprinkle with paprika. Cover and refrigerate 2 to 3 hours.

Hush Puppies ● VERY FAST ↑

  Vegetable oil
1 cup yellow cornmeal
⅓ cup all-purpose flour
1 teaspoon sugar
1 teaspoon baking powder
⅛ teaspoon salt
⅛ teaspoon cayenne, optional
1 egg
¼ cup chopped onion
1 can (8 ounces) cream-style corn
2 tablespoons buttermilk

4 to 6 servings

In deep-fat fryer or saucepan, heat oil (2 to 3 inches) to 375°. Mix cornmeal, flour, sugar, baking powder, salt and cayenne. Stir in remaining ingredients until just combined. Drop batter by tablespoonfuls into hot oil. Fry a few at a time, turning over one or two times, until dark golden brown, 4 to 5 minutes. Drain on paper towels. Keep warm in 175° oven.

Vegetables With Crumb Topping VERY FAST

Vegetable oil
1/2 cup all-purpose flour
1/4 teaspoon salt
1/8 teaspoon pepper
2 eggs
1 teaspoon milk
1 cup fine dry bread crumbs

RECIPE COATS ONE OF THE FOLLOWING:
1 large onion (about 1 pound), cut into 1/2-inch slices and separated into rings, 35 to 40 pieces
3 medium green peppers, seeded and cut into 1/2-inch rings, about 18 pieces
3 small zucchini (about 1 pound), cut in half lengthwise, seeded and cut into 2 1/2 x 1/2-inch strips, about 50 pieces
1/2 pound cheese (Colby, Swiss or Cheddar), cut into 3/4-inch pieces, about 40 pieces

4 to 6 servings

In deep-fat fryer or saucepan, heat oil (2 to 3 inches) to 375°. In paper or plastic bag, mix flour, salt and pepper. Rinse vegetables (not cheese) with water; do not dry. Shake about one-third of vegetables or cheese in bag until coated with flour. Remove; set aside. Repeat with remaining vegetables or cheese.

In small bowl, beat eggs and milk. Dip flour-coated vegetables in egg, then coat with crumbs. Fry a few pieces at a time, turning over one or two times, until deep golden brown, 1 to 1 1/2 minutes. Drain on paper towels. Keep warm in 175° oven.

Almond Crumb-Baked Tomatoes FAST

1/4 cup mayonnaise or salad dressing
2 tablespoons dairy sour cream
1/8 to 1/4 teaspoon dried dillweed
1/3 cup margarine or butter
1/2 cup dry seasoned bread crumbs
1/4 cup grated Parmesan cheese
1/4 cup sliced almonds, chopped
3 medium tomatoes, cut in half

6 servings

In small bowl, mix mayonnaise, sour cream and dillweed. Cover and refrigerate.

Heat oven to 375°. In small saucepan, melt margarine over medium heat. Remove from heat. Stir in bread crumbs, Parmesan cheese and almonds. Place tomato halves, cut side up, on broiler pan. Sprinkle crumb mixture equally on tomato halves. Gently press mixture on top of tomatoes. Bake until base of tomatoes can be pierced easily with fork and crumbs are light brown, 20 to 25 minutes. Serve with mayonnaise topping.

← Orange-Broccoli Stir-Fry

3/4 pound fresh broccoli
2 tablespoons hot water
1 teaspoon instant chicken bouillon granules
1 tablespoon sesame seed
1 small clove garlic, cut in half
2 tablespoons vegetable oil
1 tablespoon grated orange peel
1/4 teaspoon ground ginger
1 can (8 ounces) sliced water chestnuts, drained
1 cup fresh or drained canned bean sprouts
1 jar (2 ounces) chopped pimiento, drained

4 to 6 servings

Separate broccoli into flowerets. Cut stems into 1/4-inch slices. Set aside. Mix hot water and bouillon granules. Set aside. In 10-inch skillet, cook and stir sesame seed and garlic in oil over medium heat for 3 minutes. Add orange peel. Cook and stir until sesame seed is golden brown. Remove garlic. Stir in ginger. Add broccoli and remaining ingredients. Cook and stir over medium heat until broccoli is tender, about 7 minutes.

Vegetable Kabobs With Lemon Butter

4 small red potatoes (1 1/2- to 2-inch diameter)
2 small onions
1 medium zucchini or yellow summer squash
2 medium green peppers
8 cherry tomatoes
8 lemon wedges
4 metal skewers, 16 inches long
1/3 cup margarine or butter
2 tablespoons grated Parmesan cheese
1/2 teaspoon lemon pepper
1/8 teaspoon garlic powder

4 kabobs

Remove thin strip of peel from around center of each potato. In 2-quart saucepan, place potatoes and onions. Cover with cold water. Heat over low heat to boiling. Simmer until potatoes can just be pierced with fork, 5 to 8 minutes. Drain. Immediately plunge into cold water to cool.

Cut each onion into four wedges. Cut zucchini into eight chunks. Cut each green pepper into eight cubes. Alternately thread two zucchini chunks, two cherry tomatoes, four green pepper cubes, one potato, two onion wedges and two lemon wedges on each skewer. Place kabobs on broiler pan.

In small saucepan, melt margarine over medium heat. Stir in remaining ingredients. Brush evenly over each kabob. Set oven to broil and/or 550°. Broil 6 inches from heat, turning kabobs over after half the time, until potatoes are fork tender and other vegetables are light brown, 16 to 20 minutes.

Lemony Cucumber and Apple Mold ▷ LOW-FAT →

    1 package (6 ounces) lemon gelatin
    2 cups boiling water
1½ cups cold water
    1 cup chopped, seeded, peeled cucumber
    1 cup cored, chopped apple
¼ cup chopped green onion
    8 to 10 very thin slices cucumber, optional

6 to 8 servings

Dissolve gelatin in boiling water. Add cold water. Refrigerate 1 to 1½ hours until soft-set, stirring one or two times. Stir in chopped cucumber, apple and green onion. In bottom of 6-cup mold, arrange cucumber slices. Spoon gelatin mixture evenly over slices. Refrigerate until firm. Unmold onto serving plate lined with lettuce or watercress.

Creamy Coleslaw

    4 cups shredded cabbage
⅓ cup shredded carrot
¼ cup chopped green pepper

DRESSING:
½ cup mayonnaise or salad dressing
    3 tablespoons dairy sour cream
    1 tablespoon plus 2 teaspoons cider vinegar
    1 teaspoon sugar
½ teaspoon salt
½ teaspoon celery seed, optional
⅛ teaspoon pepper

6 to 8 servings

In large bowl, combine cabbage, carrot and green pepper. In small bowl, blend all dressing ingredients. Add to cabbage mixture, tossing gently to coat. Cover and refrigerate at least 3 hours.

Cabbage Vinaigrette ▷ LOW-FAT

    4 cups shredded cabbage
⅓ cup chopped green pepper
⅓ cup snipped fresh parsley
¼ cup finely chopped onion
¼ cup vinegar
    1 tablespoon vegetable oil
    2 teaspoons sugar
½ teaspoon dry mustard
¼ teaspoon celery seed
¼ teaspoon salt

6 to 8 servings

In medium bowl, combine cabbage, green pepper, parsley and onion. In small bowl, mix vinegar, oil, sugar, mustard, celery seed and salt; add to cabbage, tossing gently to coat. Cover and refrigerate 3 to 4 hours.

Frozen Fruit Salad

½ cup flaked coconut
    1 package (3 ounces) cream cheese, softened
    1 container (12 ounces) prepared frozen whipped dessert topping, thawed
    1 can (15¼ ounces) crushed pineapple, drained
    1 can (11 ounces) mandarin orange segments, drained
    1 cup chopped pecans
½ cup chopped maraschino cherries

8 to 9 servings

Set oven to broil and/or 550°. Spread coconut evenly on baking sheet. Broil 4 inches from heat until golden brown, about 1 minute. Set aside.

In large bowl, place cream cheese. Gradually blend in whipped topping at medium speed of electric mixer. Mix in remaining ingredients except coconut. Spread mixture in 8 × 8-inch baking pan. Sprinkle with toasted coconut. Cover and freeze until firm, at least 2 hours. Cut into squares.

Sauces

A good sauce enhances the taste of fish without covering the natural flavor. It can be simple or complex, but it adds a unique flavor to the cooked fish. For extra tang, substitute fish stock for water, wine or half of the milk or cream in the sauce recipe.

← Lemon-Parsley Sauce LOW-FAT VERY FAST

  1 tablespoon cornstarch
¾ cup cold water
  1 tablespoon grated lemon peel
  1 teaspoon fresh lemon juice
½ teaspoon sugar
¼ teaspoon salt
  1 tablespoon snipped fresh parsley
  1 tablespoon margarine or butter

                  ¾ cup sauce

In small saucepan, gradually blend cornstarch into water. Stir in lemon peel, lemon juice, sugar and salt. Cook over medium heat, stirring constantly, until thickened, about 3 minutes. Add parsley and margarine, stirring until margarine is melted.

Lemony White Sauce

  2 tablespoons margarine or butter
  2 tablespoons all-purpose flour
⅛ teaspoon salt
⅛ teaspoon white pepper
  1 cup half-and-half
  1 tablespoon snipped fresh parsley
¼ teaspoon grated lemon peel

                  1 cup sauce

In small saucepan, melt margarine over medium heat. Stir in flour, salt and white pepper. Blend in half-and-half, parsley and lemon peel. Cook over medium heat, stirring constantly, until thickened, about 4 minutes.

Basic Tartar Sauce LOW-FAT FAST

½ cup mayonnaise or salad dressing
  2 tablespoons chopped sweet pickle relish
  2 tablespoons dairy sour cream
  2 tablespoons fresh lime or lemon juice
  2 teaspoons finely chopped onion
⅛ teaspoon salt
    Dash curry powder, optional

                  ¾ cup sauce

In small bowl, mix all ingredients. Chill at least 30 minutes to blend flavors.

NOTE: Recipe can be doubled.

Flavored Softened Butter

CITRUS BUTTER *(pictured):*
  6 tablespoons margarine or butter, softened
  ¼ teaspoon grated orange, lemon or lime peel

LEMON-PARSLEY BUTTER:
  6 tablespoons margarine or butter, softened
  1 tablespoon snipped fresh parsley
  ¼ teaspoon fresh lemon juice

DILL BUTTER:
  6 tablespoons margarine or butter, softened
  ⅛ teaspoon dried dillweed

⅓ cup butter each

In small bowl, combine softened margarine and remaining ingredients.

Almondine Butter

  1 tablespoon margarine or butter
  ¼ cup sliced almonds
  5 tablespoons margarine or butter
  1 tablespoon fresh lemon juice
    Dash cayenne

½ cup butter

In small skillet, melt 1 tablespoon margarine over medium heat. Add almonds. Cook and stir over medium heat until almonds are light brown, about 4 minutes. Stir in 5 tablespoons margarine, the lemon juice and cayenne. Cook over medium heat, stirring constantly, until margarine melts.

Flavored Melted Butters

MARJORAM BUTTER:
  6 tablespoons margarine or butter
  ¼ teaspoon dried marjoram leaves
  1 teaspoon red wine

LEMON BUTTER:
  6 tablespoons margarine or butter
  1 tablespoon fresh lemon juice

DILL BUTTER:
  6 tablespoons margarine or butter
  ⅛ teaspoon dried dillweed

⅓ cup butter each

In small saucepan, melt margarine over medium heat. Stir in remaining ingredients. Cook over medium heat for 1 minute.

Orange Butter Sauce

  ½ cup margarine or butter
  ½ cup fresh orange juice
  ½ teaspoon dried thyme leaves

1 cup sauce

In small saucepan, melt margarine over medium heat. Stir in orange juice and thyme. Heat to boiling. Reduce heat. Cook over low heat 1 minute.

Zesty Tomato Sauce ▷ LOW-FAT ● VERY FAST →

¼ cup chopped celery
 2 tablespoons chopped onion
 2 tablespoons margarine or butter
 1 tablespoon plus 1½ teaspoons all-purpose flour
⅛ teaspoon salt
⅛ teaspoon pepper
 1 can (8 ounces) tomato sauce
½ cup chili sauce
 1 teaspoon sugar
 1 tablespoon fresh lemon juice

1½ cups sauce

In small saucepan or skillet, cook and stir celery and onion in margarine over medium heat until tender-crisp, about 3 minutes. Stir in flour, salt and pepper. Blend in remaining ingredients. Cook, stirring constantly, until thickened, about 4 minutes.

Cocktail Sauce ▷ LOW-FAT ● FAST

 1 cup chili sauce
 2 tablespoons fresh lime or lemon juice
½ teaspoon prepared horseradish

1⅓ cups sauce

In small serving bowl, blend all ingredients. Chill at least 30 minutes to blend flavors.

White Wine Sauce ● VERY FAST

¼ cup finely chopped celery
 1 tablespoon finely chopped onion
 2 tablespoons margarine or butter
 2 tablespoons all-purpose flour
⅛ teaspoon pepper
    Dash dried marjoram leaves
    Dash dried thyme leaves
¾ cup half-and-half
½ cup shredded Monterey Jack cheese
¼ cup white wine

1½ cups sauce

In small saucepan or skillet, cook and stir celery and onion in margarine over medium heat until tender, about 5 minutes. Stir in flour, pepper, marjoram and thyme. Blend in half-and-half. Cook over medium heat, stirring constantly, until thickened and bubbly, about 5 minutes. Stir in cheese until melted. Remove from heat; slowly blend in wine.

Sherried White Sauce Variation: Substitute 2 tablespoons sherry for the white wine.

Mushroom Sauce

2 cups chopped fresh mushrooms
¼ cup chopped onion
2 tablespoons margarine or butter
1 tablespoon all-purpose flour
¼ teaspoon salt
⅛ teaspoon pepper
⅓ cup milk
¼ cup dairy sour cream
1 tablespoon Dijon-style mustard
1 tablespoon white wine, optional

1½ cups sauce

In small saucepan or skillet, cook and stir mushrooms and onion in margarine over medium heat until onion is tender, about 5 minutes. Stir in flour, salt and pepper. Blend in milk. Cook over medium heat, stirring constantly, until thickened, about 3 minutes. Remove from heat. Stir in sour cream, mustard and wine.

Clam-Tomato Sauce

⅓ cup chopped celery
¼ cup chopped onion
3 tablespoons margarine or butter
1 tablespoon all-purpose flour
¼ teaspoon salt
⅛ teaspoon pepper
⅔ cup clam-tomato juice cocktail
¼ cup whipping cream
1 tablespoon white wine

1¼ cups sauce

In small saucepan or skillet, cook and stir celery and onion in margarine over medium heat until tender, about 5 minutes. Stir in flour, salt and pepper. Blend in clam-tomato juice, cream and wine. Cook over medium heat, stirring constantly, until thickened, about 3 minutes.

Mustard Sauce

1 tablespoon finely chopped onion
2 tablespoons margarine or butter
1 tablespoon all-purpose flour
¼ teaspoon salt
   Dash pepper
1 cup milk
2 tablespoons Dijon-style mustard

1 cup sauce

In small saucepan or skillet, cook and stir onion in margarine over medium heat for 1 minute. Stir in flour, salt and pepper. Blend in milk and mustard. Cook over medium heat, stirring constantly, until thickened, about 4 minutes.

Cucumber Sauce

2 tablespoons chopped onion
1 cup chopped, seeded, peeled cucumber
2 tablespoons margarine or butter
2 tablespoons all-purpose flour
⅛ teaspoon salt
   Dash white pepper
¼ teaspoon dried dillweed
½ cup hot water
½ teaspoon instant chicken bouillon granules
½ cup whipping cream
1 egg yolk, slightly beaten

1¾ cups sauce

In 1½-quart saucepan, cook and stir onion and cucumber in margarine over medium heat until tender, about 7 minutes. Stir in flour, salt, white pepper and dillweed. Mix hot water and bouillon granules. Blend into vegetables. Stir in cream. Cook over medium heat, stirring constantly, until thickened and bubbly, about 4 minutes. Stir small amount of hot mixture into beaten egg yolk. Return to hot mixture. Cook, stirring constantly, for 1 minute.

Sweet and Sour Sauce

⅓ cup water
¼ cup sugar
¼ cup red wine vinegar
1 tablespoon plus 1½ teaspoons soy sauce
1 can (8 ounces) whole tomatoes, drained, cut up
1 small bay leaf, optional
1 medium onion, chopped
1 tablespoon cornstarch
2 tablespoons cold water

1⅓ cups sauce

In small saucepan, combine ⅓ cup water, the sugar, vinegar and soy sauce. Heat to boiling. Stir in tomatoes, bay leaf and onion. Return to boiling, stirring occasionally. Reduce heat. Simmer 5 minutes.

Blend cornstarch into 2 tablespoons cold water. Stir into sauce. Heat to boiling, stirring constantly. Cook, stirring constantly, until sauce is thickened and translucent, about 2 minutes.

Index

O

Oligotrophic Lakes, 18
Overcast Weather, 46, 87, 191, 202
Oxygen Level of Water, 15, 16, 133, 177, 194

P

Pacific Salmon, see: Salmon
Palomar Knot, 32
Pan-Dressing Whole Fish, 273
Panfish, 18, 19, 292-297
  Lures for, 47-49
  See also: Crappies, Sunfish, Yellow Perch
Paternoster Rig, 156, 158
Pattern Fishing, 86, 186
Perch, see: Yellow Perch
Phosphorescent Lures, 145, 191
Photographing Fish, 278-281, 402-417
Phytoplankton, 12
Pickerel, 48, 200
Pier Fishing, 161, 270
Pike & Muskies, 10, 200-221
  Daily activities, 202, 213-215
  Equipment for, 29, 34, 44, 204, 210
  Fishing for, 47-49, 51, 204-221
  Foods & feeding, 10, 12, 14, 200, 212, 215, 221
  Habitat, 15, 18, 19, 21, 202, 203
  Ice fishing for pike, 219
  Removing Y-bones, 276
  Spawning, 203
  Trophy pike & muskies, 220-221
  Water temperature preference, 15, 202
  World records, 200
Pink Salmon, see: Salmon
Pits, 19
Planer Boards, 185, 193
  See also: Side Planers, Trolling Boards
Plankton, 136
Plastic Lures, see: Soft-Plastic Lures
Playing & Landing Fish, 62-63, 171
Plugs, 47-48
  Attaching to line, 109
  For bass, 80-81, 100, 109, 119
  For pike & muskies, 215
  For salmon, 267, 271
  For walleyes & saugers, 183
  Tuning, 109
  See also specific types of plugs
Plunge Pool, 23, 225
Plunking, 247

Pocket Water, 225
Ponds, 19, 132
Poppers, 46, 132
Popping Plugs, 119, 121
Pork-Rind Trailers, 82
Power Plants, 117, 131
Predators, 8, 10, 14
  Escaping, 14
  Fish as predators, 11, 12, 14
Propbaits, 48, 81, 91, 100, 108, 111, 121, 206
Pumpkinseed, see: Sunfish

Q

Quick-Strike Rig, 221

R

Rainbow Trout, see: Stream Trout
Recipes, 426-489
Redear Sunfish, see: Sunfish
Reels, see: Rods & Reels
Releasing Fish, 63-65, 210
Reservoirs, see: Man-Made Lakes
Riffle-Run-Pool Sequence, 22
Riprap, 92, 107, 130, 153, 159, 177, 196
Rivers & Streams, 22-23
  And bass, 97-99, 102, 107
  And catfish, 151-153, 156, 157, 160, 161, 164, 167
  And panfish, 124, 132, 137
  And pike & muskies, 203, 212, 218, 219
  And salmon, 271
  And trout, 224-225, 242-248, 254, 255
  And walleyes & saugers, 177, 187, 192, 196
  Old channel in man-made lakes, 77, 169, 203
Rocky Areas, 50
  And smallmouth bass, 104, 106
  And crappies, 137, 143
  And pike & muskies, 203
  And walleyes & saugers, 177, 190
Rods & Reels, 26-28
  Attaching line to reel, 30

S

Salad Recipes, 436-441
Salamanders, 53
Salmon, 10, 262-271

Eggs as bait, 53, 247, 250, 251, 254
  Equipment for, 269, 271
  Fishing for, 48, 51, 266-271
  Foods & feeding, 264
  Habitat, 19, 22, 263
  Migration, 10, 262, 263
  Spawning, 263, 266, 270, 271
  Water temperature preference, 15, 264, 266, 270
  World records, 264, 265
Sauce Recipes, 484-489
Sauger, see: Walleyes & Saugers
Scent Products, 11, 50
Schooling Behavior, 8, 116, 133, 148
  Fishing schools, 100, 119, 120, 143, 184
  Locating, 86, 100, 115, 127
Scud-Pattern Flies, 250
Sculpins, 246, 250, 251, 257
Searching Pattern Flies, 52
Seasonal Movement of Fish, 16-17
Senses of Fish, 8-11
Setting the Hook, 60-61, 145, 217
Shad, 21, 115-121, 155, 168
  Annual die-off, 168
Shallow Water, 87, 97
  Fishing shallow structure, 89
  Lures, baits & techniques for, 46, 49, 112, 138, 139
Shiners, 101, 108, 117, 209
Shore Fishing, 63, 160, 163, 243, 270
Shrimp, 53
Side Dish Recipes, 478-483
Side Planers, 42-43, 120, 178, 183, 243, 267, 269
  Techniques for trolling with, 185
  See also: Diving Planes
Sinker Styles, 35
Skinning Fish, 274-277
Skipping, 93, 101
Slip-Bobber Fishing, 35
  For bass, 95, 108
  For catfish, 166, 169
  For panfish, 126, 127, 130, 131, 138, 149
  For pike & muskies, 211
  For walleyes & saugers, 178, 181, 187, 189, 190, 193-195, 197
  Illustration of rig, 126, 158
  See also: Floats
Slipping, 67, 243
Slip-Sinker Fishing, 60
  For bass, 108
  For catfish, 155, 156, 158, 168
  For panfish, 131, 148
  For walleyes & saugers, 178, 180,